Sound symbolism

Sound symbolism is the study of the relationship between the sound of an utterance and its meaning. In this interdisciplinary collection of new studies, twenty-four leading scholars discuss the role of sound symbolism in a theory of language. They consider sound-symbolic processes in a wide range of languages from Europe, Asia, Africa, Australia, and North and South America. Beginning with an evocative typology of sound-symbolic processes, they go on to examine not only the well-known areas of study, such as onomatopoeia and size–sound symbolism, but also less frequently discussed topics such as the sound-symbolic value of vocatives and of involuntary noises, and the marginal areas of "conventional sound symbolism," such as phonesthemes. The book concludes with a series of studies on the biological basis of sound symbolism, and draws comparisons with the communication systems of other species.

This is a definitive work on the role of sound symbolism in a theory of language. The wide-ranging new research presented here reveals that sound symbolism plays a far more significant role in language than scholarship has hitherto recognized.

Sound symbolism

Edited by

LEANNE HINTON, JOHANNA NICHOLS,
AND JOHN J. OHALA

University of California at Berkeley

CAMBRIDGE
UNIVERSITY PRESS

CAMBRIDGE UNIVERSITY PRESS
Cambridge, New York, Melbourne, Madrid, Cape Town, Singapore, São Paulo

Cambridge University Press
The Edinburgh Building, Cambridge CB2 2RU, UK

Published in the United States of America by Cambridge University Press, New York

www.cambridge.org
Information on this title: www.cambridge.org/9780521452199

© Cambridge University Press 1994

This publication is in copyright. Subject to statutory exception
and to the provisions of relevant collective licensing agreements,
no reproduction of any part may take place without
the written permission of Cambridge University Press.

First published 1994
This digitally printed first paperback version 2006

A catalogue record for this publication is available from the British Library

Library of Congress Cataloguing in Publication data
Sound symbolism/edited by Leanne Hinton, Johanna Nichols, and John J. Ohala.
p. cm.
ISBN 0-521-45219-8
1. Sound symbolism.   I. Hinton, Leanne.   II. Nichols, Johanna.   III. Ohala, John J.
P119.S68 1995
414–dc20   93–34988 CIP

ISBN-13 978-0-521-45219-9 hardback
ISBN-10 0-521-45219-8 hardback

ISBN-13 978-0-521-02677-2 paperback
ISBN-10 0-521-02677-6 paperback

Contents

	List of contributors	*page* ix
1	*Introduction*: Sound-symbolic processes LEANNE HINTON, JOHANNA NICHOLS, AND JOHN OHALA	1

PART I *Native American languages north of Mexico*

2	Symbolism in Nez Perce HARUO AOKI	15
3	Nootkan vocative vocalism and its implications WILLIAM H. JACOBSEN, JR.	23
4	Relative motivation in denotational and indexical sound symbolism of Wasco-Wishram Chinookan MICHAEL SILVERSTEIN	40

PART II *Native languages of Latin America*

5	Symbolism and change in the sound system of Huastec TERRENCE KAUFMAN	63
6	Evidence for pervasive synesthetic sound symbolism in ethnozoological nomenclature BRENT BERLIN	76
7	Noise words in Guaraní MARGARET LANGDON	94

PART III *Asia*

8	*i*: big, *a*: small GÉRARD DIFFLOTH	107

List of contents

9	Tone, intonation, and sound symbolism in Lahu: loading the syllable canon JAMES A. MATISOFF	115
10	An experimental investigation into phonetic symbolism as it relates to Mandarin Chinese RANDY J. LAPOLLA	130
11	Palatalization in Japanese sound symbolism SHOKO HAMANO	148

PART IV *Australia and Africa*

12	Yir-Yiront ideophones BARRY ALPHER	161
13	African ideophones G. TUCKER CHILDS	178

PART V *Europe*

14	Regular sound development, phonosymbolic orchestration, disambiguation of homonyms YAKOV MALKIEL	207
15	Modern Greek *ts*: beyond sound symbolism BRIAN D. JOSEPH	222
16	On levels of analysis of sound symbolism in poetry, with an application to Russian poetry TOM M. S. PRIESTLY	237
17	Finnish and Gilyak sound symbolism – the interplay between system and history ROBERT AUSTERLITZ	249

PART VI *English*

18	Phonosyntactics JOAN A. SERENO	263
19	Aural images RICHARD RHODES	276
20	Inanimate imitatives in English ROBERT L. OSWALT	293

PART VII *The biological bases of sound symbolism*

21	Some observations on the function of sound in clinical work PETER F. OSTWALD	309

List of contents

22 The frequency code underlies the sound-symbolic use of voice pitch   325
JOHN J. OHALA

23 Sound symbolism and its role in non-human vertebrate communication   348
EUGENE S. MORTON

Index   366

Contributors

BARRY ALPHER
Journals Division, American Society for Microbiology, Washington DC

HARUO AOKI
Department of East Asian Languages, University of California, Berkeley

ROBERT AUSTERLITZ
Department of Linguistics, Columbia University

BRENT BERLIN
Department of Anthropology, University of California, Berkeley

G. TUCKER CHILDS
Department of Linguistics, University of Witwatersrand, Johannesburg

GÉRARD DIFFLOTH
Department of Modern Languages and Linguistics, Cornell University

SHOKO HAMANO
Department of East Asian Languages and Literatures, The George Washington University

LEANNE HINTON
Department of Linguistics, University of California, Berkeley

WILLIAM H. JACOBSEN, JR.
Department of English, University of Nevada, Reno

BRIAN D. JOSEPH
Department of Linguistics, Ohio State University

TERRENCE KAUFMAN
Department of Anthropology, University of Pittsburgh

MARGARET LANGDON
Department of Linguistics, University of California, San Diego

List of contributors

RANDY J. LAPOLLA
Institute of History and Philology, Academia Sinica, Taiwan

YAKOV MALKIEL
Department of Linguistics, University of California, Berkeley

JAMES A. MATISOFF
Department of Linguistics, University of California, Berkeley

EUGENE S. MORTON
National Zoological Park, Smithsonian Institute, Washington DC

JOHANNA NICHOLS
Department of Slavic Languages and Literature, University of California, Berkeley

JOHN J. OHALA
Department of Linguistics, University of California, Berkeley

PETER F. OSTWALD
*Langley Porter Psychiatric Institute, University of California,
San Francisco Medical Center*

ROBERT L. OSWALT
California Indian Language Center, Kensington, California

TOM M. S. PRIESTLY
Department of Slavic and East European Studies, University of Alberta

RICHARD RHODES
Department of Linguistics, University of California, Berkeley

JOAN A. SERENO
Department of Modern Languages and Linguistics and Department of Psychology, Cornell University

MICHAEL SILVERSTEIN
Department of Anthropology, University of Chicago

1
Introduction: sound-symbolic processes

LEANNE HINTON, JOHANNA NICHOLS, AND JOHN OHALA

Hermogenes. I should explain to you, Socrates, that our friend Cratylus has been arguing about names; he says that they are natural and not conventional; not a portion of the human voice which men agree to use; but that there is a truth or correctness in them, which is the same for Hellenes as barbarians.   Plato

1.1. Introduction

In general, linguistic theory assumes that the relation between sound and meaning is arbitrary. Any aspect of language that goes against this assumption has traditionally been considered as only a minor exception to the general rule. Over the past few decades, there has been a great accumulation of cross-linguistic data on sound symbolism. Recently, scholars interested in sound symbolism came together at a conference to attempt to synthesize the data and discuss its implications, in order to begin the determination of the rightful role of sound symbolism in a theory of language. The papers in this volume represent the findings of the conference. We must conclude, from the combined work shown here, that sound symbolism plays a considerably larger role in language than scholarship has hitherto recognized.

In this introduction, we will examine the nature of sound symbolism in general. The term "sound symbolism" has been used for a wide array of phenomena in human languages, related but each with its own distinguishing characteristics. We will begin, then, with a typology of sound symbolism. We then explore the general characteristics of sound-symbolic form and meaning.

1.2. A typology of sound symbolism

Sound symbolism is the direct linkage between sound and meaning. Human language has aspects where sound and meaning are completely linked, as in involuntary utterances such as cries of pain or hiccups. In these cases sound only has "meaning" in that it directly reflects an internal state of the body or mind. A scale can be set up between these utterances and completely conventional, arbitrary language, where sound and meaning presumably have no direct relationship at all. We have found it reasonable to divide the overall concept of sound symbolism into four different categories, which are arranged below according to degree of direct linkage between sound and meaning.

1.2.1. Corporeal sound symbolism

This is the use of certain sounds or intonation patterns to express the internal state of the speaker, emotional or physical. This category includes involuntary, "symptomatic" sounds such as coughing or hiccupping, and ranges through expressive intonation, expressive voice quality, and interjections. An argument could be made that this is not properly sound symbolism, because in this case the sound is not a true *symbol*, but rather a *sign* or *symptom*. We nevertheless give it a place in this typology and in this volume, because it lives around the edges of sound symbolism, and is related to the biological roots of sound symbolism (as well as language in general).

Much of corporeal sound symbolism is not commonly written. Either it forms part of the suprasegmental features of utterances, expressed as intonation or voice quality, or else it is expressed in unconventionalized utterances. Corporeal sound-symbolic utterances are typically structurally simple, non-segmentable vocalizations. In English writing traditions, it is primarily in comic strips that we find expressive intonation and voice quality portrayed, by visual effects such as letter size, shape and color; and such forms as *Aaugh!* and *Achoo!* are attempts to write corporeal utterances that do not fit easily into the sound system of the conventional vocabulary. Corporeal sound-symbolic utterances are directly tied to the emotional or physical state of the speaker, and as such cannot easily be objectified into referential speech. They are, therefore, generally complete utterances, rarely occurring as parts of more complex sentences (except as direct quotations). The unconventionality of corporeal utterances, their structural simplicity, and their defiance of writing makes them an understudied area of human speech. In this volume, the role of human utterances expressive of physical state is discussed in the paper by Ostwald, who develops a typology of the ways in which corporeal utterances reflect disease.

We should also mention here a type of sound symbolism related but tangential to the symptomatic utterances of corporeal sound symbolism: *vocatives* formally have certain similarities to corporeal sound symbolism, but with the function of gaining the attention of some hearer. The use of vocalization to get the attention of another individual is a basic function of vocal communication throughout the animal kingdom. There is a good deal of overlap between corporeal and vocative utterances: the crying of a child or the scream of someone in serious danger are both directly symptomatic and vocative in nature. Some corporeal utterances are regularly manipulated by speakers within linguistic interactions, as vocative or turn-taking signals. Clearing the throat or coughing are often used for these communicative functions. Vocatives, however, go beyond the bounds of corporeal sound symbolism in that they often use the normal vocabulary of language, such as names (see Jacobsen, this volume). Nevertheless, even name vocation involves such expressive features as increased amplitude and segment duration. Since vocation has the specific function of gaining someone's attention, vocatives have the special feature of being designed to suit the acoustic limitations of the external environment and the auditory and mental requisites of the hearer (in so far as the speaker can understand and perform these). Thus our use of whistles and bilabial clicks to call dogs is based on their higher center of hearing; and calls to a distant hearer are different from close-up calls.

Corporeal utterances have many universal components, both in human languages and across species. The paper by Morton discusses some of these cross-species universals, including differences between long-distance and close-up calls.

1.2.2. *Imitative sound symbolism*

This relates to onomatopoeic words and phrases representing environmental sounds (e.g., *bang*, *bow-wow*, *swish*, *knock*, and *rap*). Again, imitatives include many utterances that utilize sound patterns outside of conventional speech and are difficult to portray in writing, such as representations of bird and animal sounds, children's imitations of sirens, etc. Nevertheless, imitatives are much better represented in the linguistic literature than corporeal sound symbolism, because so much onomatopoeic vocabulary does become conventionalized. It is not directly tied to emotional or physical state, the way most corporeal sound symbolism is, but instead has a very important role in referential speech, and can be objectified in a way that expressive sound symbolism cannot. In this volume, Rhodes' paper "Aural images" sets up a scale for discussing degree of conventionalization of onomatopoeic words – his "wild" and "tame" vocabulary. And while "wild" imitative words are not found in dictionaries, there is nevertheless a huge tradition of writing them in comic strips, as discussed by Oswalt.

Imitative sound symbolism is often highly structured linguistically. Rhodes, and also Robert Oswalt in his contribution on "Inanimate imitatives in English," show how English imitative words have an internal grammar.

Very frequently, languages represent movement with the same sorts of sound-symbolic forms that they use for the representation of sounds. The movements so represented are often highly rhythmic (such as walking, swaying, repeated jerking, trembling, etc.). Certainly, rhythmic movement often directly produces sound. But beyond that, the rhythms of sound and the rhythms of movement are so closely linked in the human neural system that they are virtually inseparable. This is illustrated in the very natural human physical response to rhythmic music, in the forms of hand clapping, foot tapping, dancing, rhythmic physical labor, etc. Just as humans are capable of translating rhythmic sounds into rhythmic movements, they are also capable of the reverse: translating rhythmic movements into sounds, including sound-symbolic language forms. In the representation of repeated sounds and movements the linguistic strategy of reduplication is frequently utilized (as in English "ding-dong"), a direct imitation of the rhythm being represented. While it could perhaps be argued that these movement terms are a kind of synesthetic sound symbolism (see section 1.2.3 below), they are so closely tied to imitatives that we would rather call them *movement imitatives*, and include them in this category. Movement imitatives are discussed by Alpher, Aoki, Childs, Diffloth, Langdon, and others in this volume. Hamano's paper gives us an example of a transitional system, one where imitative symbolism is extended into synesthesia.

1.2.3. Synesthetic sound symbolism

We choose here the term "synesthetic" because this realm of sound symbolism can be defined as the acoustic symbolization of non-acoustic phenomena. Synesthetic sound symbolism is the process whereby certain vowels, consonants, and suprasegmentals are chosen to consistently represent visual, tactile, or proprioceptive properties of objects, such as size or shape. For example, segments such as palatal consonants and high vowels are frequently used for diminutive forms and other words representing small objects. Expressive intonation patterns are also used synesthetically, as in the use of deep voice and vowel lengthening in speaking of large objects. ("It was a *bi-i-ig* fish!") Besides symbolic frequency shifts and durational patterns, other acoustic parameters may also serve symbolic roles, such as rise time, fall time, loudness, continuancy, and the contrast between periodicity and aperiodicity. Segmental synesthetic symbolism is most readily subject to study, and has a large and ever-growing literature associated with it. This is partly because it is an area of sound-symbolic speech that is strongly conventionalized ("tame"), and also partly because it is one of the most interesting aspects of sound symbolism, in view of the fact that here the relation between sound and meaning is relatively indirect. Work by scholars from Sapir on (see references) shows clearly that in the case of size symbolism, there is a very significant tendency in languages throughout the world for certain types of segments to be chosen over other types of segments to represent objects of given sizes. For example, Ultan (1978) found that in almost 90% of the languages he sampled that had diminutive marking, the diminutive was symbolized by high front vowels. Nevertheless, to a much greater extent than for expressive symbolism and onomatopoeia, exceptions to these findings are also prevalent, illustrating that this sort of sound symbolism is further along the scale toward arbitrariness than the previous two types.

Introduction

Like imitative sound symbolism, synesthetic sound symbolism is often highly structured. As Silverstein demonstrates (this volume), the phonemic inventory of Wasco-Washram Chinookan is structured according to its role in demonstrating diminution and augmentation.

1.2.4. Conventional sound symbolism

This is the analogical association of certain phonemes and clusters with certain meanings: e.g. the "gl" of glitter, glisten, glow, glimmer, etc. This process is most eloquently described by Bloomfield (1895):

Every word, in so far as it is semantically expressive, may establish, by hap-hazard favoritism, a union between its meaning and any of its sounds, and then send forth this sound (or sounds) upon predatory expeditions into domains where the sound is at first a stranger and parasite. A slight emphasis punctures the placid function of a certain sound-element, and the ripple extends, no-one can say how far . . .

The signification of any word is arbitrarily attached to some sound-element contained in it, and then cogeneric names are created by means of this infused, or we might say, irradiated, or inspired element. (pp. 409–410)

Unlike the previous three categories, which are seen to exhibit many cross-linguistic similarities, conventional sound symbolism, as the name implies, may be largely language-specific in its choice of phonetic segments. These submorphemic meaning-carrying entities are sometimes called *phonesthemes*, or *phonetic intensives* (Bolinger 1965). While phonesthemes are often conventional, some have universal properties and fit into other categories described above. There is some debate as to whether these units really have a special status, or whether they should be classed as a type of morpheme instead. Rhodes (this volume) argues the latter point of view.

While conventional sound symbolism is frequently classed as sound symbolism, we are getting close here to the arbitrary end of the language scale. Yet the point must be made that in the minds of speakers, sound and meaning are always linked automatically, so that on some subjective and unconscious level we all agree with Cratylus (see the quotation which opens this chapter), that names are somehow "natural." Children feel this especially strongly, as illustrated once by Stephanie, the stepdaughter of one of the authors: she said, "English is the one true language, isn't it?" When asked what she meant, she replied, "Well, when [our Mexican friend] Lupe says 'agua,' what she *means* is 'water.' But when *I* say 'water,' I don't mean 'agua,' I really mean 'water'!"

While some of us may later learn to subjugate these linguocentric prejudices, the tension of their continued underground existence in adult minds is still often expressed in humor. ("No wonder they call it an elephant: it's so big!") It is this predilection toward the belief in the naturalness and rightness of words or their components as representatives of meaning that is probably at work in phonesthetic association and creation. Phonesthetic creation is especially obvious in the realm of blends. Another quote from Bloomfield (1895):

> I have mentioned in the past that I frequently felt tempted to blend the two words *quench* and *squelch* in a composite result *squench*, and that my attention was afterward drawn to a passage in Page's "In Old Virginia," p. 53, presenting the word in dialect "She le' me *squench* my thirst kissin' her hand." ... The slang word *swipe*, which is now heard often, is to my sense clearly a similar product of *wipe* and *sweep* and *swoop*. One can taste the ingredients.
> (pp. 411–412)

Great use of conventional sound symbolism is made in the creation of names for commercial products. The American automobile corporation Dodge has named one of its transporters the *Caravan*, which evokes the image of adventure and far-flung travel, while at the same time being a play on words by referring to a vehicle type called a "van." (The word "van" was derived as an abbreviation from "caravan" in the first place, but most people probably are not aware of that historical fact, and are more likely to see the play on words as a pun in the last syllable. Americans do not use the word as the common term for a mobile home, as British English does.) The *Nova*, famous as a naming disaster in the Spanish-speaking world ("doesn't go"), is nevertheless a very successful car name to English speakers. The word itself means an exploding star, evoking a sense of mystery, beauty, speed, and powerful light; the first part of it connotes newness (novel, novelty), and it bears the traditional feminine ending so popular among car names. Auto namers create blends, such as *Sentra*, which combines the feminine ending with a piece of the word "sentry," the watchful protector. Among shampoos, we find such names as *L'Oreal*, no doubt recognized by its creators as sounding like a very feminine-sounding name (Laura), reminiscent of a flower name (Laurel), while at the same time harking back to synesthetic sound symbolism: the name is full of continuant, "flowing" sounds to symbolize flowing hair.

At the ends of sound symbolism, then, we see the human mind at work *creating* links between sound and meaning even where such links might not be intrinsic or universal.

1.3. Metalinguistic symbolism

Cross-cutting the above categories is a sort of sound symbolism that might be termed *metalinguistic symbolism*, where segment choice and intonation patterns signal aspects of linguistic structure and function. One type of metalinguistic symbolism, highly conventionalized and abstract, comprises the various language-specific restrictions on the formal canon of individual parts of speech, including exclusion of, or preference for, particular phonemes in particular parts of speech or affixes, dealt with in this volume by Austerlitz, Diffloth, Malkiel, Matisoff, and Sereno. Diffloth shows that what he calls *expressives* are a regular phonological part of the language, yet particular vowels are infrequent in them. Yet while central vowels are dispreferred in Bahnar expressives, the central vowel /y/ is shown by Langdon to be favored in corresponding symbolic vocabulary in Guaraní; this discrepancy illustrates the language-specific and conventionalized nature of such restrictions. Matisoff discusses a set of words one might describe as involving metacommunicative synesthetic symbolism: a particular, language-specific, form is conventionally associated with a particular kind of semantics. Malkiel proposes the term *morphosymbolism* for the association of particular root-canon forms with particular parts of speech or their subclasses. Sereno shows that in English, parts of speech (nouns and verbs) are partially signaled by vowel quality. In an example that may be transitional between plain and metacommunicative conventional symbolism, Austerlitz discusses a set of etymological problems suggesting that particular sounds – including, saliently, sounds that are secondary in the language and therefore likely to have been highly marked and to have had high affective value at some earlier time – have some propensity to associate themselves non-etymologically with certain roots, and the conditions favoring the innovations involve both semantics and abstract lexical or grammatical classes. For all these and similar examples, association of particular forms with particular abstract classes functions to expedite communication in that, especially under noisy conditions, the occurrence of a particular sound, sound class, or sound sequence aids the hearer in recovering the fact that s/he has just heard, say, a noun or an accusative case or a past-tense verb. Perhaps the best-known example of this kind of symbolism is the use of phonemes, of neutralization, of abstract structural shapes, and of accent in what Trubetzkoy calls the *boundary-marking function* (Trubetzkoy 1969).

Frequently labeled as "symbolism" are various forms of consonantal and vocalic ablaut utilized to express such grammatical phenomena as tense, aspect, pluralization, etc. – such as *goose/geese* in English, or a similar kind of vowel ablaut to represent active/passive distinctions in Yana (Sapir 1922). This kind of process strains at the edges of what we would consider to be valid sound symbolism. Certainly consonant or vowel substitution is one of the most common means for producing sound-symbolic expression, but only if a non-arbitrary (either natural or conventional) relationship between a segment and its meaning can be demonstrated would we want to call the process sound-symbolic. Nevertheless, a productive process of ablaut has the potential to be a process of conventional sound symbolism.

The examples dealt with so far have all involved the non-arbitrary relations of sound to meaning. There are also instances of the non-arbitrary relation of sound to communicative function, for which a separate term such as *metacommunicative symbolism* might be proposed. In fact, it may well be that each of our types of sound symbolism also has a metacommunicative variant. Certainly the vocative and turn-taking uses of corporeal utterances (coughing, throat-clearing) discussed above are example of metacommunicative symbolism. One further example is whispering: here the acoustic form of speech is adjusted in accordance with the communicative function, namely communication at close distance and where intimacy, privacy, or some form of restraint (conventional or otherwise) on the possible audience is desired. Another example would appear to be the addition or lengthening of word-final vowels in the vocatives discussed in this volume by Jacobsen. The added acoustic prominence achieved by this device serves the communicative end of getting the hearer's attention; since in real usage vocatives sometimes function as interjections or contributors of special pragmatic coloring rather than (or as well as) attention-getters, the metacommunicative function is again distinctly conventionalized.

Another metalinguistic function of sound symbolism is described in Silverstein's article here on Wasco. He points out that diminutive–augmentative sound symbolism in Wasco does not merely denote small and large objects, but rather functions to signal the affective and evaluative relationship of the speaker to the referent.

1.4. Sound-symbolic form

There is much that is language-specific about sound-symbolic form, and most of the papers in this volume will illustrate these language-specific characteristics (termed "local sound symbolism" in Priestly's article). However, threaded throughout these papers and others listed in the references, there are aspects of sound-symbolic form that appear over and over again, and that we may thus hypothesize to be universal tendencies. Diffloth (this volume) warns against the premature naming of any sound-symbolic pattern as "universal," when the use of the term is loosely used simply to mean that it occurs in a number of languages. However, we believe that when a sound-symbolic pattern is found in a larger number of languages than one would expect if language were fully arbitrary, its presence is attributable to some explanation that is independent of the internal workings of a particular language. It is in that sense that we believe the term "universal (tendency)" to be both accurate and valuable. Such explanations of common sound-symbolic patterns are quite various. They may be extrinsic to language, as in onomatopoeia, where the choice of linguistic representation is based on the features of language-extrinsic sounds; or they may be related to deeply rooted aspects of human (or in some cases, more generally mammalian or even vertebrate) neurology and cognition, as in corporeal sound symbolism and much synesthetic sound symbolism. The explanation may also lie in universals of the pragmatics of human interaction, such as in universal tendencies of vocative forms suggested by Jacobsen in this volume.

Introduction

Three overall sound-symbolic strategies emerge from these studies as being especially noteworthy: (1) use of reduplication; (2) marked use of segments that are otherwise uncommon in the language, and the loosening of distributional constraints that are otherwise strong in the language; (3) the association of certain types of segments and suprasegmentals with certain semantic realms.

1.4.1. Reduplication

Some languages use reduplication more than other languages. But in those languages that do use it, we seem to find a strong tendency for reduplication to be associated with sound symbolism. Such use of reduplication is common but not very productive in English sound-symbolic forms (the English style of reduplication is often called "partial reduplication" since it involves vowel alternation): "ding-dong," "see-saw," "teeter-totter," "flim-flam," "dilly-dally," "wishy-washy," etc. European languages in general utilize reduplication less than the rest of the world. In this volume, examples of reduplicated forms abound in Guaraní (Langdon), Nez Perce (Aoki), Mon Khmer (Diffloth), Lahu (Matisoff), and Africa (Childs), illustrating the prevalence of reduplication around the world.

1.4.2. Use of unusual segments and suprasegmentals

As shown elsewhere (see, for example, Hinton 1986), sounds often enter a language by means of sound-symbolic words. Scholars from Grassmann on have shown that sound changes often do not affect sound-symbolic words, so that phonemes which have otherwise disappeared or become restricted to certain environments are often found thriving in the sound-symbolic vocabulary. This same tendency is shown in this volume for Huastec (Kaufman). Papers in this volume by Aoki (Nez Perce), Austerlitz (Finnish), Joseph (Modern Greek), and Matisoff (Lahu) all discuss segments or tones that are common only in sound-symbolic vocabulary. English also exhibits this tendency: Rhodes's "wild" forms exhibit marked phonology, such as the use of segments that do not occur elsewhere in the English language.

At the same time that unusual sounds may occur, there is also a tendency to use a reduced phonemic inventory in sound symbolism, as suggested by Oswalt in this volume (who makes the same claim for Pomo in Oswalt 1971).

1.4.3. Association of certain phoneme classes with certain semantic fields

This is the sort of sound-symbolic patterning that is most commonly discussed in the literature, and which is best illustrated by imitative and synesthetic sound-symbolic forms. In imitatives, for example, stops are used for abrupt sounds and acts, and continuants for continuing sounds and acts. Fricatives are used for quick audible motion of an object through air; nasals are used for ringing, reverberating sounds.

Overarching imitatives and synthesthetic symbolism is the celebrated Frequency Code (so named by Ohala 1984, and developed by Sapir 1911, 1927, Jesperson 1933, Swadesh 1970, Nichols 1971, and others), which can be summarized as follows: high tones, vowels with high second formants (notably /i/), and high-frequency consonants are associated with high-frequency sounds, small size, sharpness, and rapid movement; low tones, vowels with low second formants (notably /u/), and low-frequency consonants are associated with low-frequency sounds, large size, softness, and heavy, slow movements. Ohala carries his work on Frequency Code further in this volume, and it is well borne out by several other papers here; LaPolla and Matisoff shows its validity for several Asian languages, and Berlin and Langdon for South and Central American languages. Berlin and LaPolla have gone further, to show that the same Frequency Code can be utilized to allow English speakers to correctly guess semantic components of Chinese and Jivaro words. Diffloth, on the other hand, reminds us that there are languages which actually reverse the Frequency Code, as is the case with Mon Khmer sound-symbolic vowel usage.

1.5. Semantic and pragmatic realms of sound-symbolic vocabulary

The following semantic and pragmatic fields crop up again and again for sound-symbolic vocabulary.
(1) mimicry of environmental and internal sounds;
(2) expression of internal states of being, both physical and emotional;
(3) expressions of social relationships (as in diminutive forms and vocatives and imperatives); also the expression of opprobrium and stigma;
(4) salient characteristics of objects and activities, such as movement, size, shape, color, and texture;
(5) grammatical and discourse indicators, such as intonational markers of discourse and sentence structure, and distinctions between parts of speech;
(6) expression of the evaluative and affective relationship of the speaker to the subject being discussed.

These six areas may be seen as encompassing most of language. Only abstract relational notions (such as categories of even and odd numbers) seem to be sparse in sound-symbolic representation. The first three of these semantic fields are clearly present in the non-human animal world of communication (vocal mimicry is not a general feature of non-human communication, but is found in many species; expressions of internal state and social relationships are found quite generally in vocalizing animals). It is only the last two that are thought to be

Introduction

(almost) uniquely characteristic of human language. It is also the last two that are traditionally thought to be largely represented by arbitrary linguistic forms; yet we have seen that sound symbolism plays an important role here as well.

Given that we share many of our sound-symbolic aspects of language with other species, it is quite possible that in sound symbolism we are seeing the precursors of fully formed human language. In fact, it seems quite reasonable to say that in all advanced vocalizers (especially humans, many birds, and many cetaceans) we can see a basic sound-symbolic communication system overlaid by elaborations which could be termed arbitrary in their relationship to meaning. Morton (this volume) has demonstrated some of the sound-symbolic aspects of bird and mammal vocalizations. An "arbitrary" component of bird song has developed in the elaboration of territorial songs, just as it has in human language.

In terms of evolution, the value of a sound-symbolic basis to communication is fairly obvious, in that it allows greater ease of communication. Reaction-time experiments show that for humans, correct judgments about the meanings of words are faster for sound-symbolic words than for arbitrary words. Sereno (this volume) demonstrates this for the part-of-speech symbolism she has found in English. In the human and non-human world alike, it is generally to the benefit of speaker and hearer for accurate communication to take place; if form of vocalization is tied directly to meaning, the possibility of accurate and speedy comprehension is enhanced.

It is the evolutionary value of arbitrariness, then, that must be explained. While this interesting problem has been the focus of a fairly large body of research, it is not the purpose of this volume.

1.6. Sound symbolism as a cross-disciplinary topic

The quotation from Plato with which we began this introduction, the terminology chosen above, and the literature, issues, and terminology reviewed here and in most of the individual contributions give our theoretical analysis of sound symbolism a decidedly Western cast. Other grammatical traditions, of course, have also examined symbolism and related issues. We refer the reader to the concise survey of Chinese sources in LaPolla's paper in this volume, and to the terminological discussions by Matisoff, Diffloth, and Hamano. Matisoff and Hamano use technical concepts taken from Japanese grammar, and Matisoff also cites the Japanese terms.

Sound symbolism is a topic of cross-disciplinary interest, as shown in the array of fields our contributors come from: linguistics, anthropology, literature, biology and medicine. In medicine we find that the corporeal sound-symbolic utterances, especially involuntary cries, can give physicians cues about the physical problems of a patient. In biology we find the ethological basis of sound symbolism. In literature, the sound of the words chosen to portray meaning comes to play an important role; just to give one example, a study of consonantism in lyric poetry shows a high degree of usage of the sonorants, while Carl Sandburg uses a high percentage of obstruents to portray his rough messages. The anthropological study in this volume (Berlin) starts from the basic anthropological interest in how people of different cultures categorize the world around them, and leads to the conclusion that sound symbolism plays an important role in these categories. In linguistics, the major question leading to sound-symbolic studies is the one we posed at the beginning of this treatise: how arbitrary is language form? Or, how much can the form of language be tied to meaning? The papers that follow will show that languages around the world carry a large sound-symbolic component. Meaning and sound can never be fully separated, and linguistic theory must accommodate itself to that increasingly obvious fact.

REFERENCES

Bloomfield, M. 1895. On assimilation and adaptation in congeneric classes of words. *American Journal of Philology* 16: 409–434.

Bolinger, D. 1965. The atomization of meaning. *Language* 41: 555–573.

Hinton, L. 1986. Musical diffusion and linguistic diffusion. In C. Frisbie (ed.) *Anthropology and Music: Essays in Honor of David P. McAllester*. Detroit Monographs in Musicology 9. Detroit: Information Coordinators.

Jesperson, O. 1933. Symbolic value of the vowel *i*. In *Linguistica. Selected Papers in English, French and German*. Copenhagen: Levin & Munksgaard, 283–303.

Nichols, J. 1971. Diminutive consonant symbolism in Western North America. *Language* 47: 826–848.

Ohala, J. 1984. An ethological perspective on common cross-language utilization of F_0 of voice. *Phonetica* 41: 1–16.

Oswalt, R. L. 1971. Inanimate imitatives in Pomo. In Jesse Saweyer (ed.) *Studies in American Indian Languages*. University of California Publications in Linguistics 65: 175–190.

Sapir, E. 1911. Diminutive and augmentative consonant symbolism in Wishram. *Handbook of American Indian Languages*. Bureau of American Ethnography, Washington, DC Bull. 40, Part 1: 638–646.

1922. The fundamental elements of Northern Yana. *University of California Publications in American Archaeology and Ethnology* 13, no. 6: 215–234.

1927. Language as a form of human behavior. *The English Journal* 16: 421–433.

Swadesh, M. 1970. The problem of consonantal doublets in Indo-European. *Word* 26: 1–16.

Trubetzkoy, N. 1969. *Principles of Phonology*. Originally published as *Grundzüge der Phonologie*, Travaux du Cercle Linguistique de Prague 7 (1939). Translated by C. A. M. Baltaxe. Berkeley: University of California Press.

Ultan, R. 1978. Size–sound symbolism. In Joseph Greenberg, (ed) *Universals of Human Language*, volume 2: *Phonology*. Stanford: University Press.

PART I

Native American languages north of Mexico

2
Symbolism in Nez Perce

HARUO AOKI

2.1. Introduction

Nez Perce is a native American language spoken where the states of Idaho, Oregon, and Washington meet. In connection with the Nez Perce language the term *symbolism* can be associated with sound in at least two ways. One is as in imitative sound symbolism, and the other is augmentative–diminutive sound symbolism, a type of synesthetic sound symbolism marking the size of an object or the status, sex, age, or other characteristics of the speaker, addressee, or referent. Imitative phonosymbolism is reported in a wide range of languages, and is probably universal; the symbolic augmentative–diminutive alternation of sounds is reported in many languages of the Americas.[1] Both kinds of symbolism exist in Nez Perce.

2.2. Imitative sound symbolism

Unlike some languages such as Japanese, whose sound-symbolic words fill five-hundred-page dictionaries, Nez Perce phonosymbolic words are not many in number. The following are examples:[2]

    bear coughing   łik
    bear eating soup   łi·k̓
    burning (e.g. of tepee)   pim·
    chorus of katydids   tum·
    drum   pim
    eating cartilage   x̣ú·mx̣um
    door flap flapping in the wind   x̣alp
    flatus   ček̓
    footstep of deer   kúx

goose call   hú·
katydid   čálalal
locust   t̓ex̣
magpie flying   law
pounding (e.g. of sunflower seeds)   kút
raven   qó·x̣
rope going taut   qiʔ
thunder (boom)   t̓um·
thunder (crash)   t̓o·x̣
tumbling out of Coyote's excrement-children (a folktale incident; see p. 53 below)   yóx̣ox̣ox̣ox̣
walking through dry grass leaves   ɬox̣ɬóx̣
west wind   t̓ákakak
wind whistling through snags   tiyé·pu

One characteristic of Nez Perce phonosymbolic words is the relatively large number with initial /ɬ/ and ending in a stop. Also, there are two features that suggest that the rule of ordinary word formation does not apply to phonosymbolic words: one is the occurrence of /k/, /q/, and their glottalized variants at the end of words, and the other is the occurrence of a glottalized λ. Glottalized barred lamda is not found in non-onomatopoeic words. An example is λ́ép (sound of something falling into water).

Besides these forms, some nouns, especially bird names, appear to be imitative in origin. Examples are ʔá·ʔa "crow," ʔawí·xno "curlew," qú·ynu "dove," ʔicpó·qox "gray jay."

There are a limited number of imitative words which represent movement instead of sound. An example is ɬép, which describes movements of sheet-like objects. The word for butterfly, ɬé·pɬep, seems to be a derivative of ɬép.

2.3.   Diminutive symbolism

2.3.1.   *Consonant and vowel symbolism in Nez Perce*

Symbolism in Nez Perce is observable in both consonants and, although only in one pair, vowels. In some languages consonant symbolism is, as in the case of Wiyot (Teeter 1959, 1964), in three grades: (1) normal, (2) diminutive, (3) augmentative. In Nez Perce there are only two grades: normal and diminutive. The non-diminutive /s n k e/ are paralleled by /c l q a/ in the diminutive grade. Another device Nez Perce has in order to express diminutiveness is reduplication, which is frequently used simultaneously with consonant or vowel symbolism as in (14) (Aoki 1970: 43–44).

s > c
- (1) pé·su·yece.   "He rocks (a child)."
- (2) pé·cu·yece.   "He rocks (a small child)."
- (3) naʔyá·c   "my elder brother"
- (4) ʔirhyá·s   "your elder brother"
- (5) waswásno   "chicken"
- (6) wacwácno   "saddle horn"
- (7) ʔiskí·cuʔmix   "Coeur d'Alene"
- (8) ʔickí·cuʔmix   "Coeur d'Alene" (in derision)

n > l
- (9) hité·mñes   "book" (thing to read)
- (10) kiwkwílec   "drum" (thing to beat)

k > q
- (11) síkem   "horse"
- (12) ciq̓á·mqal   "dog" (-qal "young of an animal")

e > a
- (13) ké·tis   "spear"
- (14) katická·tic   "toy spear"

Of these diminutive shifts the last two pairs substitute the low vowel /a/ for non-low /e/, which runs counter to universal expectations that diminutives should bear high vowels. Form (12) also shifts k̓ to q̓, which goes against the general case where diminutive forms front velars. These forms exemplify another phonological mechanism that overrides diminutive sound symbolism: Nez Perce vowel harmony (Aoki 1966). The vowels /u/, /e/, and some /i/ constitute one group, which may be called *recessive*, and the corresponding /o/, /a/, and the remaining /i/ constitute the *dominant* group. When a dominant vowel is in the same word, recessive vowels /e u/ change to dominant /a o/ respectively. Terms of endearment are often in the dominant group. For example, the ordinary word for the color brown is *sukúysukuy*, but a pet name for a roan horse is *có·k̓oy*, which might be considered a kind of diminutive form. The shift of /k/ to /q/, as in examples (11)–(12), does not occur frequently. It may be considered a process of assimilation caused by the lowering of the vowel.

Of the examples above the pairs (1)–(2) and (9)–(10) may be considered cases of true diminutive symbolism: they involve variants of a *single* lexical item, and the ingredient which triggers the variation is the diminutive quality of the referent. The pair (7) and (8) is also an example of diminutive symbolism, except that what is involved is not the real diminutive quality but the contempt or belittling opinion of the speaker. The parts in the pair (3)–(4) meaning "older brother" are again two variants of the same lexical item, but they no longer appear to be a case of basic or prototypical diminutive symbolism in that they are no longer free; the pronominal prefix determines which one of the variants is used. After a first-person prefix only the diminutive variant is grammatical and elsewhere only the normal is correct.

The other examples are different from those discussed in that they should be considered *two* different lexical items, with vestiges of symbolic relationship. The normal forms represent basic items and the diminutive forms represent something similar in shape but smaller in size and often dissimilar in substance. The pairs (5)–(6) and (13)–(14) are examples.

One of the ways the Nez Perce language accommodates a new cultural item can be seen in the following pair:

(15) tiṁú·ni   "gun"
(16) walí·mtiṁuni "bow" (lit. old-time tiṁú·ni)

The procedure seems to be (1) the new item is called by the name for the old item, and (2) the old item is called by a newly created name. The pair (11)–(12) seems to indicate the same procedure. First the newly introduced horse is called *síkem*, a "dog." Then a new word for the dog is created utilizing the mechanism of sound symbolism: it is called a "little dog." The ordinary word for dogs used by adults today is *ciqá·mqal* with the diminutive grade of the suffix *-qan* which means "young of animals." (For example, *lá·qac* is a mouse and *lá·qacqan* is a baby mouse.) The unsuffixed diminutive for *ciqam* survives as a children's word.

The etymology of Nez Perce symbolic words may be considered to have three stages: (1) in the first and basic stage there exists a single lexical item which may assume its normal grade form or, when needed, assume its variant with diminutive meaning; (2) in the second the diminutive meaning is changed or lost; and (3) in the third stage the normal grade and diminutive grade forms are two different lexical items. This may be summarized as in (17).

(17)

	Single lexical item	Diminutive meaning	Examples
Stage I	+	+	(1)–(2)
Stage II	+	−	(3)–(4)
Stage III	−	−	(5)–(6)

2.3.2. *Diminutive symbolism and specialized speech genres in Nez Perce*

As in many other cultures of the Americas, the characters in traditional Nez Perce stories are animals. Most of the animals are real, but there are also mythical ones. There are rare cases of bilinguals such as Porcupine, who speaks both Nez Perce and Interior Salish, but the majority speak only Nez Perce. The character who speaks *normal* Nez Perce is Fox, who is always cast as a straight man opposite Coyote. The speeches of animals other than Fox are marked either by special prefix or by substitution of consonants. For example, Coyote's speech is marked either by the prefix ʔisci- or by replacing an /n/ with an /l/, which is the same as one of the changes involved in diminutive symbolism. Phinney records in his 1934 *Nez Percé Texts* that "boy-child" as spoken by Coyote is *lícu* (Phinney 1934: 361, line 14). The normal form is *nícu*. Phinney notes that the change of /n/ to /l/ occurs in "affected baby talk" (Phinney 1934: 144, n. 1). This change is likely to be designed to reflect the immature and infantile side of Coyote's character. The role of the villain is frequently played by Grizzly Bear. Her speech is represented by changing stops and spirants to [ł]. For example, (18), which is normal speech, is changed to (19) in Grizzly Bear's speech.

(18) ʔi·sqal memhé·te·x himsamó·siqa.   "Oh, they were telling me a lie!"
(19) ʔi·łqal memhé·łe·x łimłamó·łiqa.   (= (18) by Grizzly Bear)

I was told that the change of sounds to /ł/ is imitation of lisping. In Nez Perce lisping is associated with subnormal intelligence, which, combined with muscle power, makes the grizzly dangerous. That all of the onomatopoeic words imitative of sounds made by bears begin with a ł may not be completely accidental.³

In most examples of animal speech the rule of change does not seem to apply exhaustively. For example, in (19) the last applicable consonant in each word is left unchanged. This might be because in Nez Perce most grammatical information such as case and tense is suffixed, and modification or excessive neutralization of the suffix area could create communication problems.

2.3.3. Diminutive symbolism in comparative linguistics

Nez Perce is genetically related to Sahaptin and together they constitute the Sahaptian family. Sahaptin is divided into three dialect clusters: (1) Northwest (NW), (2) Columbia River (CR), and (3) Northeast (NE).⁴ The Sahaptin system is again only in two grades: normal and diminutive. The normal /s š n/ are paralleled by /ł s l/ in the diminutive grade.

s > ł
  (20) kúsi (NW, CR, NE)   "horse"
  (21) kúłi (?)   "pet"

š > s
  (22) yámaš (NW, CR, NE)   "mule deer"
  (23) yámas (NW)   "jumping mouse"
  (24) kušú (CR)   "pig"
  (25) kusúkusu (CR)   "new-born pig"

n > l
  (26) wíwnu (NW, CR)   "huckleberry"
  (27) wiwlúwiwlu (NW, CR)   "small huckleberry"
  (28) tkwínat (NW, CR)   "chinook salmon"
  (29) tkwiláttkwilat (NW, CR)   "jack salmon" ("little chinook salmon")

The pair (24)–(25) shows that symbolic modification occurs in loanwords just as in native ones. The Sahaptin word for "dog" is *kusíkusi* in the Northwest cluster and *kusikúsi* in the Columbia River and Northeast clusters, indicating that the same adaptive strategy as in Nez Perce is at work here: the simplex form (20) which once meant "dog" was appropriated to designate the newly introduced horse, and the old dog is now referred to by a reduplicated form which expresses diminutiveness. Although what corresponds to the second stage is not found there are Sahaptin examples of basic symbolism (Stage I) and those which show lexical split (Stage III). In a word, the mechanisms of symbolism in Sahaptin and Nez Perce are quite similar.

When we compare Sahaptin (S) and Nez Perce (NP) forms taking pairs involving /n/ and /l/ as examples, we have the following correspondence types:

(30) *n:l* S nunás   (NW, CR, ww) NP ló·las   "mariposa lily"
(31) *n:n* S išnim   (CR, NE)   NP sísnim   "black hawthorn"
(32) *l:n* S patúlpatul (Ws)   NP pátan   "brush, bush"
(33) *l:l* S q̓špalí   (NW, CR, NE) NP q̓ispaʔláya "vulture"

The number of correspondences is four if we have identity correspondence within Sahaptin, but when we consider the three dialect clusters in Sahaptin there are 2^4 or 16 n/l correspondences. This number will be further multiplied if we take individual dialects into account. A sensible way to avoid reconstructing 16 or more n-like or l-like proto-units seems to be to assume that n-to-l symbolism existed in Proto-Sahaptian. One noticeable phenomenon in the n/l correspondences between Sahaptin and Nez Perce is that the distribution of various correspondence types is not even. For example, the Sahaptin forms in the sets (30), (31), and (33) are found in at least in two dialect clusters, but in the set (32) the form that fits this pattern is found only in the Tenino and Tygh dialects, which are sometimes grouped as Warmsprings (Ws). The majority of correspondences are either identity correspondences as (31) and (33) or the type which has the *normal* grade on the Sahaptin side and *diminutive* grade in Nez Perce as in (30). The situation is quite similar in the *s*-like consonants: Sahaptin *š* and Nez Perce *s* in the normal grade and their diminutive counterparts, Sahaptin *s* and Nez Perce *c*. This suggests that there are different, language-specific, degrees of predilection for diminutive sound shift. Of the two languages Nez Perce more frequently adopted the diminutive forms.

This suggests two things that sound shifts do in historical linguistics. One is to create a dialect or language split, and the other is, for the language which adopts the forms which have already undergone the shift, death of symbolism: for, quite simply, when *n* is diminutivized to *l* there is no way to diminutivize it any further.

NOTES

1 One of the first to discuss augmentative–diminutive symbolism was Sapir (1915). Its occurrence in Northwestern California was treated by Haas (1970) and Nichols (1971). Of the eleven cultural areas north of Mexico that Sherzer surveyed, only three (Arctic, Western Subarctic, and Southeast) lack augmentative–diminutive consonantal symbolism in nominal stems (Sherzer 1976: 25, 37, 212).

2 The Nez Perce language data were collected by the author in the 1960s and 1970s under the joint auspices of the Survey of California and Other Indian Languages, Department of Linguistics, University of California, Berkeley and of the Idaho State Historical Society, Boise, Idaho. Americanist symbols that are not equivalent to IPA are: c = ts; C̣ = backed version of C, e.g. x̣ is uvular x; ƚ = voiceless lateral fricative; λ = voiceless lateral affricate; š = fortis dental fricative; y = palatal glide; ṗ, ṫ, k̇).

3 In his grammar of the Takelma language of Oregon, Sapir refers to a prefix peculiar to the bear in the form of L (1922: 8, n. 2), which is "voiceless palatalized l" (Sapir 1909: 10). This is further discussed by Hymes (1979).

4 The following classification and abbreviations of Sahaptin dialect are after Eugene Hunn (1979a, 1979b):

NW: Northwest cluster
  kt: Kittitas or Pshwanwapam
  uc: Upper Cowlitz or Taitnapam
  yk: Yakima or Mamachat
  kl: Klickitat
CR: Columbia River cluster
  te: Tenino
  ty: Tygh
  Ws = te + ty
  ce: Celilo or Wayampam
  rc: Rock Creek
  jd: John Day River
  um: Umatilla
NE: Northeast cluster
  ww: Walla Walla
  sr: Snake River
  pr: Priest Rapids or Wanapam
  pl: Palouse

REFERENCES

Aoki, H. 1966. Nez Perce vowel harmony and Proto-Sahaptian vowels. *Language* 42: 759–767.

    1970. *Nez Perce Grammar.* University of California Publications in Linguistics 62. Berkeley and Los Angeles: University of California Press.

Haas, M. R. 1970. Consonant symbolism in Northwestern California. In Earl H. Swanson, Jr. (ed.) *Languages and Cultures of Western North America: Essays in Honor of Sven S. Liljeblad*. Pocatello: The Idaho State University Press, 86–96.

Hunn, E. 1979a. Sahaptin animal terms. Unpublished preliminary version prepared for the Yakima Indian Nation.

  1979b. Sahaptin plant terms. Unpublished preliminary version prepared for the Yakima Indian Nation.

Hymes, D. H. 1979. How to talk like a bear in Takelma. *International Journal of American Linguistics* 45: 101–106. (Reprinted with revision as Chapter 2 of *"In Vain I Tried to Tell You": Essays in Native American Ethnopoetics*. Studies in Native American Literature 1. Philadelphia: University of Pennsylvania Press, 1981.)

Nichols, J. 1971. Diminutive consonant symbolism in Western North America. *Language* 47: 826–848.

Phinney, A. 1934. *Nez Percé Texts*. Columbia University Contributions in Anthropology 25. New York: Columbia University Press.

Sapir, E. 1909. *Takelma Texts*. University of Pennsylvania, The Museum, Anthropological Publications 2(1). Philadelphia: The University Museum.

  1915. *Abnormal Types of Speech in Nootka*. Geological Survey (Canada), Memoir 62, Anthropological Series 5. Ottawa: Government Printing Bureau.

  1922. The Takelma language of Southwest Oregon. In F. Boas (ed.) *Handbook of American Indian Languages* 2. Bureau of American Ethnology, Bulletin 40. Washington: Government Printing Office, 3–296.

Sherzer, J. 1976. *An Areal-Typological Study of American Indian Languages North of Mexico*. North-Holland Linguistic Series 20. Amsterdam: North-Holland.

Teeter, K. V. 1959. Consonant harmony in Wiyot (with a note on Cree). *International Journal of American Linguistics* 25: 41–43.

  1964. *The Wiyot Language*. University of California Publications in Linguistics 37. Berkeley and Los Angeles: University of California Press.

3
Nootkan vocative vocalism and its implications*

WILLIAM H. JACOBSEN, JR.

3.1. Introduction

All the Nootkan languages exhibit vocative forms in which one of the vowels of a word is changed to a long mid vowel, or a mid vowel or falling diphthong is suffixed, occasionally with truncation of the word. I will consider the languages separately in a geographical ordering from south to north: Makah, Nitinat, Southern Nootka, Northern Nootka, and related Northern Wakashan,[1] and then draw some inferences about the development of the pattern; after which, with the consideration of a sampling of other languages, I will suggest some universal tendencies that seem to bear upon the shaping of vocative forms.

The function of these forms seems to be equivalent among the Nootkan languages. Most commonly they occur in words which are labels for categories of persons, expressing kinship, sex, age, social rank, and tribal affiliation. Such forms are predominantly used in directly addressing or calling to the person(s) so labeled, as in Makah

(1) čo·kʷap šuʔukʷ   "grandson, come here!"

However, such forms may also indicate that the utterance is being called out to someone, in which case they need not label the addressee. Then one finds the formation also applied to verb forms, most commonly imperative but also indicative in mode, as well as to words for inanimate objects and to kinship terms marked for second-person possessor. We will nevertheless illustrate some specific contexts in which inanimate objects or insects are directly addressed using these forms. Because of these cases where the addressee is not referred to, the label *vocative* is less happy than Sapir and Swadesh's (1939: 210, note 4) *calling-out forms*.

This formation may be applied to two or more words combined in a phrase that is called out, as in this Nootka example of an imperative verb form and its object:[2]

(2) m̓učʔiƛʔape·ke·sta   "Keep the chamber pot covered!"

3.2. Makah

Vocative forms in Makah are formed by a change of vowel within a word, by which a vowel of quality *a* or *i* is replaced by *e·*, and one of quality *u* is replaced by *o·*. In the case of vowel change in the first syllable, the word may be clipped to the first one or two syllables. Occasionally another long vowel in the word is shortened. I list the forms that have come to my attention, grouped according to the position of the changed vowel in the word and the amount of shortening that has taken place.[3]

Several words for close relatives show a change of the vowel in the first syllable, for the vocative form together with a shortening to monosyllable. I give the full (unanalyzed) word, its meaning, and the vocative form. The following show the *a > e·* change:

	Full form	Gloss	Vocative
(3)	ʔabe·ʔiqsu (alt. ʔabe·qsu)	"mother"	ʔe·b
(4)	hade·ʔiqsu (alt. hade·qsu)	"uncle, aunt"	he·d
(5)	ba·bi·qsu	"older sibling, cousin"	be·b
(6)	dade·ʔiqsu (dade·qsu)	"grandparent, sibling of grandparent"	de·d
(7)	yaqʷi·duqʷik	"partner, mate"	ye·q̇ʷ

The form *ye·q̇ʷ* is used only between men.

The *i > e·* change occurs in:

(8)	ʔiki·	"son"	ʔe·k.

A disyllabic variant is given below.

The *u· > o·* change occurs in:

(9)	du·wi·qsu	"father"	do·w.

The full words are given in underlying form as far as final vowels are concerned. By regular rule, final short vowels are lost and final long vowels are shortened.[4] The *-u* of the kinship term absolutive suffix *-i·qsu* is lost in additional environments also. Whether the vocative forms have underlying final short vowels is an academic question, since these are never followed by a suffix that would allow them to appear. But otherwise words ending in voiced or glottalized consonants are found to have underlying short final vowels. And there is evidence that the underlying stems have final short or long vowels, e.g. *du·wi-* "father". and *ʔaba·-* "mother."

The clipping of vocative forms takes place mechanically, without regard to morpheme boundaries, and they preserve the meanings of the full forms regardless of where these are localized in them. In ye·q̓ʷ (example 7) all that is left is the remains of the relative stem yaqʷ-.

The following two words for close relatives also show these vowel changes in the first syllable, but the shortening is to a two-syllable word. The $i > e·$ change is seen in:

(10)   hitax̣wiɬuba   "daughter"   he·tax̣.

And the $u > o·$ change, along with a shortening of the second vowel, occurs in:

(11)   čukʷa·piqsu   "grandson"   čo·kʷap.

The retention of a longer form of these words is doubtless due to the need to avoid any possible ambiguity. The word for "daughter" is made up of the "empty stem" hita- plus the suffix -x̣wix̣ɬuba, which also occurs in ʔa·sicx̣wiɬuba "niece" (cf. ʔa·si·qsu "nephew") and čukʷicx̣wiɬuba "granddaughter." Thus in vocative he·tax̣ we have the stem plus just the first consonant of the suffix. "Grandson," čukʷa·piqsu, is opposed to "granddaughter," čukʷicx̣wiɬuba, with respective stem shapes čukʷa·p- and čukʷic-; patently the second syllable is required to discriminate between these forms (the vocative form of the latter word is given below). An alternative word for "grandson" shows merely shortening of the second vowel:

(12)   čukʷle·l   "grandson"   čo·kʷlel.

Some other words also show these vowel changes in the first syllable, but without any clipping. Those noted are mostly words for siblings and cousins, as differentiated by sex of relative and of speaker. These show $a > e·$ change:

(13)   x̣ačupsi·qsu   "brother, male cousin of female"   x̣e·čupsi·qs

(14)   baʔax̣si·qsu   "sister, female, cousin of female" be·ʔax̣si·qs.

The $i > e·$ change is seen in:

(15)   hitaččida   "brother, male cousin of male"   he·taččid.
       (hitaččʔida)

And the $u > o·$ change occurs in:

(16)   čukʷicx̣wiɬuba   "granddaughter"   čo·kʷicx̣wiɬub

(17)   ɬučaqsuba   "sister, female cousin of male"   ɬo·čqsub.

The variant vocative form ɬo·šx̣čaksub occurs in a myth in the speech style of Raven (regularly marked by -šx̣-).

Yet other words embody these vowel changes in non-initial syllables. An $a· > e·$ change, along with shortening of a preceding long vowel, is seen in:

(18)   wikwi·ya·k   "boy"   wikwiye·k.

The word for "woman," xadʔak, must come from an underlying form with medial vowel, xadVʔak, by regular loss of short vowel before ʔ. This loss is counteracted in the vocative form:

(19) xadʔak   "woman"   xadeʔek.

Other examples involve words for inanimate objects and insects. The a > e· change occurs in:

(20) ṫa·wisa·baċiqa·d   "this star"   ṫa·wise·baċqa·d.

This occurs in a children's song analogous to "Twinkle, Twinkle Little Star," wherein other verb forms also show this vocalism:

(21) ʔa·diyaʔa·ċiƚa·k   "you're far up in the sky"   ʔa·diyaʔa·ċi·ƚe·k

    ʔux̣ʷu·x̣ʷċaʔa·š   "it must be"   ʔu·x̣ʷu·x̣ʷċe·š.

The complete text is as follows:

    ʔa·diyaʔa·ċi·ƚe·k   You're far up in the sky,
    ṫa·wise·baċqa·d   Star!
    ʔux̣ʷu·x̣ʷċe·š   It must be
    x̣a·ƛux̣ʷaku·kʷ   the shiny
    ku·bux̣ʷsaku·b   nose-ring you have,
    ṫa·wise·baċqa·d, baċqa·d Star!

Prose forms of the fourth and fifth words have certain vowels short: x̣aƛux̣ʷakuk̇ʷ / ku·bux̣ʷsakub.

These two words for insects show an i· > e· change:

(22) qiči·da   "louse"   qi·če·d

(23) baċasi·da   "flea"   baċase·d.

A more irregular form, with the sequence -eʔe- as in "woman," is:

(24) q̇aƚa·xs   "chamber pot"   q̇aleʔexs.

The last three vocative forms given occur in a verse that was said to babies while pulling on each of their four fingers, starting with the little finger, then tickling them at the armpit:

(25) qi·če·d   Louse,
    baċase·d   flea,
    q̇aleʔexs   potty,
    ʔačx̣ʷiyo·ʔ   whale!

(The anomalous lengthening of the first vowel in "louse" makes it closer in length to the other three-syllable words.)

The change to *e·* also occurs with vowels that are final in a word. We see *a· > e·* in a name:

(26) x̣ax̣axta·   name of a whaler   x̣ax̣axte·.

A variant to a monosyllabic form given above also shows the change *i· > e·* of a final vowel:

(27) ʔiki·   "son"   ʔike·.

This shades into a type wherein the *a > e·* change applies to a final vowel which is otherwise lost. My recordings inconsistently show both long and short vowels: the latter would be due to the regular process of word-final shortening, the former imply that these vocative forms may override this rule. This is found in some reduplicative plural formations alongside the singulars:

(28) ʔu·šax̣u·da   "child"   ʔu·šax̣u·de
(29) ʔu·ʔu·šax̣u·da   "children"   ʔu·ʔu·šax̣u·de
(30) ča·bała   "rich person, upper-class person, chief"   ča·bałe
(31) ča·ča·bała   "chiefs"   ča·ča·bałe
(32) ʔi·ʔi·x̌ʷa   "big, large"   ʔi·ʔi·x̌ʷe.

The last forms occur in two similar expressions. After sneezing one said "Heavenly Father, take care of me!":

(33) ʔuča·ʔakiske   Take care of me
    ča·bałe   Lord
    ʔi·ʔ·x̌ʷe   great
    hita·ʔa·čiłatx̣   living in Heaven!

If it tickled on the right side after sneezing, one might say:

(34) čačabax̣e·ʔiske   Help me to be right at all times,
    ča·bałe.   Lord!

In the following form, it is not known whether the -*e·* replaces an underlying vowel:

(35) yukʷi·qsu   "younger sibling, cousin"   yukʷiʔe·.

The *u > o·* change is also attested in non-initial syllables, in another pair of singular and plural forms:

(36) ła·x̣ukʷ   "man"   ła·x̣o·kʷ
(37) łała·x̣ukʷ   "men"   łała·x̣o·kʷ;

in the last word of (25) above, which is based on the Clallam (Straits Salish) word *čxʷəyuʔ* "whale":[5]

(38) čxʷə́yuʔ   "whale"   ʔačxʷiyo·ʔ;

and also in an imperative verb form, where there is partial shortening eliminating the suffixes for imperative and "me":

(39) daʔuqʷsis   "take me along (in canoe, car)"   daʔo·qʷs.

Just as with final underlying *a*, the change applies to final *u* that is otherwise lost. Two words that we have met above, "boy" and "woman," have irregular plurals ending in *yu*. When no suffix follows, the *u* is lost and the *y* vocalizes to *i*. The words are then *wikwi·yałi* "boys" and *xatxa·dači* "women." The *-u* manifests itself by its assimilatory effect on the article *-°iq̓*: *wikwi·yałi ʔuqʷ* "the boys" and *xatxa·dači ʔuqʷ* "the women." The vocative forms show the regular replacement by *o·*, with word-final shortening:

(40) wikwi·yałyu   "boys"   wikwi·yałyo

(41) xatxa·dačyu   "women"   xatxa·dačyo.

Some other words containing *e·* or *o·*, although not paired off with plain forms, clearly convey this force of calling to someone. These include *ƛe·ko·*, expression of thanks for receiving a gift at a party, and *we·d* (pl. *we·dač*), a call to ascertain whether anybody is present.

3.3. Nitinat

A briefer look at the situation in related Nootkan languages to the north of Makah will help to give us some idea of the development of these forms. Nitinat is the closest language geographically, directly across the Strait of Juan de Fuca.[6] Relatively few of the available vocative forms show internal vowel changes, and some others show final *-e·*, probably reflecting a change of an underlying *a* or *i* which, as in Makah, is lost. It is interesting that, for "mother" and "father," the older source shows the latter type, *ʔabe·* and *date·*, while a recent source shows further clipping and transfer of the ablauting vowel to the first syllable: *ʔe·b* (= Makah) and *de·t*.[7] The older source also contains baby-talk words with the same first vowels: *ʔe·bašx* and *de·tašx*. The vocative form for "mother" is related to the full form *ʔabʔe·qs* (cf. also *ʔabe·ʔ* "your mother"), while that for "father" is suppletive with the form *du·ʔwaqs* (cf. *duwiʔ* "your father"). An alternative vocative for "mother," as for several other kinship terms, is formed with a suffix *-abo·*: *ʔabʔe·qsabo·*.

A changed first vowel without clipping is seen in *xe·čibisiʔqs* "brother of female" (Makah *xe·čupsi·qs*), but again a vocative form with suffix *-abo·* also occurs:

xačibisiʔqsabo·. Other vocatives formed with this suffix include *ʔi·kabo·* "son" (from *ʔi·k*) and *hadʔe·qsabo·* "uncle, aunt" (from *hadʔe·qs*). Similar to Makah is *ča·baìe·* "sir" (from *ča·baì* "chief, boss, captain, wealthy").[8] Based on *dade·ʔqs* "grandparent" is *dadeʔe* beside presumed baby-talk variants with *n*: *ne·n, nane·ʔš*, and *ne·našx*. A change of the last vowel internal to the word is seen in *λišxyu(·)ʔbe·c* "Raven's daughter" (with infixed *-šx-*), from *λiyu·ʔbc*, with regular loss of the underlying vowel. Verb forms called out take a final *-e·*: *λi·xakλide·* "we are paddling now."[9]

3.4. Southern Nootka

Turning to the third language, Nootka proper, the southerly Tsishaath and Hupachasath dialects show the same vowel changes we have met in Makah. These usually apply to the last vowel of the word. This may be in absolute final position:[10]

a > e·:
(42)	kisìa	"chamber pot"	kisìe·
(43)	λama	"house-post"	λame·
(44)	ququ·tihta	"big-nosed ones"	ququ·tihte·

i > e·:
(45)	ńuwi	"father"	ńuwe·
(46)	naneʔi	"your uncles"	nanaʔe·[11]
(47)	čiheʔi	"ghost"	čiha·ʔe·
(48)	ya·cšiʔaλi	"now set out"	ya·cšiʔaλe·

i· > e·:
(49)	ta·yi·	"older brother"	ta·ye·
(50)	mahti·	"house"	mahte·
(51)	ʔaktckʷi·	"gnawings"	ʔaktckʷe·
(52)	wiki·	"do not . . ."	wike·

u > o·:
(53)	ʔa·si·qsu	"niece"	ʔa·si·qso·
(54)	naneʔiqsu	"uncles"	naneʔiqso·

u· > o·:
(55)	wi·ʔu·	"nephew"	wi·ʔo·
(56)	čimìu·	"squirrel"	čimìo·
(57)	λułqu·	"a good one"	λułqo·.

Just as commonly the last vowel affected may be before a final consonant:

a > e·:
(58)	maʔas	"tribe"	maʔe·s

(59)	hupinwaš	"small canoe"	hupinwe·š
(60)	čiša·ʔatḥ	"Tsishaath people"	čiša·ʔe·tḥ
(61)	yaqčiʔathqas	"my neighbors"	yaqčiʔathqe·s
(62)	hahamutnaq	"bone-eaters"	hahamutne·q
(63)	λimssac	"boiling boxes"	λimsse·c

a· > *e·*:
(64)	witwa·k	"warriors"	witwe·k
(65)	ma·tma·s	"tribes"	ma·tme·s
(66)	hica·k	"floor"	hice·k
(67)	ṅa·s	"day"	ṅe·s

i > *e·*:
(68)	haẇił	"chief"	haẇeł
(69)	hina·siλ	"get on"	hina·se·λ
(70)	su·tił	"to you (pl.)"	su·teł

i· > *e·*:
(71)	haẇi·ḥ	"chiefs"	haẇe·ḥ
(72)	łu·csa·mi·ḥ	"women"	łu·csa·me·ḥ
(73)	ḥatkmi·ḥ	"high-born women"	ḥatkme·ḥ

u > *o·*:
(74)	čičišaʔaqsup	"Tsishaath women"	čičšaʔaqso·p
(75)	łu·kʷsaċus	"platforms"	łu·kʷsaċo·s
(76)	nitup	"beams"	nito·p

u· > *o·*:
| (77) | ka·ʔu·c | "grandchild" | ka·ʔo·c |

These changes of the last vowel occur regardless of the morphological analysis of the word. In many cases the vowel is part of a suffix. Thus the vowel-final examples above embody suffixes including -*ma* "... thing, being," -*'iḥta* "at the nose," -*'i·* imperative, -*ckʷi·* "remains of ...," -*i·qsu* absolutive suffix in kinship terms, and -*qu·* conditional, while the suffixes in the consonant-final examples include -*'as* "in the village," -*ʔatḥ* "belonging to ... tribe," -*naq* "fond of eating ...," -*sac* "... vessel," and -*ʔaqsup* "woman of ... tribe."

The following was given as an example of typical address during prayer in Nootka, wherein all the words exhibit this vocalism (Sapir and Swadesh 1955: 49, 54):

(78) ṅe·s   Day,
      hina·yeł   in the sky,
      haẇeł.   Chief.

And the following memorable passage (Sair and Swadesh 1955: 86, 118) illustrates an unusual situation in which inanimate objects were addressed, thus emphasizing the productive nature of this pattern. In it a low-ranking person addresses a house, including some parts and contents, vacated by its occupants, who did not wish to entertain his proposal of marriage:

(79) naʔa·tahʔaʎisim ʎame·   Now listen to me, house-post,
     čita·qme· nito·p ɬu·kʷsačo·s.   weather-boards, beams, platforms.
     ʔanik suwa·q haẃiɬ.   You are chiefs.
     ʔanik ʔu·nu·ʎ qicyu· mahte·.   That is why you are painted, house.
     hi·na·ṅuhse·m ɬukʷska·poɬ   Harpoon, lanyard,
     ʔa·ʎyaqaṅoɬ tukʷaqape·h   cedar-branch rope, bladder-floats,
     hice·k ɬu·waʔiɬe·m   floor, bedside flooring,
     ʎimsse·c ʎaṁe·qʎ   boiling boxes [and] tongs
     hahaẃiɬimčuẏe·k.   for feasting the chiefs.
     ʎuyaẏapaʎim ɬiṁaqsti   Let your heart be well-disposed,
     kiste·   chamber pot,
     ʔanik sukʷiʔatʔa·ɬa   for they take you
     mačqa·ɬačiʔaʎqu· hiyiqtup.   when everything gets dirty.
     ʎuyaẏapčipaʎim ɬiṁaqsti   Make the heart well-disposed
     yaqʷaci·k haẃiɬi·c.   of your master.

There have been only a few Nootka forms noted wherein the changes apply to the first, rather than to the last, vowel in a word. For two words, variant forms have been observed in this respect (recall Makah ʔe·k/ʔike· "son" and Nitinat ʔe·b/ʔabe· "mother"): ho·ɯ̇i beside huɯ̇e· "father" (from huɯ̇i, absolutive huɯ̇i·qsu) and ke·sia beside kisie· "chamber pot" (from kisia).¹² Other examples of changed first vowel are ʔo·ṁi "mother" (absolutive ʔumʔi·qsu) and the longer verb imperative form ʔe·xnučiʎʔis "get small," from ʔanu·čiʎʔis with -x- marking the speech of the culture-hero Kwatyat. Note that these forms are not clipped to monosyllables, but one case of this is ne·n "grandparent" (cf. Makah de·d, Nitinat ne·n) (from nani, absolutive nani·qsu).¹³ A word like ɯahe· "partner, friend, comrade" occurs only in vocative form.

In some forms the vocative vowel seems to be suffixed rather than derived from an already-present vowel: -e· in hakume· "princess" and hayu·huʔuʎe· a woman's name (lit. "Ten-in-Front-Woman"), -o· in himqa·ʔapino· "keep us out of the way,"¹⁴ and -ɯe· in ʔu·qʷiya'.aqameʔicuɯe· "you (pl.) have fine weather." And final -a is irregularly replaced by -o· in ɯa·ma·hso· "I said so."

3.5. Northern Nootka

As regards other, more northerly, dialects of Nootka, we are told by Sapir and Swadesh that "among the Tsishaath it is customary to make calling-out forms by changing an *a* or *a·* of the stem to *e·*, while further up the coast -*e·* or -*a·* is added."¹⁵ They are referring to a Hupachasath vocative form ʔiḥa·qłe· formed from ʔi·ḥa·ʔaqs, the name of Deer's wife, which in Tsishaath would be ʔi·ḥa·ʔe·qs.

These phenomena have now been carefully described in Kyuquot, one of the northernmost Nootka dialects (Rose 1981: 201–203). In this dialect the change applies to the last vowel in the word, much as in Southern Nootka. This vowel is always lengthened, but does not always become mid in quality. Here *a*(·) becomes *a·*:

(80)   haẁiła?š   "there's the chief"   haẁiła·?š,

u(·) becomes *o·* in forms that are vocative in a narrow sense, i.e. that are primary labels for the addressee:

(81)   tu·kʷu·kʷ   "sea lion"   tu·kʷo·kʷ,

but otherwise becomes *u·*, *i*(·) becomes optionally either *e·* or *i·* in the narrowly vocative forms:

(82)   quʔišinḥit   "raven"   quʔišinḥe·t/quʔišinḥi·t,

and otherwise becomes *i·*, except that in absolute final position this -*i·* becomes -*a·y* either optionally:

(83)   nani   "grandparent"   nani·/nana·y

or obligatorily under certain grammatical constraints:

(84)   wi·ninti   "warriors"   wi·ninta·y.

There is also a suffixed -*a·y* in very limited cases, such as the interjection *hawa·y* "hey!"

3.6. Northern Wakashan

North of Nootka is located (Southern) Kwakiutl, a language of the other branch of the Wakashan family. In this language vocative forms of nouns lose final *a* or *ʔ*. But when they are shouted, -*é* is added. If the word ends in *ε* it is merely accented. Other final vowels are replaced, as follows: -*a* > -*é*, -*o* > -*əwé*, -(*əw*)*eʔ* > -*aʔyé* or -*ɔʔyé*.¹⁶

3.7. Development

We can now see the outline of a scenario for the development of this Nootkan pattern. It may have originated as a suffix -*e·* or -*a·* along the lines of that found in

Kwakiutl and some Nootka. By regular rules of vowel contraction, final vowels of stems would have been absorbed into the suffix, and underlying -u would have manifested itself in a resultant -o· or -u·.

The Nootkan languages have a five-vowel inventory, *i e a o u*, but the mid vowels *e* and *o* have a distinct, highly marked, status. Only the other vowels, *i a u*, occur in basic forms of most morphemes. Exceptions include recent loanwords such as Makah *ke·bič* "cabbage" and *ko·pi·* "coffee."[17] These languages have extensive ablaut involving lengthening and shortening of vowels, controlled by various factors, that is roughly analogous to Indo-European ablaut, but this does not involve changes of vowel qualities. Vowels of quality *e*, and less commonly *o*, do, however, arise by mechanical processes of partial assimilation.

The marked mid vowels would have become favored in the southerly dialects as a signal of vocatives over competing -*a·* and -*u·*. In Kyuquot they were taken on to a lesser extent, not replacing *a·*, and being limited to strict vocatives, and this dialect developed final *e·* into the strengthened variant *a·y*.

Before the period of loss of final vowels in Makah and Nitinat, the vowel contractions would have been reinterpreted as a kind of ablaut, allowing their spread to the last vowel of words ending in consonants, much as we see in Tsishaath and Kyuquot. A further continuation of this movement in Makah and Nitinat to earlier vowels, usually first ones, especially in words for close kin, may have been encouraged by a preference for changing lowest *a* rather than other vowels. Subsequent clipping to one or two syllables of words for the very closest kin is probably a kind of baby-talk, as the infants would not be expected to handle longer words. On the other hand, the later loss of final short vowels in Makah and Nitinat would have reinforced the effect of a suffix being added at the ends of words, keeping this alternative productive to a limited extent.

3.8. Universal tendencies

Nootkan seems rather unusual in applying its vocative pattern to verbs as well as nouns. This is perhaps another manifestation of the weak differentiation of parts of speech in these languages that has often been noted (cf. Jacobsen 1979a), although this is usually thought of as going in the opposite direction, in that nouns and other parts of speech can act as predicates, whereas here we have what is thought of as a nominal category also applying to verbs.

In the Indo-European tradition the vocative is treated as part of the case inflection of nouns, but in Nootkan nouns do not inflect for case, so the vocative is a category standing distributionally rather apart from others. A number of other languages also have vocative formations that do not form part of a system of cases.

A sampling of vocative formations in different languages suggests that there are parallel tendencies constraining their shapes. Although one would not expect to find predictable forms of, for example, a genitive case suffix, the vocative stands apart in that it signals, not syntactic relationships within the clause or phrase, but rather a specific kind of interpersonal speech act, and it takes on shapes to facilitate this function.

It is true that in some languages vocatives have arisen by morphological processes, especially by specialization of an affix indicating either a first-person possessor or a second-person subject; vocatives that are embodied in prefixes probably always arise in this manner.

There seem to be two main sound-symbolic tendencies that shape vocative forms; they can be subsumed under the labels *saliency* and *brevity*. Saliency entails that the word contains a prominent syllable and that will attract the attention of the addressee. This syllable will contain a long vowel and/or a mid (sometimes low) vowel *e o (a)* or a diphthong *ay aw* perhaps with added nasalization or strong stress or falling pitch. (Non-high vowels are more salient in that they are intrinsically louder; falling pitch might be argued to be more salient because it is a *rapid change* in pitch.) At the least, a vocative suffix will end in a vowel: I know of no productive vocative formation (unless a bare consonant-final stem is used) that consists of or ends in a consonant (other than diphthong-forming *y* or *w*).

The other tendency of brevity often brings about a shortening of the word in question, and it keeps the number of salient syllables in a word down to one. (Recall that in Nootkan there is only one changed vowel per word – one would obviously get greater saliency by changing all the vowels.) Brevity arises from several functional factors, especially the opposing drives of urgency and perfunctoriness. For both reasons one wishes to get past the attracting of attention or the routine addressing and on to the conveying of information. (Note the English shortening of perfunctory *madam* to *ma'am* to *'m* in *yes'm*.) Also contributing to brevity is the more technical matter of the omission of suffixes of, say, case, number, or gender because this information is not needed. Salience coincides with brevity when such omission yields a vowel-final form. And as we have seen in Nootkan, vocative forms that arise out of baby-talk are commonly shortened to one or two syllables because of the limited capacity of very young children.

Let us now consider a few examples illustrating these tendencies, starting with saliency as manifested in vowel length. In Southern Sierra Miwok of east central California (Broadbent 1964: 50) the vocative is manifested as a lengthening of final vowels, with no effect on final consonants:

(85) ʔita-   "mother"   ita·
(86) his·ik-   "skunk"   his·ik·

In Chipewyan of western Canada (Li 1946: 403) the vocative is formed either by lengthening a final vowel and imposing a falling tone on it:

(87) sɛtá   "my father"   sɛtâ·

or by adding a suffix -i̯ which will replace a final vowel:

(88) ʔɛné   "my mother"   ʔɛni̯.

And in Mohawk (Marianne Mithun, personal communication) proper names used for address have their stressed syllables lengthened:

(89) Sóse   "Joe"   Só·se
(90) Shawátis   "John"   Shawá·tis.

Cases of final diphthongs are also common. In Gilyak of Sakhalin Island and the nearby mainland (Austerlitz 1958: 479) there are two vocative endings, -iy and more polite -a:

(91) řaŋq   "woman"   řaŋqiy, řaŋqa.

In the Inari dialect of Eastern Lappish (Collinder 1965: 56) the vocative is sometimes emphasized by the particle áy: eäččámáy "father."

And in Chukchee of Siberia (Bogoras 1922: 697) a -y is sometimes added after a final vowel, with the accent moved to this syllable:

(92) Aráro   (name)   Araróy.

Vocatives formed with mid vowels are also plentiful. Thus Classical Náhuatl (Andrews 1975: 9, 203–204, 223) forms a vocative used only by males by suffixing -é, giving the only words in the language that are not accented on the punult:

(93) cihuātl   "woman"   cihuātlé.

Rumanian has distinctive vocative forms in -e and -o (probably borrowed from Slavic):

(94) vecin   "neighbor"   vecine
(95) soacră   "mother-in-law"   soacro.

And combining length and mid vowels, Sanskrit, in those vocative forms which appear to be innovational, because they are longer than their stems, shows final ē and ō (structurally corresponding to diphthongs ai and au) according to rules like those of Nootkan:

(96) Agni   (a god)   Agnē
(97) aśvā   "mare"   aśvē
(98) dhēnu   "cow"   dhēnō.

A case of non-final vowels comparable to those of Nootka occurs in Chukchee (Bogoras 1922: 696), where the last vowel is changed to o, which takes the accent, and proper names lose their suffixes:

(99) Yétɪlɪn   (name)   Yetól
(100) Qutúwgi   (name)   Qutów.

Turning now to examples of brevity, in Taos of New Mexico (Trager 1946: 202, 206) the vocative of those nouns that have one is formed by omission of the gender–number suffixes (giving a stem ending in a vowel):

(101)   čùn'ena   "coyote"   čùn'e.

A similar situation obtains in Greek, where the vocative is just the stem, which with *o*-stems has a distinctive *e*-grade vowel:

(102)   híppos (nominative)   "horse"   híppe.

Consonant stems lack the lengthening of the nominative:

(103)   léōn (nominative)   "lion"   léon

In an anti-accusative language like Diegueño of Southern California (Langdon 1970: 157–158), with a case suffix for transitive and intransitive subjects, forms unmarked for case are used both as direct objects of verbs and as terms of address.

Shortened vocative forms of kinship terms are very common. Thus in Yurok of northwest California (Robins 1958: 23) they drop the final one or two syllables to become monosyllabic:

(104)   picowos   "grandfather"   pic
(105)   cimos   "uncle"   ciʔm.

We have seen a combination of salience and brevity already in the Chukchee names with -*o*-. Another example is found in Wororo of the Northern Kimberley, Western Australia (Michael Silverstein, personal communication), which adds a suffix -*á·y* with heavy stress and high-falling intonation while dropping the gender-indicating suffix of kinship terms:

(106)   gará·nja   "mother (etc.)"   gará·y.

Similarly, in Plains Cree of eastern Canada (Wolfart 1973: 32), among kinship terms, several show apocope:

(107)   nita·nis   "my daughter"   nita·n,

others show a suffix -*e·*:

(108)   nimis   "my elder sister"   nimise·,

and a few combine both processes:

(109)   nikosis   "my son"   nikose·.

These few selected examples from the much larger available number should serve at least to illustrate the wide applicability of the general tendencies that were suggested by the Nootkan data.

NOTES

* A preliminary version of this paper, under the title "Makah Vocative Vocalism," was presented to the Thirteenth International Conference on Salish Languages, University of Victoria, August 17–19, 1978. I am indebted for comments and relevant data to Stephen R. Anderson, Robert Austerlitz, Leanne Hinton, Margaret Langdon, Yakov Malkiel, Marianne Mithun, Johanna Nichols, Geoffrey O'Grady, Tom M. S. Priestly, Richard Rhodes, and Michael Silverstein.

1 On relationships within Nootkan and the deeper Wakashan family, cf. Sapir and Swadesh 1939: 10; Jacobsen 1969: 140–141, 1979a: 83–84, 1979b; and Embleton 1985: 52–56.
2 Sapir and Swadesh 1955: 19, 38.
3 These forms were obtained from Mrs. Nora Barker, Mrs. Viola Johnson, Mr. Ralph LaChester, and Mrs. Mabel Robertson. All cited conventional texts are from Mrs. Barker. My field work on Makah has been supported by the National Science Foundation, the Desert Research Institute of the University of Nevada, and the Research Advisory Board of the University of Nevada, Reno.
4 Cf. Jacobsen 1971, especially pp. 13ff., sec. 9ff.
5 Clallam from Thompson and Terry 1971: 262, 290. Native Makah words do not end in underlying ʔ. The prothetic ʔa- corresponds to the Nootka proscription against initial consonant clusters.
6 Unless otherwise indicated, Nitinat forms are taken from the Nitinat lexical file prepared by Mary R. Haas and Morris Swadesh, made available to me by Haas (cf. Haas 1969: 109, 1972: 84). This data was collected in 1931.
7 The newer forms are from Kess and Copeland 1984: 149, 151.
8 This also occurs in Touchie 1977: 86, no. 146.
9 Swadesh and Swadesh 1933: 205, no. 75. The authors comment: "-ä· [i.e. -e·] may be suffixed, or, more likely, -id ['we'] is really -idi or -ida with the final vowel never appearing except when it is lengthened and umlauted in vocative forms." However, the comparative data does not seem to suggest a recently present final vowel here (although if one is assumed, *-idu, from *-inu, would seem more likely), so we probably have to do here with mere suffixation.
10 The forms were extracted from the texts in Sapir and Swadesh 1939 and 1955.
11 In the forms naneʔi and čihe·ʔi, a(·) has regularly changed to e(·) before ʔi; when this i becomes e· in the vocative forms nanaʔe· and čiha·ʔe·, the a(·) is preserved.
12 For both these words there is one informant, Tom (Sayachapis), who produced both forms. In the case of "father" other informants produced each variant.
13 Sapir 1929: 118.
14 By the reasoning of note 9, this would suggest that the ending -'i-n imperative + "us" arises from underlying *-'i-nu.
15 Sapir and Swadesh 1939: 201, note 4.
16 Boas 1947: 295.
17 For additional Makah loanwords, see Jacobsen 1980: 168, sec. 3.2.

REFERENCES

Andrews, J. R. 1975. *Introduction to Classical Nahuatl.* Austin and London: University of Texas Press.
Austerlitz, R. 1958. Vocatif et impératif en ghiliak. *Orbis* 7: 477–481.
Boas, F. 1947. Kwakiutl grammar, with a glossary of the suffixes. *Transactions of the American Philosophical Society* 37(3): 201–377.
Bogoras, W. 1922. Chukchee. In F. Boas (ed.) *Handbook of American Indian Languages* 2. Bureau of American Ethnology, Bulletin 40. Washington: Government Printing Office, 631–903.
Broadbent, S. M. 1964. *The Southern Sierra Miwok Language.* University of California Publications in Linguistics 38. Berkeley and Los Angeles: University of California Press.
Collinder, B. 1965. *An Introduction to the Uralic Languages.* Berkeley and Los Angeles: University of California Press.
Embleton, S. M. 1985. Lexicostatistics applied to the Germanic, Romance, and Wakashan families. *Word* 36: 37–60.
Haas, M. R. 1969. Internal reconstruction of the Nootka-Nitinat pronominal suffixes. *International Journal of American Linguistics* 35: 108–124.
——— 1972. The structure of stems and roots in Nootka-Nitinat. *International Journal of American Linguistics* 38: 83–92.
Jacobsen, W. H., Jr. 1969. Origin of the Nootka pharyngeals. *International Journal of American Linguistics* 35: 125–153.
——— 1971. Makah vowel insertion and loss. Paper presented to the Sixth International Conference on Salish Languages, Victoria.
——— 1979a. Noun and verb in Nootkan. In B. S. Efrat (ed.) *The Victoria Conference on Northwestern Languages.* British Columbia Provincial Museum Heritage Record 4. Victoria: British Columbia Provincial Museum, 83–155.
——— 1979b. Wakashan comparative studies. In L. Campbell and M. Mithun (eds.) *The Languages of Native America: Historical and Comparative Assessment.* Austin and London: University of Texas Press, 766–791.
——— 1980. Metaphors in Makah neologisms. In B. R. Caron *et al.* (eds.) *Proceedings of the Sixth Annual Meeting of the Berkeley Linguistics Society, February 16–18, 1980.* Berkeley: Berkeley Linguistics Society, 166–179.
Kess, J. F. and A. M. Copeland. 1984. The structure and function of Nootkan baby talk. In N. Strantzali (ed.) *Studies in Native American Languages* III. Kansas Working Papers in Linguistics 9. Lawrence: Linguistics Graduate Student Association, University of Kansas, 141–164.
Langdon, M. 1970. *A Grammar of Diegueño: The Mesa Grande Dialect.* University of California Publications in Linguistics 66. Berkeley/Los Angeles/London: University of California Press.
Li, Fang-Kuei. 1946. Chipewyan. In H. Hoijer *et al.* (eds.) *Linguistic Structures of Native America.* Viking Fund Publications in Anthropology 6. New York: The Viking Fund, 398–423.
Robins, R. H. 1958. *The Yurok Language: Grammar, Texts, Lexicon.* University of California Publications in Linguistics 15. Berkeley and Los Angeles: University of California Press.

Rose, S. M. 1981. Kyuquot grammar. Dissertation, University of Victoria.
Sapir, E. 1929. Nootka baby words. *International Journal of American Linguistics* 5: 118–119.
Sapir, E. and M. Swadesh. 1939. *Nootka Texts: Tales and Ethnological Narratives, with Grammatical Notes and Lexical Materials*. Philadelphia: Linguistic Society of America.
  1955. *Native Accounts of Nootka Ethnography*. Publications of the Indiana University Research Center in Anthropology, Folklore, and Linguistics 1, *International Journal of American Linguistics* 21(4), pt. 2.
Swadesh, M. H. and M. Swadesh. 1933. A visit to the other world, a Nitinat text. *International Journal of American Linguistics* 7: 195–208.
Thompson, L. C. and M. Terry. 1971. Clallam: a preview. In J. Sawyer (ed.) *Studies in American Indian Languages*. University of California Publications in Linguistics 65. Berkeley/Los Angeles/London: University of California Press, 251–294.
Touchie, B. N. 1977. Nitinaht. *International Journal of American Linguistics* Native American Texts Series 2(3): 69–97.
Trager, G. L. 1946. An outline of Taos grammar. In H. Hoijer et al. (eds.) *Linguistic Structures of Native America*. Viking Fund Publications in Anthropology 6. New York: The Viking Fund, 184–221.
Wolfart, H. C. 1973. *Plains Cree: A Grammatical Study*. Transactions of the American Philosophical Society 63(5).

4

Relative motivation in denotational and indexical sound symbolism of Wasco-Wishram Chinookan

MICHAEL SILVERSTEIN

4.1. Introduction

To many, sound symbolism would appear to be at the margins of how – as Jakobson and Lévi-Strauss view inherently social facts – language is an "intervention of culture in nature" (Jakobson and Halle 1956: 17). To such a view, in fact, just as there were logically equivalent "Ding Dong," "Pooh Pooh," or "Bow Wow" theories of yore (see Whitney 1867: 426–427), cast in the idiom of language origin, there is a startling persistence or resurgence of essentially pre-structural views on the matter of sound symbolism. There appear to be many proponents of a notion of primordial sound iconism (in the technical, Peircean sense) for whom – notwithstanding the fact that language and culture are specific, organized semiotic systems – such iconic relations atomically motivate certain lexical forms in respect of what they denote, on grounds independent of any such sociohistorical facts of linguistic and/or cultural semiosis.

This kind of logically pre-linguistic and pre-cultural motivation of lexical denotation is, of course, what Saussure was talking about under the rubric of the "symbolic" (i.e. iconic) aspect of *absolute* motivation. The entire first two parts of the *Cours* (Saussure 1916: 97–192), by contrast, are devoted to demonstrating two truths. The first is that anything that is seriously a (denotational) sign in human language, from word-stem up through syntactic phrase, is so much more "arbitrary" in its semiotic properties than anything else, that we might as well axiomatize linguistics with this stipulation. The second is that the useful and productive opposition of "arbitrary" and "motivated" in language is a system-internal matter of degrees of *relative* motivation, from relatively arbitrary (or lexical) denotational signs to relatively motivated (or grammatically formed) ones, depending on a sign's regularity of value in, or rule-governed determination by, the whole system of language, its grammar.[1]

In many respects we are more sophisticated today, eighty-five years later, in our ability to articulate the Saussurean lessons, at least in certain areas of the problem.

For example, in the very analysis of the signal-forms, we have applied the Saussurean lessons in the realm of phonology, and can give a fairly precise descriptive account, in terms of primitives and conditions on their concatenation and projection, of what emerges at the surface as inventories and combinatorics of phonological segments that seem to comprise phenomenal denotational units – morphemes, words, phrases, sentences.

So we can examine putative sound-symbolic denotational units in any language with respect to the degree of phonologicization of pre-linguistic, pre-structural "sound substance," and with respect to the degree of violation of expectable phonological combinatorics under the Saussurean assumptions. Further, we can articulate with some precision the relationship of grammatical constructionality to semantic compositionality, given a rich enough understanding of morphosyntax of denotational language, and determine thereby what is, as a grammarian might say, "merely" lexical (hence, from a systemic point of view, totally arbitrary, and indeed the fit subject matter of non-grammatical study of sound symbolism). We can even understand something of the poetics of linguistic expression as a functional plane distinct from denotation as such, to determine the contribution of (broadly speaking) "metrically" organized form as one of the determinants of at least the native speaker's feeling of sound symbolism attached to certain expressions.[2]

But even with such advances in being able formally to describe denotational iconism in language, we remain at the same impasse of understanding that Saussure himself faced. For we are operating along the single dimension of signs as being denotationally iconic or denotationally arbitrary and, as it were, equating specific-system determination with arbitrariness.[3] Hence, on a higher plane of abstraction, many writers look for cross-systemic (i.e. cross-linguistic) universal generalizations; they immediately see in these absolute or statistical tendencies of form-denotatum correlation transparent evidence for psychological or more broadly biological motivation for linguistic form. (Haiman 1985; Givón 1984: 29–45; 1989 are two exemplars among many.) This is merely ding-dongism operating with due respect to the power of the structuralist perspective on the analysis of denotational structure. It is not really making use of the distinction between absolute and relative arbitrariness/motivation, even on the denotational plane.

For the point about *sound* symbolism in particular is that phonological or even phonetic shape is far from being merely the non-denotationally-correlatable level of "interpretation" (Chomsky and Halle 1968: 7), "representation" (Hockett 1961: 33, 41–42; Lamb 1964), or "articulation" (Martinet 1964: 22–27) of the *real* linguistic units, the morphemes, words, phrases, sentences – as in the Saussurean and subsequent grammatical views of the matter. In sound symbolism, such form is endowed with its own plane of meaning, one that, in the classic instance of denotational iconism, supersedes the power of the Saussurean grammatico-semantic system at its own functional game, symbolically mediated reference-and-predication. In other words, we must view denotational iconism as one of the "breakthrough" modes of semiosis, in which a system of sound structure (with its own, merely distributional functions of making segmental form), normally subordinated to virtual zero autonomous power with respect to reference-and-predication in the doubly articulated structure of language, undergoes a functional rank-shifting (to use a tagmemics term apt in this context) into the plane of referential-and-predicational function. That is, sound as sign becomes independently endowed with apparently denotationally relevant value *qua* signifier.

If such is the case, we must ask, what is/are the usually latent function(s) of such a system of sound signifiers? How are such signifiers organized as units in some structure? How do they manifest the same kind of relative motivation, *mutatis mutandis*, in their own functional sphere(s) as grammatico-semantic units like segmental phonological units do in theirs? Finally, what other kinds of "breakthrough" modes implicate this structure of sound as well as denotational iconism?

4.2. Functional structures of Wasco segments

I want to develop these questions – if not provide totally satisfying answers – by illustration, looking at the interplay of types of sound symbolisms in Wasco-Wishram, the easternmost Chinookan dialect once spoken in the area of present-day The Dalles, Oregon, on both sides of the Columbia River.[4] Wasco is unique among Chinookan languages as documented in having an obvious and pervasive *indexical* system of sound symbolism of the "diminutive"–"augmentative" type, as well as a number of denotationally iconic sound symbolisms, and a large number of areas of interaction of the two. The example becomes valuable, from its high degree of structuredness, for guiding us in the general theoretical area, because the interplay of indexical and denotational sound symbolisms is, I believe, the central mechanism that underlies the less obvious cases as well.

As a typical interior Northwest Coast–Plateau language, Wasco has a rich consonantal system of segment types and a very meager vocalic one, at the level of denotational phonology. As can be seen from figure 4.1, the stop-affricate-fricative inventory is particularly rich in the velar and uvular positions, only the dentals matching in elaboration (if we count the voiced *l* as part of this, not really a perfect solution). The consonants ʔ and *h* are of very limited occurrence as segmental phonemes of lexical items. The voiced series of stops, *b*, *d*, *g*, g^w, g,[5] g^w, and the corresponding voiceless series, *p*, *t*, *k*, k^w, *q*, q^w, automatically alternate in most, but not all, forms, according to a rule of voicing immediately preceding a voiced segment (except in final stressed syllable, where the voiceless member, with strong aspiration, remains); hence, the functional load of the voiced/voiceless distinction is low. There are grammatically significant alternations in the velar and uvular orders between stop and fricative series, differentiating, for example, in stem-initial

Native American languages north of Mexico

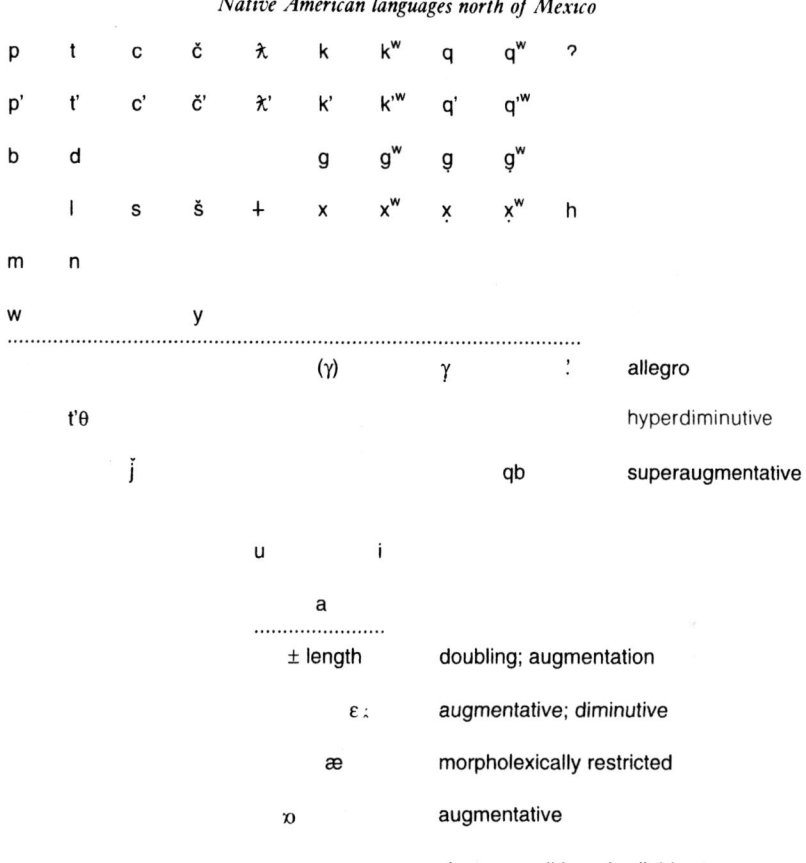

Figure. 4.1. Segmental phonemes of Wasco (Chinookan) denotational structure, with some common additional segments from other functional systems.

position, absolute vs. construct (possessed) deverbative nominals. In the vocalic system, given the rather meager inventory of phonological segments, there are, as one would expect, numerous subtle degrees of position, aperture, and gliding coarticulations conditioned by the numerous different types of syllable-onset and syllable-coda environments in which vowels are found.

As also shown in figure 4.1 below the dotted lines, there are a number of clearly "non-phonemic" segment types that occur with considerable frequency or predictability in Wasco. Firstly, among consonantal segments are allegro forms of intervocalic *g* and sometimes *g̣*, the voiced, lightly rubbed fricatives; the uvular *γ* frequently weakens further to a somewhat pharyngealized glottal occlusion, here written ˀ. Further, there are three consonantal segments outside the regular inventory that are produced as part of the indexical diminutive-augmentative system, a "hyperdiminutive" version of *c'* made as the corresponding mellow dental affricate *t'θ*, occurring particularly in "baby-talk" register, and a "super-augmentative" of both the *č* and *qʷ* orders, a voiced counterpart in the first, *ǰ*, and a true doubly articulated *qb* (the closure for the *b* occurring before the release of the *q*) in the second. Among the vowels, there are clear, morphologically dictated doubled segments occurring for double or triple segmental vowels, i.e. $-i+i+i-$ = [i:] under slow, deliberate conditions of pronunciation. These lengthened segments occur also as part of the indexical "augmentative" apparatus, and obviously in denotationally iconic forms expressing long and/or drawn-out denotata. The phonemic vowel *a* undergoes augmentative coloring by backing and slightly lowering, and diminutive coloring by raising and fronting toward lowered [ɛ^], generally with flattened, wide lip aperture. This same basic quality, with a more open lip aperture, occurs as the augmentative form of phonemic *i*, generally lengthened to a kind of [ɛː]. The segment *æ* seems to occur regularly in the stem-prefix *da-* only on certain particles for color denotata, e.g., *da-tgup* [= dætgúp] "white"; in such forms, the [a] pronunciation of the prefix vowel seems clearly to be noticed by speakers as incorrectly realized. Finally, the schwa, in its multiform colorings, occurs when an otherwise vowelless cluster requires a stress by morphological rules, or by phonological syllable constraints.

Now while in Wasco there are found many words comprised of regulation *CV(C)* syllable types, there do exist some extraordinary consonantal combinations, such as Northwest Coast languages are notorious for exemplifying, e.g., *ɬtpčkʷt* "it is now coming hither out of the water," *škčq'ʷɬx* "my two hips, flanks," etc. – because the great majority of schwa- or *a*-insertion rules are highly morphologically specific, requiring specification of certain morpheme boundaries as part of the conditions for operation, and operating only in certain classes of morphemes, though the phonological conditioning factors are similar across these contexts. Hence, to the outsider looking in, there is a *Gestalt* of phonetic plenitude to most words, intermediate between the two extremes just mentioned. And it should be clear that starting from such a system of phonology in denotational function, the native speaker's intuitions about "natural" – logically pre-linguistic and pre-cultural – "sound symbolism" are going to be quite different from those of an English speaker.

Similarly for observations about ease and difficulty of articulation, a way of talking about naturalness that colors one's perception of the phonic substance as such. For us as speakers of English – or for other SAE-language speakers – the clustering of so many consonants as was illustrated just above constitutes a kind of treacherous, error-filled terrain of articulatory–auditory intuitions, somewhat outside our universe of subtlety. Yet, in a completely volunteered fashion, one of my most interesting Wishram consultants at Yakima observed one day that a simple or "easy" word like *itq'ixʷšalx* "wood shavings," with which she had begun her remedial instruction in Wasco for her middle-aged daughter, was too much for her well-meaning student! "There must be something wrong with her throat now, from talking too much English all the time," she observed in amusement, leaving me to wonder whether or not this was vintage "Indian humor" of ironic understatement or a serious, face-value remark on the simplicity of this word. Perhaps the former, because independently a Wasco consultant on Warm Springs Reservation several times observed, both to me and to young anglophone Wascos, that the hardest word in the whole language was *i̇-ʔišaɬx* "corn tassels," certainly a word much less difficult-sounding to an outsider than a totally consonantal one (such as the two cited earlier), and perhaps strange-sounding to us only for the *-ɬx* cluster at the end. Observe the similarity of the two phonological shapes in these two words that evoked such commentaries: who could attempt to explain – much less predict – that, given the Wasco phonological inventory of segments and phonotactics, these would have special place for speakers in terms of a remarkable phonic substance, with connotational value available for "sound symbolism"?

My point is that it is extraordinarily dangerous to suppose that *our* intuitions as analysts about sound substance – which, if we learn the minimal Boasian lesson, are formed from our whole set of complex relations to it through language and other phonic media – ought in any way to be valid when approaching a system as alien as this one (and, the point could be pressed, when approaching even our own!). So we cannot merely determine from the outside what lexical items are "sound symbolic" in the sense of denotationally iconic in some fashion, even where the noises made in uttering a particular word seem to us to be icons of something presented to us by some denotatum of the word. Rather, it seems to me, we must work up to any interpretative statements in this area from a structure-conscious approach, examining all of the systems where phonic shape decidedly operates independently of denotational systematicity, and seeing how the connotational penumbra of denotation is constituted by the intersection of these various functional systems, occasionally achieving the real "breakthrough" in semiosis to real denotational iconism specific to the language in question. I illustrate this approach to the matter with the Wasco data on functional intersection and "breakthrough."

Very important to Wasco phonetic production and reception, as mentioned above, is the indexical system of "diminutive–augmentative" consonantism (sometimes accompanied by vocalic effects as indicators of "hyper-" or "super-" degrees, as will emerge below). It should be observed that such a system does not, strictly, denote small and large objects, or even take the place of adjectives (or equivalent modifiers, syntactic nouns and verbs) for "small" and "large" in the denotational structure of Wasco. Rather, the system of consonantal (and some vocalic) differences is a true indexical system, in that these special phonological or phonetic effects signal the utterer's affective and evaluative relationship to some denotatum otherwise determined by the lexical form to which the indexical system is, in effect, applied. A cluster of oppositions of a culturally salient sort form a *pragmatic metaphorical set*, or, briefly, a set of actor-centered (here, utterer-centered) enacted cultural equivalences, around the central or focal opposition of "[affectively engaging] smallness" vs. "[affectively engaging] largeness." Some of the related oppositions are "intimate; dear" vs. "distanced; off-putting"; "desirable" vs. "to-be-shunned"; "personal" vs. "impersonal"; "pleasing; satisfying" vs. "gross; disgusting"; etc. While these binarily specified oppositions would code the distinctions at the polar extremes of diminutive vs. augmentative, there is really a three-term overall system in categorical terms, "diminutive" vs. "[neutral =] non-diminutive" and "[neutral =] non-augmentative" vs. "augmentative," the two indexical effects operating formally in a gradient of degrees cross susceptible segments of the lexical forms of an expression.

In both simplex and complex expressions, there seem to be such graded effects in both indexical directions. One aspect of such graded diminutivization/augmentativization is the appearance of these effects in more and more unusual phonotactic positions in the syllable structure of forms, from simple, non-clustered consonants in pre-vocalic position to those found inside complex clusters. Another is the morphologically controlled spread of these effects in complex cross-referencing words to morphemes with denotational connection to distinct aspects of a presented entity or situation, e.g. the lexical root, then the derivational suffixes, then the grammatical prefixes, then the cross-referencing prefixes (which agree with phrasal dependent lexemes in the head-marking morphosyntactic structure). Finally, there is a clear distinction between forms affected only consonantally vs. the subtler and higher-degree effects achieved by both consonantal and vocalic changes, reflecting the salience of distinct classes of sounds within the overall configuration of availability of segments for augmentative and diminutive effects.

As shown in figure 4.2, there is, as we would expect, a high degree of overlap between the system of denotationally implemented segmental phonemes (shown above the dotted lines in figure 4.1) and the set of segment types involved in consonantal diminutivization–augmentativization. In fact, the latter system includes the three sounds qb, j, and $t'\theta$, otherwise not used denotationally, and excludes only the glides y, $\mathit{?}$, and h – the latter two in particular of extraordinarily low functional yield in the language – and the fricatives x, x^w, $\underset{\cdot}{x}$, $\underset{\cdot}{x}^w$ – these four heavily involved in the morphosyntactic signaling of verbal/nominal, absolute/construct, and voice-rection systems, and, in a sense, inappropriate for implementation as diminutive and augmentative machinery.

I have organized figure 4.2 so as to highlight the functional structure along its proper dimensions, all the while staying as close as possible to the configuration of denotationally functioning segments (as shown in figure 4.1). Note that the voiced series, generally predictable under denotational structure (as discussed above), is the maximally augmentative manner of consonantal production, while the glottalized (ejective) series is the maximally diminutive one, the voiceless non-glottalized (or "plain") series lying in the middle. Among the resonants, nasality is diminutive with respect to non-nasality, though, as shown with a connecting chain (thus:

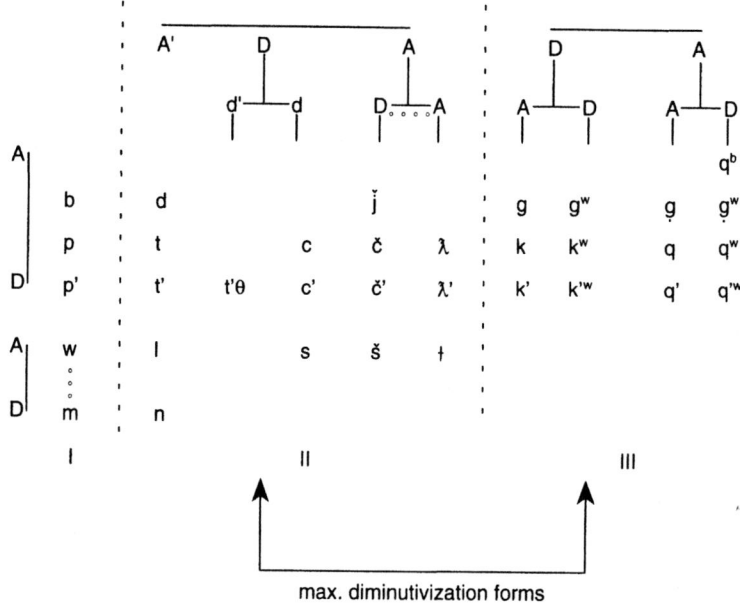

Figure 4.2. Consonantal system of indexical diminutivization and augmentativization in Wasco (Chinookan), functionally organized.

ooooo), the $m:w$ pair does not seem to function synchronically in this way. All of these, voicing, glottalization, and nasality, are shown in the horizontal dimensions of the figure, as is the "double stop" segment qb, which figures in its own series as a unique development from g^w as a kind of "superaugmentative."

Looking across the display in this figure, we can observe two properties of the system as a whole. First, the vertical interrupted lines separate three distinct *interactive regions* of the indexical system, labeled I, II, and III. The indexical effects do not create paradigms of alternating segments across these regions in the data to hand. Second, within each of these regions, there are various diminutive–augmentative polarities that organize the columns or orders of segment types. (These, recall, can be expressed as either of the pair of indexical binaries, diminutive/neutral or neutral/augmentative, in partial or attentuated form.) Note then that there is a bilabial region (I), within which only the manner-of-articulation oppositions function, as well as a coronal region (II) – dento-alveolar/palatal/lateral – with a very complex, hierarchical internal structure, and a (labio-)velar/uvular region (III), with a rather regular and proportional internal structure. Let us consider these regions in a bit more detail, particularly II and III.

Michael Silverstein

In the coronal region, there is a double relationship of the c order as diminutive to both the $č/ƛ$ order and, in a number of cases, to the t order. Further, the "hyperdiminutive" $t'\theta$ that corresponds only to c' gives a kind of vertical-horizontal interaction in the possible diminutive chains [augm./ neutr.] $> c > c' > t'\theta$. Also, the fact that there are many clear cases of fossilized augmentative $ƛ/ƛH$:diminutive $č/č'/š$ gives evidence for an historical renewal of augmentative–diminutive categories with the now-productive oppositions of $č/č'/š$:$c/c'/s$, and explains why there are doublets of indexical paradigms functioning simultaneously in the language, both $ƛ$-order:c-order and $č$-order:c-order. Within this region II, then, the c-order (and its "hyper" form, $t'\theta$) is the maximally diminutivized form, particularly the sound c' itself; by contrast d, and most particularly $ƛ$, are maximally augmentativized forms.[6]

In the (labio-)velar/uvular region, there is a regular diminutivization effect expressed by labialization, giving two parallel orders of A:D at the velar and uvular positions. Further, there is a relationship of A:D in each of the distinct uvular and velar positions, so that switching from the q/qw to k/kw orders is moving from augmentative/neutral to diminutive or from augmentative to neutral/diminutive. Operating in addition to this are the manner-of-production alternations already discussed, with the addition of the "superaugmentative" $q\dot{}$ that, in a sense, virtually overrides the q/qw distinction and serves as the neutralized maximally augmentative form in the entire region III. By contrast, the k^w-order, doubly diminutivized within the system, and its particular member k^w, is the locus of maximal diminutivization.

Vocalic segments implemented in augmentativization and diminutivization are more straightforward. All four of the segmental values $a:i:u:\emptyset$, i.e. three full vowels and deleted or zero vowel (sometimes schwa under appropriate syllabic conditions), play a role. Full V:$\emptyset$ serves as either augmentative/neutral vs. diminutive or augmentative vs. neutral/diminutive. Furthermore, there are certain characteristic qualitative differences that were indicated in discussing the system of denotationally used phonological segments, the two types of [ε] sound as diminutive of a and as augmentative of i, and the backed, lowered, slightly internally rounded [ɒ] as an augmentative form of a (accompanied by a decided shift in voice register to a somewhat pharyngealized, rasping timbre occasionally exemplified in my material, an effect seemingly outside of the regular augmentative–diminutive system) or even of u. Needless to say, stressed syllables show all of these vocalic effects more clearly than unstressed ones, since the canonical shifts are between more distinct articulations under these syllabic conditions.

It is remarkable to discover in the corpus of data to hand that even simplex lexical items frequently occur in numerous such gradations of form, each bespeaking a particular indexically signaled utterer-attitude at the moment of its recording, an attitude suggestively communicated but generally unavailable for objectified contemplation such as is presupposed by "exact" repetition of a form (see

Silverstein 1981). It is very important to remember, however, that the English (or other language) translation "equivalent" or gloss of such a form generally constitutes a "refunctionalized" (Barthes 1967: 41–42) presentation of it so as to appear to be translating a purely denotational form, not an indexically charged one.[7] Actually, we are usually misled by the fact that, for example, English has two distinct lexical items for sound-symbolically related forms of a lexeme in Wasco, or by the fact that one of the sound-symbolic polarities of an historical Wasco etymon has been lexicalized as the synchronically "neutral" form, with certain connotational baggage left over from its phonic substance, as necessarily to be evaluated against the backdrop of the functioning indexical system just outlined. The particularities of how the indexical and denotational systems of sounds interact for any lexical form in Wasco "radicalizes" the possibility of translation (Quine 1960: 28) on yet another plane of semiosis (as if Quine's referential grounds were not bad enough!), making intuitions from "outside" the system that much more shaky as bases for systematization and explanation.

Perhaps the most subtly graded example of the phenomenon is the simplex lexical stem that is glossed both as "big" and as "small." There is a kind of neutral distinction of degrees we might gloss by these translations, perhaps reinforced by the existence of distinct lexical forms in both English and Sahaptin (the long-term other language of Chinookan bilingualism). These "neutral" forms, however, show characteristic differentiation according to the diminutive–augmentative system: -gaiλ "big" vs. -ġaic "small." Observe the $g:\dot{g}$ and $λ:\dot{c}$[8] consonantism, as we would expect from figure 4.2, along with the characteristically neutral -ai- vocalism common to both. Around these two points, however, is a whole series of differentiated colorings, intergrading one into the other, from a "superaugmentative" to a "hyperdiminutive" as polar opposites of the whole set. Each of the two lexical elements, nevertheless, forms part of a series in its own right as the indexically "neutral" element. From -gaiλ we have: -qbaiλ > -gaiλ > -gʷaiλ > -g'waiλ > -g'waiλ' in order from "superaugmentative" through a certain attenuated, diminutivized lexical item we might denotationally gloss as "biggish." Starting from -ġaic we have > -k'aic or -kʷaic > -k̇ʷaic > -k̇ʷaic' > -k̇ʷεic' > -k̇ʷεit'θ in order from two alternatively slight diminutivizations through the fully "hyperdiminutivized" version of the lexical item, denotationally approximated as "teeny-weeny," appropriately in baby-talk register. Yet the two series can be joined one to the other end-to-end in a continuously gradable set, so that what we translate into English as "big" and "small" are in reality in Wasco only two way-stations along this gradient cline, any member of which might occur on a particular occasion of usage. Indeed, an extreme solution to the demand of any theory of phonology that requires a unique "lexical representation" might be to characterize this whole series as $-[III]ai[II]$ from the point of view of denotational segmentation, here obviously overridden by augmentative–diminutive indexical structure.

Having sketched the form of diminutive and augmentative indexical effects, I turn now to their structural and discursive functional vitality – the living effects for the speakers (even if few speakers are still living). We can get an idea in this way both of the net historical sedimentation of "breakthrough" semiosis and of the contextualized leading edge of this in the functional realtime of *parole*. We will reveal thereby, furthermore, the folly of essentializing "sound" as a natural stuff available to the non- or pre-cultural sensibilities, as is the case in contemporary Ding-dongism as much as it was at an earlier period.

4.3. Indexicality in morpholexical derivation

Several types of derivational pattern in this morphologically complex language, both freely productive and lexicalized, rest upon the functioning system of indexical shifts to generate connotative augmentation and diminution in understandable ways. The systematicity of the indexical meanings is brought thereby into the plane of denotationally understood form – in effect, superimposed upon it as a structuring principle.

Let us take as an example Wasco verbal derivation, which productively creates complex inflectional themes from roots by patterned use of constituent layers of prefixation (see Silverstein 1984 for a systematic exposition). By such patterns are generated various combinations of prefix-class members in appropriate order as "constant" derivational accompaniments of the (seventh-position) root of a form; at the surface, without functional insight, this yields apparently discontinuous sequences of morphemes that, together, constitute the inflectional theme of the derived verb. Thus, the root $-\sqrt{g(^w)}a_7$, together with a locative prefix $-k_{-5}$ (in fifth-position- or order-class) yields the theme $-[\ ]_3-[\ ]_4-k_5-\sqrt{g(^w)}a_7{}^9$ "[ ]$_3$ fly$_7$ over$_5$ [ ]$_4$." Any of the prefix classes 2 ("transitive subject pronominal" in a resistantly familiar, though unrevealing gloss), 3 ("transitive object/intransitive subject" pronominal), 4 ("indirect object/locative" pronominal), 5 ("locative" or postposition) can be involved in such derivation.

And in this type of derivation, the connotations of the augmentative–diminutive indexicals play a distinct and recognizable role. For example, the locative $-gl_5-$ "away from; (completely) out of" occurs in many such derivational sets, e.g. $-[\ ]_3-[\ ]_4-gl_5-\sqrt{ba_7}-$ "[ ]$_3$ come-out$_7$ (out-)of$_5$ [ ]$_4$," as in $i_3-n_4-gl_5-\sqrt{p_7}-x_{11}$ "it [sc. blood/urine/semen/etc.]$_3$ is-coming-out$_{7+11}$ (out-)of$_5$ me$_4$", a continuative form with no initial tense prefix. The obviously diminutivized counterpart of the locative, $-q\dot{\ }l_5-$, occurs as a seeming denotationally attenuated form of $-gl_5$, indicating something like "beginning to . . . out of/away from" or "partially . . . out of/away from" as a connotation on the denotational plane, as in the example $i_3-n_4-q\dot{\ }l_5-\sqrt{p_7}-x_{11}$ "it$_3$ is-growing-out$_{7+11}$ (out-)of$_5$ me$_4$," based on the verb theme $-[\ ]_3-[\ ]_4-q\dot{\ }l_5-\sqrt{ba_7}-$ "[ ]$_3$ grow-out$_7$ (out-)of$_5$ [ ]$_4$." Note that while the English

Native American languages north of Mexico

translations differ essentially in the coding of the lexical verb stem, "come out" vs. "grow out," the only formal distinction in Wasco is the diminutivization vs. non-diminutivization (= neutral/augmentative pole of opposition) of the locative-postpositional element in theme derivation; the structure of the two themes – indeed, even their basic lexical elements at the denotational morpheme level – is unitary. Precisely parallel to this form in prefixal derivation is the pair of themes -[ ]$_3$-[ ]$_4$-gl_5- -$\sqrt{}da_7$- -$q!q_{10}$- "[ ]$_3$ run$_7$ completely$_{10}$ away-from$_5$ / escape$_{7+10}$ from$_5$ [ ]$_4$" – which has the regular voiced-series form -gl_5- – and -$\acute{s}_3$-[ ]$_4$-$q'l_5$- -$\sqrt{}da_7$- -ba_9- "[a part$_3$] tear/rip$_7$ out$_9$-and-off-of$_5$ [ ]$_4$" – which has the somewhat diminutivized, ejective-series -$q'l_5$-. These examples represent numerous other similarly opposed formations where the denotational meaning plays upon the basic indexical opposition of the fifth-position locative.

This form of opposition is also regularly found in certain thematic formations of the verbal system, like "tear/rip out/off of" cited above, that employ a "fixed," non-cross-referencing pronominal morpheme as the critical derivational part of the theme.[10] A very productive such opposition uniformly signals action by animate actor with body parts, in allusional categorization, taken as generally paired things, and hence coded by a third person dual non-cross-referencing pronominal. The theme of such forms is generally built from some verbal root of motion or its equivalent, with some dative-plus-locative/postpositional derivational complex as well. For example, note -[ ]$_2$-s_3-[ ]$_4$-$k'l_5$- -$\sqrt{}la_7$- -ba_9- "[ ]$_2$ make [ ]$_4$ fall back/tip over (backwards)" and its Dative- or "indirect"-reflexive form -s_3-[ ]$_4$-x- + $k'l_5$- -$\sqrt{}la_7$- -ba_9- "[ ]$_4$ fall back/tip over (backwards)." Similarly, -[ ]$_2$-s_3-[ ]$_4$-l_5- -$\sqrt{}k'a_7$- $m(a)_{8.1}$ + it_{11}- "[ ]$_2$ poke-around-in/'goose' [ ]$_4$," constructionally, "[ ]$_2$ cause$_{8.1+11}$ [the-two-dimin.-ones]$_3$ to-become-slightly-stuck$_7$ in$_5$ [ ]$_4$" (cf. non-diminutive causative -[ ]$_2$-[ ]$_3$-[ ]$_4$-l_5- -$\sqrt{}ga_7$-$m(a)_{8.1}$ + it_{11}- "[ ]$_2$ stick$_{7+8.1+11}$ [ ]$_3$ into$_5$ [ ]$_4$." Note also -[ ]$_2$-s_3- -u_6-$\sqrt{}bna_7$- "[ ]$_2$ jump," constructionally, "[ ]$_2$ slightly-lift$_7$ [the-two-dimin.-ones]$_3$" (cf. canonical transitive verb -[ ]$_2$-[ ]$_3$- -u_6-$\sqrt{}buna_7$- -$\acute{c}k^{(w)}{}_{10}$- "[ ]$_2$ lift$_7$ (telicly$_{10}$) [ ]$_3$"). And finally -s_3-[ ]$_4$ + x- -$\sqrt{}c'i_7$- -lxa_9-gwa_{10}- "[ ]$_4$ have-grooved-notch-all-around," constructionally, "[body-part]$_3$ of-[ ]$_4$ evulse$_7$ centrifugally$_9$ all-around$_{10}$." These are representative constructions with -s_3-. It should additionally be observed of them that several of the other morphemes in these themes themselves have diminutivization effects in their basic, "lexical" citation forms: roots -$\sqrt{}ga_7$- "motion through air," -$\sqrt{}buna_7$- "raise up," and -$\sqrt{}\lambda'i_7$- "pull (on); draw" occur in these formations as -$\sqrt{}k'a_7$-, -$\sqrt{}bna_7$- (generally -$\sqrt{}p'na$- in derived forms), and -$\sqrt{}c'i_7$-, respectively, bespeaking the connotations of non-total movement or involvement and diminished scale; similarly for the locative-prepositional -gl_5-, which occurs as -$k'l_5$-.

In addition to these systematic morphological derivations, indexical sound phenomena are involved in a second major area of lexicon. They constitute the formal basis for connotatively negatively valued, embarrassing, and otherwise inherently pejorative denoting forms, where, as is to be expected, we get clearly augmentative (vs. diminutive-to-neutral) shapes. These occur both in opposition to otherwise similar, and non-charged, shapes with distinct English translations, and as unique formations the shape of which is consistent with this connotational value. Thus, for example, note the formal difference between $n_3 + x\text{-}i_4\text{-}k_5\text{-}$ $\text{-}\sqrt{t'a_7}\text{-}m[a]_{8.1} + \text{-}id_{11}\text{-}ix_{12}$ "I$_3$ skate on (some location$_4$)," constructionally, "I$_3$ cause$_{8.1+11}$ self[= x] quick-motion-on-surface$_7$ on$_5$ (location$_{4+12}$)," and the otherwise structurally identical form $n x i k d \acute{a} m i d i x$ "I (go to) squat someplace [sc. for defecation]," where the only distinction is the augmentative form of the root, $\text{-}\sqrt{t'a_7}\text{-}:\text{-}\sqrt{da_7}\text{-}$. Note also that for already embarrassing and pejoratively amusing words, such as $ig_1\text{-}i_3 + x\text{-}(a)n_4\text{-}l_5\text{-}\sqrt{qw_7}\text{-}it_{11}$ "he$_3$ (recently$_1$) farted$_{7+11}$ on$_5$ me$_4$," the telicly continuative or repetitive forms occur in the hyperaugmentative, $igixanlqbílitimčk$ "he was just repeatedly farting on me" (i.e. "he was just blasting me with wind").

Forms such as -[ ]$_3$- $\text{-}\sqrt{\check{c}ga_7}\text{-}$ -it_{11}- "[ ]$_3$ sweat$_{7+11}$" and -[ ]$_4$-x + gl_5- $\text{-}\sqrt{\check{s}gia_7}\text{-}$ "[ ]$_4$ be-fat-in-buttocks/steatopygous$_7$," moreover, seem always to occur in such lexically augmentative form. While not specifically opposed to any structurally equivalent neutral-to-diminutive forms, they are clearly compatible only with augmentative shapes within the indexical system of sound symbolism. It would also appear that the expletive $qalaqbáya$, generally glossed as "damn!" or something similar, is also an historically frozen augmentative form, with frozen connotational baggage, from the adverbial particle $qánaga$ "rather"; note -l- for -n- and -qb- for -q-, along with stretching of the final syllable in a characteristic Wasco manner, -$áya$ for -a. The segmental form $qalaqbáya$ can additionally be accompanied by extraordinary paralinguistic effects.

4.4. Textual indexicality and imagery of voice

If the sound-symbolic consistency of certain productive derivations and lexicalized forms is already sedimented in the Wasco language, by contrast we can look at phenomena that bespeak functional "breakthrough" in discursive practice, at the organizational level of text-in-context. Two such phenomena can be readily identified.

The first is rather frequent in our records of narrative, where, as Bakhtin (1981: 324–331) would say, the "voice" of a particular emplotted character breaks through the frame of narrativity itself to be potentially identifiable with the "voice" of the narrator, who is presupposed to be in the communicative frame of the receivers/ interpreters of the narrative.[11] In this way, the manner in which a narrator reports particular events being narrated can potentially duplicate, in matters of verbally coding the represented or denoted material, the way that a characterized voice would do so; or vice-versa, an emplotted character may "voice" the narrator (and note that this has little to do with the mere denotational use of *I* as a descriptor of a character in the narrative). The way that a narrator reports the particular events being narrated shows an indexical infection with, for example, attitudinal and affective characteristics, point of view, etc., of one or more of the very participants in the narrated events. Such attitudinal colorings emerge in the phonic substance of the language of narration in Wasco augmentativization and diminutivization, a kind of *pragmatic (indexical) "style indirect libre"* (indirect free style) in the narrative guise of metapragmatic description of the pragmatics of interaction that constitutes so much of narrative emplotment of character: narrating and narrated "voices" are indexically aligned, seeing things at least in part from the same point of view.

Thus, a frequent event in myth narrations about the Trickster-Transformer figure, Coyote, is his consultation with his "Two Little Sisters," who are, it turns out, two turds that he keeps in a special interior place in his lower bowel. Coyote is always getting into trouble of one sort or another, about which he needs interpretative advice and guidance on proper courses of action. At such times, when he wishes to consult his Two Little Sisters, he defecates them and consults them in rather humorous interchanges of a stylized sort. Whenever Coyote gets their opinion on a matter, he always says, "Just as I thought!" – as if he could have reached that conclusion all by himself, so obvious has the interpretation now become to him! Thus, whenever Coyote defecates his Two Little Sisters out and asks them something, they at first refuse to tell him, saying "You'll just say, 'Just as I thought!'" They always relent,[12] though sometimes only after Coyote has threatened them with being "rained" (i.e. spat) upon, which would, of course, melt them into nothing. And always, Coyote, hearing their interpretation and advice, says, "Just as I thought!" as his Two Little Sisters have claimed he would. The Shakespearian comic relief of all this notwithstanding, everyone in the society knows that Coyote has long-suffering, indeed "dear little" Sisters, on whose help he really depends, even if he cannot bring himself to say so. Thus, Coyote's attitude toward them ought to be one that characteristically would be verbally expressed by his use of diminutivized forms for all denotation of his Two Little Sisters and of their activities.

Observe, then, how the metapragmatic frame, the descriptive narration of how characters interact one with another in pragmatic modalities, absorbs this attitude, this Bakhtinian "voice." In the following portion of "Coyote Enslaves the West Wind," one of the myths recorded by Sapir from Louis Simpson in 1905 (printed in Sapir 1909: 100, lines 11–16), the critical points illustrative of the process are given in Wasco, after a contextualizing English translation of the preceding material:

Coyote woke up: No slave! Coyote went to (where the slave had been): No slave! So then Coyote looked for him. He ran around to every (possible) place, but did not get (hold of) him.

Aga kwápt gacsugícxaba isiáutxix. Aga kwápt gacsúlxam, "Mtxánitk^włičk dán yáxtau!" Aga kwápt gašgiúlxam, "..." ...

[So then he-defecated-the-two-of-them-out his-Two-Younger-Sisters. So then he-said-to-the-two-of-them, "You-two-tell/recount-to-me what *that* (is) [sc. 'what is going on here']!" So then the-two-of-them-said-to-him, "...". ..]

Notice that the framing verb *gacsúlxam* "he said to the two of them" and the whole propositional descriptor *gacsugícxaba isiáutxix* "he-defecated-the-two-of-them-out his-Two-Younger-Sisters" are in essentially diminutivized form,[13] even though these are strictly speaking the words of the narrator, not those of Coyote. And when Coyote himself speaks, it is with regular, non-diminutivized forms, as likewise both the framing description *gašgiúlxam* "the-two-of-them-said-to-him" and the Sisters' words replied to Coyote in return. Such breakthroughs of the pragmatic or indexical material as would be characteristic of the narrated characters in their events render the culturally understood parameters of the narrated situation as connotations of the denotational value of the metapragmatic frame. That is, the denotational value of the lexical expressions of narration become "sound symbolic" through the transfer, and the event of narration itself takes on the symbolisms of the narrated content.

Such a process, of course, operates on the plane of yielding connotational content – hence, "sound symbolism" – of phonic substance in the metapragmatic descriptors of speech acts, that is, acts of using performatively effective pragmatic indicators. It is a process parallel to the usual *delocutionary* process first systematically described by Emile Benveniste (1966 [original 1958]), whereby sometimes new metapragmatic denotational forms are created, both synchronically (functionally) and diachronically (etymologically).

As Benveniste pointed out, we frequently find regular creation of metapragmatic descriptors for conventional speech acts by a process of "mentioning," but not "using," a characteristic pragmatically effective formula indexically associated with the particular (type or token) speech act. For example, if one characteristically indexes (and performs) an instance of greeting by saying the expression "Hello!" one can form a grammaticalized verb-stem, (*to*) "*hello*" [someone], meaning "to perform a characteristic act of greeting [someone]", as a means of *describing* this type of speech act, though not necessarily of performing it on each occasion of use; cf. the angry "Don't you 'hello' mé, you SOB!" Such a descriptor is frequently usable to characterize the speech act, even where the actual form of greeting or whatever on some occasion at descriptive issue was not, in fact, the particular formula by which, through various processes of conventionalization, the speech act was evidenced. In other words, some delocutionaries, by degrees and through communicative practice, become the conventional ways of denoting certain types of speech act as indexically accomplishable interactional routines. In a sense, note, the delocutionary descriptor denotes the particular speech act essentially by *re-presenting* it, in a suitably grammaticalized form with the apparatus of the plane of denotational structure (i.e. grammar-as-usual), by virtue of which one can *represent*, i.e. denote, the speech act by using a form identical or at least very close to the one used in performing it.[14] In the example under discussion, likewise, we get a quasi-delocutionary connotational "indirect free style."

Under proper conditions, it seems, such phenomena observable in narrative "voicing" can become detached from their metapragmatic functional contexts. So detached and then reused with a trope of *renvoi*, they become aesthetic readymades that reveal a way-station along the path to true "sound symbolism," that is, denotational iconism in the straightforward sense. For it is only where there can be a re-presentation of phonic substance as at once *indexically effective* and as an instantiated, culturally understood *image* or *icon* of something (a cluster of aligned schematizations across modalities, for example), that we have denotational iconism that we can investigate directly. Only where sound itself has some locally understood semiotic function independent of denotation – hence as dictated by some framework of "relative motivation" for that non-denotational code type – does denotational iconism become possibly transparent to the outsider's inquiry. In the most fortunate cases, we can see the process at its source of motivation, where the indexicality laminated together with conventional iconism (emblematization) brings together schematized entities, activities, etc. with the presentation of sound itself (the *Klang an sich*?). Like any such tropic metasemiosis (compare so-called metaphor on the denotational plane), there are degrees of living and frozen functional forms at any given synchronic cross-section, so the key is to find something at once structurally locatable in denotational morphosyntax, and wholly determinate in the non-denotational system of meaningfulness.

The lexico-grammatical class of Particles in Wasco is a likely place to look. This is a noticeably huge set of lexical items (from the academically registered perspective of usage in English) that occur in predications together with an inflection-bearing predicating auxiliary, that occur paratactically alongside a complete predicate, and that sometimes occur alone in minor syntactic fragments. They sometimes seem to us to have an almost palpable sound-symbolic quality. Yet such elicitable attributions are just completely skewed with respect to our outsider's intuitions. The delight that we find in identifying something as a "sound-symbolic" Particle is much more often than not inexplicable to the native speaker, who (here compare the examples of phonic "difficulty" and "ease" noted above) is puzzled by our silliness.[15]

Discussing this class of items in Lower Chinook, the now extinct dialect of Chinookan once spoken in the region of the mouth of the Columbia River, Franz Boas professes himself to be hard-pressed to separate what he would consider Particles that are onomatopoeic from the others, though his lists of membership – many of which have near or exact correspondences in Wasco – are exceedingly interesting. Boas (1911: 627–631, 636) makes the following remarks about these words:

In some cases it appears doubtful whether the [onomatopoeic] words belong to the regular vocabulary of the language, or whether they are individual productions [of the single consultant, Charles Cultee]. This is true when the words do not form part of the sentence, but appear rather as independent exclamations. . . .

In a number of cases onomatopoetic terms which undoubtedly belong to the regular vocabulary are used in this way. . . .

It is difficult to say where, in this [regular but onomatopoeic] class of words, the purely onomatopoeic character ceases, and where a more indirect representation of the verbal idea by sound begins. I think a distinct auditory image of the idea expressed is found in the following words [here given in a modernized orthography]:

iuλ'l   "proud"
kúlkul   "light (of weight)"
k'a   "silent"
q'am   "lazy"
q'uλ   "fast"
paλ   "full"
təmən "clear"
təl: "tired"
č'pak   "loud"
gútgut "exhausted"
lúlu   "round"
wax̱   "to pour out"
gəšgəš "to drive"
λəl: "to disappear"
λax̱   "to appear"
λx̱wap "to dig"

Needless to say, these shapes are closely matched by others that denote entirely different states of affairs, their synonyms have entirely other shapes in many instances, and, where we can locate Wasco correspondents, e.g., *paλ* "full," (*sai-*)*lulu* "round," *wax̱* "pour out," *λx̱wap* "dug out," to mention only a few, we have no evidence of any felt sound-iconic or onomatopoeic quality to those particles. What sometimes does happen, however, is the accompaniment of the Particle by various paralinguistic and even connotational indexical effects in the event of denotational usage or when an interjectional form is created on these forms; these effects are easily confused by the outsider with denotational iconism, or "onomatopoeia."

It is important to see, therefore, that any analysis of such lexical items into morpheme partials, "phonaesthemes," "ideophones," or other putative structural units of denotation that violate the duality of patterning or double articulation of linguistic structure must be based on some evidence that has a structural basis within the particular language, as well as on reductionist universalism, no matter how strong the outsider's intuition of such might be. So establishing the grammatical status of onomatopoeic lexical classes would, of course, necessitate such evidence as paradigmatic sets, consistencies of grammatical class membership based on multiple distributions, or other such reasoning from grammatical data – even, as Whorf long ago pointed out, characterizable gaps or complementarities (negative "signatures" and "reactances") involving the forms at issue – as distinctively and transparently correlated with denotational iconism or emblematicity on the functional plane.

Like most such proposals one encounters, Boas's intuition about the onomatopoeic underpinnings of the class of grammatical Particles fails the methodological test. However, we can see in certain *discursive* contexts the basis of a live process of creating emblematic, Particle-like phonic forms by crossing augmentative–diminutive indexicality with epitomizing *renvoi* to narrative schematization of events.

We find wide knowledge among the Wasco-Wishram speakers of a bawdy theme of sexual wrestling between a variously characterized male-and-female couple; sometimes it is Coyote and *Adat'áliya* (Basket-Ogress Woman), sometimes others. An asymmetry of size, power, fierceness, etc. prevails as part of the dramatic tension to be resolved, and the lesser of the central pair instructs some third party beforehand to listen for the outcome. Observe that the narrator's addressee(s) – the "audience" – are thereby aligned with the third part as they are drawn into a perspective on the dramatic emplotment. "If I manage to best [i.e. get the definitive advantage over] her/him," the lesser character points out, "you [i.e., the third party, including us, the listeners] will hear '$g^wa\cdot w$'; if she/he manages to best me, you will hear '$k'u\cdot$'."[16] Of course, these phonic forms display canonical augmentative vs. diminutive sound symbolism: g^w- vs. k'^w- (the labialization swallowed up in the following vowel u), -a- vs. ∅ (with vocalization of the resulting schwa-plus-w, as is normal in Wasco). And when re-presented denotationally, the phonic substance thus "speaks" with the meaning of the opposed augmentative vs. diminutive connotations. Emblematized as a textual ready-made that can be extracted from its narrative context by the widespread familiarity of the incident/motif, the very terms $gwa\cdot w$ and $k'u\cdot$ become "onomatopoeic" lexemes for denoting David-over-Goliath vs. Goliath-over-David types of victory, capable of provoking mirth among fully cultured speakers upon utterance, with a distinct intuition of "sound symbolism": this is what such kinds of situations sound like!

Such chains of reasoning about "relative motivation" in various cultural and linguistic functional structures provide us with a way into a particular system, on the planes of both discursive textuality and grammatical system. Differentiating these planes and differentiating the semiotic functions involved in the *process* of achieving various crossings and laminations of them are the methodological *sine qua non* of investigating denotational iconism as an analytic construct. Here, for example, we have stressed the (functional) indexicality of augmentation/diminution effects in Wasco, the (structural) lamination of these effects as connotation in simplex and systematically derived lexical form in grammar, and the (discursive) processes that generate delocutionary (metapragmatic) and emblematic (conventional indexical-iconic) forms in text.

NOTES

1 This view is rephrased in the historically derived accounts of Bloomfield during the 1920s and 1930s, by the way. See, for example, Bloomfield 1923; [1934]1970: 282–286; and especially 1933, chapters 9, 10, 16, based on 1926, sections II–VII.
2 Professor Malkiel's *irreversible binomials* (1959) come to mind as such "poetic" phenomena, at least in part, where both grammatical-plane and phonological-plane factors seem to play a role. Consider also the salience and memorability of pleasingly ordered proper names in binary or larger-scope conjunctive ordering, as in firm names, or authorial topoi in bibliographic formulation and citation.
3 This, it should be noted, can be celebrated or deplored as a kind of "linguistic relativity," as many writers have recognzied about extreme approaches from Saussurean "langue"-centrism to Chomskian "autonomous syntax"-centrism.
4 Unless otherwise credited, data and analysis of Wasco-Wishram are the results of my own fieldwork in Washington and Oregon, generously supported in 1966–1974 by the Phillips Fund of the American Philosophical Society, the National Science Foundation through its Graduate Fellowship Program, the Society of Fellows (Harvard University), and the Adolph Lichtstern Fund of the Department of Anthropology, The University of Chicago, to all of which I am most grateful. Wasco-Wishram, or "Wasco" here for short, echoing speakers' usage in local English, together with other village and village-cluster dialects, comprises the Kiksht language of the Upper Chinookan branch of the more extensive Chinookan linguistic family. See Silverstein 1990: 533–535 for the relevant ethnographic and linguistic distinctions.
5 See Aoki, this volume, n. 3, for some of the Americanist symbols used here that are not equivalent to IPA. Additional symbols used in this paper are $č\,(=tʃ)$, $š\,(=ʃ)$, $ǰ\,(=ʤ)$.
6 One sees immediately the implication for use of such forms as contain, or can be modified so as to contain, these segment types to suggest characterological or other essentialized traits about which culturally conventional affect can be indexed in denoting and in quoting from represented narrative characters, as in various "abnormal speech types" (Sapir 1915) found over a wide area of the Northwest Coast and Plateau. See the discussion in the main body of the text.
7 Such a denotational refunctionalization is completely to be expected under the conditions I have discussed at length in Silverstein 1981, arising in part from the semiotic character of such pragmatic codes as the one being here discussed, and in part from an ideological view of language codes in general that seems to underlie the Western language sciences, which intensifies and essentializes the focus on denotational form into a theory of restrictively denotational meaning or content.
8 The very paradigm of $λ;c$ here reinforces the quasi-lexicalized status of the final-position alternation, justifying our distinct translations. Recall from our discussion above that $č:c$ order distinctions seem to have replaced $λ:c$ ones as freely productive "augmentative": "diminutive" alternants for the last generation of speakers.
9 The brackets mark freely filled inflectional positions for cross-referencing pronominal elements, in their respective order-classes as indicated by subscripts: $-[\ ]_2-$ is the Ergative position, $-[\ ]_3-$ is the Nominative/Absolutive position, $-[\ ]_4-$ is the Dative position. Obviously, various ordered combinations of two or three of these are the indicators of

various inflectional types of verb roots, stems, and themes. See Silverstein 1984 and refs. there.

10 This type of derivation I have elsewhere (Silverstein 1984: 281–285) termed *derivational allusion*, since the pronominal element at issue alludes to, but does not refer to, the kind of entity that is typically denoted by the particular grammatical cross-referencing pronominal as it would normally agree with grammatico-semantic categories of nouns, relative to the typical case relation (thematic role) coded in the inflectional position where the derivational pronominal occurs.

11 Appealing to the compositional analogy with music, Bakhtin's concept of voicing – whence the "polyphony" of certain texts – is not to be identified with denoted or denotable characters of narrated emplotment or of the communicative parts (role structure or turn-incumbency structure) of the event of narrating (however discontinuous in time in the case of the production of text-artifacts like printed material). It is a structure of relational projections of socially personifiable interests in a sociocultural universe that constitutes the "voicing" of a literary work. We thus note that the projection across the narrating frame – where we live – and the narrated frame – where the emplotted characters live – sets up a structure of *identification with* vs. *differentiation from* characters in both frames that underlies the composition, as it were, of a literary work.

12 Indeed, what are little sisters for in a culture where the literary themes loom large of "youngest = smartest" and "female ingenuity" ("mother-wit")? Note that the Little Sisters hilariously articulate the cultural knowledge about Coyote himself, that narrator and narrator's addresses (= the "audience" of the performance) share, as commonplace though humorous.

13 Absolute consistency of phonetic form would, by the way, demand *gacsuk'ʷícxaba*, as occurs in my own materials for this type of incident, "he-daintily/lovingly-defecated-the-two-little-ones-out."

14 Hence the similarity of our connotational "delocutionary" breakthrough of textual voicing to the so-called use vs. mention distinction at the plane of denotational language. In the latter, too, a particular presentation of a form in some specialized grammatical context signals its re-presentation and consequently its representation, though we must make much finer distinctions for any adequate semiotic discussion than this sloppy and unifunctional one of standard philosophical discourse informed by local ideologies of language.

15 Much as, one supposes, speakers of French are puzzled by the anglophone tendency to capitalize on the availability of many puns, at least in the distinct citation forms of lexical items in their language.

16 I have sometimes heard the first uttered in a deep voice, the second in falsetto.

REFERENCES

Bakhtin, M. M. 1981. *The Dialogic Imagination: Four Essays*. M. Holquist (ed.); C. Emerson and M. Holquist, transl. Austin: University of Texas Press.

Barthes, R. 1967. *Elements of Semiology*. A. Lavers and C. Smith, transl. New York: Hill & Wang.

Benveniste, E. 1966. Les verbes délocutifs. In *Problèmes de linguistique générale*. Paris: Gallimard, 277–285. [Original 1958.]

Bloomfield, L. 1923. Review of Saussure, *Cours de linguistique générale*, 2nd edn. *Modern Language Journal* 8: 317–319. (Reprinted in Hockett 1970: 106–108.)

  1926. A set of postulates for the science of language. *Language* 2: 153–164. (Reprinted, Hockett 1970: 128–138; pages cited from this reprint.)

  1933. *Language*. New York: Henry Holt.

  1934. Review of Havers, *Handbuch der erklärenden Syntax*. *Language* 10: 32–39. (Reprinted in Hockett 1970: 281–288; pages cited from this reprint.)

Boas, F. 1911. Chinook. In F. Boas (ed.) *Handbook of American Indian Languages* 1. Bureau of American Ethnology, Bulletin 40. Washington: Government Printing Office, 559–677.

Chomsky, N. and M. Halle. 1968. *The Sound Pattern of English*. New York: Harper & Row.

Givón, T. 1984. *Syntax: A Functional-Typological Introduction*, vol. 1. Amsterdam: Benjamins.

  1989. The linguistic code and the iconicity of grammar. In *Mind, Code, and Context: Essays in Pragmatists*, Hillsdale, NJ: Erlbaum, 69–125.

Haiman, J. 1985. *Natural Syntax: Iconicity and erosion*. Cambridge: University Press.

Hockett, C. F. 1961. Linguistic elements and their relations. *Language* 37: 29–53.

  (ed.) 1970. *A Leonard Bloomfield Anthology*. Bloomington: Indiana University Press.

Jakobson, R. and M. Halle. 1956. Phonology and phonetics. In *Fundamentals of Language*. The Hague: Mouton, 1–51.

Lamb, S. M. 1964. On alternation, transformation, realization, and stratification. *Georgetown University Round Table* 15: 105–122. Washington: Georgetown University Press.

Malkiel, Y. 1959. Studies in irreversible binomials. *Lingua* 8: 113–160.

Martinet, A. 1964. *Elements of General Linguistics*. E. Palmer, transl. London: Faber.

Quine, W. V. 1960. *Word and Object*. Cambridge, Mass.: MIT Press.

Sapir, E. 1915. *Abnormal Types of Speech in Nootka*. Canada, Department of Mines, Geological Survey, Memoir 62 (Anthropological Series, 5). Ottawa: Government Printing Bureau. (Reprinted in D. C. Mandelbaum (ed.) *Selected Writings of Edward Sapir in Language, Culture, and Personality*. Berkeley: Univeristy of California Press, 1949, 179–196.)

Saussure, F. de. 1916. *Cours de linguistique générale*. (Pages cited from 5th edn., 1960.) Paris: Payot.

Silverstein, M. 1981. *The Limits of Awareness*. Sociolinguistic Working Papers 84. Austin: Southwest Educational Development Laboratory.

  1984. Wasco-Wishram lexical derivational processes *vs.* word-internal syntax. In D. Testen *et al.* (eds.), *Papers from the Parasession on Lexical Semantics*. Chicago: Chicago Linguistic Society, 270–288.

  1990. Chinookans of the lower Columbia. In W. Suttles (ed.), *Handbook of North American Indians*, vol. 7, *Northwest Coast*. Washington: Smithsonian Institution Press, 533–546.

Whitney, W. D. 1867. *Language and the Study of Language: Twelve Lectures on the Principles of Linguistic Science*. New York: Charles Scribner's Sons.

PART II
Native languages of Latin America

5
Symbolism and change in the sound system of Huastec

TERRENCE KAUFMAN

5.1. Introduction

This paper will illustrate from Huastec, a Mayan language of East Central Mexico, two probably fairly common phenomena in the area of sound symbolism:
  (a) Because of their imitative sound–meaning correlation certain phonemes may not be subject to certain sound changes when these correlations are in play;
  (b) Certain firmly entrenched and not at all marginal (albeit somewhat infrequent) phonemes in a language may in fact occur only in sound-symbolic words.

5.2. Background

Over six fields seasons (1969, 1980, 1981, 1982, 1983, and 1984) I have been collecting lexical materials for a Huastec dictionary. As a modest estimate, I have over 10,000 lexical items and over 2,300 roots.

5.3. Huastec phonemes

Huastec has the following phonemic system in the native general (= non-symbolic) lexicon:

Consonants[1]

p	t	ṭ	c	k	k^w	ʔ
b	t'	ṭ'	c'	k'	$k^{w'}$	
	θ		š			h
m	n					
	l					
	y			w		

Vowels

	i		u	
	e		o	V:
		a		

63

Symbolic roots contain, in addition:

s, r, r̃

Spanish loanwords add:

d, g; f [in some varieties only]

5.4. Practical orthography

In the practical orthography that I use for writing Huastec the following equivalences hold:

#c	\<tx\>	#kʷ	\<kw\>
#č	\<ch\>	#h	\<j\>
#ṭ	\<ts\>	#š	\<x\>
#r̃	\<rr\>	#θ	\<th\>
#ʔ	\<ʔ\>	#V:	\<VV\>

5.5. Diasystems

A diaphon(em)e is a phonological category that relates the statistically significant sound correspondences among phonemes across the dialects of a single language. It is for practical purposes – but not in essence – analogous to a protophoneme (which is the product of reconstruction); still, you almost always have more diaphon(em)es than protophonemes in the respective constructs. Diaphon(em)es are indicated by a preposed # (word boundary uses # #).

5.5.1. Huastec diaphonology

Huastec has three dialects (see T. Kaufman, 1985. Aspects of Huastec dialectology and historical phonology. *International Journal of American Linguistics* 51: 473–476). In native vocabulary all varieties of Huastec have the same set of phonological contrasts (shown above), but for certain diaphonemes, in the general lexicon their realizations differ according to dialect, as follows:

diaphone	O(tontepec)	C(entral)	P(otosino)
#c	č	č	¢
#c'	č'	č'	¢'
#ṭ	ṭ ~ č̣	¢	č
#ṭ'	ṭ' ~ č̣	¢'	č'
#r̃	r̃	r̃	r

Examples

#can "snake"	čan	čan	¢an
#ʔic "chilli pepper"	ʔič	ʔič	ʔi¢
#c'ak "flea"	č'ak	č'ak	¢'ak
#c'e:n "mountain"	č'e:n	č'e:n	¢'e:n
#ṭiθ "pigweed"	ṭiθ	¢iθ	čiθ
#paṭ "pot"	paṭ	pa¢	pač
#ṭ'iṭab "comb"	ṭ'iṭab	¢'i¢ab	č'ičab
#we:ṭ' "squeak"	we:ṭ'	we:¢'	we:č'
#r̃un "whirr"	r̃un	r̃un	run

The original pronunciation of #c, #c' was [č, č'], for the following reasons (see Kaufman 1985: 474–475):
(a) #c, #c' comes from Proto-Mayan *č, *č' and *k, *k' (via palatalization);
(b) Spanish /č/ shows up in early borrowings as Huastec #c, whereas later borrowings show Huastec [č] across the board.

The original pronunciation of #ṭ, #ṭ' was probably [ṭ, ṭ'] phonetically, since (see Kaufman 1985: 475):
(a) they developed from Proto-Mayan *t, *t' and *ṭ, *ṭ';
(b) their current reflexes [ṭ, ṭ'] cannot be plausibly derived from [č, č'] or [¢, ¢'];
(c) they become /t/, /t'/ in Chicomuceltec, a descendant of Proto-Huastecan.

Nevertheless, support for [č, č'] as early pronunciations of #ṭ, #ṭ' is provided by
(d) their rendering by [č] in loans into Spanish and Náhuatl;
(e) their being spelled < ch > in the only extant sixteenth-century source written in Huastec;
(f) their occurrence today in some varieties of Otontepec Huastec.

5.5. Sound symbolism in Huastec

Huastec has a sizeable number of roots which are sound-symbolic, in that
(a) they encode meaning more or less directly via the sounds the roots are composed of;
(b) the roots do not belong to other major root classes, and have some derivational possibilities that are peculiar to what I call the class of *symbolic roots*.

Symbolic roots are of two subtypes from a semantic/typological point of view:
(a) those that directly represent sounds in nature: *imitative* or *onomatopoeic*. There are easily more than 200 such roots in any variety of Huastec. These are abbreviated ONOM in the discussion that follows.
(b) those that use Huastec phonemes to encode non-auditory phenomena (especially referring to *light* and *moving forms*) in a more or less direct conventionalized way: synesthetic sound symbolism (see introduction, this volume).

There are relatively few symbolic roots of type (b); most symbolic roots are imitative.

Symbolic roots can have the basic shapes CV(:)C and CV(:)Yʔ (where Y is /w/ or /y/). These are basically the shapes that all major root classes can have, though nouns can be phonologically more complex than this.

Symbolic roots are not expletives or exclamations; they are thoroughly integrated into the derivational and inflexional morphology of Huastec, which is a typical Mayan language in the high degree of its morphological complexity, especially in derivation.

5.6.1 Morphological/derivational traits of symbolic roots

The following derivations are unique to symbolic roots (all forms are written using practical orthography):

(1) *bare root* (P, C) *the sound*
Ex: CHAKW! – in t'ajaʔ an atx'eem toltom tam ti ijkan txabaal
"PLOP went the wet cloth when it fell to the ground"

(2) *-bix* (P, C) vi *produce the sound*
Ex: CHOMbix an lanaax aal an jaʔ
"the orange SPLASHed in the water"

(3) *-V₁y* (P, C) vt *act on (usually hit or throw) something so as to produce the sound*
Ex: u CHAKway an toltom axi atx'eem
"I made the cloth that was wet go PLOP'

The following formations are also found with other root types, mainly positional roots:

(4) -le (P, C) vi *fall making the sound*
Ex: TXEKWle txabaal an taasa ti kwajlan
"the cup fell with a THUNK when it fell"

(5) -laʔ (P, C) vt *let make the sound*
Ex: in CHIKlaʔ in Kaarujil an laab
"the Mestizo let his truck('s air-brakes) go WHUFF"

(6) -k'aʔ (P, C) vt *let fall and make the sound*
Ex: an txakam kwitool in CHONK'aʔ an t'eleʔ aal an jaʔ
"the little boy let the baby fall and go SPLASH in the water"

(7) -paʔ (C only?) vt *same meaning as #6*
Ex: u CHOMpaʔ n-u lamil aal an jaʔ
"I let my specs fall and go SPLASH in the water"

(8) $-V_I V_I l$ (C only?) adj *in a state resulting from an action producing the noise*
Ex: naaʔ CHOMool an txakam ti atsim al jaʔ
"the child is there bathing HALF-IN-HALF-OUT of the water"

(9) $-C_I V_I V_I l$ (P, C) va *move back and forth making the sound*
Ex: CHEK'cheel in pajab an yejtxel thak pat'eb
"the old man in white pants's sandals SQUEAK back and forth as they go"

(10) $CV_I C-C_I V_I C_I V_I V_I l$ (V_1 must be short even if underlyingly long) (P, C) vs *go right along making the sound*
Ex: CHURuruul an txakam t'eleʔ k'al in ubaat'
"the little baby goes along with his toy WHISTLing"

(11) $CV_I C-C_I V_I C_I V_I V_I l$ (V_1 must be short, etc.) (P only?) va *go along at a shifting pace making the sound*
Ex: CHAWʔchachaal an k'athaw
"the hen turkey goes around SQUAWKing"

5.6.2. Alternation

The term *alternation* is used here to refer to a situation where two or more root shapes that are essentially synonymous differ by one phoneme only and where the articulatory differences between the commutable non-identical phonemes are minor. There is only one known active process of phonemic alternation (or ablaut) in Huastec, and that involves changing underlying /a/ to /o/ under certain grammatical conditions. As far as I know, the types of "alternation" referred to in this paper are embedded in the lexicon and not rule-governed.

5.6.3. Anomalies in symbolic roots

Huastec symbolic roots show four anomalies when compared to the general lexicon:

1. Whereas Huastec #c, #c' shift to [¢, ¢'] in the general lexicon in Potosino Huastec, in symbolic roots this change occurs only sporadically. In the vast majority of cases, [č, č'] occur across the board in symbolic roots. Such cases are assigned to the diaphonemes #č and #č' (on the other hand, Huastec #ṭ, #ṭ' do not seem to show any anomalies of development in symbolic roots).

2. Huastec #ř occurs only in symbolic roots, not in the (native) general lexicon. Though [ř] and [r] also occur in the general lexicon in loans from Spanish, symbolic roots with #ř are fairly numerous and only occasionally of Spanish origin. There is occasional "alternation" between /ř/ and /l/. ("Alternation" is explained below.)

3. Central (but not Potosino) Huastec has both /ř/ and /r/ in imitative roots, though the latter phoneme is extremely rare: only two imitative roots containing /r/ are known.

4. Apart from Spanish loans, Huastec /s/ occurs only in symbolic roots, never in the general lexicon. Huastec /θ/ derives from earlier *s; whether this change had occurred by the sixteenth century is not clear, since Spanish <ç> and <z> were used to write [s]. In symbolic roots both /θ/ and /s/ occur and rarely or never alternate. /s/ occasionally alternates with /š/, however. Spanish borrows Huastec /θ/ as Spanish /s/.

Henceforth Huastec (dia)phonemes will be represented via the practical orthography.

5.6.3.1. #TX and CH, TX' and CH'

Out of 40 cognate pairs of ONOM roots that have [č], [č'] in Central Huastec, in Potosino Huastec 26 have [č], [č'] (= #ch, #ch'), 12 have [¢], [¢'] (= #tx, #tx') and 3 have either [č] ~ [¢] (= #tx ~ #ch) or [č'] ~ [¢'] (= #ch' ~ #tx'). The breakdown is as follows:

##ch 5	##tx 5	##ch ~ tx 0
##ch' 16	##tx' 1	##ch' ~ tx' 1
ch## 0	tx## 0	ch ~ tx## 1
ch'## 5	tx'## 6	xh' ~ tx## 1

Note that *ch'* outnumbers *ch* 21:5, and *tx'* outnumbers *tx* 7:4; i.e. glottalized outnumbers plain 28:9 (a ratio of 3:1).

Note also that while syllable-initially *ch'* and *ch* overwhelmingly predominate over *tx'* and *tx* (21:5), syllable-finally unmatched *tx'* (which can follow any vowel) barely predominates (6:5) over unmatched *ch'* (which only occurs following front vowels).

The one case of syllable-final *tx ~ ch* shows that Proto-Huastec *c was at best rare in that position in ONOM roots. The item in question, *petx ~ pech* "thump," does not even have a cognate in Central Huastec.

All this suggests that there is a strong correlation, at least syllable-initially, for the imitative value of the sound [č'] in Huastec sound symbolism, one that resisted a sound change that must have occurred at least 350 years ago (see Kaufman 1985: 475). The imitative correlation for [č] seems weaker than for [č'] since [č] and [¢] reflexes for Proto-Huastec *c are about evenly balanced (in ONOM roots). I want to point out that there is little or nothing in this data to support the notion of lexical diffusion.

5.6.3.2. Meanings encoded by CH and CH'

A survey of all roots found in both Potosino and Central Huastec that contain *ch* and *ch'* suggest that these sounds represent the following meanings (associated vowel qualities are noted in corresponding cells):

	ch	ch'
hitting metal		i
chewing forcefully		e
sound in enclosed space		
water: gurgle, glug		o
solids: rumble, rattle		o, a
sucking		o
hitting soft things		
flesh: smack		o, a
mud, shit		
plop		a
squish		i
hitting water: splash	u, a	o
animal cries: birds and bugs		
high pitch		i, e
low pitch	a	o, u

I have not done a complete catalog of the sound–meaning correlations found in Huastec ONOM roots, so I cannot say whether these meanings are encoded in any other way.[2]

5.6.3.3. #RR and #R

Huastec #*rr* is unusual in that in native words it occurs only in symbolic roots. I have not established any sound correspondences between Huastec #rr and phonemes in other Mayan languages, and do not expect to be able to. As mentioned above, it may bear some relationship to Huastec /l/. The Otontepec and Central dialects have both /ř/ and /r/ as phonemes, both occurring in loans from Spanish as well as in ONOM roots (however, /r/ is not yet attested in ONOM roots in Otontepec Huastec); Potosino, on the other hand, has only /r/ corresponding to Spanish /ř/ and /r/, as well as in symbolic roots. While some might imagine that [r] is more "natural" than [ř], and suspect that Potosino is phonetically more conservative, the arrow of implication says that Proto-Huastec *ř > Potosino /r/, and to assume that [r] is older would complicate the picture in ways such that the possible avantage is unclear. There are two Huastec rs and both become Potosino /r/.

Huastec #r is found in only two (or three) ONOM roots both meaning "grunt, snore." Such an infrequent element may be suspected of being recent and not showing uniform treatment across informants. We can only wait to see if more instances of it show up. While I have, I believe, collected a large part of the ordinary vocabulary of Huastec, the corpus of ONOM roots is hardly closed.

5.6.3.4. S

Though Proto-Mayan and Proto-Huastecan *s goes to /θ/ in Huastec, the /s/ that is found in symbolic roots does not show any clear relation to /θ/. The fact that Spanish borrows Huastec /θ/ as /s/ and that some words have been borrowed back with /s/ into Huastec again (by some speakers) is irrelevant to determining the function of /s/ in non-borrowed vocabulary. In a number of cases /s/ "alternates" with /š/. Huastec /š/ (from Proto-Mayan *š) is phonetically [š] perhaps for most speakers, but in some towns [ṣ] and/or [ṡ] are typical pronunciations. Our one sixteenth-century source (de la Cruz) freely uses both <x> and <s> for Huastec /š/, <x> predominating over <s> by a rate of 2:1 or even 3:1 (in sixteenth-century Spanish <s> stood for ṣ and <x> stood for [š] and possibly also [ṡ]). Thus, Huastec /š/ may always have been varying among [ṣ], [š], and [ṡ]. Huastec /s/ is [s], with no retraction, retroflexion, or grooving.

5.6.4. Summary of previous discussion

The above discussion shows that the symbolic meaning of a sound may make it able to resist sound change, and that phonemes not used in the general lexicon may nevertheless be part of the phonology and lexicon of a language. It is not clear whether any generalizations should be drawn nor how they should be formulated, but the following claims are at least supported, even required, by the facts of Huastec:

(a) There need not be total overlap in the set of phonemes used in symbolic roots with those of the general lexicon.

(b) The semantic associations of certain sounds in symbolic roots may exempt them from certain sound changes (i.e. presumably such as would destroy established sound–meaning correlations) undergone by the general lexicon.

These may be fairly run-of-the-mill observations, but, while such peculiarities may not be *very* peculiar, many languages are not even *this* particular. I doubt very much whether the phenomena discussed above are highly *likely* to have analogs in some other unstudied language; they are merely *possible*. These phenomena do not threaten the historical linguist's axioms concerning the regularity of sound change. The phenomena under (a) could not even be recognized without the existence of such axioms. The scope of these axioms, however, may need to be more tightly defined.

5.7. Steps toward an analysis of Huastec onomatopoeia

In order to get some idea of what the sound–meaning correlations are that are manifested in the ONOM roots of Huastec, three kinds of examination of the data have been carried out.

(a) All sounds peculiar to, or peculiar in, ONOM roots have been sorted together;

(b) All sounds, and VC # # sound combinations, that have, seem to have, or might have establishable sound–meaning correlations have been brought together and subgrouped semantically;

(c) The total lexical file has been surveyed to determine (impressionistically) the relative frequencies of root-initial phonemes. This was done by estimating for each letter the proportion of a file box that the slips beginning with that letter occupied. The smallest proportion was assigned a factor of *one* and all other proportions are multiples of *one*. The relative frequencies of initial phonemes in ONOM roots was then determined (by counting) and the two situations compared. In ONOM roots some initial phonemes occur much oftener, others much less often, than in the general lexicon. For results see table 5.1.

5.7.1. Analysis

The following phonemes occur initially more often in ONOM roots than in the general lexicon:

phonemes of frequent occurrence: tx, tx', j, (k)

non-frequent phonemes: u, n, s, rr.

The following phonemes occur initially less often in ONOM roots than in the general lexicon:

frequent phonemes: p, t, m, t'

non-frequent phonemes: o, a, e, y, ts.

The following phonemes occur initially at about the same frequency in ONOM roots as in the total lexicon:

Table 5.1. *Results of Sort C*

	Impressionistic frequencies of initial phonemes in total lexicon (including ONOM roots and Sp. loans)		Real frequencies of initial phonemes in ONOM roots (!! = higher than expected, ! = lower than expected)	
Phoneme	Factor	Rank	Rank	Number
p	27	1	2	19
k	20	2	2	19
t	20	2	5!	11
tx/ch	15	3	1!!	26
k'	15	3	3	16
m	15	3	5!	11
t'	15	3	7!	7
tx'/ch'	13	4	1!!	29
j	13	4	2!!	18
w	13	4	3	16
th	13	4	5	12
l	11	5	6	9
x	10	6	5	10.5 ~
b	10	6	6	9 ~
a	10	6	10!	3
o	7	7	9!	4
y	7	7	12!	0
u	5	8	6!!	9
kw'	5	8	7	7
i	5	8	9	4
e	5	8	11!	1
n	4	9	6!!	9
kw	4	9	8	5
ts	4	9	12!	0
s	2	10	7!!	7.5 ~
rr	1	11	8!!	5
ts'	1	11	11	1

frequent phonemes: k', w, (k)
somewhat frequent phonemes: th, l, x, (b)
non-frequent phonemes: kw', i, kw, ts'

5.7.2. Discussion

Higher than expected frequency initial phonemes:

tx and *ch*, *tx'* and *ch'* and *j* are frequent root-initial phonemes which are even more frequent initials in ONOM roots. These sounds must be especially useful in Huastec sound symbolism.

u and *n* are non-frequent root-initial phonemes which have a much higher than expected frequency in ONOM roots. To these should probably be added *k*, because although it is relatively frequent root-initially in the general lexicon, a large proportion of these stem-initial *k*s occur in Spanish loans. Huastec /k/ comes from Proto-Mayan *q, which was not frequent in root-initial position.

s and *rr* are non-frequent root-initial phonemes that occur only in ONOM roots and Spanish loans.

Initial phonemes which are less frequent than expected:

t, *t'*, *p*, and *m* are frequent root-initial phonemes which occur much less commonly in ONOM roots than in the general lexicon. *t* and *t'* occur only about half as often as expected, and *p* and *m* only about two-thirds as often as expected. They must be of limited value to Huastec in representing sounds in nature.

o, *a*, and *e* are non-frequent "root-initial" phonemes whose occurrence in ONOM roots is even lower than expected. All are vowels (preceded by a glottal stop which is never missing, and never written in the practical orthography; in fact there are no vowel-initial roots in Huastec, but it is improbable that the phonemic /ʔ/ these roots begin with carries a semantic feature). Note that # #*u*, on the other hand, occurs unexpectedly frequently.

y and *ts* do not occur at all root-initially in ONOM roots. *ts* is rare anyway, but *y* is moderately common in the general lexicon. They must be especially unsuitable for sound symbolism in Huastec.

About as frequent as expected:

b calls for some remarks. Although nine ONOM roots begin with *b*, all of them have variants with *p*, *m*, or *w*. Only two ONOM roots are known that end in *b*, and only in Potosino. *b* is clearly disfavored in onomatopoeia in Huastec.

5.8. Conclusions and prospects

The main conclusions that can be drawn from my work so far on this topic are the following:

In ONOM roots:
1. *rr*, *r*, and *s* occur only here.
2. **c* and **c'* were very common, and in Potosino resisted shifting to [¢, ¢'] in them, though they shifted virtually without exception in the general lexicon.
3. Initially *h*, *k*, *u*, and *n* occur more frequently than in the general lexicon.
4. initial *o*, *a*, *e* are disfavored.
5. *b* is disfavored.

6. Initially *y* and *ts* are disallowed (or at least non-occurring).
7. Initially *t*, *t'*, *p*, and *m* occur much less commonly than in the general lexicon.
8. In final position, unless in combination with the frequent initials *tx/ch*, *tx'/ch'*, *j*, the following consonants are extremely rare (no more than five cases each): *w*, *t*, *k* (except in *Cok*), *k'* (except in *Cok'*), *p* (except in *Cop*).
9. *p* and *t* have a very depressed frequency when compared to the general lexicon (this follows from 7 and 8).

It should be stressed that Huastec *s*, *rr*, and *r* – which occur only in ONOM roots – have no known Mayan origin, but it is inconceivable that they are of Spanish origin. Because of "alternations" they show, it is tempting, but perhaps misguided, to think of /s/ as having developed out of /š/ and /ř/ out of /l/. If their origin needs to be located in some other language – and it is not clear that this *is* necessary – then some of Huastec's current and former neighbors should be examined with these facts in mind. While we are at it, we should seek origins for *kw* and *kw'*, which are also not of Mayan origin, but are not limited to ONOM roots. Candidates will naturally include Náhuatl (which has /s/ and /k^w/, but no native /ř/ or /r/), Totonacan (which has /s/, but none of the others), and Oto-Pamean (which has *p from earlier **k^w, *s, and *r or *d).

Further work:
1. Figure out specific sound–meaning correlations.
2. Try to distinguish between active and fossilized sound–meaning correlations.
3. Study onomatopoeia in Náhuatl, Otomí, Pame, and Totonac(an) to see to what extent sound–meaning correlations are shared across languages in this area, hence possibly diffused.

As a final note, I would like to stress that I think it is impossible for general or universal claims about the effects of sound symbolism on the lexicon of any language to be properly evaluated without a clear understanding of the language-specific facts of the lexicons of particular languages in the contexts of their *genetic origins* and *foreign contacts*. To the extent that sound symbolism manifests itself in the lexicon of a particular language, some traits will be inherited from near and remote ancestors, some will be language-specific and relatively recent, and some will be borrowed (or the result of borrowing) – and this does not exhaust the particularistic possibilities.

I would like to add to this caution the opinion that the details of sound symbolism in particular languages will always be *largely* language-specific (or language-family-specific) and traceable to universal or general tendencies only to a *lesser* degree. A language that clearly violated the above generalization would be of considerable interest for the puzzle it would pose.

NOTES

1 /c/ varies between [ȼ] (an apicodental affricate, also written as [t͡s] in IPA) and [č]; /ṭ/ varies between [ṭ], [ȼ̣] and [č̣]. Other symbols are explained in the text of this paper. See this volume, Aoki note 3, for IPA equivalences to these symbols.
2 Glosses given to ONOM roots are neither definitive nor exhaustive, though mostly correct as far as they go.

6
Evidence for pervasive synesthetic sound symbolism in ethnozoological nomenclature

BRENT BERLIN

Nomina debent naturis rerum congruere.   St. Thomas Aquinas

"In establishing a harmony between a thing and its name, we conform to a psychic habit as old as humanity."   J. Vendryès (1925): 183

6.1 Introduction

Sapir's important study of sound symbolism (Sapir 1929) marks the beginning of an interest in the natural association of sound and meaning for twentieth-century linguistics.[1] Building on Sapir's work, a large literature has developed on the subject of what the great linguist called "the expressively symbolic character of sounds quite aside from what the words in which they occur mean in a referential sense" (1929: 225).[2]

Most of the experiments that have been carried out on sound symbolism in the last half century have been designed so as to require subjects to match pairs of words from one language with denotatively or connotatively equivalent words in an unknown language. The pairs of words utilized in these studies have almost invariably been *antonyms*. In spite of a number of methodological criticisms (see especially Taylor 1963; Taylor and Taylor 1965, 1967), the great majority of these experiments demonstrate unambiguously that certain sensations (such as relative size, movement, shape, texture, color) are regularly associated with the acoustic quality of specific phonetic segments.

The sound-symbolism experiment outlined in the present chapter, drawing on lexical data from Huambisa (one of the major speech communities of the Jivaroan language family in north central Peru) is in the tradition of word-matching studies, but differs from earlier experiments in that it deals not with antonymic pairs but with a large portion of zoological vocabulary.

Table 6.1 *Pairs of bird and fish names used in word-matching experiment (see text for explanation)*

1.	chunchuíkit	máuts		26.	kungkuí	chantsém
2.	katísh	waikiách		27.	kanímu	makakít
3.	weáhai	tsakanána		28.	hinumánch	sécha
4.	taúsh	wáncha		29.	kúpi	yuwímas
5.	yákakua	kashíkunim		30.	wahák	hápatar
6.	súnga	maparátu		31.	sánti	pútu
7.	iyáchi	ápup		32.	shári	étsa
8.	shuwi	úushap		33.	kunángket	pinínch
9.	kantut	shingkián		34.	táwai	kúmar
10.	tsutsum	wichíkuat		35.	kumpáu	shíru
11.	pítsa	champerám		36.	kunángkit	ungkuchak
12.	wáikia	kanúskin		37.	shanáshna	nukúmp
13.	máchikan	isíp		38.	titím	kuíntam
14.	huitám	mamayák		39.	tingkísh	káashap
15.	píshi	páni		40.	yasáng	kuntsít
16.	chuíntam	suiyám		41.	paumít	kiátsa
17.	tampirúsh	sukuyá		42.	chichikía	katán
18.	tsárur	wáuk		43.	tukímp	kánir
19.	chíimpa	waunchíp		44.	terés	takáikit
20.	chúwi	tséep		45.	áau	tsapáum
21.	wapurús	yúsa		46.	máshu	tsapakúsh
22.	chawít	kángka		47.	ispík	sháip
23.	pirísh	kúum		48.	tuukía	yantsahíp
24.	yawarách	tuíkcha		49.	púwa	aúnts
25.	chanúngkerap	ímia		50.	cháke	yáuch

6.2 The experiment

The experiment had the form of a basic word-matching test where pairs of terms in an unknown language (in this case, Huambisa) were presented to subjects who were required to match them with words for familiar concepts in English. Names used in the experiment were drawn from the complete inventory of Huambisa terms for *birds* (chíngki) and *fish* (namák). These inventories represent 253 and 101 names for birds and fish, respectively.[3]

From these inventories, a representative sample of 50 pairs of words was produced, each pair comprising the name of a fish and the name of a bird, arranged in random order by flipping a coin. All terms used in the experiment were unitary in their linguistic structure, i.e. the terms selected were linguistically analogous to *robin, jay, crappie*, and *bass*. Linguistically complex words structurally analogous to compound terms such as *mocking bird, king fisher, sting ray*, and *gold fish* were excluded from the sample. There are 175 linguistically simple names for birds in Huambisa and 85 such names for fish. The pairs of terms used in the experiment are seen in Table 6.1.

The 50 pairs of names were typed as a list and organized into a small pamphlet of three pages. A practical orthography was used to represent all names. The instructions for the experiment appeared at the top of the first page and read as follows:

"The following list of words are terms for birds and fish from an Indian language of the Peruvian rainforest. In each pair, one word is the name of a fish and one word is the name of a bird. Please check the word in each pair that you believe sounds like the name of a bird."

The experiment was carried out in an introductory anthropology class of approximately 600 students. After the test booklets had been distributed, the experimenter read the instructions and proceeded to pronounce each pair of terms twice. The whole experiment required approximately ten minutes to administer.

6.2.1 Results

One hundred sets of the 600 completed booklets have been analyzed thus far. Results indicate that subjects have a 58% accuracy rate in correctly distinguishing (or identifying) bird names from fish names. This level of accuracy is not high, but is much better than chance and is extremely significant statistically ($p = 0.005$) given the large number of individual comparisons involved, in this case exactly 5000.

6.2.2 Discussion

What might account for the above findings? An obvious first clue is suggested by a linguistic analysis of those pairs of names where much better than chance results were achieved. There are 29 such pairs, with ranges of accuracy from a high of 98% to those just a bit better than chance. All of these 29 pairs, rank-ordered by their accuracy scores, are seen in Table 6.2.

The first and most notable difference in those pairs showing high levels of accuracy is the greater proportion of high front vowels in bird names than in fish names.[4] Almost 3/4 (or 72%) of the bird names recognized with greater than chance accuracy include the high front vowel [i] in one or more syllables. The contrasting fish names in these pairs differ markedly. Less than half of them (44%) show syllables with vowel [i].

There is, furthermore, a remarkable distinction in the *syllabic distribution* of vowel [i] in bird and fish names in these pairs. Ten of the 25 bird names recognized with 57% or greater accuracy exhibit the vowel [i] as their first syllabic, or 40% of the total. In contrast, only two forms, or 8%, of the names for fish are formed with

Table 6.2 *Pairs of Huambisa bird and fish names, accuracy scores ranging from 98% to 51%, in sound-symbolism experiment (correct answer [bird name] in italics, see text for explanation)*

1.	*chunchuíkit*	máuts (98%)	16.	*táwai*	kúmar (72%)
2.	*chichikía*	katan (95%)	17.	*chuíntam*	suiyám (70%)
3.	terés	*takáikit* (94%)	18.	*tingkísh*	káashap (73%)
4.	yawarách	*tuíkcha* (92%)	19.	kunángket	*pinínch* (67%)
5.	*waíkia*	kanúskin (89%)	20.	*tuukia*	yantsahíp (64%)
6.	kanímu	*makakít* (87%)	21.	*kántut*	shingkián (65%)
7.	*chawít*	kángka (86%)	22.	kumpáu	*shíru* (65%)
8.	katísh	*wáikiach* (84%)	23.	*píshi*	páni (65%)
9.	*yákakua*	kasháikunim (83%)	24.	*kúpi*	yuwímas (59%)
10.	tsúsum	*wichíkuat* (82%)	25.	kunángkit	ungkuchák (57%)
11.	*tukímp*	kánir (79%)	26.	*weáhai*	tsakanána (53%)
12.	*iyáchi*	ápup (78%)	27.	paumít	*kiátsa* (53%)
13.	tsárur	*wáuk* (77%)	28.	*pirísh*	kúum (51%)
14.	*áau*	tsapáum (74%)	29.	*chúwi*	tséep (51%)
15.	*wahák*	hápatar (78%)			

syllabics that show [i] in the first syllable. On the contrary, names for fish in this set of pairs favor another first-syllable vowel entirely, the low central vowel [a]. A full 60% of the forms (11 names) are formed in this manner.

Could it be that bird names are marked for [i] and that fish names are marked for [a], and, if true, what is so bird-like about [i] and so fishy about [a]? In order to answer the first question, the full inventories of 175 bird and 85 fish names were examined to determine if the pattern seen in the test sample continued to hold for the complete vocabulary.

Figure 6.1 displays the relative distribution of initial syllabic vowels for the complete inventory of Huambisa bird and fish names. The generalization suggested by the terms in the experimental inventory appears to hold: in comparison with fish, bird names favor [i] as a first syllable (33% of the full inventory) while names for fish appear to actively avoid this vowel as an initial syllabic (fewer than 8% of fish names are formed with first syllable [i]). By contrast, 54% of fish names exhibit the central vowel [a] as their first syllabic.

A number of other important differences can be noted about the names for animals in these two zoological domains. Considering the full ethnozoological vocabularies for both birds and fish, one observes that the obstruents [p], [t], [ts], [tš], and [k] occur as word-initial segments with about equal frequency. Slightly more than half of all bird names (90, or 52%) take one of these obstruents as an initial segment and fish names show only a slightly higher proportion (48 or 56%). However, the relative distribution of obstruents of *high acoustic frequency* (acute [p]

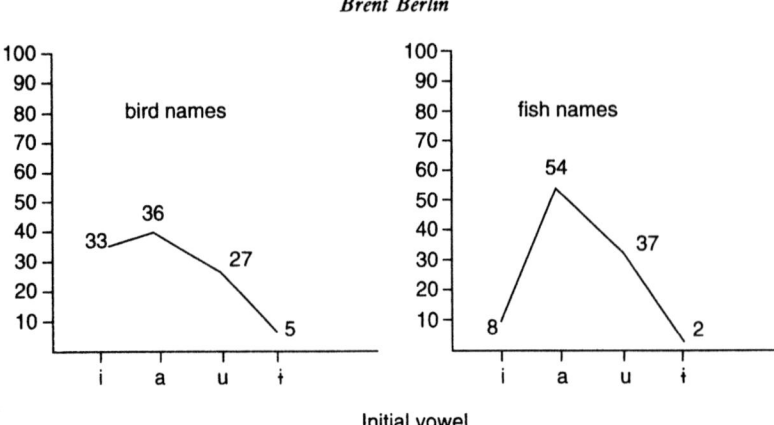

Figure 6.1. Relative distribution of initial vowels in the complete inventory of linguistically simple names for birds and fish in Huambisa.

Table 6.3 *Distribution of initial obstruents in Huambisa bird and fish names by relative acoustic frequency*

	Relatively high	Relatively low
Bird names	(p = 12 before i) t = 16 ts = 7 ch = 20	(p = 11 before a, u) k = 20
Fish names	t = 3 ts = 6 ch = 4	p = 6 k = 29

$p \leq 0.0001$, Fisher's Exact Test

NB: [i] occurs only once in fish names as the initial vowel segment of names that begin with one of the non-nasal obstruents

(before [i]), [t], [ts], and [tš]), and the obstruents of *low acoustic frequency* (grave [k] before [a], [u], and [ɨ] is markedly distinct for fish and bird names, as can be seen in Table 6.3.

It appears as if the bias toward the acoustically high-frequency [i] in bird names is reinforced by the selection of comparable high-frequency obstruents, while just the reverse is true for fish names. In the latter case, lower-frequency [a] combines with the low-frequency [k] as the favored sequence of segments.

Nasals also show distinctive distributional patterns in terms for fish and birds. More than 40% of the 85 fish names show final nasal stops in word-final position, either as a final segment or as the initial segment of the final syllable. In contrast, only 17% of the total inventory of bird names show such a pattern for final nasals.

Furthermore, in comparison with birds, 18% of the fish names prefer final consonants to be continuants ([s], [ts], and [r]) while a meager 8% of the bird names show this pattern. On the other hand, bird names commonly show word-final obstruents (28%). The proportional figure for fish names is 15%.

Finally, while a quarter of the fish names end with open syllables, nearly half of all bird names are so formed (49%). These contrasting distributional phonetic features make it possible to imagine prototypical bird and fish names in Huambisa, and the expressions in the first two pairs of terms receiving the highest accuracy rates on the word-matching experiment come close: *chunchuíkit–máuts* and *chichikía–katan*.

6.3 Universal sound symbolism or simple onomatopoeia?

The striking phonetic differences in the composition of Huambisa bird and fish names suggest a number of possible interpretations. As already mentioned, experimental evidence indicates that certain sensations (movement, size, texture) are associated with the acoustic qualities of specific sound segments of natural languages. Jespersen notes that the concept of "quickness" is widely associated with front vowels, especially [i], e.g., Danish *kvik*, *livlig*, Swedish *pigg*, French *vite*, *vif*, *rapide*, Italian *vispo*, *listo*, Japanese *kirikiri* (Jespersen 1933: 299). Swadesh has pointed out the meaning association of "[a] for something that moves on and on" (Swadesh 1971: 114). Swadesh also contrasts the sound symbolic association of voiceless obstruents with *sharp* and *rapid movements* which contrast with the *heavy* and *slow* continuity of nasals. The data reported in the present chapter strongly indicate that Huambisa zoological nomenclature linguistically marks the contrast of angular avian agility with smooth and continuous piscine flow. A universalist perspective would account for these associations in terms of abstract sound symbolism in Sapir's sense, or as Ohala would put it, "sound/meaning correlations where the meaning does not seem to be one that is capable of imitation by speech sounds" (Ohala 1983b: 5).

An alternative interpretation would suggest that the data are better understood as a result of simple onomatopoeia, i.e. where the words for specific organisms (in this case) are phonetic representations of the sound that these organisms emit. Jespersen referred to such terms as "echoic words" in that "the echoic word designates the being that produces the sound" (Jespersen 1921: 399).

Table 6.4 *Examples of onomatopoeic Huambisa bird names formed with vowels [a] or [u]*

Scientific name	Huambisa name	Vocalization*
Daptrius ater	*shanáshna*	[shá.shá.shá.]
Ortalis guttata	*wakáts*	[wakatará wakatará]
Aburria pipile	*kúyu*	[kúyu.kúyu.kúyu]
Opisthomcomus hoazin	*sãsã*	[sã.sã.sã.sã.sã]
Aramides cajanea	*kunchár*	[kunchár.kunchár]
Ara manilata	*kãyãk*	[kiák.kiák.kiák.kiák]
Amazona ochrocephala	*awarmás*	[áura.áura.áura]
Crotophaga ani	*kuákua*	[sak. au. kúR]
Nyctibius aethereus	*autám*	[aúu. aúu. aúu]
N. griseus	*aúhu*	[áuhu.áuhu.áuhu]
Trogon viridis	*táwai*	[táta.tá.tá.tá.tá.tá]
Ceryle torquata	*tarásh*	[tarásh tarásh tarásh]
Baryphthengus ruficapillus	*yukúru*	[hu.rú. hu.rú]
Bucco capensis	*maukáatarar*	[mo.ka.ta.rár.]
Capito aurovirens	*púr*	[púrrr púrrr púrrr]
Pteroglossus flavirostris	*kakarpát*	[kár.kat.kár.kat.kár.kat]

* Linguistic representation of onomatopoeic vocalizations employs a practical orthography and only roughly approximates the actual phonetic qualities of the calls

It is true that onomatopoeia plays a large role in Huambisa ornithological vocabulary. Berlin and O'Neill (1981) made taped recordings of 206 Huambisa bird names and their human vocalizations and found that 34% of these names were onomatopoeic in origin. The disproportionate presence of [i] in Huambisa bird names could be interpreted primarily as onomatopoeia, and hence the primary factor at work in accounting for the better-than-chance results of the word-matching experiment. Following this line of reasoning, my colleague, Paul Kay, on first hearing pairs of bird and fish names exclaimed, "Oh, yeah, the bird names are the ones that go 'tweet-tweet.'" Quite independently, Dwight Bolinger, after having read an earlier draft of this paper, made a similar observation: "Listen for onomatopoeia and what you will hear, when birds are concerned, will be high sounds" (personal communication).

These intuitions are correct but capture only part of the truth. While a substantial number of bird names of onomatopoeic origin are formed with [i], an equally large number of onomatopoeic names are formed exclusively with vowels [a] and [u], as seen in table 6.4.

Table 6.4 indicates that onomatopoeia in Huambisa bird names takes full advantage of low central and back vowels. Another factor in addition to simple

Table 6.5 *Association of bird length (size) and vowel quality: total inventory of Huambisa bird names (N = 175)*

	Vowel quality				
	[i]	[a, e, u]		[i]	[e, a, u]
≤ 10"	60	32	≤ 7"	37	16
≥ 11"	35	48	≥ 15"	14	30
	p = ≤ 00.001, gamma = 0.44			p = ≤ 0.0001, gamma = 0.66	

onomatopoeia appears to be at work in the ornithological lexicon and, as we will see later, in the fish lexicon as well. This factor is abstract *size–sound symbolism*.

Of all of the sense associations of sound and meaning, size–sound symbolism is perhaps the best established, building on Sapir's 1929 experiment and even earlier work (see Tolman 1887, 1904). Ohala summarizes the acoustic parameters of size-sound symbolism as follows:

Words denoting or connoting SMALL or SMALLNESS ... tend to exhibit a disproportionate incidence of vowels and/or consonants characterized by high acoustic frequency. Words denoting or connoting LARGE use segments with low acoustic frequency. In consonants, voiceless obstruents have higher frequency than voiced because of the higher velocity of the airflow, ejectives higher than plain stops ... and dental, alveolar, palatal and front velars higher than labials and back velars. In the case of vowels, high front vowels have higher F_2 and low back vowels the lowest F_2. (Ohala 1984: 9)

If vowel quality plays a systematic part in abstract size–sound symbolism, it should be possible to test such an association quantitatively should a standard metric be available. Fortunately, for birds, just such a metric (average length from beak to tail) has been recorded for all of the major species of birds in South America (de Schauensee 1970). The first panel in Table 6.5 indicates the association of length (size) and vowel quality for the total inventory of 175 Huambisa bird names. The second panel in table 6.5 shows the association of length and vowel

Brent Berlin

Table 6.6 *Huambisa bird names exhibiting vowel [i] for species ≤ 10" in length and their vocalizations*

Vocalizations of bird calls are rough phonetic transcriptions of taped recordings made by the author from formal interviews with three Huambisa males in 1979 and 1980 on the Santiago River, Amazonas, Peru. Entries marked with an * are judged to be non-onomatopoeic, given the author's strict definition of onomatopoeia.

Scientific name	Size	Huambisa name	Vocalization
Myromotherula obscura	3.2"	*chunchuíkit	[chí.chí.chí] voiceless, starts slowly, builds to rapid peak
Pipra coronata	3.2"	*wisham	[whispered whistle]
Pipra pipra	4.0"	*kaawia	[no call]
Sporphila sp.	4.2"	*shaíp	[tsúng.tsúng.tsúng]
Cyanerpes spp.	4.2"	*himpíkit	[tsíp.tsíp.tsíp.tsíp]
Hylophalax naevia	4.2"	pishipísh	[písh.pish.písh.pish]
Mymotherula axilaris	4.2"	kiátsa	[kiátsa.kiátsa.kiátsa]
Hypocnemis hypoxantha	4.0"	*wakíach	[whistled imitation only]
Microcerculus marianatus	4.5"	tingkísh	[tí.ti.ti.tí.ti.tí.ti.tí.ti]
Forpus xanthoperygius	6.0"	nuínuí	[núi.nui.nui. núi.nui.nui]
Chlorophanes spiza	6.0"	*ukúnchkit	[tsíng.tsíng.tsíng.tsíng]
Atticora spp.	6.0"	*shúrpip	[mbís.mbís.mbís.mbís]
Glyphorhynchus spirurus	6.5"	*tushimp	[tsí.tsi.tsi., voiceless]
Thamophilus schistavesus	6.5"	chickikía	[chichikía.chichikía]
Chaetura spp.	6.0"	*chiním	[shí.shi.shí.shi.shí.shi]
Icterus croconotus	6.0"	huitám	[huí.huí.huí.huí.huí]
Veniliornis passerinus	6.0"	*nái	[kí.kí.kí.kí.kí.kí]
Touit huetii	6.0"	shai	[shái.shái.shái]
Eubucco bourcierii	6.5"	tíwa	[tí.wa.tí.wa.tí.wa]
Piranga rubra	6.5"	píchurkik	[píchurkik.píchurkik]
Hoploxyterus cayanus	6.5"	*tuentuí	[no call]
Formacarius colma	6.0"	*chiwachíng	[pá.pi.re.re.re]
Laterallus malanophaius	6.0"	*shíru	[no call]
Attila spadicius	6.0"	ukurpíp	[kuru.ku.pí.pí.pí.pí]
Grallaria dignissiona	6.0"	wíahai	[no data]
Tringa solitarius	6.0"	*kiángkia	[no call]
Formacarius analis	6.1"	tukímp	[tekímp.tekímp.tekímp]
Cymbilaimus lineatus	6.2"	*tseretsíng	[whistled imitation]
Automolus spp.	6.5"	*kuíntam	[chip.chip.twa.rú]
Actitus macularia	6.5"	piampía	[suí.suí suí.suí.suí.suí]
Pitylus grossus	6.5"	*wichikuat	[pis.pis.pis. áá]
Capito niger	6.5"	*takáikit	[tuntú tuntú.tuntú]
Brotogeris cyanoptera	8.0"	chimp	[chirím.chirím.chirím.]
Icterus chrysocephasus	8.0"	pikít	[no information]
Laniocera hypopyrrha	8.5"	chíntam	[chuí.chuí.chuí]
Xiphorhychus guttatus	8.5"	*yukaikua	[tsuá.tsuátsuá]
Saltator maximus	8.5"	tukía	[tú.tu.tú.tu.tú.tu]
Pionopsitta barrabandi	10.0"	muí	[muí.muí.muí muí muí.]
Pyrrhura picta	10.0"	kírus	[kíru.kíru.kíru.kíru]
Geotrygon sapphirina	10.0"	*pupuí	[whistled imitation]
Falco rifigularis	10.0"	tsiártik	[tsi.tsi.tsi.tsi]
Lipaugus cinerascens	10.5"	pápainch	[kui.kui.pá pánch.aaa][1]

quality when one looks at the extreme ends of the continuum. In both tests, the association of [i] with relative size of bird species is strongly confirmed.

Onomatopoeia and size-sound symbolism could work hand in hand, of course. As Kay might now respond, "O.K., so it's the *small* birds that go 'tweet-tweet.'" In this regard, notice that the significant disproportion of terms with [i] versus all other vowels (65%) is in the *top half of Table 6.5*, namely those birds that are 10″ in length or less. However, in examining bird names formed with [i] one finds that only about half of them are onomatopoeically derived, as seen from the list of terms given in Table 6.6.

Moving one step further, by removing all bird names for species 10″ or less which can be shown to be onomatopoeic in origin one might get a better notion of the relative weight of onomatopoeia versus strict size–sound symbolism. Working with the inventories in both cells A and B of Table 6.5, the reduced inventory of non-onomatopoeic bird names reveals 23 terms formed with [i] and 10 terms formed with other vowels. The relative proportion of birds 10″ or less in length with names formed with [i] is now even higher, namely 71%. These data suggest clearly that onomatopoeia alone cannot account for the association of size and vowel quality.

6.4. Comparison of other ethnoornithological vocabularies

Are the patterns apparent in Jívaro ornithological nomenclature unique? In an effort to answer this question, I have been gathering new data on a number of other languages for which relatively complete ethnoornithological vocabularies are available. Thus far, data from three unrelated languages have been compiled. Two

---

[1] (Table 6.6) A distinction is made here between literal *imitation*, where the sounds of some animals are rendered by whistling, humming, grunting, hissing, smacking or clicking (cf. the whistled rendition of the call of the Bobwhite quail, *Colinus virginianus*) and *onomatopoeia*. Onomatopoeia is present when the call of some animal, for example, is phonologically vocalized by humans employing the resources of the regular speech sounds of their respective languages in combination with such paralinguistic processes as stress, intonation, tempo, and vocalic quality.

An *onomatopoeic phonological vocalization* of a particular animal's call and the *name* of that animal may be related in at least one of two ways: (1) the vocalization may bear no resemblance to the name, as in the stereotypic calls of certain domesticated animals, e.g. the English vocalizations for the calls of the cat (*meow-meow*), the dog (*woof-woof*), and the pig (*oink-oink*); (2) the vocalization may be similar to the name in that some or all of the speech sounds of the name comprise a fragment of the vocalization (cf. the British English name *cock* [synonym *rooster*] and the call *cockadoodledoo*; or the name *Bobwhite*, which is a complete phonological replication of the call of *Colinus virginianus*. In the present treatment, a name is not considered to be onomatopoeic unless it can be demonstrated that native speakers, when phonologically vocalizing the name of some animal, produce vocalizations that bear a phonetic resemblance to the name itself. This definition is not shared by most linguists, who are far less explicit about the criteria to be used in determining whether a particular term shows onomatopoeia.

Table 6.7. *Distribution of Wayampí (Tupian) and Apalái (Cariban) bird names by length of species and vowel quality (data from Jensen [1988])*

	Wayampí			Apalái	
	\[i\], \[e\]	Vowel quality \[a\], \[o\], \[u\], \[I\]		\[i\], \[e\]	\[a\], \[o\], \[u\], \[I\]
≤ 10"	48	18	≤ 10"	45	15
≥ 11"	35	35	≥ 11"	40	32

$p \leq 0.005$ (both by Fisher's Exact Test) $p \leq 0.03$

languages are from South America, the Wayampí (Tupian) and the Apalái (Cariban). These materials are drawn from Arthur Jensen's doctoral dissertation (Jensen 1988). The third language is Tzeltal (Mayan) and I incorporate the data given in Eugene Hunn's *Tzeltal Folk Zoology: The Classification of Discontinuities in Nature* (Hunn 1977). The association of vowel quality with size in these three languages is given in Tables 6.7 and 6.8. In each of these languages, the association of vowel quality with relative size is confirmed, leading to the tentative conclusion that the Huambisa materials are not unique but part of a wider pattern of sound-symbolic marking in ethnoornithological lexicon in general.

6.5. Fish, again

The most convincing argument for size–sound symbolism in ethnozoological vocabulary must ultimately be made by reference to animals whose sound-emitting abilities are non-existent, or at least not auditorily noticeable by human beings. Here we return once again to consider Huambisa fish. Unlike birds, no single standard metric exists for the measurement of the relative "size" of fish species. (Which is "larger"? The slender freshwater electric eel or the flat long-tailed stingray?) Lacking a standard measurement, I have relied on simple length measurements from our ethnoichthyological research in investigating possible size–sound meaning associations in this domain. Table 6.9 presents the distribution of Huambisa fish names by length of species and vowel quality for those species for which reliable length measurements could be obtained.

Table 6.8 *Distribution of Tzeltal bird names by length of species and vowel quality (data from Hunn 1977)*

Stems with [i] [e]		Stems with [a] [o] and [u]	
		tz'unum	3.5" "hummingbirds"
		xlux	5" *Catharus aurantiirostris*
chayin	5" *Vireo flavoviridis*	xpurowok	7" *Scardafella* sp.
ulich	5" "swallows"	solsol	7" *Melozone biarcuatum*
xmayil	5" *Seiurus* spp.	x'ub	8" *Colinus virginianus*
p'itp'it	5" *Empidonax* spp.	k'orochoch	8" *Melanerpes formicivorus*
xch'iht	5" *Vermivora* spp.	ot'ot'	9" *Amblycercus holosericeus*
chonchiw	6" *Zonotrichia capensis*		
toytoy	6" *Glaucidium* spp.		
wirin	7" "flycatchers" (in part)		
sik'	7" "swifts"		
k'usin	7" *Atalaptetes albinucha*		
tzokoy	7" *Campylorhynchus zonatus*		
†kulkulina	8" *Agelaius phoeniceus*		
chochowit	8" *Saltator coerulescens*		
xch'e	8" *Dumetella carolinensis*		
*k'owesh	8" *Pipilo erythrophthalmus*		
†chiboriáano	8" *Sturnella magna*		
tz'ihtil	8" *Dendrocopos villosus*		
purkuwich	9" *Caprimulgus vociferus*		
ti'	9" *Centurus aurifrons*		
≤ 9"			
chulin	10" *Melanotis hypoleucus*	toht	9.5" *Turdus* sp.
		tukut	10" *Colaptes auratus*
		kurunkuts	10.5" *Otus* spp.

Table 6.8 (cont.)

	Stems with [i] [e]		Stems with [a] [o] and [u]	
	pu'kuy	11" *Nyctidromus albicolis*	stzumut	11" "doves"
			puyuch'	11" *Pionus* sp.
	liklik	10.5" *Falco sparverius*	k'uk'	11" *Trogon* spp.
	wanchil	10.5" *Dives dives*	xkuj	14" *Cccaba virgata*
≥ 10"	†chiktawilon	11" *Crypturellus cinnamomeus*	xoch'	14.5" *Tyto alba*
			kutzukutz	16" *Momotus momota*
	*tuntzerek'	12" *Dryocopus lineatus*	x'uman	18.5" *Geococcyx velox*
	*peya'	17" *Psilorhinus morio*	pan	16–18" "toucans"
	*ch'ekek	24" *Penelopina nigra*	jojkot	22.5" *Ortalis vetula*
	*xulem	24" *Cathartes aura*	tza'los	24" *Coragyps atratus*
	*usel	30" *Sarcoramphus papa*	joj	25" *Corvus corax*
			mo'	32" *Ara* spp.
			tuluk'	33"–47" *Meleagris gallopavo*

$p \leq 0.013$ by Fisher's Exact Test

* note possible scaled association of [e] vs. [i]
† likely loans from Spanish

Table 6.9 Distribution of Huambisa fish names by length* of species (in inches) and vowel quality

Stems with [i]		Stems with [a], [u], or [e]	
(fish species 10" or less in length)			
íspik	2" *Brachychalcinus nummus*	kuntsét	3" *Rivulus* spp.
hinumánch	3" *Thoracocharix stellatus*	kantásh	4" *Aequidens syspislus*
kánir	3" *Hemonomus* sp.	kusúm	4" *Characidium* spp.
kanúskin	3" *Paragoniates alburnus*	tsapakús	4" *Leporinus striatus*
yautsaháip	4" *Moenkhausia cotinho*	tsárur	4" *Creagrutus* spp.
máchikan	4" *Tetragomopterus argenteus*	maparátu	4" *Centromochlus heckelii*
shári	4" *Panaque* spp.	hápatar	5" *Chaetostoma* sp. nov.
yuwínas	5" *Copeina guttatus*	cháke	6" *Hypostomus madeirae*
kúnchi	5" *Pimalotus* spp.	mamayák	6" *Astyanax* spp.
shúwi	6" *Lasiancistrus* spp.	púwa	8" *Microglanic parahybae*
nukúmpi	7" *Heptapterus* sp.	wapurús	8" *Cichlasoma bimaculatus*
tampirúsh	7" *Cynaptomus* spp.	tsapáum	8" *Triportheus angulatus*
paumít	7" *Myleus* spp.	katán	10" *Auchenipterus nuchalis*
kátish	8" *Leporinus* spp.	teres	10" *Trichomycterus* sp.
chúwi	8" *Cremicichla* spp.		
kanímu	8" *Erythrinus erythrinus*		
kasháitum	8" *Gladium* sp.		
yutui	8" *Pimelodella* spp.		
(fish 12" or more in length)			
suiyám	12" *Cynaptomus* spp.	kumpáu	12" *Rhamdia* sp.
páni	12" *Serrsalmus* spp.	kúum	12" *Curimata* spp.
shingkián	12" *Callichthys callichthys*	hácham	12" *Chaetostoma* spp.

Table 6.9 (cont.)

wampíkus	12" *Ancestrorhynchus falcatus*	yawarách	12" *Curimata* spp.
kugkuí	24" *Hoplia malabaricus*	pápe	16" *Duopalatinus allalae*
kuír	24" *Megalonema* spp.	ápup	18" *Pseudotylosurus angusticieps*
titím	24" *Soribum lima*	karachám	20" *Loricaria* spp., *Rineloricaria* spp.
numkúmpia	36" *Symbranchus marmoratu*	champerám	24" *Cynodon gibbus*
		kushám	24" *Pimelodus ornatus*
		wáncha	24" *Gymnotus* spp.
		kángka	30" *Prochilodus* spp.
		máuts	30" *Pseudocetopsis* sp.
		káshap	36" *Potamotrygon* sp.
		tunkáu	36 +" "large river catfish"
		múta	36 +" "large river catfish"

p = ≤ 0.05 by Fisher's Exact Test

* Length represents maximum length in inches for mature adults. Estimates are based on data derived from informant elicitation and field collections. Scientific determinations were provided by Camm C. Swift, Ichythyology Section, Los Angeles Museum of Natural History, Los Angeles, California. Data from Berlin, Swift, and Stewart (in preparation).

Table 6.9 reveals that the patterns of size–sound symbolism observed for ornithological vocabulary appear to hold, as well, for the names for fish in Huambisa. What better names for the small angel fish and minnow-like gasteropod than *ispík* and *hinumanch*? Likewise, can the assignment of the terms *tunkáu* and *múta* to the two large free-swimming doradid catfish be totally without psychological motivation?

6.6. Conclusions

The phonetic characteristics of the names of birds and fish in Huambisa suggest the workings of universal sound-symbolic processes. First, birds and fish differ on the basis of the differential distribution of phonetic segments of high and low acoustic frequency. Bird names show a disproportionate number of segments that are of acoustically high frequency, which, it is claimed, connote quick and rapid motion (i.e. "birdness"). This contrasts with the lower-frequency segments in fish names which lead to connotations of smooth, slow continuous flow (i.e. "fishness"). Secondly, both bird and fish nomenclature demonstrate a prominent internal pattern of size-sound symbolism where vowel quality and relative size are positively associated at high levels of statistical significance. Smaller birds and fish show disproportionate numbers of high-frequency vowel [i] stems while larger birds and fish show disproportionate numbers of lower frequency vowel [a] and [u] stems. Comparable patterns of size–sound symbolism have been found in the ethnoornithological vocabularies of at least three other languages, Wayampí, Apalái, and Tzeltal, leading to the conclusion that the phenomenon is likely to be widespread and general.

The most plausible explanation of these findings has been elaborated by Ohala (1982, 1983b, 1984) who, building on the work of Morton (1977), has proposed a universal and innate cross-species "frequency code" where "high F_0 signifies (broadly) smallness ... and low F_0 conveys [the meaning] of largeness" (Ohala 1984: 12). (The frequency code also provides a framework for the interpretation of certain universals of intonation, facial expressions [in association with vocalization], as well as the anatomical sexual dimorphism of the vocal apparatus in human and non-human species.)

In a perfect world, names for the creatures of nature should reflect their natural, inherent qualities. These data suggest that to a large extent, the Huambisa, and perhaps other peoples like them who maintain close ties with the natural universe, are unconsciously motivated to develop systems of zoological nomenclature whose sound–meaning associations take full advantage of the frequency code innate to many living species. It is not without some importance to note that the greatest biological nomenclator of all times, Linnaeus, intuitively shared this same view when, in considering the nature of generic names, he claimed that all "should be apt in meaning, easy to say and remember, and pleasant to hear" (Stern 1959: 8).[5]

NOTES

1 See especially John Ohala's unpublished 1983 "Bibliography on sound symbolism" (Ohala 1983a) available from the Phonology Laboratory of the University of California, Berkeley, which contains more than 200 entries.
2 Dwight Bolinger (personal communication) indicates that Alber H. Tolman "grasped the size–sound symbolism earlier than [Sapir]" in a piece titled "The laws of tone color in the English language," *Andover Review* 7: 326–337 (1887).
3 The region inhabited by the Huambisa is quite rich biologically. Zoological collections, carried out as part of the Second Ethnobiological Expedition of the University of California to the Upper Marañón River, are extensive, although of course incomplete. There are probably more than 400 species of birds in the region and approximately 200 species of fish (see Berlin, Boster and O'Neill, in preparation and Berlin, Swift, and Steward, in preparation).
4 An erroneous first impression, from a quick perusal of the test items, is that bird names are generally longer than fish names. Actually, bird and fish names are of comparable length when the total inventories for each domain are examined. If there is a major difference, birds differ from fish in the somewhat greater proportion of monosyllabic terms. Twenty-three single-syllable bird names compare with but three single-syllable fish names. Of bird names, 52% are bisyllabic, closely comparable to 61% of bisyllabic fish terms. The two lexicons are essentially identical in the relative distribution of three- and four-syllable expressions.
5 This paper was originally presented to the Berkeley Linguistics Group in April, 1983, and later to the Society of Ethnobiology in its seventh annual meeting in Seattle. I am especially grateful for the encouragement of John J. Ohala, who was the first to point out to me the ways the data presented here might relate to broader ethological questions. Without the support of my colleagues John P. O'Neill (ornithology) and Camm Swift (ichthyology), I would never have come to grips with the complexities of the world of birds and fish. I am grateful for the comments of Paul Kay, Terrence Kaufman, Dwight Bolinger, Leanne Hinton, Eugene Hunn, Mary LeCron Foster, George Lakoff, Marianne Mithun, Yakov Malkiel, Cecil Brown, and Richard Ford. Luisa Maffi has read a final draft of the paper and has offered important substantive and editorial suggestions that I much appreciate. Jack Potter allowed me to conduct the word-matching experiment in his introductory anthropology class, and I thank him as well as the students who took part in it. Finally, some debt is owed to Mel Brooks, whose classic phonograph record, *The 2000 Year Old Man*, convinced me more than ever that the names *for* animals should sound like the names *of* animals.

REFERENCES

Berlin, B. and J. O'Neill. 1981. The pervasiveness of onomatopoeia in the Jivaroan language family. *Journal of Ethnobiology* 1: 95–108.
Berlin, B., J. Boster, and J. O'Neill. In preparation. Huambisa bird classification.
Berlin, B., C. Swift, and D. Stewart. In preparation. Principles of Huambisa fish classification.
de Schauensee, R. M. 1970. *A Guide to the Birds of South America*. Wynnewood, Penn.: Academy of Natural Sciences of Philadelphia.
Hunn, E. 1977. *Tzeltal Folk Zoology: The Classification of Discontinuities in Nature*. New York: Academic Press.
Jensen, A. A. 1988. *Sistemas Indígenas de Classificação de Aves: Aspectos Comparativos, Ecológicos e Evolutivos*. Belém: Museo Paraense Emílio Goeldi.
Jespersen, O. 1921. *Language: Its Nature, Development, and Origin*. London: Allen and Unwin.
  1933. Symbolic value of the vowel i. In *Linguistica. Selected Papers of O. Jespersen in English, French, and German*. Copenhagen: Levin and Munksgaard, 283–303.
Morton, E. W. 1977. On the occurrence and significance of motivational–structural rules in some bird and mammal sounds. *American Naturalist* 111: 855–869.
Ohala, J. J. 1982. The frequency code and its effect on certain forms of speech and facial expressions. In *International Congress of Linguistics*. Tokyo, International Congress of Linguistics Editorial Committee, 199–208.
  1983a. Bibliography on sound symbolism. Unpublished ms. Phonology Laboratory, University of California, Berkeley.
  1983b. Cross-language use of pitch: an ethological view. *Phonetica* 40: 1–18.
  1984. An ethological perspective on common cross-language utilization of F_0 of voice. Unpublished ms. Berkeley: Phonology Laboratory, Department of Linguistics, University of California.
Sapir, E. 1929. A Study in phonetic symbolism. *Journal of Experimental Psychology* 12: 225–239.
Stern, W. 1959. The background of Linnaeus' contribution to the nomenclature of methods of systematic biology, *Systematic Zoology* 8: 4–22
Swadesh, M. 1971. *The Origin and Diversification of Language*. Chicago: Aldine and Co.
Taylor, K. I. 1963. Phonetic symbolism reexamined. *Psychological Bulletin* 60: 200–209.
Taylor, K. I. and M. M. Taylor. 1965. Another look at phonetic symbolism. *Psychological Bulletin* 64: 413–427.
  1967. Phonetic symbolism in four unrelated languages. *Canadian Journal of Psychology* 16: 344–356.
Tolman, A. H. 1887. The laws of tone color in the English language. *Andover Review* 7: 326–337.
  1904. Symbolic value of English sounds. In *Views about Hamlet*. New York: Houghton Mifflin.
Vendryès, J. 1925. *Language: A Linguistic Introduction to History*. Translated by Paul Radin. New York: Knopf.

7
Noise words in Guaraní*

MARGARET LANGDON

7.1. Introduction

This paper presents a preliminary analysis of a set of sound-symbolic words in Guaraní, the national language of Paraguay. A few of the phonological characteristics of the language are outlined to orient the reader and to place the data in their structural setting. Additional morphological and syntactic information will be provided as necessary in the course of the exposition.

The phonemic inventory is given in Table 7.1. The units are listed in the practical orthography developed in a field-methods class at the University of California, San Diego in the academic year 1984–1985. Segments whose phonetic character is not obvious from the symbols are given a phonetic explanation next to

Table 7.1 *Phonemes of Guaraní*

Consonants					
p	t		k	ku [kʷ]	'[ʔ][1]
mb	nd		ng [ŋg][1]	ngu [ŋgʷ][1]	
(b)	(d)	j [dʒ]	(g)		
m	n	ñ			
(f)	s	x [ʃ]			h
v					
	r [ɾ]				
w	l	(ll [j])			
Vowels					
i	ĩ			u	ũ
e	ẽ		y [ɨ]	ỹ	o	õ
		a	ã		

[1] Does not occur initially.

them in square brackets. Items in parentheses occur only in words of Spanish origin, of which Guaraní has a very large number.

A pervasive process of nasalization exists in the language. If a word contains an underlying nasal vowel, the feature of nasalization spreads both left and right to produce nasalization of the other vowels, or full nasalization of the pre-nasalized stops which then surface as pure nasal stops. For the purposes of this process, /j/ and /ñ/ form a pair, just like /mb/ and /m/. Nasalization can also spread across word boundaries until it runs into certain apparently syntactically determined boundaries, though the exact conditions are not well understood. The process is inhibited when it encounters non-nasal obstruents. The mid-central unrounded vowel /y/, both plain and nasal, is extremely common.

7.2. Features of Guaraní noise words

This paper focuses on a class of words in Guaraní which can be characterized phonologically and semantically as follows. They all have the canonical shape $CV_1rV_1rV_1$, and they all refer to noises. They share with other words of the language the preferred syllable structure CV, and the vowels all agree in nasality, i.e. they are either all plain or all nasal, following the normal pattern. They also obey other phonological constraints: the initial consonant is never one of the consonants which cannot be initial in native Guaraní words, (i.e., ', ng, and ngw), nor can it be one of the sounds borrowed from Spanish. This is evidence that these words are part of the native lexical inventory of the language, a fact supported also by the meanings, which are as difficult to convey exactly in Spanish as they are in English. However, unlike other words in the language, they cannot begin with r, l, m, n, ñ, h, v; in other words, these lexical items can begin only with stops and voiceless fricatives, i.e. obstruents, plus /w/ which may in fact be an obstruent /gw/ underlyingly. The absence of initial nasals (as opposed to pre-nasalized stops) is a consequence of the fact that, in my corpus, no forms appear which contain both a nasal vowel and a consonant with a nasal component. Whether this is an accidental gap remains to be determined. The initial syllable of noise words, therefore, is one of the optimal syllable types, with maximum closure at the onset, and maximal opening at the coda. The noise words are characterized by vowel harmony: that is, a single vowel is repeated in all syllables of the word. This can be any vowel in the language, although no instance of /ẽ/ has been found, probably an accidental gap. Some consonantal gaps (e.g. none of the items begin in /ku/), are probably accidental also.

Noise words are true words of the language; in fact they are verbs. They are therefore more like English *rumble*, *clap*, or *reverberate* than they are like *kaboom*, *kerplunk*, or *ding-dong*. Only those forms known to Marina Dos Santos are presented in this paper.

Table 7.2 Evidence for semantic content of individual segments in Guaraní noise words

	/p/ "sharp, snappy"	/t/ "neutral (?)"	/x/ "friction"	/s/ "pressure"	/w/ "irregular noise"	/mb/ "deep, ponderous"	/k/ "?", /j/ "?"
/i/ "high-pitched, intense"	piriri "fire burning dry grass; crackle of new money"	tiriri "splintering glass, just one crack"	xiriri "water coming out of faucet"		wiriri "high-pitched giggle; branches scraping"		
/e/ "?"	perere "lumpy things in box; chicken flapping wings"						jerere "round and round" (perhaps not a noise word)
/a/ "lower pitched than /i/"		tarara "chattering teeth; shivering; pecking"	xarara "animal walking through dry leaves; congested chest"		warara "echoing thunder"	mbarara "loud, deep; big drum; heavy books falling"	
/o/ "burst"	pororo "popcorn; sparks"		xororo "torrential rain"	sororo "splitting open"			
/y/ "random"		tyryry "dragging; shuffling"	xyryry "grease spatter; sizzle"	syryry "flowing, dragging gently"	wyryry "crumpled paper; ferreting through box"		

/u/ "soulful"	tururu "low whistle"; Indian bamboo flute	sururu "tight-fitting parts; forcing into tight slot"	mbururu "lowing of bull"	
/ĩ/ "?"				kĩrĩrĩ "quietly"
/a̰/ "tinny"	pãrãrã "rocks in tin can"	xãrãrã "tinny, no tone; shooting at tin can"		
/õ/ "rumble"	tõrõrõ "monumental water fall"			kõrõrõ "snoring; rumbling stomach"
/ỹ/ "?"	pỹrỹrỹ "jumping, spinning top"			
/ũ/ "?"	pũrũrũ "biting a ripe grape, cherry tomato; starched petticoat"			

Given that all these words are descriptive of noises, we can assume this semantic trait to be conveyed by the canonical structure described above, which sets off these forms from all others in the language. Within this set, then, we can assume that the remainder of the semantic content of each word is carried uniquely by the distinctive CV element. The existence of minimal sets, i.e. sets differing by only the initial consonant or the vowel, even suggests that it might be possible to give a semantic characterization of each of the occurring segments.

Table 7.2 presents the full corpus available to me at this time, and is organized in such a way as to exhibit vertically all forms showing the same consonant, and horizontally those showing the same vowel. Glosses are given in as concise a form as possible, but an attempt is made to capture the flavor of each. In all cases, it should be remembered that a full gloss would have to include the introductory phrase "to make the sound of . . .".

This analysis must certainly be taken with a grain of salt, and some of the proposals are less likely than others to be correct. Work with more speakers would undoubtedly allow refinement or change in the analysis. Nevertheless, some at least of the generalizations must be more than accidental; the meaning "high-pitched" for /i/ is clearly iconic and so universal as to require no further comment. The contrast between /p/ and /mb/ reflects the phonetic nature of these sounds. The sharp explosive connotations of /p/ is also found in English *pop, plop, ping,* French *paff,* etc., with /b/ being deeper, the voicing of the consonant corresponding to more reverberating environmental sounds, as in *boom, bong,* etc. The prenasalization of /mb/ in Guaraní makes it even more appropriate, adding to the ponderousness of the effect. Another general observation is that nasal vowels convey more muffled, less musical sounds than plain vowels, another instance of acoustic iconicity.

7.3. Noise words with other internal consonants

It should be noted that a few words were found whose shape is reminiscent of the noise words, but instead of a syllable frame with /r/ they have either /l/ or /n/. Thus

walala "noise of stomach growling from hunger"
xinini "noise of rattle of rattlesnake"
sununu "noise of echoing thunder"

These are clearly part of the noise-word set. It would be interesting to find out whether they are archaic residues of an earlier more complex system, particularly in view of other known sound-symbolic systems which also use sets contrasting r, l, and n (Haas 1970, Langdon 1971, Nichols 1971). Two of these three words form a minimal pair with an "r" word. Thus, *walala* "stomach growling from hunger" contrasts with *warara* "echoing thunder." Semantically, however, it is not clear that these two words form a set; in fact, Marina Dos Santos spontaneously compared *walala* to *kõrõrõ* "snoring, rumbling stomach," noting that *walala* describes a more watery sound than *kõrõrõ*, while sharing the "growling stomach" association. On the other hand, *xinini* "rattle of rattlesnake" and *xiriri* "water coming out of a faucet" are a plausible set, but probably only because they share the feature "friction" conveyed by /x/. *Sununu* "noise of echoing thunder" was compared to *warara* "noise of echoing thunder" semantically (for obvious reasons), rather than to *sururu* "forcing into tight slot."

A topic for further research would be to find out whether less acculturated dialects of Guaraní have more of these l and n words. In fact, the extent of the whole system in other dialects of Guaraní would be of considerable interest.

7.4. Noise words vs. dissyllables

In some cases, noise words are paired with two-syllable forms of the shape CV1rV1, from which they are perhaps derived by reduplication of the final syllable. The original word may, but need not, be descriptive of noise; in the cases where the semantic relationship is clear and the notion "noise" is common to both, the reduplicated form seems to indicate a more prolonged sound than the non-reduplicated one. Thus

> sunu "first thunder clap" vs. sununu "echoing thunder"
> xiri "needlepoint spray" vs. xiriri "prolonged spray."

However,

> pere "liver spots" vs. perere "lumpy things in box"

are not obviously semantically related, and

> tiri "a crack in a piece of glass" vs. tiriri "splintering glass, just one crack"

seem to contrast more on a stative-vs.-active parameter. On further investigation, *tiri* was found to be a verb in its own right, as in

> o-tiri ha o-sununu la ara (3-crack and 3-thunder the weather) "It was crashing and thundering."
> piri "thatch" (a noun) vs. piriri "fire burning dry grass; crackle"

do not appear to be related. However, when it is noted that summer bedding is made of *piri*, which crackles under pressure, the connection becomes obvious. On further investigation, *piri* turned out to be a verb also, with basic meaning "crackle," as in

Table 7.3 *Sample paradigms of various Guaraní verb types*

	Transitive with third-person object wereko "to have"	Intransitive (regular) puka "to laugh"	Noise verb perere "to make flapping noise"	Intransitive attributive kyra "to be fat"
I	a-wereko	a-puka	a-perere	xe-kyra
you	nde-wereko	nde-puka	nde-perere	nde-kyra
he/she/it	o-wereko	o-puka	o-perere	i-kyra
we (inc.)	ja-wereko	ja-puka	ja-perere	ñande-kyra
we (exc.)	ro-wereko	ro-puka	ro-perere	ore-kyra
you all	pe-wereko	pe-puka	pe-perere	pende-kyra
they	o-wereko	o-puka	o-perere	i-kyra

xe-pire o-piri (my-skin 3-crackle) "My skin is full of static electricity."

Only one word of the appropriate canonical shape does not seem to fit into the semantic class of noise words: *terere* "a type of drink." Marina Dos Santos did not feel any noise association in this word.

7.5. Grammar of noise words

Grammatically speaking, noise words form a cohesive class. They are all verbs and can take the same inflections and fulfil the same functions as other Guaraní verbs. They are inflected for person, tense, and aspect, and can form causatives by prefixation of the very productive causative prefix *mbo-*. In their non-causative form, they are all intransitives. It should be noted here that Guaraní has two types of intransitive verbs, overtly distinguished by different sets of subject-agreement markers. The opposition is between verbs that convey qualitative/attributive notions (appropriately translated by English adjectives) and all other intransitive verbs. Attributive verbs take person markers which are more similar to the object forms of transitive verbs than to subject forms. Noise verbs are all of the general rather than the attributive type. Producing a noise is certainly not interpreted in Guaraní as a quality or attribute. This is not necessarily self-evident, in view of the fact that so many seem to describe canonical sounds of natural phenomena, like the noise of thunder, which one could readily conceive of as an attribute. Table 7.3 exhibits sample paradigms of the various classes of verbs.

Guaraní has various nominalizing processes, among the most productive of which is the formation of relative clauses. For illustrative purposes, I will use an example of subject relativization which is achieved by taking the verb with its subject prefix (i.e. the form the verb would have as a main verb) and suffixing it with -*va*. Together with its nominal head, which precedes, it forms a relative clause. Thus

la kuimba'e o-purahei (the man 3-sing) "The man sang."

is relativized as

la kuimba'e o-purahei-va (the man 3-sing-NOM) "The man who sang."

Attributive verbs, however, can modify nouns without any special morphological apparatus; in fact, the bare stem acts essentially as an adjective:

la kwimba'e i-põrã (the man 3-attributive-good) "The man is good."
la kuimba'e pora "The good man."

A puzzling situation was encountered where all spontaneously offered sentences containing noise verbs as noun modifiers exhibited the bare stem form, as if they were attributive verbs. Thus

nd-a-ipota so'o xyryry (NEG-I-want meat sizzle) "I don't want fried meat."

This was at first interpreted as an indication that noise verbs might be grammatical hybrids, combining properties of both verb classes. However, further investigation revealed first of all that noise verbs can, in fact, relativize like other verbs. It is indeed possible to say

la rywasy o-perere-va (the chicken 3-flap-wings-NOM) "the chicken that is making noise flapping its wings."

Secondly, it was found that regular verbs can, in fact, also modify nouns with no overt morphology, i.e. in their bare form. Thus, it is possible to say both

(1) a-hendu la kuimba'e purahei (I-hear the man sing) "I heard the man sing"

and

(2) a-hexa la kuimba'e o-purahei-va (I-see the man 3-sing-NOM) "I saw the man who sang."

On being asked to characterize the difference between these two sentences, Marina Dos Santos explained that there is a difference in focus, so that in (1) the focus is on "sing" (what I heard was singing) while in (2) the focus is on "man" (what I saw was a man). What remains to be explained is why all spontaneous noise verbs used as noun modifiers were in the bare form. The answer, I believe, lies in their special semantic content, highly expressive and iconic, which it seems intuitively more appropriate to use as focus of an event rather than simply as descriptive of another focused element. Be that as it may, this is an example of the usefulness of investigating the syntactic behaviour of sound-symbolic words.

7.6. Noise words and metaphor

Noise words seem to be particularly prone to metaphorical extension, especially in one semantic area. While many of the basic meanings describe noises produced in nature, by inanimate objects, or involuntarily by human bodies, it is often possible to use these verbs to refer to human emotions, expressing a whole range of types of anger – an emotion which is of course often accompanied by sounds not fully under rational control – as well as other unacceptable types of behavior. Examples illustrate the differences between some of the verbs:

> perere "to be angry, make noise like a flapping chicken"
> mbururu "to be angry, make sounds like a bull, but not totally out of control"
> walala "to get angry, lose control all of a sudden"
> tyryry "to behave to someone as if one were wiping the floor with him"
> mbo-sururu (causative-sururu) "to make someone eat his words, to ram someone's words down his throat"
> sororo "to emote uncontrollably, be hysterical"
> syryry "to be slippery, devious"
> kõrõrõ "to be snorting with anger"
> xyryry "to be sizzling mad."

7.7. Conclusion

Turning now to how the facts of Guaraní compare with those of other languages where sound symbolism is known to play a systematic part, a first observation based on my own experience is that the Guaraní facts are not reminiscent of the size symbolism found in languages of western North America (except in their use of the segment /r/ and the few instance of /l/ and /n/ as well). They are somewhat more like what I have called elsewhere "expressive 'say' constructions", which are reminiscent of such English expressions as "Pop goes the weasel" but with a form of the verb "say" instead of "go." These commonly involve reduplication, and may describe sounds (although they are not limited to this area). Sound-symbolism systems tend to be areally distributed; in fact, both size symbolism and "expressive say constructions" are areal phenomena of native California (Haas 1970; Langdon 1971, 1977). This leads me to suspect that parallels to the Guaraní facts should be looked for elsewhere in South America. Specialists in South American languages I have talked to all seem to feel that the languages they are familiar with abound in sound-symbolic words. Whether the particular type described here is in fact an areal feature of part of South America remains to be ascertained. Obviously, in this area as in so many others, the study of South American Indian languages promises to reveal a rich array of challenging data.

NOTES

*A partial presentation of the material in this paper was made at the 1985 meeting of the American Anthropological Association as "Sound Symbolism in Guarani" by Margaret Langdon, Marina Dos Santos, and Brenda Gossett. The data were obtained from Marina Dos Santos, a native speaker of Guaraní, formerly a resident of Asunción, Paraguay, and currently residing in San Diego. Her vivid and imaginative description of the semantics of the words here described are an indispensable contribution to this paper. Possible misinterpretations are of course my own.

REFERENCES

Haas, M. R. 1970. The Northern California linguistic area. In M. Langdon and S. Silver (eds.) *Hokan Studies*. Janua Linguarum, Series Practica 181. The Hague: Mouton, 347–357.

Langdon, M. 1971. Sound symbolism in Yuman languages. In J. O. Sawyer (ed.) *Studies in American Indian Languages*, ed. by Jesse O. Sawyer. University of California Publications in Linguistics 65: 149–173.

1977. The semantics and syntax of expressive 'say' constructions in Yuman. *Proceedings of the Third Annual Meeting of the Berkeley Linguistic Society* 3: 1–11.

Nichols, J. 1971. Diminutive consonant symbolism in Western North America. *Language* 47: 810–825.

PART III
Asia

8
i: *big*, a: *small*

GÉRARD DIFFLOTH

8.1. Introduction

From the start, one must admit that the study of sound symbolism has a tarnished reputation in current linguistics. Among several reasons, the poor quality of the evidence is sufficient to explain why many theoreticians show a definite lack of interest in this topic.

Instances of sound symbolism found in languages like English tend to be limited in number, and scattered pell-mell through the language; the iconic patterns themselves are ill-structured, timidly developed, and often difficult to identify and describe. Nevertheless, the more uncertain the data the more daring the theories tend to become, and sober-minded linguists have good reasons to remain skeptical.

Among the more reasonable statements made about sound symbolism, it is often said (Sapir 1929; Newman 1933; Jespersen 1933; Tarte 1974) that if vowel quality is used for size symbolism, [i] will symbolize smallness, and the lower vowels, especially [a], will symbolize largeness, with degrees in between. Casual remarks are often made about this being another set of language "universals," even though one major effort in this area (Ultan 1978) led only to guarded statements. Furthermore, there are suggestions (Ohala 1984) that this trait belongs not to the cultural but to the natural, innate domain.

This last point appears to be headed in the wrong direction, as I try to show below. Regarding the claim of universality, I will not have much to say, beyond deploring the incorrect use of the term "universal" to mean simply "found in a number of languages." One learns to take such grandiloquent terminology for what it is. The real problem is in the first claim, the apparently reasonable one.

The records show that there are well-developed sound-symbolic systems where vowel quality is used with systematic results exactly opposite to those predicted. Furthermore, there is really no point in considering the first type of sound symbolism as somehow being normal, while this second type would be aberrant or language-specific; both, as I will argue, find equal justification in the physiology of speech and in the principles of iconicity, explored and applied differently in different languages.

In order to sway the skeptical, I will use evidence from languages where iconicity is rich, well-structured, and encoded in such a way as to make its presence quite certain. I am referring to languages which possess a class of words variously called "descriptives" (Smith 1973), "impressifs" (Durand 1961), /iy-te-ɔ/ (Korean linguistic terminology; Martin 1962) /gitaigo/ (Amanuma 1974), "tượng hình" (Vietnamese linguistic terminology), "obraznye slova" (Kile 1973), /olikkurippu/ (Sadasivam 1966), among others. The term "ideophone" has also been used to cover a wide variety of African linguistic phenomena, some of which correspond to what will be discussed here. I have used the term "expressives" to refer to this basic part of speech, which is alien to Western tradition but can be defined in the traditional way by its distinct morphology, syntactic properties, and semantic characteristics; these have been discussed elsewhere (Diffloth 1972, 1976, 1979).

Some non-native linguists, especially in Japanese and Korean studies, have proposed that expressives be considered a subclass of adverbs. In passing, I must mention that similarities between expressives and adverbs do exist, but are quite superficial. The differences are profound and more relevant. For instance, English adverbs are inherently negatable (un-fortunate-ly, in-tolerabl-y, superficially vs. deeply, etc.). This is not an accidental but a fundamental property of the class "adverb," which points to its close relationship with the class "adjective." Expressives, on the other hand, though they may on occasion be used in sentences containing negatives, cannot be themselves negated. It is not possible to say that this tree trunk, in Semai, is floating down-river in an "un-/dyɔ̄ɔl-yɔ̄ɔl/" manner, that there is something "un-/pika-pika/" about this Japanese lantern, or that this Korean girl is smiling in an "un-/paŋgil-paŋgil/" way. Such expressions are rejected not simply on morphological or syntactic grounds; they are obnoxious and baffling to the native speaker because they are semantically ill-formed. They have no meaning, and their use (by non-natives or inquisitive linguists) betrays a misunderstanding of what expressives are for.

Adjectives and adverbs, like predicates, function in the conventional semiotic domain, where having truth values and being negatable are fundamental characteristics. Expressives do not operate in that domain; instead, they represent an attempt at fully exploiting the semiotics of iconicity, in order to convey various sensations in as direct a manner as speech makes possible. Because of this, it is not sufficient to say that expressives form a distinct basic part of speech: they actually constitute a parallel sublanguage grafted on, and parasitic on, the conventional one. This can explain many of the strange linguistic properties of these words; it accounts for their large but indefinite numbers, for their creativity and semantic elusiveness. The presence of expressives also gives us a chance to study sound symbolism in its finer grade and its more purposeful development.

Asia

8.2. Expressives in Bahnar

Bahnar, a Mon-Khmer language of Vietnam, has a large class of expressives, which is conspicuous for having plural and dual suffixes. This is all the more noticeable in that Mon-Khmer languages show a variety of both prefixes and infixes, but almost never have suffixes, except, precisely, in expressives; moreover, in this family generally, morphological plurals or duals are never found in nouns and verbs. In spite of these rather obvious pointers, the class of expressives has usually been neglected or even ignored by linguists, in this and similar languages. We are fortunate to have, in print, a very large dictionary of Bahnar (Guilleminet and Alberty 1959) which gives a great number of expressives (probably around two thousand). They are labeled as "mot descriptif" or "réduplication descriptive," as the case may be.

Examples ("D. red." = "Descriptive reduplication"):

(1) /blɔɔŋ-blɔɔŋ/ "D. red. of the numerous reflections caused by rays of light on a small object"
(2) /blɔɔŋ-blɛɛɛw/ "D. red. of the numerous reflections caused by a single ray of light on a small shiny object"
(3) /blɛɛl-blɛɛl/ "D. red. of small flames appearing intermittently but remaining vivid"
(4) /blɛɛl-ɲep/ "D. red. of a small scintillating fire, of the last intermittent flashes given by a small fire about to die off"
(5) /khɛɛŋ-cəkhɛɛŋ/ "D. red. of someone carrying a small burden on his shoulder"
(6) /teel-hleel/ "D. red. of a very light movement, of something moving after being lightly brushed by something passing by (*affleuré*)"
(7) /rəhyəl/ "Descriptive word of a light movement, like that of grasses a wild animal is cautiously stealing into"
(8) /jəhaah/ "D. word of something small and gaping (a wound, a mouth)"
(9) /hleep/ "D. word for what disappears, hides itself"

In expressives, as these examples attempt to show, onomatopoeia plays only a minor role and is sometimes not involved at all, as in (1–4), (8). Bahnar has, in addition to expressives, many onomatopoeic expressions which are separately labeled as such in the dictionary. And yet, in expressives as in onomatopoeia, the phonetic substance of the word has something to do with its meaning. This may not be obvious at first to the non-speaker of Bahnar: in order to understand and use these expressives properly, one must know the Bahnar iconic system, i.e. one must learn to focus on those specific resemblances between sound and meaning which its speakers have selected and exploited.

It is important to notice that, in most languages, expressives use only phonic material which is already given by the phonological system of the language. This is true not only in terms of inventory, but also, for the most part, in terms of distribution. Expressives are phonologically well-formed words of the language, and when there are unusual sound combinations, the phonological violations appear limited, and clearly iconic (Diffloth 1979). In this obvious way at least, the iconicity of expressives is language-specific: Korean exploits the three degrees of aspiration in initial stops which its prosaic phonology provides, whereas Bahnar utilizes its large number of vowels.

The Bahnar vowel system is typologically normal for mainland Southeast Asia, at least in Mon-Khmer and Southwestern Tai languages:

iə		uə			
ii	ɯɯ	uu	i	ɯ	u
ee	əə	oo	e	ə	o
ɛɛ	aa	ɔɔ	ɛ	a	ɔ

Bahnar expressives tend to cluster into small networks of semantically and phonologically related forms, which are cross-referenced to each other in Guilleminet and Alberty's dictionary. These related forms differ mostly in the quality of their vowels. By far the most common pattern is a pair of expressives, one with a low vowel, the other with a mid-high or a high vowel, length and fronting remaining the same. The semantic difference has to do with size, and the pattern is invariably as follows:

	ii	uu	i	u
"BIG"				
	ee	oo	e	o
"SMALL"	ɛɛ	ɔɔ	ɛ	ɔ

(Central vowels are not very common in expressives.)

Examples:

(10) /bloŋ-bloŋ/ "D. red. of numerous reflections caused by rays of light on a large object, elongated in shape"
vs. /blɔŋ-blɔŋ/ "id., small object," cf. (1).

(11) /bloŋ-blɛɛw/ "D. red. of the numerous reflections caused by a single ray of light on a big shiny object"
vs. /blɔŋ-blɛɛw/ "id., small shiny object," cf. (2)

(12) /bleel-bleel/ "D. red. of large flames appearing intermittently but remaining vivid."
vs. /blɛɛl-blɛɛl/ "id., small flames," cf. (3)

(13) /bliil-ɲip/ "D. red. of a large scintillating fire, of the last flashes of a large fire about to die"

vs. /blɛɛl-ɲɛp/ "id., small fire," cf. (4)

(14) /kheeŋ-cəkheeŋ/ "D. red. of someone carrying a heavy burden on his shoulder"
vs. /khɛɛŋ-cəkhɛɛŋ/ "id., small burden," cf. (5)

(15) /jul-kəjul/ "D. red. of a large creature, or an important person, trotting about"
vs. /jɔl-kəjɔl/ "id., small creature."

There is usually no way to predict, in the "large" variety, whether the high or the mid-high vowel will be used. There are a number of cases where both are given, and with the same meaning:

(16) /rəmut/ "D. word for lovely big objects equal in size"
(17) /rəmot/ "id."
(18) /rəmɔt/ "D. word for lovely small objects equal in size"
(19) /təbriil/ "D. word for a pair of big spherical objects"
(20) /təbreel/ "id."
(21) /təbrɛɛl/ "D. word for a pair of small spherical objects"
(22) /cəriil/ "D. word for a large source of light"
(23) /cəreel/ "id."
(24) /cərɛɛl/ "D. word for a luminous point, a far-away light."

Often, the high vowel /uu/ is further distinguished from /oo/ by a nuance of reverence, social importance or fear:

(25) /guun-təguun/ "D. red. of a tall and impressive man, of an imposing and awe-inspiring person, who is bending under a heavy load or is hunchbacked"
(26) /goon-təgoon/ "D. red. of a tall man or important person, who is hunchbacked or bending under a heavy load; (tiger) arches its back"
(27) /gɔɔn-təgɔɔn/ "D. red. of a small man bending under a heavy load"

(28) /jəhuuh/ "D. word for something large, gaping, and awe-inspiring"
(29) /jəhooh/ "D. word for something large and gaping"
(30) /jəhɔɔh/ "D. word for something small and gaping," see also (8).

But there are examples where a three-way gradation is given, with high vowels providing a third degree: "enormous." The fact that such triads of expressives are not as frequently found in the dictionary as pairs are may have more to do with elicitation procedures than with the actual structure of the lexicon; further work on Bahnar would probably produce a good many more, and fill in a number of obvious gaps. The actual iconic system of Bahnar vowels is then likely to look like this:

	ii	uu	i	u
"ENORMOUS"	ii	uu	i	u
"BIG"	ee	oo	e	o
"SMALL"	ɛɛ	ɔɔ	ɛ	ɔ

Examples:

(31) /halul/ "D. word for an enormous wedged-up (*coincé*) object, immense overfilled premises, a vast filled-up container, impressive or frightening-looking"

(32) /halol/ "D. word for a big wedged-up object, wide but overfilled premises, a large filled-up container"

(33) /halɔl/ "D. word for a small wedged-up object, small cramped premises, a small filled-up container"

(34) /gəluuŋ-gəlaaŋ/ "D. red. of very big heaps, very great pilings, of a confused, awe-inspiring scuffle"

(35) /gəlooŋ-gəlaaŋ/ "D. red. of big heaps, great pilings, in disorder"

(36) /gəlɔɔŋ-gəlaaŋ/ "D. red. of small heaps, small pilings, in disorder"

(37) /dəbuuŋ/ "D. word of the curved ridge of an immense (*très vaste*) roof, the center of the curve being below the ridge"

(38) /dəbooŋ/ "id., large roof"

(39) /dəbɔɔŋ/ "id., small roof"

(40) /cəwiir/ "D. word of a very large twisted mouth in a grimacing face (due to joy or suffering)"
(the expected /cəweer/ "id., large mouth" is not found in the dictionary)

(41) /cəwɛɛr/ "id., small mouth"

(42) /ɲəɲiir/ "D. word, superlative of /ɲəɲeer/, of a person annoyed by the sun, blinking eyes a great deal, or unable to keep them open"
[/ɲəɲeer/ is missing in the dictionary]

(43) /ɲəɲɛɛr/ "D. word of a person annoyed by the sun, blinking eyes a little bit."

8.3. Conclusions

Whether it is this more elaborate system or the simpler two-way division which is at the basis of the vowel gradations of Bahnar expressives is not crucial to the point made here. In either case, the iconic values of the vowels are, roughly speaking: High = Big and Low = Small, exactly opposite to the English /i/ = Small and /a/ = Big, claimed to be universal. There is nothing peculiar about this Bahnar system, and one can easily find an iconic basis for it.

In the articulation of high vowels, the tongue occupies a much larger volume in the mouth than it does for low vowels. The proprioceptive sensation due to this, reinforced by the amount of contact between the sides of the tongue and the upper molars, is available to all speakers and is probably necessary to achieve a precise articulatory gesture. The most direct form of iconicity relies on finding similarities between two different kinds of sensations: articulatory feedback sensations (or proprioception of articulation) on the one hand, and the various sensations conveyed by expressives on the other.

In this perspective, two different languages may easily use the same phonetic variable (vowel height) to convey the same range of sensations (size), and come up with exactly opposite solutions, both being equally iconic; all they need to do is focus upon different parts of the rich sensation package provided by articulatory gestures, in our case the volume of the tongue instead of the size of the air passage between it and the palate. Iconicity can be both physiologically motivated and culturally relative at the same time.

It follows that iconic patterns, being fundamentally language-specific, must be described in the grammars of particular languages. But at the moment, we do not have the formal linguistic tools necessary for describing iconicity. One problem is that current models do not allow us to show a direct relation between phonetics and semantics. This could easily be arranged by modifying formal conventions about rules and features. However, the real difficulty is not in mapping or deriving various kinds of notations, but in showing resemblances. A phonetic feature and a semantic one are entirely different linguistic objects; how can we show that there are actual similarities between them if there does not exist a common medium where such similarities could reside?

In any case, as the Bahnar example suggests, the phonetic parameters needed for iconicity, for example perceived size of the tongue in the oral cavity, are very different from those needed to represent the phonological contrasts of prosaic phonology; and a similar point could probably be made on the semantic side. Thus, even our notation systems are inappropriate to describe the iconic systems found in expressives.

Iconicity belongs to a different semiotic domain from the one usually described in our grammars. As far as expressives are concerned, the phonic and the meaning elements must be described in terms of certain elementary sensations. Iconicity consists here in exploiting similarities between the sensations of speech and other kinds of sensation. This kind of synesthesia must be described in a distinct component of grammar, the esthetic component, which is distinct but not isolated, as it somehow must be plugged into the conventional components which have received much of the attention of theoreticians so far.

REFERENCES

Amanuma, Y. 1974. *Dictionary of Onomatopes and Expressives* (in Japanese). Tokyo: Tokyodo.

Diffloth, G. 1972. Notes on expressive meaning. *Papers from the Eighth Regional Meeting of the Chicago Linguistic Society*: 440–448.

―――. 1976. Expressives in Semai. In *Austroasiatic Studies*. Oceanic Linguistics, Special Publications 13:1. Hawaii: University Press, 249–264.

―――. 1979. Expressive phonology and prosaic phonology in Mon-Khmer. In *Studies in Thai and Mon-Khmer Phonetics and Phonology*. Bangkok: Chulalongkorn University Press, 49–59.

Durand, M. 1961. Les impressifs en Vietnamien, étude préliminaire. *Bulletin de la Société des Etudes Indochinoises*. Nouvelle Série 36:1. Saigon.

Guilleminet, P. and J. Alberty. 1959. *Dictionnaire Bahnar-Français*, 2 vols. Paris: Ecole Française d'Extrême-Orient.

Jespersen, O. 1933. Symbolic value of the vowel *i*. In *Linguistica. Selected Papers of O. Jespersen in English, French and German*. Copenhagen: Levin and Munksgaard, 283–303.

Kile, N. B. 1973. *Obraznye slova nanajskogo jazyka*. Leningrad: Nauka. (In Russian.)

Martin, S. E. 1962. Phonetic symbolism in Korean. *Uralic and Altaic series*, 13: Bloomington: Indiana: University Press; 177–189.

Newman, S. S. 1933. Further experiments in phonetic symbolism. *American Journal of Psychology* 45: 53–75.

Ohala, J. J. 1984. An ethological perspective on common cross-language utilization of F_0 of voice. *Phonetica* 41: 1–16.

Sadasivam, M. 1966. *Olikkurippakarāti*. (Dictionary of Expressives, in Tamil). Pāri Nilaiyam.

Sapir, E. 1929. A study in experimental symbolism. *Journal of Experimental Psychology* 12: 225–239.

Smith, R. L. 1973. Reduplication of Ngeq. *Mon-Kmher Studies* 4: 85–112.

Tarte, R. D. 1974. Phonetic symbolism in adult native speakers of Czech. *Language and Speech* 17: 87–94.

Ultan, R. 1978. Size-sound symbolism. In J. H. Greenberg, C. R. Ferguson, and E. A. Moravcsik (eds.) *Universals of Human Language*, vol. 2. Stanford: University Press, 527–568.

9
*Tone, intonation, and sound symbolism in Lahu: loading the syllable canon**

JAMES A. MATISOFF

9.1 Feature shuffling and tonogenesis in Sinospheric languages

The development of full-fledged tonal systems of the "omnisyllabic" type seems to be unique to East and Southeast Asia. In a language with an omnisyllabic tone system, virtually every syllable occurs with a distinctive tone that is not predictable either in terms of the syntactic structure of its phrase or phonotactically in terms of neighboring syllables. These tones are not just oppositions of higher vs. lower pitch, but are complex bundles of prosodic features including pitch, contour, vowel length, and "phonation type" (clear, creaky, breathy voice). Omnisyllabic tone languages usually have a minimum of three distinctive tones, and some have as many as 10 or 12.[1]

There appears to be a necessary connection between omnisyllabic tone and monosyllabic morphemes. The stronghold of these tone systems is precisely the monosyllabic languages that are typologically similar to Chinese: what I have called the "tone-prone" or "toniferous" languages of the "Sinosphere."[2] Some of these languages are genetically related to Chinese (those of the Tibeto-Burman family), but others (Tai, Hmong-Mien [Miao-Yao], Vietnamese) have developed their tones – and indeed their monosyllabicity – secondarily, through contact influence from Chinese.

Diachronically, the development of tonal contrasts – *tonogenesis* – has been shown to result compensatorily from losses or mergers in the consonantal system. Loss of a voicing contrast in pre-vocalic consonants can be transphonologized into a contrast between higher and lower tones; while loss of a postvocalic laryngeal (-ʔ or -*h*) can lead to a phonemic contrast between rising and falling tone.[3] "There is something about the tightly structured nature of the syllable in monosyllabic languages which favors the shift in contrastive function from one phonological feature of the syllable to another" (Matisoff 1973: 78), and the birth of tones is only the most spectacular of these "feature shufflings."[4]

Lahu is a typical omnisyllabic tonal language of the Loloish subgroup of the

Table 9.1 *Tones in Black Lahu*

OPEN			CHECKED		
ca ^{33}	[mid level]	"look for"			
cá ^{35}	[high rising]	"to boil"	câʔ	[high]	"string"
câ ^{53}	[high falling]	"eat"			
cà ^{21}	[low falling]	"ferocious"	càʔ	[low]	"push"
cā $^{11(2)}$	[very low]	"feed"			

(The numbers $^{33,\ 35}$ etc. indicate relative pitch on a scale from 1 (lowest) to 5 (highest), with the first number representing the beginning, and the second the end, of the tonal contour. Note that the very low tone has a slight "allotonic" rise in phrase-final position.)

Tibeto-Burman branch of the great Sino-Tibetan family. The standard Black Lahu dialect has seven tones, five of them synchronically "open" and 2 of them "checked," i.e. accompanied by a glottal stop (Table 9.1).

Syllables under the checked tones derive historically from syllables with final stops */-p -t -k/, though synchronically it is far preferable to regard the glottal stops as tonal (prosodic, suprasegmental) features rather than as post-vocalic consonants. (For one thing, -ʔ disappears in *singing*, as do all other tonal features.) In fact it is best to consider the open versus checked tones as two quite independent subsystems. The symbols /ˆʔ/ and /ˋʔ/ are to be regarded as unitary digraphs, with no connection implied between them and the open-tone marks /ˆ/ and /ˋ/.[5]

Since Lahu has no initial consonant clusters (syllables can also begin with no consonant at all), and no final consonants by this analysis, we are left with an extremely simple *CORE syllable canon*:

    T
(C) V

9.2. Intonation in an omnisyllabic tone language

Even in languages with elaborate omnisyllabic tone systems, *intonation* certainly exists as a phenomenon independent of tone. Since intonational contours usually extend over a much larger stretch than a single syllable, and in any case are determined by "fortuitous" syntactic structure rather than any inherent property of particular lexical items, the effect of intonation is to overarch the tones of the individual syllables in an utterance. In Y. R. Chao's felicitous metaphor, intonations are like ripples on the surface of the tone-waves.[6]

Still, there may also be highly perceptible intonational effects even on single syllables. Chao describes e.g. how Mandarin syllables under the fourth tone /ˋ/, which in "neutral" intonation has a simple falling contour like ^{51}, can acquire a complex rise-fall at the end under "exasperated intonation":

qù ^{51} "go" / bù qù-ú-ù ^{5121} "I'm not going, dammit!"

Similarly, a Lahu syllable under one of the high tones /´/ or /ˆ/ may acquire a lengthened vowel and a superhigh contour for special emphasis, which for male speakers may mean lapsing into falsetto:

ô ^{54} ɔ̄ ^{112} "over there"
ôoo ^{66} ɔ̄ ^{112} "wa-a-ay over there."

In Lahu humorous or emotional conversation, in the incantatory style of animist prayers, and especially in women's speech, a special tripartite intonation is often encountered. Starting with the high-falling contour, it rapidly descends to the very low tone, whence it rises again to the mid range:

pò-thô-ō-o "Good grief"[7]

For us non-native speakers of tone languages, dramatic cases of interference can arise between the tones of the target language and the ingrained intonational habits of one's own, non-tonal language. On the simplest level, anyone who has tried inserting a Chinese word into an English sentence quickly runs into trouble – e.g. when ending an English yes–no question with a quoted word in the Mandarin falling tone:

"Did you say qù??"

Lahu has an interjection under an intonationally exaggerated high-falling tone hâi ^{51}, whose function is to indicate that one has not understood the previous utterance, and that a repetition is desired, much like American English huh? To American ears (or at any rate to mine) this interjection creates a bizarre first impression, simply because the falling tone of the particle sounds so positive or asseverative, not at all like the rise in pitch that we habitually associate with uncertainty or a request for repetition. (The strangeness of this word is accentuated by the allophonic nasalization of its vowel [hâin ^{51}], characteristic of syllables with initial h-, a phenomenon I have called *rhinoglottophilia*. See below, section 9.6.5.)[8]

9.3. Non-prosodic "canonical" strategies for conveying affect in tone languages

Although intonation certainly exists in tone languages, it seems clear that tonality favors the use of something else besides mere pitch or contour to help perform the communicative jobs that intonation handles in non-tone languages. Thus Lahu does not need to have a special intonation for interrogative sentences, since it has a set of sentence-final particles whose sole function is to signal various kinds of questions: *lâ* "yes–no question," *le* "substance (WH-) question," *nā* "indirect or rhetorical question." More strikingly, omnisyllabic tone languages typically have a repertoire of particles whose only job is to convey the emotion or affect of the speaker – syllabic exclamation points, as it were. Thai has several of these, e.g. *rɔ̀ɔk*, *mâj paj rɔ̀ɔk* "I'm not going!" (*mâj* "not," *paj* "go," *rɔ̀ɔk* "!"), while Lahu boasts many more, including *qôʔ-ma*, *lēʔ*, *vâ*, *nē*, *yâ*, *Èʔ*, *qôʔ-yò-Èʔ*, and several others, with sequences of three or four possible in the same clause.[9]

Such particles, it must be stressed, are fully canonical syllables or polysyllables, with meaty consonants and vowels in addition to their tones. They are indistinguishable in their phonological shape from ordinary items of root vocabulary.[10]

Many other subtle nuances of affect or attitude are conveyable by segmental particles in tone languages. Thai is well known for its sentence-final "politeness particles" (*khráp* for males, *khâa* for females). Lahu has several attitudinal particles whose meanings are so abstract that they are not readily apparent without many examples taken from elaborate contexts. At first I assumed that the morpheme *qha-pâʔ(-a)* was just another of the innumerable final emphatic particles, and translated it by such expressions as "dammit!" or simply by an exclamation point, as in:

âa, chɔ-há-pā là qha-pâʔ   "Ah, here come the guys!"
ŋà nâʔ chi^ʔ qha-pâʔ-a   "My shot fizzled, dammit!"

Only gradually did it become clear that *qha-pâʔ* always refers to *an affective attitude toward auditory perception*, either its presence (a striking sound one hears) or its absence (a "deafening silence" when an expected sound is not perceived). The above sentences should be translated something like "Ah, I can hear the guys coming (they're making a racket)!"; and "My shot fizzled (with a little anemic sound, instead of going off with a bang)!" (See *GL*: 681, n. 355.)

Similarly in a raunchy Trickster story recorded in 1965–1966 (see Matisoff 1979): as the Trickster, having been caught by his enemies, is tied to the rump of a water buffalo and is being dragged face downward over rocky ground, there occurs the sentence:

"*qâ-càʔ, qâ-càʔ, qâ-càʔ*" *qôʔ ve*.

Clearly the thrice repeated *qâ-càʔ* is an interjection of some kind, but the subject of the sentence is not expressed (*qôʔ ve* means only "[somebody] said"), and the situational context makes it equally likely for the speaker to be the Trickster or his enemies. At first I opted for the Trickster, and translated the sentence as

"Ouch, ouch, ouch!" he said.

Upon rechecking this in 1970, I was amusedly corrected by my informant, who explained that it was the enemies who were speaking, and the interjection was a gloating taunt, not a cry of pain, so that the sentence really meant

"Nyaah, nyaah, nyaah!" they said.

Note that *qâ-cà⁷* is a perfectly canonical dissyllabic word, and is not marked by any special intonational contour – in sharp contrast to the American English taunt conventionally spelled *nyaah*, whose peculiar phonological features stamp it as an item of affective vocabulary: initial /ny-/ does not otherwise occur before [æ], the exaggeratedly prolonged vowel is strongly nasalized, and most notably there is a special "sing-song" intonational pattern that can be symbolized musically as *F D G F D* (where the key is B-flat, and the rhythm is quarter, dotted eighth, sixteenth, quarter, quarter).

So far, then, we have not had to stretch our basic Lahu syllable canon at all in order to accommodate these items of affective or interjectory vocabulary. We are still operating within the basic framework of

(C) $\begin{matrix} T \\ V \end{matrix}$

and have not yet quite entered the realm of sound symbolism.

9.4. Canonical onomatopes and attitudinals

Languages like Japanese and Korean abound in reduplicated sound-symbolic expressions, traditionally dichotomized by Japanese scholars into two great classes: on the one hand *giseigo* or *giongo* (lit. "imitate-sound-words") and on the other hand *gitaigo* ("imitate-attitude-words") (Amanuma 1974). *Giseigo* (e.g. *kotokoto* "sound of muffled, scampering footsteps, as of a mouse or small barefoot child") correspond closely to our notion of *onomatopes*. For *gitaigo*, which express subjective attitudes toward aspects of visual or auditory experience, I suggest the translation "attitudinals" (e.g. *pera-pera* "fluently," *pocha-pocha* "plump," *pika-pika* "glittering").

Despite the huge number of these expressions in Japanese and Korean, they are certainly not infinite (they can be listed in dictionaries), and they are not freely inventable by the ordinary speaker. By and large they are also canonical in their phonological shape.[11]

In Lahu, *giseigo* are fairly numerous, though this is not a particularly salient feature of the language. They are mostly reduplicates:

pô⁷-pô⁷   "pop-pop" (fried millet); "chug-chug" (motorcycle)
vɨ-vɨ   'bzz-bzz" (bees); "vroom-vroom" (motor)
tɛ⁷-tɛ⁷   "scratch-scratch" (crabs on bamboo-sheaths)

qáy-qáy	"arf-arf; yip-yip" (little dog)
qáw-qáw	"bow-wow; woof-woof" (big dog)

Some Lahu *gitaigo* are non-reduplicated disyllables, but the disyllables as a whole may be reduplicated:

pÈ-ši pÈ-ši	"zigzag"
cɔ́-cí cɔ́-cí	"tingly; prickly"

Rather similar, though not usually reduplicable, are "intensified adjectives," where an adjectival root is coupled with an otherwise meaningless syllable that conveys a nuance of intensity (*GL*: 295–297):

nâʔ-tɔ́	"jet-black"	(nâʔ (black"))
cɔ́-nÉʔ	"skinny as a rail"	(cɔ́ "thin")
hE-tɔ́ʔ	"hard but resilient (like a pig's sternum)"	(hE "hard").

Even more typically Tibeto-Burman are four-syllable "elaborate expressions," where the first and third, or second and fourth, syllables are identical, as in the following group with the symbolic morpheme -*li*, all having to do with dangling or bouncing, or with skewed or disorderly appearance:

ɔ-li-a-li	"jouncing from side to side"
tú-li-pā-li	"head over heels; tottering, stumbling"
pi-li-khɔ-li	"rough and uneven; bestrewn with extraneous objects (as a road with rocks)"
pɨ-li-tâʔ-li	"cluttered, messy; at sixes and sevens"
hɔ́-li-thE-li	"zigzag; every which way"
qu-li-chíʔ-li	"dangling down, hanging free"
ju-li-jâ-li	"id."
də-li-dà-li	"id."

Syntactically, all these canonical sound-symbolic expressions function as adverbials, typically occurring directly before a "dummy" verb of very general meaning for its adverbiality to rest upon, usually *qay* "go" (e.g. *qáw-qáw qay ve* "go bow-bow" – note the similarity to English idiom!), *phÈʔ* "be," or *te* "do."

9.5. Core and margin in the Lahu syllable canon

As we have seen, the basic or core Lahu syllable canon is extremely simple – an (optional) initial consonant, one of nine monophthongal vowels /a i u e o E ɔ i ə/, and a tone:

```
        T
   (C)  V
```

Asia

However, once we include a variety of "marginal" phonological phenomena, several of them sound-symbolic in nature, we end up with a canon of considerably greater complexity:

Lahu SECONDARY or EXPANDED syllable canon:

```
           T    (y)
                (w)
(C)  (w)   V    (ʔ)
                (ɛ)
          (N)   (ː)
```

The parenthesized elements (except for the initial consonant) will all be discussed below. Here we simply assemble them for ease of reference, with the following remarks:

T includes the glottal component of the checked tones /ˆʔ ˋʔ/. The parenthesized (ʔ) refers to sound-symbolic imperative glottal stop (9.6.4).

(N) (vowel nasalization) occurs in loanwords, in rhinoglottophiliac syllables, and in sound-symbolic adverbs (9.6.5).

Post-vocalic (y) and (w) appear in loanwords or as the result of the "fusion" of two contiguous vowels in originally separate syllables. In the case of /-y/, some of these fusions involve sound-symbolic diminutivization (9.6.2, 9.6.3).

Prevocalic (w) occurs in loanwords, and in sound-symbolic fusions where a back vowel is deprived of syllabicity (9.6.3).

The low front vowel (ɛ) occurs as second element of a complex vocal nucleus only if /i/ precedes. Many of the words with this diphthongal vocalism /iɛ/ show diminutive sound symbolism (9.6.2).

Lengthened vowels, symbolized by (ː), appear in "echo-vowel adverbials," yet another sound-symbolic phenomenon (9.6.6).

9.6. Exploitation of otherwise marginal phonetic features for sound-symbolic purposes

9.6.1. *A symbolic value for the Lahu high-rising tone / ́/*

There is much evidence to suggest that it is the lexically rarer tones in a language which are typically exploited for special jobs: in morphophonemic processes, in incompletely assimilated loanwords, or for affective/symbolic purposes.[12] The relatively low functional load of a rare tone ensures that these special tasks will not overburden the system by creating large numbers of new homophones – and the

Table 9.2 *Diminutive forms of "extentive" Lahu NPs*

Extentive verb		Neutral extentive		Diminutive	
ɨ̄	"be big"	chi hɨ	"this big"	chi hɨ́ɛ/hɨ́y	"only this big"
mâ	"be many"	chi ma	"this many"	chi máɛ/máy	"only this much/many"
yɨ̂	"be long"	chi ši	"this long"	chi šɨ́ɛ/šɨ́y	"only this long"
vɨ̂	"be far"	chi fɨ	"this far"	chi fɨ́ɛ/fɨ́y	"only this far"

salience afforded by their very rarity makes them appropriate for grammatical or symbolic duty.

Tones may be lexically rare[13] synchronically because they arose under particularly constrained tonogenetic circumstances. The Lahu very-low tone /¯/ arose only from Proto-Lolo-Burmese (PLB) tone *2 syllables that began with *pre-glottalized or *sibilant initials. As the rarest of all Lahu tones it is available to accommodate messy polysyllabic loanwords from English or Burmese: e.g. kɔ̄mīti̍ "committee," lɔ̄lī "motor vehicle" (< Eng. *lorry*), šā-lā-gūn "doctor" (< Bs.), šānlōn "olive" (< Bs.).

The second rarest tone, high-rising /´/, arose from PLB syllables with final */-p -t -k/ that also had *pre-glottalized initials, so that "glottal dissimilation" could apply (see note 5). To its rarity it joins its highness, which makes it appropriate for a sound-symbolic *diminutive* function. A few high-frequency Lahu verbs of "extentive" meaning have morphophonemically related variants that occur with the determiner *chi* "this" to form NPs of extent, both neutral and diminutive. The diminutive forms are under the high rising tone (*GL*: 129–130) (Table 9.2).

9.6.2. *Diminutive fusional diphthongs with central vowels*

I have recently reconstructed three homophonous palatal suffixes */-y/ for Proto-Sino-Tibetan/Proto-Tibeto-Burman, each of which can be shown to be a phonological reduction of a different root morpheme (Matisoff 1989b). One of these putative suffixes had a diminutive/affective function, and I believe it to have been a reduction of the full morpheme *za ⪤ *ya "child; baby; son."[14] Each of the palatal suffixes is conceived of as having a more vs. a less stressed variant, with the latter showing a strong tendency to amalgamate with the preceding nuclear vowel.

Of the nine simple vowels (see section 9.5), only the six non-front vowels seem to have been capable of taking the diminutive palatal suffix. (This seems reasonable on dissimilatory or saliency grounds: there is not much contrast between /i/ and /i-y/, or between /e/ and /e-y/, or even between /ɛ/ and /ɛ-y/.)[15]

The peculiar diphthongal vocalism of the Lahu diminutive extentives just cited (section 9.6.1) illustrates both degrees of fusion, with the central vowels /ɨ/ and

/a/.[16] The less fused variants (hɨ́ɛ, máɛ, etc.) end in the mora /-ɛ/, which is undoubtedly to be identified with the free morpheme ɛ́ (< Proto-Lolo-Burmese *ya ²) "baby; small object," which occurs both independently with the ɔ̀-prefix (ɔ̀-ɛ́ "baby") and as the last element in innumerable compounds designating objects which are "smaller than the norm," or "the smaller/-est of two or more comparable entities," as in ɔ̀-gǜ-tɛ́ʔ-ɛ́ "small intestine," và̀ʔ-ɛ́ "piglet," yâ-ɛ́ "human baby," lɔ̄lī-ɛ́ "child's tricycle" ("little lorry").

In the more fused variants (hɨ́y, máy, etc.) the second mora is reduced to the palatal semivowel. Both degrees of diminutive fusion are also exemplified elsewhere in the lexicon with items of root vocabulary.

Complete fusion has occurred in words like mɛ́ʔ-g̈ɔ́y "hand-mirror" (< mɛ́ʔ-g̈ɔ́ʔ "glass"), ɔ̀-kɨ́y "(little) scar" (ɔ̀-kɨ́ "scar"), qáy "doubled or forked digit," as in là̀ʔ-nɔ-qáy "forked finger" (< qá "branch").

Partial fusion in diminutive/affective vocabulary is especially common in syllables with barred-i vocalism and sibilant initials. Lahu has no /s/ or /ts/ phoneme, though [s] and [ts] exist in the language as allophones of /š/ and /c/ before /i/. In order to get an [s] – a sound which seems to play a major role in sound-symbolic processes worldwide[17] – the Lahu speaker must insert a barred-i /ɨ/ before any other vowel (much as a Japanese speaker must insert an *u* to get an [f], as in *fuirumu* "film"). For whatever reason, we do find a large number of diminutive/affective vocabulary items with the partially fused diphthong /iɛ/ after phonemically shibilant (but phonetically sibilant) initials:

mû-yè	[siɛ̂ʔ-siɛ̂ʔ]	là	ve	"It's drizzling rain."
RAIN	DRIZZLINGLY	COME	PRT	
g̈âʔ –	[siɛ̂ʔ]			"measles"
tɔ̂	[tshiɛ̂ʔ]	te	ve	"to whisper"
WORDS	WHISPERINGLY	MAKE	PRT	

9.6.3. *Diminutive fusional diphthongs with back vowels*[18] (GL: 19)

One of the major sources of Lahu "canon-busting" pre-vocalic /-w-/ is sound symbolic in nature: the result of the fusion of a diminutive palatal suffix to a back vowel /u o ɔ/. When this happens, the back vowel is deprived of its syllabicity, but maintains its original height [u̯ o̯ ɔ̯]. The second, palatal element acquires the same vowel height as the original nuclear vowel, and this second mora becomes more prominent, yielding the *rising diphthongs* [u̯i o̯e ɔ̯ɛ], which I write abstractly as [wi we wɛ/.

The diminutivization of syllables with back vowels is a fairly productive process, and is applicable even to loanwords, as in the last two of the following examples:

ŋâ-ku	⚹	ŋâ-kwi	"dried fish"
yɛ̀-mí-tɔ̃	⚹	yɛ̀-mí-twɛ̄	"bear"
cɔ	⚹	cwe	"era, period of time" (< Shan)
lɔ́ʔ	⚹	lwɛ̂ʔ	"terraced field" (< Shan)

The diminutively fused variant usually conveys a more colloquial, vivid, or folksy tone than the variant with a simple vowel. In a few cases the monophthongal form has been completely displaced, as in *chi-pí-qwɛ̀ʔ* "barking-deer" (but not **chi-pí-qɔ̀ʔ*). (The barking-deer [*Cervulus muntjac*], a small species with delicious flesh, figures prominently in the Lahu imagination, and is regarded by all with hungry affection.)

The fusional diphthongs described in sections 9.6.2 and 9.6.3 represent the same basic morphophonemic process – suffixation of a palatal diminutive element. These phenomena furnish a further teeny-weeny bit of corroboration for the universal sound-symbolic connection between high-front vowels and notions of smallness.

9.6.4. *Imperative glottal stop (GL: 353–354)*

Any Lahu action-verb that is under an unchecked tone may be imperativized by adding glottal stop. The onset of the glottal stop comes after the completion of most of the verb's tonal contour, so that there is no question of confusing imperative open-toned verbs with other verbs having intrinsically checked tones:

mɨ	"sit"	á-qhɔ mɨ-ʔ	"Sit in the house!"
dɔ̀	"drink"	là-g̈ɨ dɔ̀-ʔ	"Drink some tea!"
chɛ̂	"stay"	chò kàʔ chɛ̂-ʔ	"Stay here!"

Verbs already under a checked tone may be used imperatively with no further particle (e.g. *bɔ́ʔ* "shoot," *hâʔ bɔ́ʔ* "hurry up and shoot!"). (One could of course claim that there is an underlying geminate glottal stop in these cases!) Clearly this imperative glottal stop is intonational, but it is also sound-symbolic: there is a nice iconicity between the brusque cutoff of phonation caused by a glottal closure and the abruptness of the "imperative mood."

Despite its special phonological shape, it is convenient to treat imperative glottal stop as a post-verbal particle, in the same class as several other morphemes of conventional segmental shape (e.g. *a*, *yâ*, *vɨ*). The glottal stop may in fact appear after one of these "other" imperative particles, rather than directly after the verb:

šɨ́ʔ-bá chi hâʔ yù a-ʔ   "Hurry up and give me that board!"

9.6.5. *Vowel nasalization as a symbolic feature*

Many Lahu syllables have nasalized vowels (symbolized by a lower-case "n" written after the vowel), though the systematic status of this feature differs from case to case.

It is never true that a Lahu nasalized vowel reflects an inherited syllable-final nasal consonant */-m -n -ŋ/.[19] All these etymological final nasals disappeared in Lahu, usually after affecting the quality (but not the orality) of the preceding vowel. Thus PTB *-am > Lahu -o, *-an > Lh. -e, *-aŋ > Lh. -ɔ.

Loanwords (from Thai, Burmese, Chinese, or English) with original syllable-final nasal consonants are sometimes pronounced with nasalized vowels, especially in the more careful speech of those who have a fair knowledge of the donor language: ɔ̀-yâ(n) "time" (< Shan), šā-lā-g̈ū(n) "doctor" (< Bs.), mɔ̄(n) "10,000" (< Thai < Chinese), gôšé(n) "Goshen" (< missionary Eng.). The nasalization is always optional in these cases, though occasionally it is favored in a certain context to avoid confusion with an otherwise homophonous native word. Thus the pair ɔ̀-yâ "child" / ɔ̀-yâ(n) "time" would be ambiguous in such sentences as ɔ̀-yâ cɔ̀ mâ ve lâ "Is there much time?"/"Do you have many children?"

Quite different is the phenomenon I have called *rhinoglottophilia* (Matisoff 1975): automatic, non-distinctive vowel nasalization in syllables beginning with *h*- or zero-consonant initial. This nasalization is particularly salient with the low non-front vowels /a ɔ/, and some speakers are more noticeably rhinoglottophiliac than others: ɔ́(n) "four," ɔ́(n)-qā "water buffalo," ɔ̀-hɔ́(n) "under," hɔ(n) "elephant," hɔ́(n)ʔ "to coil," hâ(n)ʔ-hâ(n)ʔ "quickly," etc. (As the last two examples show, this nasalization can occur simultaneously with the glottal occlusion characteristic of the stopped tones.) There is every reason to consider rhinoglottophilia to be grounded in universal articulatory fact – but at any rate it cannot be ascribed to sound symbolism.

The one type of syllable where nasalization has a genuine sound-symbolic value is in "vivid adverbials" (*GL*: 302–303). A few verbs are adverbializable by nasalizing their vowels and postposing the particle *kàʔ*:

ŋá   (V) "spread open" > ŋán kàʔ qay ve "go wide open"
mɛ̂ʔ-šī ŋán kà qay ò
"His eyes suddenly flew open!"

thê   (V) "straight" > thên kàʔ qay ve "go straight"
šɨ̂ʔ-cɛ̀ thên kàʔ qɔ̀ʔ qay ò
"The trees snapped back straight as arrows!"

Note that the dummy verb used after these adverbials is *qay* "go," as is the case with other types of onomatopes and attitudinals (section 9.4 above).

Japanese occasionally makes similar use of nasality in its expressive vocabulary, where it sometimes conveys an intensitive meaning:

zukizuki itamu   "have a throbbing (head)ache"
zukinzukin itamu   "have a throbbing splitting (head)ache"
(See Amanuma 1974: 168.)

9.6.6. *Echo-vowel adverbialization and secondary vowel length*[20]

Finally, Lahu has another class of *gitaigo*-like adverbials which are characterized by a lengthening of their last vowel to "a mora and a half," with the last segment usually ending up under the midtone. This secondary vowel-length is hard to hear (I was not aware of the phenomenon until my third field trip in 1977!), but there are firm examples with all nine vowels:

i	:	nɔ-vî-i	"light green"
ɨ	:	kɨ-chɨ̂ʔ-ɨ	"all scarred up"
u	:	qhò ʔ-tū-u	"emaciated"
e	:	qɛ̀ʔ-lè-e	"all scraped up"
ə	:	ɨ-ló-mə-ə̀	"grandiosely"
o	:	tɛ̀ʔ-pô ʔ-o	"stumpy, squat"
ɛ	:	šâʔ-qɛ̀-ɛ	"raspy-voiced"
a	:	chê-qâ-a	"too watery"
ɔ	:	phɨ̄-phɔ̀ʔ-ɔ	"grayish"

Again, the drawling or prolongation of the vowel has sound-symbolic significance, in the sense that it is consistently correlated with the expressive portion of the vocabulary, and occurs nowhere else.

9.7. The bulging monosyllable

As we have seen, there is no reason to feel sorry for the lean little monosyllables of languages like Lahu. They are actually teeming with the seeds of new life, bursting with all sorts of marginal phonetic features that are just waiting to be exploited and transphonologized. Many of these acquire sound-symbolic functions along the way.

Once all these ancillary phenomena worm their way into the core of the phonological system, an explosive critical mass may be reached. Then one had better watch out, because

the syllable canon goes *Boom!*

NOTES

* This paper was presented at the Conference on Sound Symbolism at U.C. Berkeley, January 16–17, 1986. It was first published as Matisoff 1989c.

1 Tone systems elsewhere in the world – e.g. Africa or Mesoamerica – are generally much more rudimentary, in the sense that there are fewer contrasts (often just a two-way high vs. low opposition), a high degree of predictability in terms of neighboring syllables or

position in the syntactic phrase, and/or a low functional load in distinguishing utterances. ("Pitch-accent" systems like that of Japanese are a limiting case.) Some Tibeto-Burman languages have intermediate systems, where the domain of tone is not the individual syllable but the dissyllabic word, i.e. there are fewer tone-pattern possibilities in dissyllables than the product of the possibilities in two separate monosyllabic words. One such language is Kham of Nepal (Watters 1985).

2 The terms *omnisyllabic*, *toniferous*, *Sinosphere*, and *Indosphere* are introduced in Matisoff (in prep.).

3 The first coherent explanation of these phenomena is due to Haudricourt 1954. The term *tonogenesis* itself was coined by Matisoff, and first appeared in print in 1970.

4 The term "feature shuffling" was introduced in Henderson 1985.

5 The transmutation of syllable-final stops into tonal features is a gradual and ongoing process in the Loloish languages. An original final oral stop may decay until it has even less occlusion than a glottal stop, becoming merely constriction or "creakiness" on the vowel; or it may ultimately leave no overt trace of its former stoppitude at all. This is what happened in the case of the Lahu high-rising tone, e.g. $cá^{35}$, which is now totally open, with no glottalization, but derives historically from syllables with final */-p -t -k/ under special conditions where "glottal dissimilation" applied (Matisoff 1970).

6 Chao did pioneering work in comparing intonational phenomena in tonal and non-tonal languages (cf. Chao 1932). A recent contrastive study by Shen Xiaonan (1985) compares Chinese and French interrogative intonation.

7 This interjection is borrowed from Thai *phút-thôo* "by the Buddha!" See Matisoff 1973b (hereafter *GL*): 37–38.

8 The mastery of this particle has an immediate payoff during my first period of fieldwork on Lahu in 1965. Before that time I had wondered why people were constantly barking [hâin ^{51}] at me whenever I tried to say anything! When I wanted to ask for a repetition myself I would painfully say something like [à-thò?-ma qô? ve le], literally "What are you saying?" which was so unidiomatic that people usually gave up, or at any rate resorted to a simpler paraphrase. Once I learned [hâin ^{51}], however, people automatically repeated what they had just said, in exactly the same words. This marked the beginning of the end of my intonational dependence on English.

9 See the section on "interjectory final unrestricted particles" in *GL*: 383–384.

10 We do not of course wish to claim that the existence of this type of particle is restricted to omnisyllabic tone languages. Japanese not only has an interrogative particle *ka*, but also a number of purely affective final particles that are fully syllabic (*wa, yo, sa, ze, zo, na*). Yet it seems safe to say that the proliferation of these entities is especially characteristic of the tonal languages of Southeast Asia.

11 Though certain phonemes (e.g. Japanese *p-*) occur here with much higher frequency than in normal vocabulary. Some Mon-Khmer languages appear to have even richer sound-symbolic systems, to the point where it is claimed that their "expressive vocabulary" is *non-discrete* – i.e. freely inventable by native speakers via "analog" rather than "digital" processes, so that it would be impossible to list "all" of them in any dictionary. See Diffloth 1976.

12 Such diachronically secondary, and thus synchronically rare, tones include Jingpho falling tone /ˆ/, and Burmese creaky tone /'/, both of which figure prominently in morphophonemic processes. (See Matisoff 1974 and Thurgood 1981.) This phenomenon

is reminiscent of the generalization of Germanic umlaut to be the marker of such grammatical processes as pluralization or diminutivization.
13 Tones may be lexically rare (i.e. occurrent in few lexical items) but textually quite frequent (if they occur e.g. in a few particles or other high-frequency morphemes).
14 Other allofams of this etymon include *dza and *tsa. See Benedict 1972: 27, 30, 100, 111, 154, 158, 169, 188, 189.
15 Lahu does have a marginal distinction between long and short vowels, including -i vs. -i -i, though this is restricted to "echo-vowel adverbials" (see section 9.6.6).
16 As illustrated by the examples to follow, the mid-central vowel /ə/ admits only the more-fused palatal suffix /-əy/. The combination */əE/ seems not to occur at all in Lahu.
17 E.g. in Japanese baby-talk, where [ch] is systematically substituted for [s], as in *chiichai* "teeny-weeny" (< *chiisai* "little"), *-chan* "affectionate suffix" (< *-san* "honorific suffix"), as in *Áya-chan* "little Miss Aya."
18 This discussion supersedes the treatment in *GL* (p. 19) and in Matisoff 1989a (pp. 169–170). In the latter article (which was actually written in 1980 though not published until 1989) the palatal element of these diphthongs is referred to unrevealingly as "a meaningless extrusion or extension from the original nuclear monophthong ... a benign bulging of the syllable's substance." In general, I now feel my previous treatments of this phenomenon to have been ass-backward: instead of referring to "pre-labialized" vocalic nuclei, I should have considered them to be "post-palatalized."
19 In this respect Lahu nasalized vowels are quite different from those of Modern Burmese, which do indeed go back to earlier syllable-final nasal consonants.
20 These echo-vowel adverbials are discussed at length in Matisoff 1989a.

REFERENCES

Amanuma, Y. 1974. *Giongo-Gitaigo Jiten* (Dictionary of Onomatopes and Attitudinals). Tokyo: Tokyodo Publishing Co. (In Japanese.)

Benedict, P. K. 1972. *Sino-Tibetan: a Conspectus*. Contributing editor, James A. Matisoff. Cambridge: University Press.

Chao, Y. R. 1932. A preliminary study of English intonation (with American variants) and its Chinese equivalents. *Bulletin of the Institute of History and Philology*, Academia Sinica, Supplement I: 105–156.

Diffloth, G. 1976. Expressives in Semai. In P. N. Jenner, L. C. Thompson, and S. Starosta (eds.) *Austroasiatic Studies*, Part I. Honolulu: University Press of Hawaii, 249–264.

Haudricourt, A.-G. 1954. De l'origine des tons en viêtnamien. *Journal Asiatique* 242: 68–82.

Henderson, E. J. A. 1985. Feature shuffling in Southeast Asian languages. In Suriya Ratanakul et al. (eds.) *Southeast Asian Linguistic Studies, Presented to A-G. Haudricourt*. Bangkok: Mahidol University.

Matisoff, J. A. 1970. Glottal dissimilation and the Lahu high-rising tone: a tonogenetic case-study. *Journal of the American Oriental Society* 90(1): 13–44.

——— 1973a. "Tonogenesis in Southeast Asia." In Larry M. Hyman, ed., *Consonant Types and*

Tone, Southern California Occasional Papers in Linguistics, no. 1, pp. 71–95. Los Angeles: University of Southern California.

1973b. *The Grammar of Lahu.* (*GL*). University of California Publications in Linguistics, no. 75. Berkeley and Los Angeles: University of California Press. (Reprinted 1982.)

1974. The tones of Jinghpaw and Lolo-Burmese: common origin vs. independent development. *Acta Linguistica Hafniensia* (Copenhagen) 15.2: 153–212.

1975. Rhinoglottophilia: the mysterious connection between nasality and glottality. In C. M. Ferguson, L. M. Hyman, and J. J. Ohala (eds.) *Nasálfest: Papers from a Symposium on Nasals and Nasalization*. Stanford, California. 265–287.

1979. Trickster and the village women: a psychosymbolic discourse analysis of a Lahu picaresque story. In *Proceedings of the Fifth Meeting of the Berkeley Linguistic Society*: 593–636.

1988. *The Dictionary of Lahu*. University of California Publications in Linguistics, no. 111. Berkeley and Los Angeles: University of California Press.

1989a. The bulging monosyllable, or the mora the merrier: echo-vowel adverbialization in Lahu. In J. H. C. S. Davidson (ed.) *Southeast Asian Linguistics: Essays in Honour of Eugénie J. A. Henderson*. London: School of Oriental and African Studies, 163–197.

1989b. The three palatal suffixes of Sino-Tibetan. Paper presented at the 21st International Conference on Sino-Tibetan Languages and Linguistics. Honolulu.

1989c. Tone, intonation, and sound symbolism in Lahu; loading the syllable canon. *Linguistics of the Tibeto-Burman Area* 12(2): 147–163.

(in prep.) *The Languages of Mainland Southeast Asia*. Cambridge: University Press.

Shen Xiaonan. 1985. A contrastive study of Mandarin Chinese and French interrogative intonologies – a contribution to the prosody of Chinese. PhD dissertation, University of California at Berkeley.

Thurgood, G. 1981. *Notes on the Origins of Burmese Creaky Tone*. Monumenta Serindica no. 9. Tokyo: Institute for the Study of the Languages and Cultures of Asia and Africa.

Watters, D. E. 1985. Emergent word tone in Kham: a Tibeto-Burman halfway house. *Linguistics of the Tibeto-Burman Area* 8(2): 36–54.

10
An experimental investigation into phonetic symbolism as it relates to Mandarin Chinese[1]

RANDY J. LAPOLLA

10.1. Introduction

10.1.1. General

About the time Plato was writing *Cratylus*, in which the protagonist argues that the relationship of sign to signified was one of object to imitation (Fowler 1977), that is, less than arbitrary, discussion of this question was also going on in China, especially among the Confucianists. The Chinese, in general, came to a different conclusion than Plato's Cratylus. The writer who spoke most directly to this question was Xun Zi (d. 221 BC) (Hong 1982). He felt that an object and its name had a totally arbitrary relationship, that no name was any more "suitable" than any other, that all names are "suitable" only as a result of convention and popular usage. Though there were some Chinese philosophers (from the Han Dynasty on) who attempted to find the *true* sound–meaning correspondences for words, going against Xun Zi's principle of non-suitability of names, the mainstream of Chinese linguistics to this day still does not really question the concept of total arbitrariness. Almost all of the general books on linguistics now in use in the People's Republic (e.g. Gao and Shi 1963; Ye and Xu 1981; Ma 1981) use the same quote from Xun Zi and another, from *Capital*, where Karl Marx says "The name of a thing is entirely external to its nature" (Fowkes 1977: 195).

In the West, although Saussure felt that "No one disputes the principle of the arbitrary nature of the [linguistic] sign" (1966: 68), there have been many since that time who have tried to show that the assignment of signifier to signified is not always completely arbitrary. Jespersen (1922) went to great lengths to show that among the languages he was familiar with there were definite correlations between certain types of sounds and certain categories of meaning, such as size, movement, feelings, and distances. Jespersen also felt that people have an instinctive feeling for what are the best sounds for the different meanings in each category.

10.1.2. Experimentation

Much of the debate between those who support the idea of sound symbolism and those who do not, and between those who support its universality and those who do not, has centered around methodology of experimentation.

Sapir (1929) was the first to try to prove the latter of Jespersen's hypotheses experimentally (particularly a feeling for "large" and "small" among English speakers), and was followed by Newman (1933), who tried to support Sapir's findings and expand on them by including the feeling for "bright" and "dark," and by examining the lexicon for sound–meaning correspondences. Though these two studies came under some criticism, the conclusions they felt their results led to set the tone for much of the discussion of sound symbolism that has taken place since that time. The five conclusions they drew were that

(1) Phonetic elements tend to be rigidly patterned on a non-linguistic symbolic scale ... (2) The factor of age ... has little effect on the subjective scale ... (3) The basis of phonetic symbolism is fundamentally objective ... (4) Diverse types of phonetic patterns are formed by unlike symbolisms[2] ... (5) These symbolic judgements are not produced by linguistic associations (Newman 1933: 75).

Since that time there have been some experimental investigations that have claimed to have disproved the theory of sound symbolism (Bentley and Varon 1933; Maltzman et al. 1956; Brackbill and Little 1957), but these results can often be explained as being due to important procedural problems (Brown and Nuttall 1959; Weiss 1963).

Starting with Brown et al. in 1955, a ten-year debate on the pros and cons of various types of methodology of experimentation and evaluation of results ran through the *Journal of Abnormal and Social Psychology* and later the *Psychological Bulletin* (Brackbill and Little; Brown and Nuttall 1959; Miron 1961; Weiss 1963; Taylor 1963; Weiss 1964; Johnson et al. 1964; Taylor and Taylor 1965), but no agreement on the best method was reached.

At least ten experiments have been done on sound symbolism using either the Chinese language (Mandarin) or Chinese subjects. (Sapir 1929;[3] Brown et al. 1955; Brackbill and Little 1957; Brown and Nuttall 1959; Weiss 1963; Huang et al. 1968; Tsien-Lee 1969; Klank et al. 1971; Lester 1973, 1974.) Of these, nine had results supporting the sound-symbolism hypothesis, and only one (Brackbill and Little 1957) had results which did not support the hypothesis. With all of these experiments I believe there were problems of methodology and procedure serious enough to warrant a new set of experiments.

10.1.3 Tonal morphology

10.1.3.1 Monosyllabic

A distinctive feature of a large group of languages, including many Southeast Asian languages and several Chinese dialects in the southeastern part of China, is the use of tone change to mark morphological or semantic change. Though this use of tone is not always limited to marking the hypocoristic or diminutive,[4] this is one of its more common uses. This is true of Lahu, Yi (Lolo),[5] and the Hui, Wu (that of southern Zhejiang), and Yue dialect groups of Chinese (Hirata 1983). In the Canton dialect (one of the Yue dialects), for example, which is one of the most representative and best attested of the Chinese dialects using tone change to mark the hypocoristic, a change to a high level or high rising tone is used to mark the diminutive or familiar.[6]

In standard Mandarin Chinese the hypocoristic of nouns is marked only with the affixation of a retroflex suffix,[7] with no change in the original tone. Even so, if there is a universal tendency to associate high frequency with "smallness" (the diminutive in general), then Mandarin speakers also should be sensitive to tone differences such as those in Cantonese.[8]

10.1.3.2. Disyllabic

A second use of the change to a high tone in Cantonese is to change the intensity of reduplicated adjectives. This can be done to different degrees depending on which syllable the changed tone is assigned to. Lengthening of the vowel is also used for extreme intensification. For example, [hong^{21}] "red" can be modified to [ho:ng^{35} hong^{21}] "very red" or [hong^{21} hong^{35} tei^{35}] "a little red."[9] (Yue-Hashimoto 1972: 95; Whitaker 1955–1956: 31) The first type of tone change is also obligatory on the first syllable of a three-syllable adjective formed by reduplication of the first syllable of a disyllabic adjective for the purpose of intensification, as in [søn^{35} søn^{21} pan^{35}] "very good tempered" from [søn^{21} pan^{35}] "good tempered." The second type of tone change is possible for onomatopoeic (either in the metaphysical or real sense) phrases with an initial reduplicated syllable, as in [lap^{33} lap^{35} lyn^{33}] "disorderly"[10] (Yue-Hasimoto 1972: 95).

The change of the first syllable to a high tone is obligatory when reduplication is used for extreme intensification, and can apply to syllables in all of the nine tones of Cantonese because of the lengthening of the syllables. The tone change in the second type of reduplication, though, is optional, and can only apply to syllables with low tones (Yue-Hashimoto 1972: 99). Because with the tone change the resulting tone pattern (i.e. low-high) is the same as that for familiarity, it is possible that the changed form is less intense or serious, as with the phrase [t'an^{21} t'an^{35} tsan^{44}] "shivering," because the change puts it in the field of the hypocoristic. It is also the case, in Thai and the Hainan form of the Southern Min dialect of Chinese, that modification of the first syllable of a reduplicated adjective by raising the tone and often lengthening the vowel is used for the purpose of intensification. In Thai, there is [dii^{55} dii^{33}] "very good," from [dii^{33}] "good" (Li 1977: 8; Haas 1946: 128–30), and in Hainan Chinese there is [bui^{55} bui^{33}] "very fat" from [bui^{33}] "fat" (Woon 1979: 87). According to Lien Chinfa (personal communication), this is also the case in mainland Southern Min.

What is significant in all these languages is that for extreme intensification, modification must be of the first syllable and the resulting tone pattern is high-low.[11] In Cantonese and in Thai, other types of adverbial compounds or marked disyllabic words will be marked by modification of the second syllable, so generally have a low-high tone pattern. In Cantonese this is also the case for marking familiarity, especially family relation terms, such as [pa^{22} pa^{55}] "daddy" or [mui^{22} mui^{35}] "sis" (Gao 1980: 22–23).

In Mandarin, the tone on the second token of a reduplicated adjective changes to a high level (55) tone, but this change of tone is not usually thought to be semantically significant. Although this is probably the case, I wanted to see if native Mandarin speakers would also be sensitive to the tone pattern-to-meaning correspondences in Cantonese.

10.1.4. The hypotheses

The hypotheses we attempted to test in this investigation are similar to those tested by other researchers: (1) that English speakers should have better-than-chance-expectancy success at matching Chinese antonymic word pairs, thereby showing that Chinese exhibits sound-symbolic patterns which are perceptible to English monolingual speakers, and (2) that Chinese native speakers would have enough of a common innate sense of sound–meaning correspondences to give a common pattern of responses when asked to assign meanings to sounds.

10.1.5. General methodology

The method we used in the first experiment of the investigation was one of those that is generally most supported, matching antonymic pairs, being careful to eliminate or reduce any of those factors that have been called into question.[12] But for one part of the investigation using Chinese subjects (Experiment 2, Part a), we used a new method that gave the subjects much more freedom in making sound–meaning choices, while at the same time allowing us to analyze the choices into grave and non-grave segments, a key parameter of sound symbolism (Jakobson 1978).

10.2. Experiment 1

10.2.1. Method

10.2.1.1. Part a

The first part of the first experiment was designed to test the ability of native English speakers who had never been exposed to Chinese to match the correct word out of a pair of antonymic Chinese words and the written English translation of one of them. A significant number of correct answers would point to the existence of sound-symbolic patterns in the Chinese lexicon, and would also be evidence that English speakers are sensitive to them.

A list of 40 English words that are members of common antonymic pairs was given to each of the subjects.[13] Beside each word were the numbers 1 and 2, and the word "neither."[14] A tape recording of a list of antonymic pairs that were the Chinese equivalents of each English word and its commonly accepted antonym, spoken by a native speaker of Mandarin from Taipei,[15] was played for the subjects. Each pair was spoken with two seconds between the members of the pair, and there was a five-second pause between pairs. The subjects were asked to circle 1 or 2, depending upon which word of each antonymic Chinese pair they thought had the same meaning as the English word given, or "neither," if they felt that neither of the words "felt right." They were told that some pairs might be similar in meaning to other pairs, but to judge each pair separately. The word list used, and the Chinese words[16] spoken for each item, are given in table 10.1.

The Chinese words were spoken because giving a romanized transliteration of the Chinese words would not give linguistically naive subjects a good idea of what the sound was really like, especially the tone. This could also lead to the subjects matching the words because of orthographic similarities.

Only one English word was given for each pair, for three reasons. First, it simplified the answering process for the subject, comparing one word with two instead of two with two. Second, it reduced the possibility of the subject just matching up the vowels of one or both of the English words with that/those of the Chinese words, or basing his/her choice on the English–Chinese pair that was not being asked for.[17] Third, it allowed us to use the other half of some of the English pairs later on in the test, with the same Chinese pair, either in the same order or not, depending on randomization. This third point was analyzed separately, and used as a kind of double check. Since the subjects were told that many pairs were possibly somewhat synonymous, they might not have noticed the same pair being given twice. If they did not notice, but got the correct answer on both, then it would reinforce the findings of the experiment; if they did not notice and had opposite results for the two times a pair was used, then any positive results would be cast in doubt. To find out if the subject noticed or not, the question was asked at

Table 10.1 *The antonymic pairs tested*

ugly	měi	chǒu	cold	lěng	rè
long	duǎn	cháng	shallow	shēn	qián
many	duō	shǎo	concentrated	dàn	nóng
thick	báo	hòu	micro	wēi	jù
big	dà	xiǎo	friend	dí	yǒu
sharp	ruì	dùn	few	shǎo	duō
bright	liàng	àn	small	xiǎo	dà
coarse	xì	cū	narrow	kuān	zhǎi
fat	pàng	shòu	hard	yìng	ruǎn
soft	ruǎn	yìng	skinny	shòu	pàng
heavy	zhòng	qīng	macro	jù	wēi
weak	qiáng	ruò	strong	ruò	qiáng
wide	zhǎi	kuān	hot	rè	lěng
tall	gāo	ǎi	diluted	nóng	dàn
fast	kuài	màn	thin	hòu	báo
drunk	xǐng	zuì	short	ǎi	gāo
joy	xǐ	bēi	high	gāo	dī
dry	gān	shī	fine	cū	xì
low	dī	gāo	slow	màn	kuài
quiet	xuān	jìng	sorrow	bēi	xǐ

the end of the test: "Did you feel any of the separate pairs you heard on the tape was the same as any other pair, though possibly not with the same internal order? If so, which ones?"

10.2.1.2. Part b

For the second part of the first experiment, a second group of ten native English speakers was given the same test as in Part a, except that a second recording, using a different native Mandarin speaker from Taiwan,[18] was made in which the tones were reversed on the words in those pairs whose members differed in tone. This was done to see if the tones of the words could have been instrumental in the choices made by the first group of subjects.[19] This is of course assuming that the second group of English speakers would have roughly the same results as the first group if given the exact same test.

10.2.2. Results

The number of right and wrong answers[20] from Part a out of the total non-"neither" responses were calculated and are presented in line 1 of table 10.2. The

Table 10.2 *Results of Experiment 1*

Type	No. of responses	Right	Wrong	
Part a	359	190	169	($p < 0.30$)
Part b	337	187	150	($p < 0.05$)

Table 10.3 *Comparison of items from Parts a and b*

word	Part a	Part b	Part a result	Part b result
big	dà	dǎ	9/0	4/4
coarse	cū	cù	6/2	9/0
soft	ruǎn	ruàn	9/1	2/6
wide	kuān	kuǎn	1/8	6/1

subjects in general only noticed one or two repetitions, and were not sure which ones had been repeated, so it seems this did not interfere with the results. The number of correct answers was approximately the same for both halves of those antonymic pairs that were split up and tested separately.

The results for Part b, calculated the same way as for Part a, are given in line 2 of Table 10.2.

These results tell us that tone could have been an important criterion for the subjects' judgments.[21] It seems here that the change in tone made it easier for the subjects to pick the correct Chinese word. This could mean either that the tones assigned to some words are not the ideal ones from an English speaker's point of view, or that something about the difference between the two recordings or the two groups of subjects influenced the results.

For some pairs the difference before and after the tone switch was quite startling. Table 10.3 contains some of the pairs that experienced the biggest change in response. The number to the left of the slash in each column is the number of right responses, and to the right is the number of wrong responses.

Some of the differences here match up with the results from Part a of Experiment 2 (see 10.3.2.1): as the high level tone is favored for the "small" category, the better scores for *coarse* and *wide* follow logically. The results for *big* also follow logically from our results showing a preference for the falling tone for the "big" category, but for *soft*, the effect is the opposite. The better score for *soft* before the change to a falling tone seems to contradict the tendency for the use of the falling tone for "big" category words, unless the "big" category is not a monolith, and can be subdivided into several different semantic subgroupings, such as "soft," "warm," and "big." In this case, it seems the falling tone might be less suitable for those words connoting softness.

10.3. Experiment 2

10.3.1. Method

10.3.1.1. Part a

The second experiment was designed to test the subjective sensitivity of Chinese speakers to sound symbolism. In Part a, a list of 48 English words that are all members of antonymic evaluative pairs[22] was printed on the answer sheets, with a blank line next to each word. A separate group of 50 nonsense syllables was taken from a list of all possible Chinese syllable types (from Zhong 1980) and printed in five columns of ten words each. They were chosen because they were simple CV syllables, with the vowels all monophthongs and the consonants all stops or fricatives, all of which could be easily classified as [± nasal] and/or [± grave]. No recording was made of the words.

The subjects were five native Mandarin-speaking graduate students from Taiwan. They were instructed: "Please say these words to yourself, then assign these words to the meanings given on the answer sheet, based only on how appropriate you feel they sound for the given meaning. Also assign tones to the words, based on the same criterion."

10.3.1.2. Part b

For Part b, a list of 25 Cantonese words or phrases was compiled from Chao 1947, Whitaker 1955–1956, Yue-Hashimoto 1972, and Kam 1977, from their lists of words and phrases that can be either made diminutive/familiar or, in the case of adjectives and adverbs, changed with regard to intensity by a change in the pronunciation to a high- or high-rising tone. Questions were then formed to contrast the semantic differences between the minimal pairs. Each question was then recorded (spoken by myself), followed by the relevant minimal pair, the order having been randomized, spoken by a native speaker of Cantonese from Hong Kong.[23] The subjects, all native Mandarin speakers from Beijing or Taiwan who had no knowledge of Cantonese, were told that they would hear a tape of Cantonese words, and that they should answer only "A" or "B" after hearing each pair, based on which one they thought was the best answer to the question asked.

10.3.2. Results

10.3.2.1. Part a

The 48 English words used for this part of the experiment were divided into "small" category words and "big" category words. Out of the total 210 choices (initial and vowel) made by the subjects for the "big" category words, grave segments were chosen 151 times, much greater than chance probability ($p < 0.001$), but for the "small" category words, grave segments were chosen only 103 times, no better than chance probability. The number of grave initials and grave vowels chosen by the subjects for each category are given in table 10.4.

The results show a clear tendency on the part of the subjects to assign grave consonants and vowels to "big" category meanings, and not to the "small" category meanings. This agrees with the findings of Solomon 1959: 494, which showed that subjects' judgments of "heavy" or "high magnitude" relate to the lower octave bands, while judgments of "light" or "low magnitude" relate to the higher octave bands. It also correlates well with the findings of Huang *et al.* 1969, which showed that when asked to produce words meaning "large" or "small," subjects produced words that overwhelmingly favored the acute vowels for "small" and grave vowels for "large."

Two other measurements were done, one on the nasals and one on the tones. A count of the number and type of nasal used for each category is given in table 10.5.

From this table we can see that the subjects made a clear choice of the grave nasal for the "big" category, and the acute nasal for the "small" category.

The number of times each tone was used for each category is given in table 10.6. The numbers 1, 2, 3, 4, and 5 refer to the high level, high-rising, falling-rising, falling, and neutral tones respectively.

We can see at least two tendencies here. One is the preferred use of the high level tone for the "small" category meanings, and the other is the preferred use of the falling tone for the "big" category meanings.

It is interesting to note that the tendency on the part of the subjects to use the high-level and falling tones more than the other tones correlates well with the findings of Yue-Hashimoto 1980 and Li and Thompson 1977. These studies showed that the high-level and the falling are the first two tones to be mastered by a child learning to speak Mandarin as its native language. Tse (1977) has reported that for Cantonese speakers as well, the high-level tone is the first to be acquired. It would be hard to determine if this is because this tone is easier to learn and produce (the "Difficulty Hypothesis"[24] of Li and Thompson), or because it is compatible with the size and defenselessness of the child (see discussion of "frequency code" below).

Table 10.4 *Analysis of grave segments*

Type	No. of responses	Grave initial	Grave vowel
big	105	71	80
small	105	52	51

Table 10.5 *Comparison of nasals*

Type	No. of responses	No. of [m]	No. of [n]	
big	23	17	6	($p < 0.01$)
small	29	9	20	($p < 0.01$)

Table 10.6 *Results for each tone-type*

	N	1(55)	2(35)	3(214)	4(51)	5(var.)	
big	105	13.3	16.2	15.2	50.5	4.8	($p < 0.001$)
small	105	35.2	16.2	16.2	20.9	11.4	($p < 0.01$)

10.3.2.2. Part b

To analyze the results of this part of the experiment, the questions were divided into four types, depending on what was being tested: (a) the hypocoristic (i.e. size-to-sound and monosyllabic familiarity); (b) "onomatopoeic" intensification; (c) disyllabic familiarity; and (d) intensification of reduplicated adverbs. Out of the 150 responses to type (a) questions, 87 were the same as they would be for a native Cantonese speaker (the definition of "correct") ($p = 0.05$). If we break this down into the subtypes, we see that of the size-to-sound responses, only 51 out of 100 were correct. Of the 50 responses to the questions testing monosyllabic familiarity, 36 were correct ($p < 0.01$).

Fifteen responses out of the twenty for type (b) pointed to a feeling on the part of the subjects that the unmodified form was the more intense of the two ($p < 0.05$). As I pointed out in section 10.1.3.2, this is the same for some native Cantonese speakers. Twenty-one of the 40 responses were correct for type (c).

The results for type (d) were much more straightforward and strongly support the universality of the feeling for the high-low pattern as an extreme intensive. Thirty-four of the 40 responses were correct ($p < 0.001$).

10.4. Discussion

I would like to explain these results by reference to the "frequency code" theory as developed in Ohala 1982a, 1982b, 1982c, 1983, 1986, and Morton 1977. As mentioned in the introduction of this volume, "frequency code" refers to the universal communication of size by frequency between vocalizing animals in close-contact competitive encounters. In such an encounter, an aggressor would try to make itself seem as large as possible to intimidate its opponent into submission. If this were successful, the opponent would try to make itself seem as small and unthreatening as possible, sometimes even acting infantile, to avoid being hurt. One of the ways for both sides to achieve their different ends would be by altering the frequency of their vocalizations. By using low-frequency, staccato vocalizations, the aggressor makes himself seem larger and more threatening, as generally the larger any object or animal is, the lower and more irregular the sound it will emit. In the same way, an animal that wants to capitulate needs to appear non-threatening, so would use high-frequency, tone-like vocalizations to appear smaller or infant-like. This code is not something that is learned, but is innate (Morton 1977, 1986).

In human language there is a universal use of similar pitch contours for statements and questions that are not lexically or syntactically marked (Bolinger 1964, 1978). Many languages also use high pitch for polite speech (Brown and Levinson 1987: 267–268). Just as an animal seeks to mollify its opponent by using a high-pitch tone-like cry, it is possible that human languages use a high or rising pitch for questions and polite speech because in asking a question, or in being polite, the speaker defers to the addressee, in a sense admitting that the other party is stronger, at least as regards the situation or topic of conversation. The other part's answer is in a falling-pitch pattern, again to reflect this power relationship. Friendliness is also shown by using high-frequency (especially low-high) patterns more, to show that the speaker is not a threat to the other party.

We have seen from the results of these experiments that there is a cross-linguistic tendency toward associating acute segments with "small" category words, and grave segments with "big" category words. As acute sounds have energy largely in the high frequencies, and grave sounds mostly in the low, this could be related to the "small" ~ high frequency and "big" ~ low frequency relationships mentioned above. Just as objects and animals emit sounds of different frequency corresponding to their sizes, it seems natural that people, by extension, would name these things, or adjectives of size, etc., according to the same criterion.

This theory does much to explain some heretofore unexplainable facts of nature and language, such as the origin of the smile and some other facial features (Ohala 1980), the reason for sexual dimorphism in the vocal anatomy of many species of vocalizing animals and birds (Ohala 1983, 1986), and size–sound symbolism in language (Ohala 1982a, 1982b, 1982c, 1983, 1986). This could also help explain the more frequent use of rising intonation in "women's speech" (Lakoff 1975: 17) and why, as Whitaker (1955–1956) and Haas (1946: 130) have pointed out for Cantonese and Thai respectively, women are more likely than men to use the changed tone patterns in optional cases. The fact that the changed tone form of Cantonese is used more frequently in informal speech (Wong 1982) might also be explained by reference to this.

This theory does not explain everything to do with sound symbolism, though, such as why *soft* is usually grouped with the "big" category words. It may be (as mentioned in section 10.2.2) that the "big" category is not a monolith, but is comprised of smaller categories that overlap in their use of sounds, even if the source of the sound–meaning correspondence is very different. This would be the case, for example, if *soft* became associated with grave sounds because the sound of a mother's heartbeat that a fetus or infant hears is a low non-tone-like sound.[25] For many vocalizing animals and birds, the mother's call to the young is a low soft sound. For some of these creatures there is a change in voice quality (to soft) and/or a drop in the pitch of the voice of the female that accompanies the birth of the young (Collias 1960).

The relationship of amplitude and pitch, and other related questions, could be solved with enough research. It would be interesting to do further experimentation to see if, as reported in Hata 1983, some phonetic features have tighter sound–meaning correlations than others, and also to repeat these experiments using color terms (cf. Solomon 1959; Fischer-Jørgensen 1978).

NOTES

1 I would like to thank Leanne Hinton, Robert Blust, John J. Ohala and Johanna Nichols for valuable comments on earlier versions of this paper, and Jing Fang Wang for her help on the experiments.

2 Points (3) and (4) are based on the experimenters' attempt to explain their findings using either the kinesthetic factors of articulation, acoustics, or a combination of the two.

3 Sapir used seven Chinese subjects for his experiments, but did not give any more information about them (such as age, native dialect, time in US, etc.) other than the fact that they were "Chinese." (Li Fang-Kuei, personal communication, has informed me that he was one of the seven Chinese subjects.) He gives the age and status, but not the race or nationality, of his other subjects. The results for the seven Chinese subjects were not included in the general results, but were reported to be similar to those for the other subjects.

4 For a discussion of the different uses of tone change in Cantonese other than for the hypocoristic, see Kam 1977 and 1980.

5 In Lahu there are two parts to making the diminutive-extensive: affixation of a non-low unrounded front vowel, and a change of tone from the mid level (33) (tones here are

marked with the five-point scale first introduced in Chao 1930) tone of the neutral extensive to the high-rising (45) tone of the diminutive-extensive, e.g.

[chi^{33} hi^{33}] "this size" – [chi^{33} hii^{45}] "such a small one" (Matisoff 1973: 18).

In Yi, there is a raising of tone and a devoicing of some vowels to mark the hypocoristic, e.g.

[a^{11} mæ^{33} zu^{11}] "a girl" (you do not particularly like) – [a^{11} mæ^{55} zu^{33}] "a small girl" (you like). (Ma Xueliang, personal communication.)

6 Cf. Solomon 1959: 496, which showed that for the subjects of that experiment, "sounds with energy concentrated in the lower octave bands are reliably judged as 'strange' ... while sounds with energy concentrated in the higher octave bands are judged 'familiar'."

7 For discussion of the relationship of the retroflex final to the changed tone and the possible source of the changed tone, see Kam 1980; Chao 1945; Hirata 1983; Whitaker 1955–1956; and Wong 1982.

8 It is interesting to note the differences in the tone systems of the two languages. In Cantonese, there are three pitch levels that are significant, and most of the tones are in the lower two levels. Gandour (1981) has shown that contour and direction, in general, are more salient features than height for native speakers' distinguishing of the different tones in Cantonese. This is contrary to the findings of Vance 1976, but is logical given the closeness in register of the four non-stopped low tones. For showing markedness, though, the most salient feature of the changed tones is the change from [– high] to [+ high]. This correlates well with two of Maddieson's universals of tone: "3. Phonetically Central tones are unmarked, Extreme tones are highly marked ... 4. Systems in which high tones are marked are more frequent than systems in which low tones are marked" (Maddieson 1978: 341–342). This is reflected also in the fact that the low tones are statistically more likely to undergo this change (Wong 1982). In Mandarin, though it is possible to see the third tone as a low tone (Hashimoto 1981), register is not very important, possibly because all of the tones can at some point in their production be in the [+ high] register. This is supported by the findings of Victor Zue (reported in Klatt 1973), where even when compressed into a four-kHz range the tones on synthetic Mandarin syllables were judged correctly by the subjects 90% of the time. Even when compressed to two kHz the level and the falling tone were still judged correctly, while the other two tones were confused. Wu (1984) also showed that register was not necessary in an autosegmental analysis of Mandarin tones.

9 According to Samuel H-N. Cheung (personal communication), there is another type of modification of some adjectives using reduplication of an onomatopoeic syllable after the adjective. With this type of modification, a reduplicated high-tone onomatopoeic syllable will usually give the adjective positive connotations, and a low-tone syllable will give the adjective negative connotations, as in [fei^{21} tyt^{55} tyt^{55}] "plump" or "fat (like a nice fat baby)" and [fei^{21} than^{21} than^{21}] "fat" (as a derogatory reference to fat people).

10 According to Whitaker (1955–1956), there is an intensified form of this phrase, with the tone change on the first syllable, but it is not a reduplicated form: [lap^{35} kam^{33} lyn^{33}] "very disorderly."

11 It could be argued that these languages are all related, but as Haas (1946: 130) points out, high-low tone is also used by some speakers of English. She gives the example of

Louisiana, where adjectives such as "good" can be intensified by reduplication where the first syllable is lengthened and its tone is raised, as in *goo-ood good*. In English the low-high pattern for familiarity (especially when talking to babies) is also very common.

12 See Gebels 1969 for a discussion of some of the possible problems associated with this methodology.

13 The words were actually 25 pairs of antonyms split up, with redemption of 15 out of the 25 semantic fields represented by the 25 pairs. The words were chosen from Brown *et al.* 1955, and Lu 1981. Some of the pairs Brown used, such as "many~one," are not normal antonymic pairs, and so were not used.

14 The subjects were given the choice "neither," so that they would not be forced into making choices they were not comfortable with. As even proponents of the theory of phonetic symbolism do not claim that all words are symbolic, I feel allowing the subjects this option is necessary. After running these experiments I came across an interesting study by Asher Koriat (1975) that took the subjects' "feeling of knowing" into account by asking them to rate how certain they felt about each choice they made. The findings show that there was an awareness on the part of the subjects of phonetic symbolism, so the choices with the higher confidence scores were also the ones judged correctly most often. It is suggested that these higher scores are the more relevant ones. If I were to do these experiments over, I would also use the confidence-rating test instead of giving the "neither" choice.

15 I do not feel that having a native speaker (not connected with the experiment) say the words could possibly undermine the results of the experiment. If the native speaker (unaware of the purpose of the experiment) emphasizes those aspects of the speech sounds s/he feels most crucial to correct perception of the meaning of the word, such as those mentioned by Jespersen (1922), and the subjects respond to the same parameters, then this is further proof of the universality and direction of phonetic symbolism. It would be possible to do a test just asking speakers to emphasize or de-emphasize certain words, to see what sounds they change and in what way. The recreation in English of *tini* [tini] after the Great Vowel Shift changed *tiny* [tini] to [taini], and the creation of words like *humongous* from *huge* probably reflect this tendency to emphasize certain sounds for certain meanings. It would also be interesting to see, if sound changes diffuse across a lexicon, as discussed by Chen and Wang (1974) and Wang (1979), whether or not sound-symbolic words would be more resistant than non-sound-symbolic words to any change that would make them less sound-symbolic. This might partially explain why some words would undergo a certain sound change earlier than others.

16 The Chinese is given in pinyin romanization. The tone symbols are ā high level, á rising, ǎ falling-rising, and à falling.

17 For example, if I wanted the meaning of the italicized word in a pair, such as "*beautiful*~ugly" Chinese "měi~chòu," I might get the right answer not because the subject felt there was a relationship between "beautiful" and "měi," but because he felt one between "ugly" and "chou." This could still happen using our methodology, but we are attempting to reduce the likelihood of it happening.

18 Ideally, the original native speaker should have been used for both of the recordings, but this was not possible.

19 Given enough time and subjects, this second part could have been repeated two or three more times, each time reversing a different set of segments (such as the initials) to see

which segments and which position in the syllable structure has the greatest effect on the subjects' choice.

20 Here "right" represents the subject's picking the correct segmental form with the altered tone, and "wrong" represents the opposite case.

21 This contradicts the findings of Lester 1974, though as Lester's test presented the subjects with English words and Chinese tone marks written on paper, I do not feel the results can be valid.

22 The list was the same as that for the base list in Experiment 1, but without the pair "wet~dry" (left out because I wasn't sure how to analyse these words in terms of "big"~"small"). Fifty Chinese syllables were used because this was the number of syllables in Chinese that fit the criteria. English was used, and not Chinese characters, to diminish the chance that the subjects would match up sound and character.

23 There is no difference in this aspect between the Canton dialect and the Hong Kong dialect (Kam 1977; Cheung 1969).

24 If the "Difficulty Hypothesis" is valid, the use of the high-rising tone for markedness could possibly be explained by reference to the relative difficulty of producing it, as a tone that is more difficult to produce might seem less natural, and so therefore marked. As Gandour (1977: 60) has reported that it is natural for syllables with low tones to be longer than syllables with high tones, the lengthening of the initial syllable that accompanies the change in tone for extreme intensification of reduplicated adjectives might also be explained by reference to ease or naturalness of production and markedness.

25 Brown and Levinson (1987: 268) discuss creaky voice as a feature of "positive politeness" (as opposed to the deferential use of high pitch, which is a feature of "negative politeness"): "[C]reaky voice, having as a natural source low speech energy, can implicate calmness and assurance and thence comfort and commiseration..."

REFERENCES

Bentley, M. and E. J. Varon. 1933. An accessory study of phonetic symbolism. *American Journal of Psychology* 45: 76–86.

Bolinger, D. L. 1964. Intonation as a universal. In H. G. Lunt (ed.) *Proceedings of the Ninth International Congress of Linguists, 1962*. The Hague: Mouton, 833–844.

1978. Intonation across languages. In J. H. Greenberg (ed.) *Universals of Human Language II: Phonology*. Stanford: University Press, 471–524.

Brackbill, Y. and K. Little. 1957. Factors determining the guessing of meanings of foreign words. *The Journal of Abnormal and Social Psychology* 54: 312–318.

Brown, P. and S. C. Levinson. 1987. *Politeness: Some Universals in Language Use*. Cambridge: University Press.

Brown, R. W., A. H. Black, and A. E. Horowitz. 1955. Phonetic symbolism in natural languages. *The Journal of Abnormal and Social Psychology* 50: 388–393.

Brown, R. W. and R. Nuttall. 1959. Methods in phonetic symbolism experiments. *The Journal of Abnormal and Social Psychology* 59: 441–445.

Chao, Y. R. 1930. A System of tone letters. *Le Maître Phonétique* 45: 24–27.

1945. The morphemic status of certain Chinese tones. *The Transaction of the International Conference of Orientalists in Japan* 4: 44–48.

Chen, M. Y. and Wang, W. S.-Y. 1974. Sound change: actuation and implementation. Paper presented at First International Conference on Historical Linguistics, Edinburgh, September 1973. Revised March 1974.

Cheung, Y.-S. 1969. A study on the upper even tone and changed tones in Cantonese as spoken in Hong Kong. *Hong Kong Chinese University Chinese Culture Research Institute Journal* 2: 81–107. (In Chinese.)

Collias, N. E. 1960. An ecological and functional classification of animal sounds. In W. E. Lanyon and W. N. Tavolga (eds.) *Animal Sounds and Communication*. Washington DC: American Institute of the Biological Sciences. Publication no. 7, 368–391.

Fischer-Jørgensen, E. 1978. On the universal character of phonetic symbolism with special reference to vowels. *Studia Linguistica* 32: 80–90.

Fowkes, B. (trans.) 1977. Karl Marx, *Capital: A Critique of Political Economy*, vol. I. New York: Random House.

Fowler, H. N. (trans.) 1977. *Plato in Twelve Volumes, 4: Cratylus, Parmenides, Greater Hippias, Lesser Hippias*. London: William Heinemann Ltd.

Gandour, J. 1977. Interaction between tone and vowel length. *Phonetica* 34(1): 54–65.

1981. Perceptual dimensions of tone: evidence from Cantonese. *Journal of Chinese Linguistics* 9(1): 20–36.

Gao, H. 1980. "Research on the Canton Dialect." Hong Kong: Commercial Press. (In Chinese.)

Gao, M. and A. Shi. 1963. "A Survey of Linguistics." Beijing: Zhonghua Shuju. (In Chinese.)

Gebels, G. 1969. An investigation of phonetic symbolism in different cultures. *Journal of Verbal Learning and Verbal Behavior* 8: 310–312.

Haas, M. R. 1946. Techniques of intensifying in Thai. *Word* 2: 127–130.

Hashimoto, M. J. 1981. A phonological characterization of syllabic intonations in the so-called tone languages. In A. B. Gonzalez and D. Thomas (eds.) *Richard S. Pittman Festschrift*. Manila: De La Salle University Press.

Hata, K. 1983. Two experiments in sound symbolism. ms. University of California at Berkeley.

Hirata, S. 1983. "Diminutives" and tone sandhi. *Computational Analysis of Asian and African Languages* 21: 43–58. (In Chinese.)

Hong, C. 1982. "Readings in Chinese Linguistics from Different Historical Periods." Nanjing: Jiangsu People's Press. (In Chinese.)

Huang, Y. H., S. Pratoomraj, and R. C. Johnson. 1969. Universal magnitude symbolism. *Journal of Verbal Learning and Verbal Behavior* 8(1): 155–156.

Jakobson, R. 1978. (J. Mepham, trans.) *Sound and Meaning*. London: MIT Press.

Jespersen, O. 1922. *Language: Its Nature, Development and Origin*. London: George Allen and Unwin.

Johnson, R. C., N. S. Suzuki, and W. K. Ohls. 1964. Phonetic symbolism in an artificial language. *The Journal of Abnormal and Social Psychology* 69: 233–236.

Kam, T. H. 1977. Derivation by tone change in Cantonese. *Journal of Chinese Linguistics* 5(2): 186–210.

1980. Semantic-tonal processes in Cantonese, Taishanese, Bobai, and Siamese. *Journal of Chinese Linguistics* 8(2): 205–240.

Klank, L. J. K., Y.-H. Huang, and R. C. Johnson. 1971. Determinants of success in matching word pairs in tests of phonetic symbolism. *Journal of Verbal Learning and Verbal Behavior* 10: 140–148.

Klatt. D. H. 1973. Discrimination of fundamental frequency contours in synthetic speech: implications for models of perception. *Journal of the Acoustic Society of America* 53: 8–16.

Koriat, A. 1975. Phonetic symbolism and feeling of knowing. *Memory and Cognition* 3(5): 545–548.

Lakoff, Robin. 1975. *Language and a Woman's Place*. New York: Harper & Row.

Lester, D. 1973. Phonetic and graphic symbolism. *Perceptual and Motor Skills* 37: 592.

—— 1974. Symbolism in the Chinese language. *International Journal of Symbology* 5(1): 18–21.

Li, C. N. and Thompson, S. A. 1976. The acquisition of tone in Mandarin-speaking children. *Journal of Child Language* 4: 185–199.

Li, F. K. 1977. *A Handbook of Comparative Tai*. Honolulu: University Press of Hawaii.

Lu, J. 1981. The classification and use of monosyllabic antonyms. In Peking University Chinese Department, *Yuyanxue Luncong* Editorial Committee (eds.) *Collection of Papers in Linguistics*, no. 8. Beijing: Commercial Press, 34–49. (In Chinese.)

Ma, X. 1981. "A Survey of Linguistics." Wuchang: Huazhong Gongxueyuan Press. (In Chinese.)

Maddieson, I. 1978. Universals of tone. In J. H. Greenberg (ed) *Universals of Human Language* II: *Phonology*. Stanford: University Press, 335–365.

Maltzman, I., L. Morrisett, L. and L. Brooks. 1956. An investigation in phonetic symbolism. *The Journal of Abnormal and Social Psychology* 53: 245–251.

Matisoff, J. A. 1973. *The Grammar of Lahu*. University of California Publications in Linguistics 75. Berkeley: University of California Press.

Miron, M. S. 1961. A cross-linguistic investigation of phonetic symbolism. *The Journal of Abnormal and Social Psychology* 62: 623–630.

Morton, E. S. 1977. On the occurrence and significance of motivation-structural rules in some bird and mammal sounds. *American Naturalist* 111: 855–869.

—— 1986. Sound symbolism and its role in non-human vertebrate communication. Paper given at the Conference on Sound Symbolism, University of California at Berkeley, January 16–18, 1986.

Newman, S. S. 1933. Further experiments in phonetic symbolism. *American Journal of Psychology* 45: 53–75.

Ohala, J. J. 1980. The acoustic origin of the smile. *Journal of the Acoustic Society of America* 68: S33.

—— 1982a. Physiological mechanisms underlying tone and intonation. In H. Fujisaki and E. Garding (eds.), *Preprints of the Working Group on Intonation, Thirteenth International Congress of Linguists, Tokyo*. Tokyo: ICL Editorial Committee, 1–12.

—— 1982b. The phonological end justifies any means. *Preprints of the Plenary Session Papers, Thirteenth International Congress of Linguists, Tokyo*. Tokyo: ICL Editorial Committee, 199–208.

—— 1982c. The frequency code and its effect on certain forms of speech and facial expressions. In A. S. House (ed.) *Proceedings of the Symposium on Acoustics, Phonetics and Speech Modelling*. Paper 23/81. Princeton: Institute for Defense Analysis, 1–31.

—— 1983. Cross-language use of pitch: an ethological view. *Phonetica* 40: 1–18.

—— 1986. Sound symbolism in an ethological context. Paper presented to the Conference on Sound Symbolism, University of California at Berkeley, January 16–18, 1986.

Sapir, E. 1929. A study of phonetic symbolism. *Journal of Experimental Psychology* 12: 225–239.

Saussure, F. de. 1966. *Course in General Linguistics*. Edited by C. Bally and A. Sechehaye in collaboration with Albert Reidlinger. Transl. and notes by Wade Baskin. New York: McGraw-Hill.

Solomon, L. N. 1959. Search for physical correlates to psychological dimensions of sounds. *Journal of the Acoustic Society of America* 31: 492–497.

Taylor, I. K. 1963. Phonetic symbolism reexamined. *Psychological Bulletin* 60: 200–209.

Taylor, I. K. and M. M. Taylor. 1965. Another look at phonetic symbolism. *Psychological Bulletin* 64: 413–427.

 1967. Phonetic symbolism in four unrelated languages. *Canadian Journal of Psychology* 16: 344–356.

Tse, J. K-P. 1977. Tone acquisition in Cantonese: a longitudinal case study. *Journal of Child Language* 5: 191–204.

Tsien-Lee, M. 1969. Sound and meaning in Chinese language: a study of phonetic symbolism. *Psychologica Belgica* 9(1): 47–58.

Vance, T. J. 1976. Tone and intonation in Cantonese. *Phonetica* 33: 368–392.

Wang, W. S-Y. 1979. Language change – a lexical perspective. *Annual Review of Anthropology* 8: 353–371.

Weiss, J. 1963. The role of "meaningfulness" vs. meaning-dimensions in guessing the meanings of foreign words. *The Journal of Abnormal and Social Psychology* 66: 541–546.
 1964. Phonetic symbolism re-examined. *Psychological Bulletin* 61: 454–458.

Whitaker, K. P. K. 1955–1956. A study on the modified tones in spoken Cantonese. *Asia Major* 5: 9–36; 184–207.

Wong, M. K. 1982. Tone change in Cantonese. PhD dissertation, University of Illinois at Urbana Champaign.

Woon, W.-L. 1979. A synchronic phonology of Hainan dialect: Part I. *Journal of Chinese Linguistics* 7: 65–100.

Wu, Y. 1984. On register in a tonal theory of Mandarin. Paper presented to the Seventeenth International Conference on Sino-Tibetan Languages and Linguistics, University of Oregon, Eugene, September 7–9, 1984.

Ye, F. and T. Xu. 1981. "An Outline of Linguistics." Beijing: Peking University Press. (In Chinese.)

Yue-Hashimoto, A. O. 1972. *Phonology of Cantonese*. Studies in Yue Dialects 1. Cambridge: University Press.
 1980. Word play in language acquisition: a Mandarin case. *Journal of Chinese Linguistics* 8(2): 181–204.R.

Zhong, Q. 1980. *On Chinese Phonetics*. Beijing: Commercial Press.

11
Palatalization in Japanese sound symbolism

SHOKO HAMANO

11.1. The sound symbolism of palatalization

Japanese has an extensive set of lexical items commonly known as *giongo, giseego,* and *gitaigo* "mimetic words." These lexical terms are used most frequently in colloquial speech, and they form a system with distinct syntactical, morphological, and phonological characteristics (Hamano 1986).

Consonant palatalization is a conspicuous feature of this mimetic system, and the semantic association of palatalization extends over a semantic continuum of "childishness, immaturity, instability, unreliability, uncoordinated movement, diversity, excessive energy, noisiness, lack of elegance, and cheapness." A large number of minimal pairs, as in (1) below, demonstrates this clearly.

(1) a. pata-pata   "hitting a flat surface with a large flat object such as a fan"
       patya-patya "hitting the surface of the water with a big splash"

    b. peta-peta   "with something sticking on"
       petya-petya "to talk on and on about insignificant matters (by moving the tongue all over)"

    c. horo-horo   "weeping elegantly"
       hyoro-hyoro "looking thin and weak"

    d. tara-tara   "thick creamy liquid drips"
       tyara-tyara "flashy and cheap"

    e. toro-toro   "thick liquid"
       tyoro-tyoro "unreliably"

    f. suru-suru   "something passes smoothly"
       syuru-syuru "something goes through a narrow space and makes a noise"

g.	noro–noro	"slow movement"
	nyoro–nyoro	"a snake's wriggly and curving movement"
h.	koro–koro	"something hard and round rolls on"
	kyoro–kyoro	"to look around curiously without focusing on one thing"
i.	kata–kata	"something solid and square hits a hard surface and makes a homogeneous sound"
	katya–katya	"hard objects such as keys hit each other and make a variety of noises"

11.2. The distribution of palatalization

McCawley (1968) sets up four strata of phonology in Japanese, the native, the Sino-Japanese, the onomatopoeic, and the foreign, and lists the permitted combinations of vowels with palatalized and non-palatalized consonants as in table 11.1.

In Table 11.1, Sino-Japanese and onomatopoeic, or mimetic, morphemes are treated together. This gives the impression that the Sino-Japanese and the onomatopoeic strata are identical as to the features of palatalization. A closer look at the distribution of palatalized syllables proves otherwise.

In monosyllabic mimetic roots, there is only one location where palatalized and plain syllables can contrast, and most consonants that are permitted initially are palatalizable, as in (2) below.

Table 11.1 *Permitted vowel-consonant combinations in Japanese*

	Native	Sino-Japanese and onomatopoeia	Foreign
Cu	×	×	×
Cyu		×	×
Co	×	×	×
Cyo		×	×
Ca	×	×	×
Cya	×	×	×
Ce	×	×	×
Cye			×
Ci			×
Cyi	×	×	×

(McCawley 1968: 65)

(2) pyoN-pyoN "jumping joyfully"
 byuN-byuN "going fast against a strong wind"
 hyoi to "jumping over something casually"
 tyuu-tyuu "sucking with noise"
 syaN to "in a firm posture"
 zyuQ to "with the sound of water on a heated plate"
 kyaQ to "with a scream"
 gyuQ to "holding hard onto something"
 nyaa-nyaa "cat's meowing"

In bisyllabic mimetic roots, on the other hand, the following stringent constraints on the distribution of palatalized syllables exist.

First, palatalization cannot appear twice in the same root; that is, roots of the form */CyVCyV/ do not exist. The permissible strings are either /CyVCV/ as in (3a) or /CVCyV/ as in (3b). The sequences [pi, bi, tʃi, ʃi, zi, ki, gi, ni, mi, ri] are treated as /Ci/ and not as /Cyi/ in this paper.[1] Glosses given above are not repeated below.

(3) a. pyoko-pyoko "something light flip-flops"
 kyoro-kyoro
 tyara-tyara

 b. pitya-pitya "to move something thin, flat, and flexible like a hand over the surface of water or a watery object in such a way that a splashy noise is made"
 petya-petya
 kusya-kusya "crumpled"
 katya-katya

Secondly, in the second syllable of bisyllabic mimetic roots, only the alveolar sounds /t, (d), s, z, n/ can be palatalized, as in (4a) below.[2] The flap /r/ is alveolar, but it is not palatalizable in the second syllable. Since it does not appear in the first syllable, the flap /r/ is not palatalizable anywhere in bisyllabic mimetic roots. For lack of a better term, the term "alveolar" will be used to refer to only /t, (d), s, z, n/ in this paper. In the first syllable, by contrast, most of the consonants that are allowed to appear initially may be palatalized, as in (4b).

(4) a. kutya-kutya "to chew something like gum in a messy way"
 kasya-kasya "dry light objects scratch each other and make noise"
 uzya-uzya "to swarm around"
 kunya-kunya "something like a melted iron bar bends"

Table 11.2 *Consonantal combinations of basic reduplicative adverbs*

C₁ \ C₂	ty	sy	zy	ny	r	k	b	p	t	d	s	z	g	m	n	w	y	Total	
py								1										1	
hy					2	1												3	7
ky					1				1									2	
gy					1													1	
ty					4	6	2	1										13	
sy					3	3	2											8	31
zy					3	3	1											7	
ny					2	1												3	
p	4	5																9	
b	5	5																10	
h			1															1	
k	3	2	1															6	
g	4	4	2															10	48
m		3	2	2														7	
w/θ	1		1															2	
n	2																	2	
t																			
d		1																1	
s																			
z																			
y																			
Total	19	20	3	6	16	15	5	1	1										
	48				38													86	

b. pyoko–pyoko   "to flip-flop"
    hyoko–hyoko   "to flip-flop"
    kyoro–kyoro
    gyoro–gyoro   "to look around inquisitively and indeterminately with eyes bulging out"

    tyara–tyara
    syuru–syuru
    zyoki–zyoki   "to cut with scissors unhesitantly"
    nyoro–nyoro   "the winding movement of something like a snake"

The third constraint is as follows. If palatalization occurs in a root that contains an alveolar, it must be the alveolar that is palatalized, whether it is in the first syllable or in the second syllable. Other sounds in the first syllable may be palatalized only in the absence of an alveolar in the second syllable. The only apparent exception to this rule is /kyoto-kyoto/ "to look around indeterminately," whose semantic identity with /kyoro-kyoro/ "to look around indeterminately" allows us to hypothesize that it was formulated analogously to resemble the latter. A "correct" form /kotyo-kotyo/ "touching lightly" also exists, but semantically it resembles /koto-koto/ "hitting lightly" more than /kyoto-kyoto/.

The second of the constraints on palatalization above states that, while palatalization of alveolars is allowed in both the first and the second syllable, palatalization of non-alveolars is limited to the first syllable. This, coupled with the third constraint (the preference of alveolars over non-alveolars for palatalization) works to ensure that non-alveolars are less frequently palatalized than alveolars. The limited scope of palatalization of non-alveolars is clear statistically.

Table 11.2 breaks down the consonantal combinations of the 86 bisyllabic reduplicative adverbs in my data which have palatalized syllables.[3] The consonantal elements in the first and the second syllable are represented by C_1 and C_2 respectively. They may be Cy or C. Under C_1, all consonantal elements that appear in the first syllable are listed. To the right of C_2, on the other hand, all consonantal elements that appear in the second syllable are listed.

Of these 86 adverbs, only seven involve palatalization of non-alveolars. The rest involve alveolars. Within the latter category, 48 involve palatalization in the second syllable and 31 in the first syllable.

The oddity of palatalization of non-alveolars is also statistically clear when we consider the vowels that accompany the consonants. Tables 11.3 and 11.4 show the combinations of vowels in the 86 items used for table 11.2. Table 11.3 shows that, after /ty, sy, zy, ny/, 52 cases involve /a/, 21 cases /o/ and six cases /u/. The vowel /a/ is the predominant vowel in palatalized syllables. As for the vowels that follow simple consonants in these bisyllabic mimetic morphemes, all vowels except /e/ are involved more or less equally.[4]

When we shift our focus to the seven cases with /ky, py, hy, gy/ in the first syllable, we find that the situation is quite different from the above. In table 11.4, there are only two combinations of vowels: namely, /-o-o/ and /-u-u/. And, of the seven cases, six are of the former type, /-u-u/ being limited to only one case.

Interestingly, none of the above constraints and tendencies applies to Sino-Japanese morphemes, which came into Japanese as erudite words. First of all, in bisyllabic words from the Sino-Japanese stratum, one finds numerous examples where palatalization appears in both syllables:

Table 11.3 *Forms containing /ty, sy, zy, ny/*

V in CV \ V in CyV	i	e	a	o	u	Total
i			11	7		18
e			5	1		6
a			14			14
o			10	11		21
u			12	2	6	20
Total			52	21	6	79

Table 11.4 *Forms containing /ky, py, hy, gy/*

V in CV \ V in CyV	i	e	a	o	u	Total
i						
e						
a						
o				6		6
u					1	1
Total				6	1	7

(5) kyasya   "to be fragile"
    kyooryuu   "dinosaur"
    kyuukyo   "hurriedly"
    gyaQkyoo   "adverse circumstances"

Moreover, in the Sino-Japanese stratum, there is no difference between the role of the first syllable and the role of the second syllable. Nor is there any difference between the alveolars and the non-alveolars. Palatalization appears in both syllables with an essentially identical set of consonants: /py, by, hy, ty, (dy), sy, zy, ky, gy, my, ny, ry/.

The same thing can be said about the vowels that accompany palatalized consonants. In Sino-Japanese morphemes, of the three vowels /a, o, u/, /o/ is most frequent, and /a/ is least frequent. In the dictionary by Suzuki *et al.* (1975), of the 855 Sino-Japanese morphemes that involve palatalization, 516 entries involve /o/;

254 /u/; and only 85 /a/. The contrast is clear. In palatalized syllables in the Sino-Japanese stratum, /o, u/ appear more frequently than /a/. In the mimetic stratum, on the other hand, /a/ is over-represented. Thus, the Sino-Japanese and mimetic strata are quite dissimilar in the distribution of palatalization.

11.3. Diachronic interpretation of the constraints

The peculiar distributional constraints on palatalization in mimetic words are related to the role of palatalization in mimetic words, i.e. its sound symbolism.

As stated at the beginning of this paper, the sound-symbolic association of palatalization extends over a semantic continuum of "childishness, immaturity, instability, unreliability, uncoordinated movement, diversity, excessive energy, noisiness, lack of elegance, and cheapness."

The semantic continuum of palatalization can be reduced to a basic association of palatalization of alveolar stops and fricatives with "childishness" or "immaturity." Studies of language acquisition report palatalization as one of the universal characteristics of early stages of children's language acquisition. It is also reported as one of the commonest devices of baby-talk, i.e. adult modification of speech to children (Snow and Ferguson 1977).

The peculiar distributional pattern of palatalized syllables may be reinterpreted by taking into account the primacy of alveo-palatals and their meanings. The predominance of palatalization of alveolars points to a stage when palatalization occurred only with alveolars with the sense of "childishness." As the meaning was extended to the other end of the semantic continuum, palatalization would have been separated from alveolar stops and fricatives. That is, it would have been reinterpreted as an independent sound-symbolic factor. It would have spread to other consonants at this stage to add one or the other of the above meanings to the string. When this happened, palatalization of forms containing no alveolars naturally went to the first syllable instead of the second syllable because of the general preference of the first syllable as the site of semantic contrast in the Japanese mimetic system.

The phonotactic constraints on bisyllabic mimetic morphemes with palatalized syllables may be reformulated to reflect the above hypothesis as below.

(6) a. Palatalization is marked underlyingly in the following way: /y-CVCV/. Its position need not be specified underlyingly.

b. Alveolar stops and fricatives are first palatalized.

c. If (b) does not apply, palatalization goes to the first syllable.

The derivations of /pyoko/, /tyara/, and /pitya/ are as below.

Asia

(7) a. y-poko   y-tara   y-pita
    b. ———   tyara   pitya
    c. pyoko   ———   ———

11.4. Historical implications for Japanese sound change

When the inventory of palatalized syllables is expressed in terms of /Cyi, Cye, Cya, Cyo, Cyu/, the Sino-Japanese and mimetic strata seem to share a similar kind of palatalized syllable. However, as we have seen so far, the phenomena of palatalization in the two strata are qualitatively quite different: the phonotactic constraints on palatalized syllables, so powerful in the onomatopoeic stratum, are irrelevant in the Sino-Japanese stratum.

Based upon the documentation of palatalization after the massive borrowing and incorporation of Chinese words, it is often flatly stated that palatalization was added to Japanese under the influence of Chinese loanwords. (See, for example, Mabuchi 1971.) However, the differences between the Sino-Japanese and the mimetic strata lead us to the claim that palatalization in the mimetic words is a spontaneous process indigenous to Japanese rather than a product simply triggered by Chinese loanwords. What erudite Chinese loanwords probably did in this regard was to legitimize the existing palatalization in colloquial speech.

NOTES

1 In table 11.1, McCawley treats these phonetic strings as /Cyi/ phonologically; there are no Ci-syllables for the onomatopoeic stratum in table 11.1. On the other hand, the present analysis of the constraints on palatalization in the mimetic stratum critically depends upon the treatment of such strings as /Ci/; if this analysis were rejected and McCawley's treatment accepted, /pitya-pitya/ in (3b), for instance, would have to be reanalyzed as /pyitya-pyitya/, invalidating my entire argument about the phonotactic constraints of palatalization. Bisyllabic mimetic morphemes of the form */CVkyi-, CVryi-, CVbyi-, CVmyi-, pyitV/, and so on, which are not possible in the current analysis, would also have to be accepted.

It should first be pointed out that the distinction between /Ci/ and /Cyi/ in the foreign stratum in table 11.1 is made on the basis of the existence of such pairs as [ti:mu] "team" vs. [tʃi:zu] "cheese," which are phonemicized as /ti:mu/ and /tyi:zu/ respectively. Following this lead, McCawley phonemicizes such syllables as [pi, bi, ki, gi] in the native, Sino-Japanese, and mimetic strata as Cyi-syllables /pyi, byi, kyi, gyi/ instead of /pi, bi, ki, gi/. This is because, in these strata, [tʃi] exists but [ti] does not; phonemicizing the phonetically simple syllables as phonologically sharp syllables simplifies the phonotactics of these strata.

Shoko Hamano

In the present analysis, on the other hand, only /Cyu, Cyo, Cya/ are treated as palatalized syllables in the mimetic stratum; */Cyi/ is not considered to exist in mimetic words.

One reason for rejecting /Cyi/ for the mimetic stratum is the absence of bisyllabic morphemes */CyaCya-, CyoCyo-, CyuCyu-/, etc., which contain two unambiguously palatalized syllables. Such forms would be expected if [Cyaki, Cyari, Cyobi], etc. were interpreted as */Cyakyi-, Cyaryi-, Cyobyi-/, etc., since (e.g.) */CyVkyi/ is a form of */CyVkyV/ and this implies the possibility of */CyVkya/, etc. The absence of such morphemes proves that the constraint is real and that [Ci] cannot be interpreted as */Cyi/.

A similar reason is the absence of bisyllabic morphemes */CVkya-, CVrya-, CVmya-, pyatV-/, etc., in which non-alveolars are palatalized in syllables containing /a, o, u/. As we will see shortly, there is a general constraint banning the palatalization of non-alveolars. However, such forms would be expected if [CVki, CVri, CVbi, CVmi, pitV], etc. were interpreted as */CVkyi-, CVryi-, CVbyi-, CVmyi-, pyitV-/, since (e.g.) */CVkyi/ is a form of */CVkyV/ and this implies the possibility of */CVkya/, etc. The absence of such forms again proves the correctness of the present analysis. The constraints generally set up for palatalized syllables consistently apply in the case of the unambiguously palatalized syllables /Cya, Cyo, Cyu/; it would not make sense to allow */Cyi/ and say that the constraints do not apply only in the case of this problematic sequence.

2 The contrast between /d/ and /z/ is neutralized before /y/.

3 The following is the list of 86 bisyllabic mimetic adverbs used in tables 11.1, 11.2, and 11.3: pitya-pitya, petya-petya, patya-patya, potya-potya, pisya-pisya, pesya-pesya, pasya-pasya, posya-posya, pusyu-pusyu, pyoko-pyoko, bitya-bitya, betya-betya, batya-batya, botya-botya, betyo-betyo, bisya-bisya, besya-besya, basya-basya, bosya-bosya, bisyo-bisyo, hyoro-hyoro, hyuru-hyuru, hyoko-hyoko, hunya-hunya, tyari-tyari, tyara-tyara, tyoro-tyoro, tyuru-tyuru, tyapo-tyapo, tyobi-tyobi, tyobo-tyobo, tyaki-tyaki, tyoki-tyoki, tyaka-tyaka, tyoko-tyoko, tyoku-tyoku, tyuku-tyuku, dosya-dosya, kyoro-kyoro, katya-katya, kutya-kutya, kyoto-kyoto, kotyo-kotyo, kasya-kasya, kusya-kusya, kunya-kunya, gyoro-gyoro, gatya-gatya, gotya-gotya, gutya-gutya, gotyo-gotyo, gasya-gasya, gosya-gosya, gusya-gusya, gusyo-gusyo, gunya-gunya, gonyo-gonyo, syari-syari, syara-syara, syuru-syuru, syobo-syobo, syabu-syabu, syaki-syaki, syoki-syoki, syaka-syaka, zyari-zyari, zyori-zyori, zyara-zyara, zyabu-zyabu, zyoki-zyoki, zyaka-zyaka, zyuku-zyuku, mosya-mosya, musya-musya, mosyo-mosyo, mozya-mozya, mozyo-mozyo, munya-munya, monyo-monyo, nyoro-nyoro, nyuru-nyuru, nitya-nitya, netya-netya, nyoki-nyoki, itya-itya, uzya-uzya.

4 The distribution of /e/ is limited in the native and the mimetic stratum in general.

REFERENCES

Hamano, S. 1986. "The sound-symbolic system of Japanese." PhD dissertation, University of Florida.

Mabuchi, K. 1971. *Kokugo On-in-ron*. ["Japanese Phonology."] Tokyo: Kasama Syoin. (In Japanese.)

McCawley, J. D. 1968. *The Phonological Component of a Grammar of Japanese.* The Hague: Mouton.

Snow, C. E. and C. A. Ferguson (eds.) 1977. *Talking to Children: Language Input and Acquisition.* New York: Cambridge University Press.

Suzuki, S. *et al.* (eds.) 1975. *Kadokawa Saisin Kanwa Ziten.* ["Kadokawa's Newest Sino-Japanese Dictionary."] Tokyo: Kadokawa. (In Japanese.)

PART IV
Australia and Africa

12
Yir-Yoront ideophones*

BARRY ALPHER

12.1. Introduction

Yir-Yoront (hereafter YY) and the other languages of its area (central to southwestern Cape York Peninsula, Australia) feature a high frequency of *ideophones* in ordinary and mythic narrative. Ideophones are word-like elements that suggest the *sound*, in a highly conventionalized sense, that accompanies an action. An example is *trrra*, as in *Kalq 'trrra yoyrrin* "[he] gathered together the spears [suddenly, with a *trrra* sound]."[1] The relation of the sound of the ideophone to the sound of the action it represents is frequently more remote and arbitrary: *tor* (of hitting), as in *Par-poq 'tor piw 'y* "I hit it on the head, tor!" *pup* (of falling), as in *Pup thilhth* "pup! [it] fell"; *chan* (of hanging, as in a tree), as in *Lalpuym chan wenhth* "chan! [he] hung up the bundle."

Some ideophones seem to represent the *feel* of an action at least as much as the sound, like *cha'warrq* (of picking something up), as in *Kalq cha'warrq yiw 'l* "chawarrq! he got the spear." At the extreme of the scale of arbitrariness is a form like *tak* (of finishing an action), as in *Lalpuym tak kuy* "tak! [he] tied up the bundle," which doesn't appear to represent any typical sound at all.[2]

As with ideophones in other languages, the status of ideophones in a linguistic analysis of YY is problematic. I examine some of the problems below, particularly with regard to phonology (12.2) and syntax (12.6). YY ideophones are also of interest in the study of historical-comparative problems (discussed in 12.4) and of semantics (12.5). Excluded from this discussion are conventionalized animal calls and interjections of pain, surprise, etc. – both, like ideophones, deviant in their phonology from the rest of the words in the language.

12.2. Phonology

The sound system of YY ideophones is based on the phonemic inventory found in ordinary words plus and minus a few sounds, and with expanded phonotactic possibilities. The sounds of YY (in non-ideophones) are the bilabials /p, m, w/, the lamino-dentals /th, nh, lh/, the apico-alveolars /t, n, l, rr/, the apico-post-alveolars (retroflexes) /rt, rn, rl, r/, the lamino-alveopalatals /ch, ny, y/, the dorso-velars /k, ng/, glottal catch /q/, and the vowels /i, e, a, o, u/, /v/ (schwa).[3] The liquid *rr* is a single flap unless followed by another apical; *r* is a retroflex glide. Fricatives are absent, except as the occasional realization in older men's speech of *k* and *ch* (both normally pure stops with no affrication). Except in loanwords, initial *t* (= *rt*), *n* (= *rn*), *r*, *ch*, and *ny* are rare (together accounting for roughly 2% of lexical headwords), and initial *rr* and *lh* do not occur. Of the pair *t*/*rt*, the latter is the unmarked member, occurring to the exclusion of *t* in neutralizing positions and nearly exclusively following a stressed vowel. Syllable-final *k* is extremely rare, having been replaced historically by glottal catch at the end of a stressed syllable and by zero elsewhere. A syllable begins with a single consonant (with certain vowel-initial exceptions, most of which have consonant-initial alternants); every stressed syllable contains a vowel as nucleus, and stress is on the first syllable of a word. Schwa never occurs stressed.

With ideophones, on the other hand:
(i)   Initial *lh* occurs: *lhop* (of being swallowed).
(ii) Final *k* occurs: *lak* (of knocking someone down).
(iii) A mid-central vowel occurs stressed: *tvk* (of finishing).
(iv) Final *t* occurs to the exclusion of *rt*: *kvt* (of spearing).
(v)   Disyllables, if not reduplicatives, stress the second syllable: *chu'rup* (of a manta ray landing on the water).

The statistical distribution of initial consonants (list frequency) in ideophones differs dramatically from that in ordinary words:
(vi) For all words, the frequency of initial consonants is *p* 17%, *k* 15%, *w* 13%, *th* 12%, *m* 12%, *y* 7%, *l* 7%, *ng* 6%, *nh* 4%, *t* 2%, *ch* 1%, and each of the others less than 1%.
(vii) For ideophones, the frequency of initial consonants is *p* 30%, *t* 25%, *ch* 18%, *th* 10%, *k* 4%, *w* 4%, *l* 2%, *ny* 2%, *m* 1%, and *lh* 1%, and with *n*, *ng*, *nh*, *r*, and *y* absent.
(viii) Ideophones comprise 4% of all headwords; they comprise 100% (N = 1) of all words beginning with *lh*, 60% of those beginning with *ch*, 50% (N = 4) of those beginning with *ny*, 47% of those beginning with *t*, 8% of those beginning with *p*, 4% of those beginning with *th*, 1% of those beginning with *w*, *l*, and *k*, and less than 1% of those beginning with *m*. In summary, initial *ch*, *t*, and *p* are conspicuously favored for ideophones, and *k*, *l* and the glides and nasals are conspicuously disfavored.[4]

Australia and Africa

There is no doubt a large iconic component in the selectivity among initial consonants for ideophones; one thinks of the inappropriateness of sonorants for elements representing impact and sudden movement. Even among YY's near linguistic neighbors, however, there are different norms. In Wik-Ngathana, for example (Sutton 1978: 301–302) there are vowel-initial and *ng*-initial ideophones (e.g. *ngupan* [of a splash]) and in the geographically and linguistically more distant language Dalabon, the ideophone of running is *yonggi yonggi*. Aside from the elegant onomatopoeia of some of the YY ideophones, there does not seem to be much in the way of sound symbolism in the particular choice of initial or final sound,[5] unlike the strong statistical association that McGregor (1985) has found between particular final consonants in verb stems and particular action-types in the distantly related Australian language Kuniyanti. The fact that some 42% of YY ideophones end in one or another stop (including glottal catch) is probably of significance, since YY verb roots (by and large)[6] and verbs with inflectional endings do not end in stops. Ideophones (the non-reduplicative ones) associate almost exclusively with verbs in one of the past tenses and with perfective aspectual sense, and the attestation with non-past verbs is mostly perfective in sense. The final stop in many ideophones can then be seen as symbolizing perfectivity. Note, however, that sonorant-final ideophones of short, swift, and perfective actions occur routinely (e.g. *chan, chor, churr*), and that YY's neighboring languages, including its sister dialect Yir-Thangedl, are equally ideophone-rich and yet allow consonant-final verb roots and verb endings.

Besides having their own statistical pattern for initial sounds, YY ideophones exhibit sound and syllable types not found in ordinary words:

(ix) Vowelless syllables occur: *trrrt* (of entering).

(x) A syllable can begin with a cluster: *nychip* (of being pierced by a catfish spine).

(xi) Fricatives occur: *ffffi* (of blowing a fire) contains a drawn-out voiceless bilabial fricative; *puww* (of burning) terminates in a drawn-out voiced bilabial fricative. Note that such sound types occur as realizations of ordinary phonemes in neighboring languages such as Uw-Oykangand.

(xii) Trills of odd types occur: *pppp* (of handcuffs falling off) contains a voiceless bilabial trill producing tone with the lips (like a Bronx cheer).

(xiii) A voiced bilabial trill occurs: *pbbbp* (of falling; an alternant of *pup*).

(xiv) There is an incipient voicing contrast: *prrr* (of sliding on a salt-pan) vs. *pRRRq* (~ *parr*) (of a quick cutting motion); cf. also the examples in (xi).

There are, moreover, patterns of sound alternation absent from non-ideophones:

(xv) Final glottal catch varies freely with nothing in a number of forms: *purr* ~ *purrq* (of flopping down).

(xvi) Various free vowel alternations occur: *lhop* ~ *lhvp* (of being swallowed), *puy* ~ *poy* (of leaving), *kvt* ~ *kat* (of spearing). Note that the vowels of *tor* (of hitting), *tvk* (of finishing), *chan* (of hanging), *tuk* (of spearing), and *wirr* (of pulling) are unvarying and always kept distinct; *e*, the least frequent of the five full vowels (accounting for less than 10% of occurrences of these in connected text), is not recorded in ideophones.

(xvii) Final *y* hardens to a stop under great emphasis: *puy ~ puch* (of taking leave); in ordinary words there is a lenition process with the opposite effect in certain contexts.

Ideophone phonology does seem to parallel the regular sound system of the language, however: Olgol (Sommer 1972: 154–156), Yir-Yoront's neighbor and a language that has a tense/lax distinction for stops, has ideophones recorded as *kat* (of spearing, cf. YY *kat*), *bub* (of falling, cf. YY *pup*), and *djur* (of plunging into water, cf. YY *chur* or *chuy*).

In all of these general properties, YY ideophones are similar to "normal" ideophones recorded elsewhere.

12.3. Morphology

Of morphology of ideophones in YY there can be said to be none, save its marginal presence in the verb-derivational prefix system (see below); it is stretching a point to speak of compounding in the isolated case of *thvt* (*thvt thvt . . .*) (of chopping) and *thvtpppfff* (of hitting someone with a thrown boomerang).

12.4. Comparative ideophonics in Australia

Ideophones are recorded from languages all around Australia, as for example the north coast of Western Australia (Nyangumata: see O'Grady 1964: 2, 5). Items very like ideophones ("root forms," to use Heath's terminology, 1980a: 44) occur in the languages (Yuulngu group) of northeast Arnhem Land (Gupapuyngu: see Lowe 1960: lesson 92 and Lowe n.d.; Dhuwal: see Heath 1980a; Ritharrngu: see Heath 1980b); of these more below. But clear cases of ideophones seem to occur with greatest text frequency in languages of the western Cape York Peninsula area. They are well attested in the Wik-Mungkan texts of McConnell (1936a: 472–477, 1936b: 91–105); in Sutton's Wik-Ngathana materials (1978: 301–302, 305–325); in Hall and Foote's Kuuk-Thaayorre lexicon (1983; list rather than textual attestation), and in Sommer's Olgol textlet (1972: 154–156).

Cross-language resemblances in sound and meaning permit the use, in a nontechnical sense, of the term "cognates" with regard to ideophones. Such a resemblance is recorded for languages as geographically distant as Yir-Yoront and Gupapuyngu, both with *thut* (spelled *dhut* in Gupapuyngu; of sitting). Compare also YY *that* (of chopping) with Gupapuyngu *djat*. Between close languages, like YY and Olgol, "cognate" ideophones are numerous (see examples cited in section 12.2 above).

Australia and Africa

As with ideophones in other language areas, those in this area violate the sound correspondences that are regular for ordinary words. Take for example correspondences of word-initial segments. Olgol, like its sister dialect Uw-Oykangand (UO), is an initial-dropping language: from the uniformly consonant-initial proto-words of the common ancestor of YY and these languages, Olgol and UO words have lost all initial consonants. Hence there are correspondences like Olgol *alka*, UO *alk*, YY *kalq* "spear," all from *kalka, and Olgol *abma*, UO *abm*, YY *pam* "person," all from *pama. These correspondences fail for ideophones: UO (Sommer 1968: 27) *kat* (of spear hitting), YY *kvt* (of spearing); UO *piw* (of a shot or a sharp crack), YY *piw* (of breaking with a snap); UO *puy* ("go!"), YY *puy* (of sudden departure). From the available data it cannot be determined whether these facts result from a failure of regularity in sound changes applicable to commonly inherited ideophones, or from borrowing. It seems, at any rate, that ideophones and ideophone-like elements are borrowed with ease, to judge from the occurrence of the item *rdutj* (of returning; to return) in both the Dalabon and Dhuwal languages of Arnhem Land, which are geographically close but only very distantly related.

Of interest are the grammatical roles played by forms that are "cognate" with YY ideophones or are otherwise ideophone-like, especially in north-central Australia (including various parts of Arnhem Land). Here a construction, for which I will use the term *verb-particle*, appears in languages belonging to diverse genetic subgroups, including the Pama-Nyungan family to which YY also belongs. In this construction, an uninflected "particle" carries most of the specific meaning of a lexical verb, while more general properties are carried by an inflection-bearing "verb." A (probably minor) source of such "particles" appears to be "cognates" of what show up as ideophones in Cape York, as for example in the Djaru (Pama-Nyungan; Tsunoda 1981) construction *yut nyina-* "to sit," in which the pre-verb *yut* "sit," occupying the "particle" slot, bears an unmistakable sound/meaning resemblance to YY *thut* (of occupying a stable relative position, prototypically of sitting); with these compare the non-inflecting *dhut* (of sitting down) in Gupapuyngu and Dhuwal.

Verb-particle constructions differ in various details in various of the languages spoken in the area from northeast Arnhem Land southwards and southwestwards towards the territory of Djaru in northern Western Australia. In Djaru the "particle" is known as a *pre-verb* in the descriptive literature (Tsunoda 1981: 177) and its construction with a verb as a *verb complex*; verbs, of which there are some 40 in the language, take inflection for tense-mood-aspect. Pre-verbs are nounlike in taking inflection for case, but "like verbs they describe action or state" (ibid.). They occur as the entire predicate of a clause (180) or associate with verbs in a "close" or "loose" fashion (189–190). Where the association is close, the verb immediately follows the pre-verb, which cannot in this position be inflected for the oblique nominal cases, and "only the pre-verb carries the semantic load" (183). Examples: with the verb *bung-* "hit," *djunggudj bung-* "to walk away," *dulg bung-* "to get up"; with the verb *gang-* "carry," *badj gang-* "to fly," *gidj gang-* "stop (of rain, wind)"; with the verbs *nyin-* "sit" and *yaan-* "put," *dany nyin-* "to hang (intransitive)" and *dany yaan-* "to hang (transitive)." Where the association of pre-verb and verb is loose, the pre-verb can in fact come second, and other material can separate it from the verb (185); the semantic load is shared by both elements (189–190). There are some pre-verbs whose association with verbs is always close; others for which it is always loose; and there are at least some that appear to be used in both ways. Of the last-mentioned type is, apparently, *badj*, which with *gang-* "carry" means "to fly," as in *Djiyiga badj gangan* "a bird flies" (185), but which can be used, in a very ideophonic fashion, outside of any grammatical construction: *Badj badj badj* [a speaker, illustrating by waving his arms, describes the flight of a particular bird] (180). Djaru pre-verbs have the shape of closed monosyllables with significantly greater frequency than forms of other classes, and they condition phonological processes (turning the initial nasals and glides of following verbs into their corresponding stops) that occur in no other contexts (177–178). They are well attested (unlike YY ideophones), in both close and loose associations with verbs, in subordinate clauses: *Ngumbirr-u mawun nyang-an yud-gu-la nyinang-u-la* "the woman [*ngumbirr-u*] sees [*nyang-an*] the man [*mawun*] sitting" (*yud nyin-* "sit," with participial marking followed by the locative ending *-la*) (188).

The languages of northeast Arnhem Land, which like Djaru belong to the Pama-Nyungan family, have a verb-particle construction of a somewhat different type; the Dhuwal dialects (Heath 1980a: 44) are typical in this regard and will serve as an illustration. Here any of a large number of "particles" (or *root forms*, in Heath's terminology) can occur alone or with the thematizing element *-dhu-* ~ *-yu-*.[7] Certain others of these root forms are seen as suppletive for inflecting verbs of classes other than that of *-dhu-* or for a combination of *-dhu-* with another root form; such for example are *dhut* (for *nhiina-* "sit"), *djut* (for *dharpu-* "spear"), *bur* (for *buna-* "arrive"), *rdatj* (for *gulk-dhu-* "cut"). A root form is regarded as "an abbreviation for a regular verb form" (44), but frequently a root form occurs, in an ideophone-like manner, in the same clause as the related verb stem, as with *bur buna-n* "arrived" (44). Another recurrent pattern of usage, as attested in the texts Heath has collected, is for a verb to be introduced as new information in its "root form" to be followed after intervening material and one or more terminal intonation contours by the fully inflected verb, which gives the tense: *rlup ngarra, mayang'-lil, rulup-dhu-rr ngarra* . . . "I [*ngarra*] bathed [*rlup*; root form], to the river [*mayang'lil*], I [*ngarra*] bathed [*rlup-dhu-rr*]" (84). Dhuwal root forms, like Djaru pre-verbs, have the structure of single closed syllables with far greater frequency than forms of other classes, and a root form is "usually pronounced sharply (like an interjection)" (44).[8]

In the region between northeast Arnhem Land and the territory of Djaru are spoken a number of languages whose relationship to Pama-Nyungan (and to each other) is a very distant one. Some of these languages also attest a verb-particle construction: one such is Mangarayi (Merlan 1982: 123–124), whose verbs are of three types: monomorphemic (there are just 36 of these in the language), compound (some 270 are recorded), and particle-plus-auxiliary. In constructions of the last of these types (the "verb-particle" construction in the terminology of the present essay), the auxiliaries are verbs and carry verbal inflections, including prefixation for person-number and suffixation for tense-mode. Particles are clearly distinct from nouns and less clearly so from adverbs (124); a derivational suffix can convert a particle into a gerund (173). When a particle occurs with an auxiliary it always immediately precedes it; in these constructions, "the particle contributes most of the lexical meaning" (124). A particle can also occur as an entire predicate, in which case tense-mode is construed as that of the verb in a preceding clause (164–165). Particles end with glottal stop with greater frequency than forms of other classes (126).

In each of these languages, Djaru, Dhuwal, and Mangarayi, there is a class of "particles" with verb-like meaning, some of which exhibit ideophone-like properties. They appear to be integrated into the verb-derivational system and into various other morphological systems. The YY ideophone system, by contrast, plays almost no part in verbal derivation and differs from the verb-particle systems of these languages in a number of other regards, as will be seen below. There appear at present to be no strong reasons to argue that either of these types is historically prior to the other. (See, however, Heath 1976 for an evolutionary scenario accounting for the various subtypes of the verb-particle construction in several languages of the Arnhem Land region.)

12.5. Semantics as revealed in co-occurrence with verbs

Ideophones associate in sentences with a single verb or with one or another of a set of verbs. For example, *kvt* (of spearing) occurs with *kal* "to spear," and *chan* (of hanging) occurs with *mar* "to hang (intr.)" and with *wenhth* and *marlon* "to hang (tr.)." *Chor* (of splitting or ripping open) is recorded with several different verbs: *Chor yeng 'y* "chor! I cut [*yeng*] it [the belly] open," *Ngerr chor yiyawrrnh 'l* "the belly [*ngerr*] split open, chor!," *Ngul chor, anhth yawrronl ungnh, thaw maq marrpiy* "then [*ngul*] chor! where [he] opens [*yawrronl*] it [*ungnh*] up, [he] tore [*marrpiy*] the mouth [*thaw*] at the bottom [*maq*]." *Chor* occurs verblessly (see below) in *Purrthurr 'y yapa, chor, chor . . . lalpuym* "I put it down [*purrthurr*] in the leaves [*yapa*], cut it up, and [tied it up] in a bundle [*lalpuym*]."

The association of one ideophone with a number of verbs reveals something about the semantic commonality of these verbs which is not necessarily the same as that revealed by other techniques of association (such as correspondence of a number of verbs with a single respect-register verb, as outlined in Dixon 1971). For example, *thut* (of occupying a stable relative position) associates with *wa* "go" (respect-register *larrma*; the position of two parties traveling together), *nhin* "sit" (respect-register *larrolhth*; the position relative to others in which one sits), *than* "stand," *le* "set standing," *kal* "spear, pierce" (respect-register *walpon*; the resting position of the pointed instrument or the impaled object), *wany* "throw" (the landing position of the thrown object), and such other verbs as can be construed to involve a stable relative position of two items, whether as part of the action or as a result of it. Equally able to associate with *wany* "throw" and *wa* "go" is *puy* (of sudden separation), which co-occurs also with *yaw* "go, with definite direction" and *yam* "carry" (the sudden departure of the carrier from a rest point, to take the bundle home); with *wany* "throw," *puy* alludes to the separation of the thrower and the object. *Wany* "throw" also associates with *mot* (of waves submerging one), which co-occurs also with *moylon* "cause to submerge," and *purr* (of flopping down), which co-occurs also with *wun* "lie down" and *tharr* "put." With *kal* "spear" associate not only *thut* (of stable relative position) but also, and more typically, *kvt* (of spearing) and *tuk* (of spearing). The ideophone with the widest set of associative possibilities is *tvk* (of finishing an action). The network of associations casts an extra light on the ways in which actions are conceived and reveals some very interesting associations.

Many ideophones nonetheless have a prototypical association with a single verb or family of nearly synonymous verbs: *puy* (of sudden departure) with *wa* "go" (and other "go" verbs), *kvt* (of spearing) with *kal* "spear," *thut* (of occupying a stable relative position) with *nhin* "sit" and *than* "stand." There are also ideophones (see *chirr, churr,* and *pow* in the list below) whose association with a single verb is so close that their sub-senses parallel precisely the sub-senses of these verbs. Close associations of these types doubtless make possible the use of ideophones in a verbless context.

12.6. The question of the status of ideophones as a part of speech in the grammar of YY

Ideophones occur in YY sentences according to patterns that are amenable to grammar-like statement. They occur
(a) Immediately before the verb: *Ngoyo tor piw ungh* "tor! I hit him," *Ngoyo kat kil ungnh* "kat! I speared it";
(b) Intonation- (usually clause-) finally, usually separated from the verb by a comma or falling intonation-contour: *Piw 'y ungnh, tor!* "I hit him, tor!", *Kil 'y ungnh, kat!* "I speared it, kat!"; or
(c) With no verb in evidence, with a semantically appropriate action understood: *Ngoyo kvt!* "I [speared it], kat!", *Puy 'l* "[he got up and left] puy!"

In all these contexts, ideophones are the center of intonation, i.e. they take the highest stress (usually extra-loud), in the intonation contour.

With regard to distribution and intonation, ideophones resemble (among other things) manner adverbials, such as for example *kalpn* "hard": *Ngoyo kalpn piw ungnh* and *Piw 'y ungnh kalpn* "I hit him hard," *Ngoyo kalpn* "I [hit him] hard." It is reasonable, furthermore, to construe a direct quotation as a manner adverbial in construction with a verb of speaking, because the manner question-word *warruwrr* "how," when used with the speech verbs, can appropriately be answered with the quotation: Q: *Nholo warruwrr yirrl* "what did he say?", A: *Nholo ngey yirrl* "he said 'yes'." It is tempting, therefore, to regard an ideophone as a kind of manner adverbial, the direct quotation emitted by the action itself. But this view is mistaken, for two reasons. One is that adverbs but not ideophones occur in subordinate clauses and with negatives and imperatives. Another reason is that, when considered as "answers" to the question

(1) Q: *Nhorto warruwrr piw ungnh.*
        you how hit him
        "In what manner did you hit him?"

the following are not equally appropriate:

(2) A: *Ngoyo kalpn piw ungnh.*
        I hard hit him
        "I hit him hard."

(3) A: *Ngoyo tor piw ungnh.*
        I ! hit him
        "I hit him, tor!"

Here only (2) is pragmatically "happy."

Note also that manner adverbials can be graded: *kalpn morr* "very hard," whereas ideophones cannot: **tor morr*.

Ideophones therefore cannot count as manner adverbials; other considerations prevent classing them as modal particles (their resemblance to both of these is an artifact of the propensity of items of all these types to occur in the "New" information positions; see below). Nor can they be classed with verb-derivational prefixes, which they resemble to an extent. An example of a prefix is *polh-*, which with *mow* "to jump" produces *polhmow* "to boil," with roughly equal stress on both syllables – most usually the secondary stress (relative to what precedes) that is typical of verbs in context. Unlike ideophones, prefixes are inseparable from their verbs. Verbs derived by prefixation contain just one prefix, and yet ideophones occur with such derived verbs (e.g. *chor* with *yiyaw* "to split open" in one of the examples above). And prefixes, unlike ideophones, take the same level of stress as the verb root to which they are attached.

There are, however, a couple of prefixes that appear to come from ideophones, or to be intermediate cases: *to*, with primary stress and an initial *t* (rare in non-ideophones), attaches to *tharr* "to put" in *to + tharr* "put aside for good," but is clearly attested as an ideophone in *Ngul ngarr thurr pinn, inhqa; to* "then they just set it aside, for good." *Purr* combines as a prefix with *tharr* to give *purrtharr* "put down," but occurs with ideophone-like repetition, stress, and syntactic position in *Blanket 'purr 'purr 'purr thurr* "[they] put down blankets all around" and *Tharrlwalnh, 'purr* "[they] used to put it down, purr!"

Ideophones have probably been a minor source of prefixes in the history of YY. It appears that ideophone-like elements enter into the derivation of verbs in other Australian languages where they are recorded (see section 12.4). However, it makes no sense to speak of YY ideophones in general as combining with verbs to form new lexical items (with the exceptions *to + tharr* "put away" and *purrthurr* "put down" as noted above), since a collocation like *chan wenhth* "chan! hung it up" simply represents an act of hanging something up (*wenhth*), and is not a lexical item; contrast Djaru, where *yaan-* means "put," but *dany yaan-* means "hang." There is, moreover, no YY counterpart (verb or suffixial element) to the thematizing element *-dhu- ~ -yu-* in Dhuwal, which functions as a tense-carrier for any ideophone-like particle and can be said to combine with such particles in a derivational way.

Another type of derived verb in YY is the *phrasal verb*, which consists of a noun, e.g. *thaw* "mouth," separably in construction with a verb, e.g. *luw* "to break": *thaw luw* "to yawn," as in *nholo thaw luw* or *thaw olo luw* "he yawned." However, the noun in a phrasal verb differs from ideophones in (among other ways) being able to precede the main-stressed item before the verb, as with the stressed *wanh* "who" in *Thaw wanh luw* "who yawned," and in being unable to follow the verb (**Olo luw, thaw* "he yawned").

In terms of their placement within the clause, ideophones behave like adverbials, non-adverbial nouns in some of their uses, and modal particles. These classes do not constitute a grammatical superclass from any other standpoint. Although the rule that governs the placement of items of all of these types has to mention as context the true grammatical class of verbs, it is not so much a rule of syntax as one of information structuring in discourse.

Unlike items of any of the other types mentioned, ideophones are reported to occur as the only vocally produced signs in sign-language discourse both in the Wik languages (P. Sutton, personal communication) and in the Centralian languages (D. Bell, personal communication). In this characteristic they are in a sense extra-linguistic.

Within the context of the linguistic system strictly speaking, it is perhaps useful to consider YY ideophones as a part of the "punctuation component" (as suggested by K. Hale, personal communication), which includes the intonation system. It is this suggestion that I wish to explore in the remainder of this paper.

Intonation in YY includes the terminal contours (fall, fall-rise, half-fall-and-continue ["comma"], rise, and sustain),[9] contour-initial pitch-levels (normal, extra-high, and extra-low), and, most importantly in the context of this discussion, the high stress and pitch point, or *center of intonation*, that is realized (most usually) in the word just before the verb. At issue here is the extent to which segmentally spelled items can be considered part of this system, and there are certain items that appear to be characterizable as segmentally spelled punctuation. These include the interjectional particles *ey* and *ow*, which function as exclamation points in high-volume speech, *ey* terminating the initial utterance and *ow* the interlocutor's reply. Ideophones, however, constitute a more difficult case, since they are a large class and an open one (with the introduction of handcuffs as an item of technology, for example, comes the ideophone *tik*, of handcuffs locking).

Consistent with the characterization of ideophones as punctuation is the fact that they occur exclusively in positive declarative main clauses in narrative. Consider now the relevance of their role as occupiers of the center-of-intonation position. In YY discourse, New (as opposed to Given) information is introduced either at the center of intonation or just after the verb, separated from it by a comma or falling intonation. These are precisely the positions where ideophones occur, and ideophones are mutually exclusive with any other carriers of New information. Where it is the verb itself that carries the New information, the center of intonation is occupied by the particle *a*: it carries the main stress and signals that the following verb is new information. Pre-verbal ideophones are mutually exclusive with this *a*. Furthermore, ideophones are absent from YY clauses of *recapitulation*, which are uttered for the most part on a continuous level pitch (without a center of intonation or gradual pitch contours), which end with the segmental punctuation *e*—, a drawn-out vowel with non-fall pitch, and which function as hesitation forms before the utterance of the next episode:

(4) *Thel*   *yaw*   *'l*   *yirr*   *e*—
    again   went   he   away
    Chur   *yungrnaw.*
    !   swam
    Yungrnaw   *'l*   *e*—
    swam   he
    "Again he went off – Chur! he swam. He swam –"

Do the ideophones themselves carry what can be described as New information, or are they rather commentaries on and pointers to the verb to follow, in effect redundant emanations of the action? The latter alternative seems to me the correct one; the fact that (at least some) ideophones occur at the center of intonation with no following verb seems to depend on the typical co-occurrence of a prototypical verb with these ideophones.

Taking this to be so (for the sake of discussion), what then of the particle *a*? It is mutually exclusive with ideophones at the center of intonation, and with its usual vowel-initial realization[10] it seems like a candidate for the status of "the null ideophone," or perhaps an "anti-ideophone." That it is not such, however, is apparent from the following of its characteristics, in all of which it differs from ideophones: (a) it occurs quite routinely with imperative verbs; (b) it occurs following nominal (verbless) predicates, with emphatic force; (c) it is often used explicitly to contrast its following verb with one in a preceding clause; (d) it participates in a contrast-set with *wuw*, which either marks a clause as a yes-or-no question or, like *a*, explicitly contrasts its following verb with one in a preceding clause; and (e) like *wuw*, it can be followed by the unstressed particle *waw* "might be," yielding *a* + *waw* "I think that" and *wuw* + *waw* "I wonder if."

On this view, in sum, ideophones in YY constitute a part of speech that belongs in an entirely different realm from the familiar nouns, verbs, and particles, and from bound morphemes. The members of this class are phonologically aberrant in certain patterned ways, are apparently exempt from regular sound change, tend to be onomatopoeic and sound-symbolic in certain limited ways, and constitute the only vocal communicative noises that are permitted in social contexts where "speech" is forbidden.[11]

12.7

List of ideophones

The phonetic value of the symbols is as explained above; note that *ll*, as in ordinary YY words, is pronounced [dl].[12]

CHAN [Var. *chang* and *cham*] Of hanging or being suspended.
CHAWARRQ [Var. *chawarr*] Of picking up and carrying off.
CHICHICHI [Continued ad lib. Var. *chuchuchu*.] Of a dog running.
CHIKCHIKCHIK [Continued ad lib.] Of the sex act.
CHIP Of going along a course.
CHIRR [The [rr] is trilled.] Of the separation of the shaft and butt of a spear or harpoon.
CHIRR [Parallels the senses of *lar* "emerge."] 1. Of emerging. 2. Of arriving or coming into the center from the outside.
CHIRRR Of a boat's fast motion.
CHOK Of slicing through something.
CHOQ Of a bird's sudden take-off.
CHOR [Var. *chorq*] Of cutting or splitting or ripping open.
CHUL [The senses of this ideophone parallel those of *pul* "flow; go down; go across."] 1. Of liquid gushing forth. 2. Of going downwards to water. (Cf. also *chur* ~ *chuy*, of plunging into water.) 3. Of crossing a creek.
CHURUP Of a manta ray landing on the water.
CHURR Of spearing a man.

Australia and Africa

CHUY [Var. *chur*] Of plunging into water.

CHVP Of lightning striking. (This form seems to evoke the actual touch of the lightning, as opposed to the ideophone *taaa*, of the entire flash.)

FFFFT Of blowing a fire.

KARRKVRRKVRR [Continued ad lib.] Of spearing multiple times at an object in water.

KARRQ Of scraping.

KITKITKIT [Continued ad lib.] Of a snake's tongue darting in and out.

KVT [Var. *kat*] 1. Of spearing. 2. Of hitting. [Near syn. *tor*, *tala*]

LAK [Var. *lak*] Of throwing, knocking, or falling heavily to ground.

LAW Of breaking off a leaf from a twig. (Contrast *piw*, of breaking a stiff object.)

LHOP [Var. *lhvp*] Of being swallowed by the Rainbow Serpent.

MOT Of waves submerging one. (Cf. *mort* "heap.")

NYCHIP Of foot being pierced by catfish spine.

NYOM 1. Of losing one's footing as one's legs go rubbery, or when deep in water. 2. Of falling dead. 3. Of going under water, deliberately.

PARR [Var. *prrrq*] Of a quick cutting motion.

PARRQ [Var. *parr*] Of finishing up food.

PILL Of shooting star's flight.

PILLII Of woman's sexual arousal.

PITH Of spitting.

PIW Of a twig or stick breaking with a snap. (Cf. *tony*, *toll*.)

POLPOLPOL [Continued ad lib.] 1. Of a fish's tail flopping on the ground. 2. Of waves lapping.

POQ Of picking up and carrying off a corpse.

POR [Usually lengthened: [poooor].] Of floating up to surface of water.

POR Of scraping out the center of a wild date tree.

PORRL Of dumping waterlily from container to ground.

POTH Of smoke puffing up from a fire.

POW [Co-occurs with *yow* "get" in all extensions.] 1. Of getting, fetching, picking up. 2. Of reciting a name.

PPPP Of handcuffs falling off after being cut with a file.

PRRR 1. Of sliding on a salt-pan. 2. Of going down to the waterside in a large group. 3. Of a particular mythic incident of eating maggots.

PUM Of covering over or burying.

PUP [Var. *pbbbp* and *pvp*] Of falling or hitting bottom.

PURR [Var. *wurr* and *purrch*] Of emerging or appearing or rising. (This form exhibits the very general semantic association of "upward" and "outward.")

PURR [Var. *purrq*; used also as a verb-forming prefix in *purr pon* "pour out," *purr tharr* "put down," *purr wany* "throw down"; it is attested quasi-prefixially (with stress greater than the following verb root) in *purr + tharr* (as for *purr tharr*) and *purr + wany* (as for *purr = wany*)] 1. Of putting something down with a flopping motion. 2. Of making camp.

PURRT [Var. *prrrt*] Of throwing.
PUT Of pushing.
PUT Of tinder catching fire.
PUU Of starting a fire. (Possibly to be identified with *puww*.)
PUUT Of farting.
PUWW [Var. [*pupuWWuWWuWWuWW*]] Of burning.
PUY [Var. *poy*] 1. Of setting off and going away. 2. Of turning aside from something finished.
PVRR Of beating someone up.
TA [Voiceless vowel] Of a spear breaking. (See also *piw*.)
TAAA [Voiceless vowel] Of lightning striking. (The ideophone *chvp*, of lightning striking, evokes the actual touch of the lightning.)
TAK [Var. (apparently free; the same individuals use both) *tvk*, q.v.] Of biting.
TALA TALA Of beating someone up.
TAP [Var. *tak*] Of dying. (See also *to*, of dugong dying.)
TATL Of the cracking of a tree about to fall from chopping.
TIK Of handcuffs locking.
TITITITI [Continued ad lib.] Of a dog shaking water off.
TO Of death spasms of dugong. (See also *tap*, of dying.)
TO Of putting aside for good.
TOLL [todl] Of a rope breaking. (See also *thony*, of a stiff object breaking, *piw*, of breaking with a snap.)
TOLL [todl]. [Var. *tull* and *tvll*] Of popping or bursting.
TONY [Var. *thony*] Of the breaking or sudden severing of a straight rigid thing. (Near syn. *piw*; contrast *toll*.)
TOR Of striking a blow with an implement. (See also *kvt*, *tala tala*.)
TRRRA Of gathering together things that clatter.
TRRT 1. Of entering. 2. Of waking up. 3. Of running.
TRTRTRT [Continued ad lib.] Of running a flame along a line.
TU TU TU [Continued ad lib., with falling intonation after each repetition.] 1. Of repeated blows, as in smashing wood in the water to poison fish. 2. Of kicking while swimming. 3. Of gunshots.
TUK [Continued ad lib. with mid to high level intonation after each repetition. Free alt. *tvk* in repetitions; the vowel quality is constant throughout the repetition.] 1. Of spearing or hitting with a thrown object, with emphasis on the knocking down of the target. 2. Of smashing something up.
TUP [Var. *tvp*] Of setting something on fire or cooking it. (See also *trtrtrt*.)
TURR [Var. *churr*, *thurr(q)*] Of jumping.
TUWW Of the bursting of Moon's testicles.
TVK [Var. *tak*] Of finishing an action.
THAK Of a sudden strike.
THARR [tends to fuse with *mom* "grab" as *tharr* + *mom*.] Of grabbing or catching.
THARRCH [Var. *parrch*] 1. Of sudden upward motion. 2. Of fronting up for a fight.

Australia and Africa

THUP Of closing something.
THUP Of a thrown stick hitting the water.
THUT [Var. *thot*] Of assuming a stable relative position.
THVK [Var. *thak*] Of biting.
THVT Of chopping.
THVTPPPFFF Of the blow of a thrown boomerang.
WIRR [Continued ad lib. with close transition; when uttered without repetition the [rr] is usually trilled and devoiced.] Of pulling or dragging something.
WURLWURLWURL [Continued ad lib.] Of running from water in a panic.
WURR [the [rr] is usually trilled, sometimes voiceless. Var. *purr*] Of emerging. [Near syn. *chirr*.]
WUUUU(T) Of tree beginning to fall.

NOTES

* Earlier versions of this paper were presented at the April 1969 conference of the Southwestern and Rocky Mountain Division, American Association for the Advancement of Science and the Arizona Academy of Science in Tempe; at the August 1984 conference of the Australian Linguistic Society in Alice Springs; and in November 1984 at the Linguistics Department, University of Sydney. I wish to thank Diane Bell, Ken Hale, Peter Sutton, Philip von Bretzel, and Michael Walsh for comments and suggestions; they are not responsible for errors.

1 The apostrophe "'" is written in the first, second, and third person subject pronominal clitics, respectively *'y*, *'r*, *'l*, and represents a schwa in those positions. the symbol "'" is written before the onset of a syllable to indicate that that syllable bears high stress not otherwise expectable. Double or triple "w" indicates a prolonged voiced bilabial fricative; triple "f" indicates a prolonged voiceless bilabial fricative; tripled vowel letters indicate a greatly prolonged vowel; other tripled letters indicate trills prolonged ad lib.

2 Setting aside the question of vocal imitation of soundless processes, the forms under discussion here are examples of "imitative sound symbolism" in terms of the typology set forth in the introduction to this volume. The repetition ad lib. of many of these items (see for example *kitkitkit*, *wirr*, *purr*) is clearly imitative, although quite distinct from the reduplication that is important in the morphology of YY nouns and verbs. Regarding (synesthetic) sound symbolism, see note 5. There is also in YY a metalinguistic symbolism in the segmental phonology of verbs: a sequence of vowel followed by stop does not occur at the end of any verb and occurs internally to a verb only in the participial (see also note 6).

3 Displayed in tabular form, the inventory is:

p	th	t	rt	ch	k	q	i		u
m	nh	n	rn	ny	ng		e	v	o
	lh	l	rl					a	
		rr							
w			r	y					

175

4 Recall, however, that these figures are for list frequency, and that *kvt* (of spearing) is one of the most frequently encountered ideophones in texts.
5 McGregor (1985: 45) holds that "the final consonant [of YY ideophones, among others] tends to be symbolic"; readers are invited to try their own analyses of the list in section 12.7.
6 In a sound change conditioned by the destressing of YY verbs in context (see section 12.6), final stops in pre-YY verbs have become glides at the corresponding points of articulation, and *k has disappeared. The only exceptions to the resulting sonorant-final canon for verb roots in the modern language are verbs ending in *nhth*, *lhth*, *rnt*, and *lt* (Alpher 1988 and n.d.).
7 This *-dhu-* is probably cognate with the verb *tju-* "to put" in the Western Desert languages. In the languages of northeast Arnhem Land, it has other uses than that mentioned here, functioning for example as a thematizer for English verbs, as in Dhuwal *married-dhu-* "to marry (someone)."
8 On the basis of my own hearing of similar forms in the closely related Dhuwala dialects, I would qualify this last statement as applying only to root forms not in construction with thematizing *-dhu-*.
9 The phonetic call among fall-rise, comma, fall, and sustain can be a close one. The domain of rise and sustain is the entire pitch contour; the others commence after the center of intonation, with the fall of the fall-rise varying in the position of its onset. See also Alpher 1991: 9–10.
10 It is *nga* after vowels and, occasionally, intonation-initially; it is occasionally *qa* intonation-finally after a verb.
11 I leave aside here questions as to whether ideophones can be said to enter into syntactic construction with other segmentally realized forms without the clause, and whether ideophones can be said to "refer."
12 These forms are listed with exemplification and cross-referencing in Alpher 1991.

REFERENCES

Alpher, B. 1991. *Yir-Yoront lexicon: Sketch and dictionary of an Australian language*. Berlin: Mouton de Gruyter.

1988. Formalizing Yir-Yoront lenition. *Aboriginal Linguistics* 1: 188–197.

n.d. The origin of ablaut as a morphological process in Yir-Yoront. ms.

Dixon, R.M.W. 1971. A method of semantic description. In D. D. Steinberg and L. A. Jakobovits (eds.) *Semantics: An Interdisciplinary Reader in Philosophy, Linguistics, and Psychology*. Cambridge: University Press, 436–471.

Hall, A. and T. Foote. 1983. Lexicon: Thaayorre/English. ms; printed for the Queensland Department of Education, Brisbane.

Heath, J. 1976. North-east Arnhem Land. In R. M. W. Dixon (ed.) Grammatical Categories in Australian Languages, 735–740. Linguistic Series No. 22. Canberra: Australian Institute of Aboriginal Studies.

1980a. *Dhuwal (Arnhem Land) Texts on Kinship and Other Subjects with Grammatical Sketch and Dictionary*. Oceania Linguistic Monographs No. 23. Sydney: University of Sydney.

1980b. *Basic Materials in Ritharngu: Grammar, Texts and Dictionary*. Pacific Linguistics Series B, no. 62. Canberra: Australian National University.

Lowe, B. 1962. Lessons in Gupapuyngu. ms.

n.d. Temporary Gupapuyngu dictionary. ms, compiled by Michael Christie.

McConnell, U. 1936a. Totemic hero-cults in Cape York Peninsula, North Queensland. Part I. *Oceania* 6(4): 452–477.

1936b. Totemic hero-cults in Cape York Peninsula, North Queensland. Part II. *Oceania* 7(1): 69–105.

McGregor, W. 1986. Sound symbolism in Kuniyanti. ms.

Merlan, F. 1982. *Mangarayi*. Lingua Descriptive Studies, vol. 4. Amsterdam: North-Holland.

O'Grady, G. N. 1964. *Nyangumata Grammar*. Oceania Linguistic Monographs, no. 9. Sydney: University of Sydney.

Sommer, B. 1968. *Kunjen Phonology: Synchronic and Diachronic*. Pacific Linguistics Series B no. 11. Canberra: Research School of Pacific Studies, Australian National University.

1972. *Kunjen Syntax: A Generative View*. Canberra: Australian Institute of Aboriginal Studies.

Sutton, P. 1978. Wik: Aboriginal society, territory and language at Cape Keerweer, Cape York Peninsula, Australia. PhD. dissertation, University of Queensland.

Tsunoda, T. 1981. *The Djaru Language of Kimberley, Western Australia*. Pacific Linguistics Series B, no. 78. Canberra: Research School of Pacific studies, Australian National University.

13
African ideophones

G. TUCKER CHILDS

13.1. Introduction

Hàlí kól mùèìyáŋ lé pààléŋ kpêŋ. Tófá ndú hùnɔ́ɔ́ hyáŋ-hyáŋ*
Hali drink liquor for day all look him come Idph

"Hali has been drinking cane juice all day long. Look at him reel from side to side as he approaches!"

In the above utterance *hyáŋ-hyáŋ* is an ideophone. As opposed to other words in the utterance, it exhibits unusual phonological properties (e.g. its raised pitch range or register), morphological properties (e.g. reduplication), syntactic properties (e.g. its sentence-final position set off from the rest of the utterance), semantic properties (e.g. the translation is inexact as given above), and historical properties (e.g. its origin is obscure and it may be a nonce creation). In this paper I survey and document more fully these and other properties which set ideophones off from the elements of language that are the more common focus of linguistic descriptions.

Although they constitute a robust word category in African languages, ideophones are relatively neglected and are rarely integrated into linguistic descriptions. Their differences from the rest of language constitute much of their appeal as well as their challenge to description. In reality, the features of ideophones are not unique, or even qualitatively different from those possessed by other word categories. No feature is unique to ideophones, but they do function somewhat apart from the matrix language, possibly due to their greater reliance on universals and lesser reliance on language-specific conventions.

This paper aims to familiarize the reader with ideophones as they appear in African languages and to supplement the very fine and comprehensive survey of Bantu ideophones by Samarin (1971). Although most writers today use the term *ideophone* (for the African phenomenon), many other terms have been used in the past. An inventory of names for African languages is given in Samarin 1970b and Samarin 1971: 131–133; he lists, for example, *echo-words* in Semitic languages (including the Ethiopic languages Amharic, Tigrinya, and Tigre). Names not listed by him include *emphatics* (in use by the Lutheran Bible Translators in Liberia), and *expressives* and *impressifs* in analyses of both Asian and African languages, e.g. for Vietnamese (Durand 1961) and for Malagasy (Alexandre 1966). Swahili terms can underscore the onomatopoeic or imitative component: *vielezi miigo* (Kapinga 1983) "imitative exclamations or comments" and *tanakali za sauti* (Saidi 1976) "copy? of sounds," and *takwidi* (C. N. Chacha, personal communication).

On the other hand, the term *ideophone* has been used not solely for the African word category. Smithers (1954: 73, footnote 1) claims that he is the first to use the term for Middle English words such as those listed in (1).

(1) *liklakyng* "clashing of weapons in battle"
 tukke "pull sharply, jerk at"
 gabbe "mock, deceive, lie, act glibly"

Most of his examples are verbs or verb-like words, exhibiting a somewhat different phonology from other words. The first example shows the characteristic apophony and reduplication, and the other two show the typical form of ME ideophones, i.e. $C_1VC_2C_2e$. These features are not dissimilar to those possessed by African ideophones, but the term *ideophone* is not widely used with reference to English.

Ideophones have probably been neglected because of their intractability to analysis. They can be highly variable and difficult to elicit away from the field and often need to be studied *in situ*. They do not regularly show up in written texts. In addition, they have little in the way of morphosyntax and rely heavily on context for interpretation.

They deserve attention, however, because of their widespread distribution in the languages of the world (Samarin 1970b: 155). They are found in Aboriginal Australian languages (Courtenay 1976: 13), Mayan languages (Durbin 1973; Maafi 1990), Russian (Andersen, personal communication 1989), Malay (Carr 1966), and Lahu (Matisoff, this volume), as well as in pidgins and creoles in the New World, e.g. Jamaican English (DeCamp 1974) and in Africa, e.g. Pidgin Sango (Noss 1975) and (pidginized) Lingala (Samarin 1979: 56), Liberian English and (Sierra Leone) Krio (Childs 1994).

Furthermore, ideophones often represent a sizeable proportion of a language's lexicon: 8,000 to 9,000 in Gbaya (Samarin 1979: 55); 25% of the lexicon in Nupe (R. Blench, personal communication 1988); 2,600 in Zulu (Fivaz 1963, revised upward to over 3,000 in Von Staden 1977). In Kisi a lexicon of 4,000 words contains 363 ideophones. Bohnhoff (1982) finds comparable numbers for Yag Dii: 535 ideophones in a lexicon of 4,244 words.

In addition, ideophones constitute an open and productive class in many languages, e.g. Yoruba (Awoyale 1988), Igbo (Maduka 1983–1984), Nembe (Maduka 1988b), and Yag Dii (Bohnhoff 1982). Although not necessarily numerous in every African language, e.g. Swahili (Ottenheimer and Primrose 1989), ideophones generally represent a significant part of the lexicon, a part that cannot be ignored in any adequate analysis of a language.

Ideophones are also of interest for their apparent iconism, especially sound symbolism, raising the broad issue as to the arbitrariness of the sound–meaning association. Although they exploit non-arbitrary associations, as do other parts of the language, they do so much more extensively and directly.

Finally, the peculiar pragmatics and the aesthetics of ideophones challenge investigators. Since ideophones convey more than purely referential information, their study must be grounded in a theory of expressiveness. Understanding language as a form of human behavior requires us to consider ideophones as an important manifestation of the expressive and perhaps poetic functions. In sum, if we wish to describe all the data and to understand language as it is used, ideophones need to function prominently in the analysis.

13.2. Definitional

A starting point is Doke's familiar definition:

A vivid representation of an idea in sound. A word, often onomatopoeic, which describes a predicate, qualificative or adverb in respect to manner, colour, smell, action, state, or intensity. The ideophone is in Bantu a special part of speech, resembling to a certain extent in function an adverb. (1935: 118)

Doke further notes the special distribution of ideophones as well as their unusual phonological properties. In another entry ("Reduplication"), Doke notes that the reduplication of ideophones is common (1935: 185). This combination of phonological, morphological, semantic, and pragmatic criteria has guided later investigators and serves as a preliminary definition, to be discussed and expanded upon below.

Do ideophones form a separate word category[1] on a par with other categories such as nouns and verbs? In some languages they do not. For example, Hausa ideophones form subclasses of other categories: "[G]rammatically there are no ideophones as such, but only ideophonic nouns, ideophonic verbs, ideophonic adverbs, etc" (Newman 1968: 108). In some languages ideophones can be located in just one or two (already established) classes, i.e. no separate class is needed. In Tera ideophones function (syntactically) as adjectives (Newman 1968: 113), in Shona as verbs (Fortune 962: 4), in Gbaya[2] as adverbs (Samarin 1965: 118), and in Bambara as nouns and verbs (Courtenay 1974).

Even within the same language there are different analyses. In Yoruba, ideophones are placed in multiple word categories according to Courtenay (1976), yet Awoyale (1981) argues for the uniqueness of the class on morphosyntactic grounds. Still further, Fordyce (1983) argues that Yoruba ideophones form a "phonosemantic" class. Noss notes the confusing and conflicting literature on Zande ideophones; they are sometimes classified as adjectives, other times as adverbs. Furthermore, onomatopoeic ideophones are often completely excluded despite their functioning as adjectives or adverbs (Noss 1975: 142–143).

In the vast majority of cases, however, ideophones perform an adverbial function and are closely linked with verbs. Belonging to the content end of a content–function continuum, they are semantic rather than syntactic in their orientation. Ideophones rarely function as heads of constructions (e.g. Lyons 1968: 344) or as, say, adpositions. In some cases they represent the epitome of content words in showing almost pure content and no syntax.

If we can separate ideophones as a word class either universally or language-specifically, the next question is what conditions define these words as a class. Undoubtedly the criteria partake of the phonological and semantic peculiarities these words exhibit, but syntactic and pragmatic criteria will work as well. Occasionally ideophones violate these criteria in a particular language, but these violations do not vitiate the generalizations achieved on a broad consideration.

Within a particular language further definitional problems arise. We will have to say that no one feature can be considered criterial; a constellation of characteristics differentiates ideophones from other word categories. Each token possesses only a subset of these features. For example, one ideophone may not exhibit the typical phonological irregularities, but because it possesses other ideophone features it must be included in the category. Ideophones also share features with other word categories, even with items outside language proper, such as gesture (cf. Kita 1992). It is thus best to think of ideophones as a prototype category with a core of good members. The full set of ideophones also contains less optimal members radiating outward from this core type and becoming less and less ideophone-like. They may become more and more verb-like along the ray bridging the juncture with verbs, or even depart into paralinguistics along another dimension.

13.2.1. Phonological

Few detailed phonetic studies, including instrumental ones, have been performed on ideophones, with the exception of those by Mphande and Rice (1989), who discuss the acoustics of ChiTumbuka ideophones, and Greenberg and Sapir (1978), who analyze the vowels in Diola ideophones.

All investigators note the peculiar phonology ideophones feature, yet few claim that phonological features uniquely and exclusively define the class. Mphande and Rice 1989, however, represents an approximation to such a claim. They find that necessary and sufficient conditions cannot come from syntax, semantics, or discourse considerations. What is unique about ChiTumbuka ideophones, they claim, is their phonological features. Tone is contrastive in ideophones, as it is nowhere else in the language (ChiTumbuka has penultimate stress).[3] Nasalization of vowels is contrastive in ideophones; elsewhere it is predictable. Vowel length is also uniquely contrastive in ideophones. The paper does not make clear whether or not these three features exhaustively categorize all ideophones in the language. The expectation is that not all ideophones possess these features. In other languages ideophones display aberrant phonological features, but not all ideophones have all features. Further consideration might lead to a prototype definition, such as that sketched above.

Courtenay (1976) also opts for a phonological delimitation of ideophones in Yoruba because other word classes can also be defined phonologically. Ideophones function syntactically with multiple word classes, but phonologically they maintain a separate identity. Only verbs have a CV syllable structure, and only nouns are VCV(CV); ideophones never assume these forms and differ, for example, in being segmentally longer or in containing syllabic nasals.

As indicated by Courtenay's description of Yoruba, ideophones typically violate the segmental and prosodic constraints of the matrix language. There can be fewer or more segments. For example, Nguni ideophones have segments not found elsewhere in the language (Lanham 1960). Most Hausa syllables are open, but ideophones are commonly of the structure CVC (with a high tone) (Moore 1968: 8–9). Bulu ideophones allow [p] initially, a sound found elsewhere only as an allophone of /b/ in final position (Alexandre 1966: 16). In Southern Bantu ideophones favor monosyllables, as opposed to the general tendency in the rest of the language (Doke 1954: 29). In the Central Sudanic language Lulubo, ideophones have a different phonemic inventory (Andersen 1987: 57–58).

At the same time as there are more features or contrasts, there can also be fewer. Contrasts prominent elsewhere in the language may not be so important among ideophones. Phonetically dissimilar words may mean the same thing; the phonetic substance they share may be reanalyzed as a submorphemic partial or *phonestheme* (Bolinger 1949; see section 13.2.4.4 below). This leads to an accretion of sound and meaning correspondences that can eventually lead to sound symbolism (Childs 1989).

(2) Clusterings of sound–meaning correspondences

Gbaya   *ham hɛm hal hɛl pal pɛl*   "light"   (Samarin 1991)

Ijo   *gẹẹn*   of an even, unblinking light
      geen   of a steady light, brighter than *gẹẹn*
      gọọn   of a light which is brighter than *gẹẹn*, but does not bother one like *geen*
      goon   of a light which is brighter than *geen* or *gẹẹn*   (Williamson 1965)

Hausa   *lip   rip*   "smooth, flat"
        buzuu-bùzùu/muzuu-mùzùu   "hairy"
        cik/cif   "stopped completely"   (Moore 1968: 19)

Kisi   *càm-càm/cáŋ-càŋ*   "lukewarm (of a liquid)"
       kɔ́cu/dɔ́cù   "knocking"   (Childs 1989)

Yoruba *rogodo* "bulging (as eyes)"
       rugudu/rúgúdú "small and spherical (as buttocks)"
       rógódó "large, round (as yams)"
       rogbodo "fine and plump"
       roboto "fat – much more than *rugudu*" (Courtenay 1976: 25)

There can also be a lack of contrast between the absence and presence of a sound, as in the Kisi examples below in (3).

(3) a. Final /l/
     pál/pál   "dripping"
     fú-fú/fúl-fúl "rushing (of air)"

     b. Final /ŋ/
     yéŋgé-yéŋgé "delicately balanced"
     yéŋgéŋ-yéŋgéŋ "delicately balanced"

Another common feature of ideophones is vowel assonance or harmony, as in Zulu for example (Van Rooyen *et al.* 1976). Vowels are similarly identical in Bulu ideophones: *COCO* is the ideophone pattern as opposed to the regular pattern of *COCo* (Alexandre 1966). In Kisi ideophones of two or more syllables, the vowels are usually identical.

(4) Identical vowels in polysyllabic ideophones
     téŋ géŋ (-teŋ geŋ) "erect, as when a cobra rises"
     bílí-lí (-lí . . .) "heavily flowing"

In Temne, as in many other languages, ideophones are pronounced on a higher or lower pitch than other words and are more susceptible to individual manipulation (Wilson 1961: 43). The same exaggeration occurs with length. For example, the Kisi ideophone for "extensive in time," *hã-ã-ã-ã* . . . is not only pronounced with a raised pitch register but is also lengthened considerably more than other syllables. (The vowel is also nasalized as is no other Kisi vowel in this environment, cf. [háà] "this.") Vai ideophones also allow extra-long syllables only with ideophones (Welmers 1976: 137). Ideophones in Southern Bantu generally disobey the regular rules of stress assignment. Doke (1954: 43) gives examples of exceptional initial stress assignment in Zulu ideophones.

Prosodic features such as syllable structure and tone, rather than segmental ones, will generally be more important for marking ideophones as different. For example, Hausa ideophones end in consonants appearing only at the end of ideophones, and Tera ideophones are marked by the absence of glottalized stops and nasal resonants in word-initial position, as well as by a high incidence of consonants in word-final position (Newman 1968: 115).

Tone systems are generally simpler in Bantu ideophones (Samarin 1971: 139). The same is true of Kanuri (Hutchison 1989) and Hausa (Newman 1989), where ideophones have identical (level) tones throughout. Toura tones on ideophones are usually identical throughout: high, mid, or low, even when reduplicated more than once (Bearth 1971: 203–204). Kisi ideophone tones are generally the same (usually high), but there are proportionately more contour tones on ideophones than on other words in Kisi.

Phonological oddness may be realized on any phonological aspect. I give below the entire range of features in a single language.

(5) Phonologically odd features of Kisi ideophones
1. Raised or lowered register (F_0 or pitch range)
2. Rapid modulation or exaggerated range of register
3. Phonation: breathy voice, creaky voice, voicelessness and whisper
4. Duration: overly short or long
5. Rate: faster or slower than normal
6. Set off from the rest of the sentence by a pause[4]
7. Using phones not belonging to regular phonemic inventory, lacking regular phonemic oppositions
8. Violating phonotactic constraints of language

Not all ideophones have all of these features, but every ideophone usually has at least some of them.

Ideophones undergo few phonological rules. Usually the ideophonic subsection of a language has few rules of its own. Ideophones represent exceptions to what are characterized as lexical rules in the framework of lexical phonology (Kiparsky 1982; Mohanan 1986). For example, exceptions to Dahl's Law in Kikuyu are confined to ideophones and loanwords (Myers 1974, as cited in Pulleybank 1986: 22). Since ideophones possess little morphology, there is little of the interaction at morphological interfaces where (morpho-)phonological rules usually operate. If rules do operate on ideophones, they are generally more phonetic, that is, late-operating rules, of the sort assigned to the post-lexical component. Even downstep, which is usually a "phonetic" rule, i.e. ordered after the post-lexical rules (Pulleyblank 1986), does not affect Shona ideophones (Fortune 1962: 8). Ibibio ideophones are similarly unaffected by downstep (Ekere 1988b).

Although there has been little discussion of the topic, it seems unlikely that ideophones interact with other words at domains beyond the word level (as in a prosodic domain treatment [Selkirk 1980]). This would certainly be true in languages where ideophones are syntactically and phonologically isolated, such as Bulu (Alexandre 1966) or Shangaan-Tsonga (Jaques 1941, as noted in Samarin 1971: 136). In Hausa, on the other hand, where ideophones do not constitute a separate word category (Newman 1968), they condition the polarity rule determining the tone on the copula *nee*.

(6) Ideophones affecting tonal polarity in Hausa

Australia and Africa

fàrú́ fát nèè	"It's really white."
white Idph Cop	
gáràm née	"It's the sound of something falling."[5]
Idph Cop	

But ideophones are also exceptions to the rule of Low Tone Raising in Hausa (Newman and Jagger 1989). In Akan ideophones unexpectedly conform to a general palatalization rule (Boadi 1988). These facts suggest that ideophones are not in principle immune to phonological rules.

Furthermore, ideophones are often isolated by a (preceding) pause or accompanied by a paralinguistic gesture. Ideophones may also be introduced by a particle or dummy verb (discussed below in section 13.2.3, "Syntactic"). Kisi ideophones are introduced by a pause, as if the speaker were gathering strength for the demanding phonological features of the ideophone. The pause could be interpreted as a reset mechanism, comparable to that used between clauses in English (Ladd 1988). ChiTumbuka ideophones are also set off by a pause (Mphande and Rice 1989) and Hausa ideophones by a "pronounced juncture" (Moore 1973: 13). This feature is probably more widespread than the few references indicate. For example, Samarin (1971: 136) quotes Jaques on Shangaan-Tsonga: "An ideophone is an entity by itself, which interrupts the course of ordinary speech" (Jaques 1941: 210). This interruption surely takes the form of a pause.

13.2.2. *Morphological*

Ideophones display very little morphology. For example, despite its being classified as a "non-verb verbal," the Southern Bantu ideophone is never declinable (Marivate 1985). Similarly, Chitumbuka ideophones bear no affixes (Rice 1987). The only productive process at work with ideophones in general is repetition, sometimes morphologized as reduplication (or lengthening, lexicalized as extra-length). In the sense I use these words, repetition refers to an expressive phenomenon controlled by the individual. There is no limit on how many times a form can be repeated or on how long a segment may be prolonged (except the physical limitations of the system or speaker). Some examples of repetition and prolonged vowels from Kisi appear in (7).

(7) Ideophones which can be repeated more than once or lengthened indefinitely
    gbúŋ gbúŋ ...   "sound of rice beaten by one person"
    dóŋgú dóŋgú ...   "going on for a long time"[6]
    pùkl-ɛ́-ɛ́   "sound of rice falling into fanner"
    fìyú-ú-ú-ú   "moving rapidly"

Repeated or prolonged ideophones generally possess an iconic component in that the elongation represents extension in time or space.

Expressive lengthening must be differentiated from its lexicalized counterpart, extra-length. In many languages ideophones feature extra-long vowels, e.g. the Southern Bantu languages Zulu and Shona (Doke 1954: 43–44). I give two examples from Kisi in (8).

(8) Ideophones with extra-long vowels
    sîi   "continuing for a short distance or period"
    píàà   "quickly cutting through water"

Reduplication, on the other hand, is more restricted than repetition in the forms it can apply to and affects forms earlier on in a derivation. It is a morphological process that can affect stems or partials and can copy prosodic features, no differently from any other morphological process (Steriade 1988).

In Kisi, as in many other languages, e.g. Hausa (Newman 1989), reduplication takes many forms, as shown in the Kisi examples in (9) and (10).

(9) Reduplication
    a. Ideophones which may be reduplicated only once
       pílíkò (-pílíkò)   "going by in a series"
       cíŋ (-cíŋ)   "closely or keenly, intently"
       dóŋ (-dóŋ)   "quietly, silently"

    b. Ideophones which *must* be reduplicated
       félé-félé   "slowly and steadily"
       cám-cám   "lukewarm"
       bákàlà-bákàlà   "rain falling in single, heavy droplets"

Another type involves only part of the stem, usually only the final syllable (example a in (10)), infrequently an initial partial (example b).

(10) Partial reduplication
    a. *fóndó-ndó-ndó*   "describing something very close"
    b. *hìŋa-húŋâŋndó*   "involving back and forth movement"

Reduplication is more tractable and regular in other parts of the language. For example, noun stems are repeated in the distributive construction, but the process applies to *all* nouns, not just a subset of the total nouns.

Some derivational processes can be identified. The close relationship between verbs and ideophones manifests itself in the cross-linguistic commonness of derivational relationships between verbs and ideophones. The directionality is at times difficult to identify, but new ideophones from verbs seems to be the more commonly attested direction (Childs 1989, but cf. Samarin 1971: 141 for an opposing interpretation for Bantu). Onomatopoeic ideophones in particular augment the lexicon as, for example, names for animals and machines (see discussion below).

13.2.3. Syntactic

The comments above illustrate the different opinions as to word-category assignment and as to the existence of a separate word category. Full resolution of these questions can be achieved only on a language-specific basis. Southern Bantu languages feature verbal ideophones (e.g. Marivate 1985), while in other Benue-Congo languages ideophones belong to many different classes. Louw (1965), on the other hand, divides word categories of Southern Bantu into two groups, verbals and nominals (three if interjections are counted); in his schema ideophones represent one of the two types of verbals. Kisi and Temne, two Atlantic languages, follow the general pattern of Bantu. In Kanuri, a Nilo-Saharan language, ideophones qualify adjectives, verbs, and less frequently nouns (Hutchison 1989). In Hausa (Chadic, Afro-Asiatic) ideophones are generally adverbial; and in Tera, another Chadic language, ideophones cannot be differentiated from adjectives, except on phonological grounds (Newman 1968). The conclusion from these facts is that ideophones cannot be defined as a word class solely on the basis of their syntactic features.

Nonetheless, syntactic generalizations exist. The typical observation is that ideophones are set apart from the rest of an utterance, often so dramatically that they can be treated as a separate element. This isolation has been analyzed as resulting from their derivational history. Noss suggests that ideophones are all that is left of an embedded clause with everything else deleted (1985b: 249). Bohnhoff (1989: 19) proposes that ideophones represent a branch off a higher node at the same level as the sentence itself. Others have suggested that ideophones constitute full predicates (Awoyale 1981: 143).[7] These analyses taken together demonstrate the relative lack of integration of ideophones into any lower structures.

Other, more general, discussions underscore this fact. Kunene (1965) comments on the "syntactic aloofness" of the ideophone in Southern Sotho, and Moshi (1993) advocates treating ideophones as an "adjunct" in KiVunjo Chaga since they appear "syntactically unattached" (cf. Ekere 1988a for a similar characterization of Ibibio ideophones). In general, ideophones have also been regarded as a semantically optional element, unnecessary in any referential or information-theory sense.

Another syntactic feature of ideophones is that they are often introduced by a dummy verb with meanings such as "do," "say," "quote," or "think." In Kanuri the verb *-ŋin* "say, think" is used for this purpose and has (diachronically) combined with ideophones to form a large class of verbs in the language. Other dummy verbs in Kanuri are glossed as "go," "fall," and "beat" (Hutchison 1989: 4). The words *waka* "only" and *-ti*, translated simply as "V[erb]",[8] are used in ChiTumbuka (Mphande and Rice 1989). In Hausa the verb *yi* "do, make" can be used in comparable constructions (Hutchison 1981: 229). ShiNzwani ideophones are set off by *mba* "he said, quote" (Ottenheimer and Primrose 1989), and Yag Dii has the possibly related form *mbàà* "sit, is," as well as *mòò* "speak" and *kÓ* "do," to introduce ideophones (Bohnhoff 1989: 12). Igbo ideophones can be preceded by an indefinite verb meaning "has the qualities of" (Emenanjo 1978).

Tight collocational restrictions also characterize ideophones. In languages where they co-occur with verbs or adjectives, ideophones usually occur with only one or two such items. For example, Grebo ideophones each occur with only a few verbs, in some cases only one (Innes 1964: 48). Wolof ideophones also appear with only a limited number of verbs (Samarin 1970: 168). The Swahili ideophones *tititi* (underscoring "blackness") and *pepepe* (underscoring "whiteness") can only be used, respectively, with the verbs *-eusi* "to be black" and *-eupe* "to be white."

Another common observation is that ideophones appear only in a few sentence types. Although no absolute restrictions exist, ideophones commonly appear in declarative sentences. Newman suggests that the restriction is "probably a common syntactic feature of ideophones in all African languages" (1968: 116). For example, Kisi ideophones are generally not found in questions and negative sentences, nor in topicalized or focused sentences. These restrictions are likely related to pragmatic considerations discussed below.

In summary, syntactic features are not the most useful in delimiting ideophones as a class because of wide cross-linguistic variability. Ideophones can be variably assimilated into a language, and this fact determines their diffusion into other word classes or their isolation in their own word class. Ideophones rarely possess any syntax unique to their class except the relative absence of any syntax. Typically they are set apart by grammatical and phonological devices. What little ideophones have in the way of syntax is determined primarily by collocational restrictions.

13.2.4 Semantic

Welmers finds semantic definitions less than useful because they are impossible to specify precisely (1973: 462). The semantics of ideophones are indeed problematic, but it is a criterion often invoked. Ideophones often simply underscore the meaning of a verb, as in Bulu (Alexandre 1966: 14) or Ngambai/Ngambay-Moundou (Vandame 1963). In traditional elicitation sessions, native speakers will have great difficulty in explaining the meaning of an ideophone, especially if it is limited to occurring with one verb. They will say only that it *emphasizes* the meaning of the verb.

Ideophones can be quite specific, usually evoking some concrete imagery. They often appeal to the senses and have a narrow meaning. The rice-beating and rain ideophones from Kisi illustrate the narrowness possible. Note the phonetic differences despite the semantic closeness in the first pair of examples given in (11).

(11) Rice-beating ideophones
    gbuŋ gbuŋ . . . "rice beaten by one person"
    pim pim . . . "rice beaten by two or more people"

The two ideophones above in (11) are restricted to use only with *cuu* "to beat or pound (usually rice) in a mortar with a pestle."

(12) Rain ideophones
 wa-a-a- ... "sound of rice being sown or gentle rain"
 bia-a-a ... "sound of soft rain"
 bakala-bakala "sound of rain falling in single droplets"

Both the rice-beating and rain ideophones appeal to one's sense of hearing; appeals to other senses are made in the ideophones listed in (13) below.

(13) Ideophones appealing to senses other than sound
 Sight: *hiaŋ-hiaŋ* "loose-jointed, floppy"
 Touch: *cam-cam* "lukewarm"
 Taste: *paŋ* "tasteless, insipid, unpalatable"
 Smell: *kpiini-kpiini* "offensive smelling"

Alexandre (1966) categorizes ideophones semantically as to: sense appealed to; comportment, for living things (moral or physical); and the position, shape, etc. of objects. The largest category is the last, followed by the physical comportment of human beings, then by aural ideophones. Ideophones for touch, taste, and smell, he finds, are limited in number.

Another aspect to the semantics of ideophones is their reliance on *non-arbitrary* relations between sound and meaning, as opposed to the conventional arbitrariness (*l'arbitraire du signe* of Saussure 1915) assumed to characterize language in general. In fact ideophones differ only quantitatively from the rest of the lexicon in this respect. Non-arbitrariness can be found elsewhere; it is simply more common with ideophones. Such relationships characterize only some ideophones. If sound symbolism is the general name for this iconic relationship, its subtypes are onomatopoeia, synesthesia, and conventional (or language-specific) sound symbolism. The first two rely on shared, perhaps universal, facts about sound and meaning, while the last is particular to individual languages.

13.2.4.1. Onomatopoeia

Onomatopoeic forms directly imitate sounds in nature. Although languages constrain possible onomatopoeic forms, this form of expressive language has shared forms cross-linguistically, i.e. there are universals of onomatopoeia, as can be seen in words for a rooster's crow (English *cock-a-doodle-doo*, Japanese *kokekoko*, Hebrew *kukuRiku*, and Kisi *kukuluukuu*). Onomatopoeia clearly plays an important role in the composition of ideophones, especially in terms of animal cries and engine noises, illustrated in (14).

(14) Onomatopoeic ideophones
    Bhacu   *mhu*   "mooing of a cow" (*h* represents breathy voice)

    KiVunjo Chaga *DiDiDiDiDi*   "rapid loud/deep/sharp sound"
                   tutututu   "rapid dull sound like that of an idling engine" (Moshi 1989: 10)

    Yag Dii   *ŋ*   "snoring" (Bohnhoff 1982: 9)

    Bulu   *miook*   "meowing of a cat" (Alexandre 1966: 15)

Names of animals and machines often reflect an onomatopoeic origin, likely mediated by ideophones, as shown by the Gbaya and Ibibio pairs in (15) below.

(15) Animal and machine names derived via onomatopoeia
    Swahili   *piki-piki*   "motorcycle"
               ting'a-tin'a   "tractor"

    Kisi   *nyaayoo*   "cat"
               ŋ ɔɔŋ ŋ ɔɔŋ ndo   "bullfrog"

    Gbaya   *kutu-kutu-kutu*   "rumble of a car motor"
               kutu-kutu   "automobile" (archaic)
               kɔkeŋ ge-kɔɔ   "cock-a-doodle-doo"
               kɔkeŋ ge   "rooster" (literary) (Noss 1985b: 246)

    Ibibio   *toi-toi-toi-toi*   "the sound a motorcycle makes"
               akpokko-toi-toi   "motorcycle" (Ekere 1988b: 9)

Labial fricatives are associated with the sound of moving air. Note that the last item in the Kisi examples (16), *vwum*, contains a sequence only found in this word, as is the situation with the labio-dental flap in the Gbaya examples.

(16) Onomatopoeia: labial fricatives and moving air
    Kisi   *fa-fa-fa . . .*   "sound of scything grass"
               faka-faka   "moving fast"
               fee/fee-fee   "being blown, a whistle, a horn, breathing"
               foo   "wind whistling"
               vwum-vwum   "sound of a robe swishing or of flames blazing up as when kerosene is added"

    Hausa   *fir*   "flutter of wings" (Moore 1968)
               fur
               fir-fir-fir
               jirif

    ShiNzwani *fwii*   "sound of rapidly passing by" (Ottenheimer and Primrose 1989)

Yoruba	*fakafiki*	"sound of a train"[9]
Gbaya	*v̂uu*	"sound of water breaking and rushing through a dam"[10]
	hiv̂ik	"sound of plunging under something as under water"
	kuv̂uv̂uv̂u	"mad rushing, great speed as running or an automobile" (Noss 1975b: 143)

But not all ideophones are onomatopoeic, and one language's onomatopoeia may not be another's; some conventionality is involved (e.g. Frei 1970). Nonetheless, onomatopoeia plays an important role in the formation of many ideophones.

13.2.4.2. Synesthesia

Synesthesia represents another non-arbitrary mating of sound with meaning, but this time with regard to other human senses. It is a metaphorical extension of onomatopoeia to sight, touch, and taste. In the way I will use the term, synesthesia refers to the pairing of certain words with non-auditory sensations (cf. Jakobson and Waugh 1987: 192).

Westermann's well-known (1937) description of sound symbolism in West African languages (Ewe, Twi, Gã, Guang, Nupe, and Temne) illustrates the typical manifestation of the phenomenon. For example, "bright" is associated with front vowels and "dark" with back vowels. High tone is used to represent small things and low tone large things. Fischer-Jørgensen (1978) demonstrates that the vocalic correspondences hold among Danish students as well. More recent evidence comes from Nembe, where [i] conveys a meaning of [− large] (Maduka 1988b).

Before discussing more conventionalized instances of synesthesia, mention must be made of the "frequency code." The frequency code represents a universal non-onomatopoeic association of sound and meaning. The "frequency code [is] a cross-species association of high pitch vocalizations with smallness (of the vocalizer), lack of threat, and of low pitch vocalizations with the vocalizer's largeness and threatening intent" (Ohala 1983: 1). The examples in (17) show how the high front vowels /i/ and /e/ are associated with small things (the first three Kisi examples), while a vowel such as /O/ suggests something large (last Kisi example). The significant correspondences in the Yag Dii examples are between smallness and high tone, largeness and low tone.

(17) Ideophones using the "frequency code"

Kisi	*díìyè-díìyè*	"cry of baby chickens"
	wéé-wéé	"cut into small pieces"
	kílì-kílì	"describing quick footsteps of small animals in the night"
	cɔ́bɔ̀-cɔ́bɔ̀	"sound of heavy rain or poured water"

Yag Dii   High tone is associated with:
(1) small, thin; (2) empty, shining; (3) high; (4) tight; (5) complete
Low tone is associated with:
(1) abnormal (inflated, swollen, paralyzed, stiff, etc.); (2) fear (scary, big, deep, oily, frightful, terrifying, etc.); (3) early (Bohnhoff 1982: 12)

Gbaya ideophones with a high tone are also associated with a small object, while ideophones with a low tone are associated with a large object (Noss 1985b: 242).

The frequency code serves as a default mode for sound–meaning correspondences. If no language-specific associations override it, then the frequency code will operate. In experimental situations, e.g. Sapir 1929, subjects make use of the association; it thus seems likely that it is a universal association to which all speakers have access.

More conventionalized associations are illustrated in Zulu. Increasingly more powerful action is conveyed as one moves through the series ejective (the initial /p t k/ in the examples below in (18)), aspirated stop /ph th kh/, and breathy-voiced or plain voiced stop /gh d g/ with ideophone-like verbs in Zulu.

(18) Consonantal sound symbolism in Zulu
paku   "slap lightly"
phaku   "flutter"
bhaku   "be excited"

tapu   "touch something soft"
thaphu "take something"
daphu   "grab"

kete   "chatter"
khethe "babble"
gede   "chatter loudly" (Van Rooyen *et al.* 1976: 38)

Tonal iconicity also illustrates a partially conventionalized set of correspondences in exhibiting a non-arbitrary association between tones and meaning. Wescott (1973) illustrates tonal iconicity in Bini, shown in (19) below, and claims that it also occurs in Igbo and Twi. (Note how some of the vowels in (19) disobey the pattern of the frequency code shown in (17).)

(19) Tonal iconicity in Bini

Tall		*Short*	
(with uniform high tone)		(with uniform low tone)	
gadagbaa	"long and lanky"	*bɛtɛɛ*	"short and fat"
gisigbii	"big and high"	*giɛghɛgiɛghɛ*	"short"
gbokoo	"tall and portly"	*giɛɛnriɛn*	"small"

gbɔhuun	"tall and fat"	giɛgiɛɛgie	"tiny"
gegeege	"lofty"	kpɛkurlu	"short"
geletee	"towering"	kpukurlu	"cringing"

Tonal iconicity has also been demonstrated in Gbaya and Ewe (Samarin 1965) and in Yoruba (Courtenay 1976, Awoyale 1983–1984). Ideophones in Diola follow this same pattern with respect to vowels. For example, the concepts of "more" or "larger" take the "High" set of vowels (Greenberg and Sapir 1978).

In addition, ideophones with non-uniform tone (alternating high and low) in Bini denote irregular shape or motion.

(20) Non-uniform tones in Bini and irregular shape and motion
   rhúrhùrhú   "staggering"
   tíghítìghìtíghí   "twisted" (Wescott 1973: 201)

Courtenay (1976) has found the same generalization to hold true for Yoruba and Maduka (1983–1984) for Igbo.

13.2.4.3. Iconic lengthening

A common type of universal iconicity is that associated with expressive lengthening or (unlimited) reduplication common with ideophones. In each case the prolongation represents a lengthy or repeated action or state, in some cases standing in contrast with a non-prolonged form. I give below some additional examples not presented during the discussion of morphology.

(21) Iconic lengthening and reduplication in ideophones

Gbaya	fɛɛ	"a breath of air"
	fɛɛɛ	"a long breath of air"
	dirr	"a rumble like thunder"
	dirrr	"a long rolling rumble like thunder or like an earthquake"
	kpuk	"a rap on a door"
	kpuk-kpuk-kpuk	"insistent rapping on the door"
	bit	"to miss once"
	bít-bít-bít	"to miss repeatedly, everyone missing" (Noss 1985b: 242–243)
Toura	pĩĩ-pĩĩ-pĩĩ	"en très grande quantité (Bearth 1971: 203)
Vai	cɔɔɔ	descriptive of liquid pouring in a steady stream
	a be sɛ i kE-na cɔɔɔ	"he is urinating, 'cOOO'" (Welmers 1976: 137)

To be sure, lengthening can be found elsewhere in the language; it is just more common with ideophones.

13.2.4.4. Conventional sound symbolism

Conventional sound symbolism represents the most common type of association between sound and meaning in languages with a large inventory of ideophones. The association here is consistent within the language (perhaps only in the ideophonic subsection), but it is not universal (cf. Brown 1958: 111). The partials that illustrate conventional sound symbolism may be segmental or prosodic, or even non-concatenative. Recombinatory phonesthemes (Bolinger, e.g. 1949) make the class of ideophones infinitely large in languages with such forms, as illustrated by Nembe in (22), Igbo in (23), and Yoruba in (24).

(22) Nembe phonesthemes (tones not shown)
$m_1 \rightarrow [+\text{SOFT}]$
$kp_1 \rightarrow [+\text{WELL-MARKED}]$
$gb_1 \rightarrow [+[+\text{WELL-MARKED}]$
kpokoeokpokoeo   LARGE(R) *and* ROUND *and* WELL-MARKED
gdodoroo   LARGE(R) *and* ROUND *and* WELL-MARKED
mõgolomõgolo   SOFT *and* SMALL *and* THIN
mũgurumũguru   SOFT *and* LARGE *and* ROUND (Maduka 1988b: 107)

(23) Igbo phonesthemes (tones not shown)
k_m (medial [k] or [g]) "back and forth"
regerege   "swinging side to side"
kwakakwaka   "shaking side to side" (Maduka 1988a)

(24) Yoruba phonesthemes
i   "hard, solid"   *u*   "sealed off"
r-g-d-   "largeness"   *p-l-b*   "flatness"
gbirigidi   "of solid matter rolling with much impact"
rigidi   "round, solid, massive"
ragada   "very wide" (Awoyale 1988)

This section on the semantics of ideophones has illustrated the types of sound–meaning associations found with ideophones. The importance of non-arbitrary associations of sound and meaning has proved significant, more so than in other parts of the lexicon but not to the exclusion of conventional associations.

13.2.5. Pragmatic

In that ideophones serve an expressive function, it is not unexpected that they should appear in limited environments, ones where expressiveness would be expected to occur. As mentioned above, they are generally found only in declarative sentence types. Furthermore, they are restricted (but not exclusively, cf. Bohnhoff 1989) to certain types of discourse, especially involving some sort of performance, and they correlate with social factors such as age and sex (e.g. Ottenheimer and Primrose 1989), as well as degree of Westernization or urbanization (e.g. Samarin 1971: 135). Highly educated informants with whom I have worked have denied the existence of ideophones in their languages, dismissing them as "childish." In some contexts ideophones are even prohibited. Speakers of Biakpan consider ideophones inappropriate for scripture text (Noss 1985a: 424). Fortune claims that formality is the sole conditioning factor, Shona ideophones being featured only in "free expression" or informal style (1962: 4).

It is also not unexpected that a great deal of individual variation exists in the frequency with which different speakers use ideophones. Here it is useful to note that while serving the general function of expressiveness, ideophones serve *individual* expressiveness (in the sense of Billings 1987), as opposed to group-oriented expressiveness, such as that exemplified in the work of Labov and his colleagues (e.g. Labov 1972).

The issue of variation, both interdialectal and intradialectal, is a vexed one (Samarin 1991). The problem is illustrated by Moore's difficulties in collecting a sample of ideophones based on Abraham's (1962) Hausa dictionary. Although over 1,000 ideophones were listed in the dictionary, Moore found that only 405 were deemed acceptable by native speakers. She guesses that many of the forms in the dictionary are "archaic or are dialectal or idiolectal variants" (1968: 2). Undoubtedly this variation serves as a linguistic resource, however problematic it may be for the analyst.

Dialectal variation is considerable, as in Southern Bantu, in "striking contrast" to the affinities found elsewhere (Doke 1954: 86–87). Bulu ideophones similarly show little correspondence with the neighboring, and genetically related, languages Fang and Ewondo (Alexandre 1966: 26). In his survey of the Nguni languages Lanham writes:

From the aspect of historical phonology, there is the fact that normal reconstruction on a comparative basis is almost impossible when applied to ideophones and begins to break down even at the low level of Proto-Nguni. In the realm of the ideophone it is clear that alternation, fluctuation and innovation proceed at the level of dialect or even lower, with a latitude which, if permitted in the regular structure, would reduce at an alarming rate the communicative efficiency of the languages. The common vocabulary of Xh[osa] dialects, for example, is, relatively speaking, found to be far smaller with regard to ideophones than with other normal items of the vocabulary. At the highest level of "Nguni" there is only a relatively small central core of cognate ideophones (in form and meaning) and the difficulties encountered in trying to trace in them the threads of patterned historical changes, differ sharply from the ease with which this can be done in more regular items of the vocabulary.

(1960: 176)

Ideophones have a curious connection to context not found with other words. They do not refer to context as do deictic words, but rather they can derive meaning from their context. A typical comment is that the meanings of Igbo ideophones are vague out of context but are always understood in actual use (Okonkwo 1974). This is an area, however, which has not been systematically investigated.

13.2.6. Ideophones and gesture

Ideophones show close connections with gesture (see McNeill 1992 for a discussion of the links between gesture and speech). The problem in exploring this connection is that linguists typically do not comment on this relationship. It can be seen, of course, in the pause isolating the ideophone (discussed above) and in the dramatic prosodic changes characteristic of many ideophones. In Bulu, besides being set off by a pause and preceded by a particle *ne*, ideophones can be preceded by a snap of the fingers or a click (*click vélaire*) (Alexandre 1966). In some cases, ideophones are accompanied by paralinguistic gestures. In Kisi the ideophone *kpiini-kpiini* "stinky" is accompanied by a crinkling of the nose, as is the Venda ideophone *thuu* "smelling horribly" (Mamphwe 1987: 33). In Ibibio gestures co-occur with ideophones and represent a concomitant resource to the narrator (Ekere 1988b).

13.2.7. Summary

Ideophones possess a number of different distinguishing characteristics, not all of which apply to all languages. For example, most but not all ideophones have unusual phonological characteristics. In some languages ideophones constitute a syntactically separate category, while in others they do not. This situation suggests a prototype definition with less good members of the class on the periphery and a core of "best" ideophones at the center. As one moves outward members become less and less "good," leaving the ideophone category and joining another word class, or even joining forms of non-linguistic expressiveness such as gesture. This definition can be used cross-linguistically and can be adapted to individual languages.

13.3. Other work and issues in ideophone research

The discussion of definitional issues has demonstrated the availability of a detailed descriptive apparatus. A taxonomy of types has emerged and further comparative work can be undertaken. For example, using the semantic taxonomy of Alexandre (1966), further work can make a cross-linguistic comparison of senses appealed to by ideophones. Their distribution might be found to follow a species-specific pattern. The sense most important from an evolutionary perspective, sight, would constitute the largest group, with the other sense categories having proportionately fewer members according to the sense's relative importance to the species.

Much work needs to be done, of course, in comparing ideophones cross-linguistically in Africa and elsewhere. Because ideophones are a fragile phenomenon, field techniques need refinement, following the important lead of Samarin (e.g. 1970a). The greatest need, of course, is for research done by native speakers.

Greater attention should be dedicated to examining the expressive function, as well as to looking at comparable classes of words in the world's languages.[11] Such investigations would contribute insights as to language universals, especially as to the ways languages exploit iconicity as a linguistic resource.

A phonetic study would probably demonstrate that the phonetic features of ideophones represent a subset of universal speech sounds. Bilabial trills were at one time thought not to be part of the speech sounds of the world's languages, except insofar as they were associated with ideophones or other expressive language. Subsequent investigation showed them also to be used linguistically (Ladefoged 1985: 10). A phonetic survey of ideophones, then, can supplement the set of sounds known to be used linguistically to yield a maximal true linguistic inventory. The major thrust of research on ideophones has concentrated on analyzing ideophones as constituting a separate system. This approach assumes that ideophones belong outside language proper. The opposite assumption would surely prove as productive. Still to be scrutinized is the exact nature of the relationship between ideophones and the rest of the language, as well as the place of ideophones in a language.

Another area of interest is ideophone derivational relationships. Childs (1989) pursues suggestions by others as to the closeness between verbs and ideophones to show how ideophones arise from verbs through processes of reduplication and reanalysis. Hutchison (1981, 1989) discusses a large set of verbs in Kanuri which are derived from ideophones.

The absence of ideophones in Khoisan is another puzzling area. The Khoisan languages, uniquely in Africa, seem to have no ideophones, at least on a level with their Nguni neighbors (O. Köhler, personal communication 1990; J. Snyman, personal communication 1990; A. Traill, personal communication 1991). The one exception may be Nama, a widely spoken Khoisan lanugage of Namibia. Although the crop is not rich, there are non-onomatopoeic ideophones *xawi* "acting suddenly, swiftly," *nurub* "disappearing suddenly." Nama also has a dummy verb *ti go mí* "(it) so said" introducing ideophones, functionally identical to Bantu (Hacke and Eiseb to appear, W. Haacke, personal communication 1990). Interestingly Khoisan has been important for providing Nguni with ideophones. In his study of Khoi borrowings into Xhosa, Louw gives numerous examples of borrowed Khoi verbs becoming Xhosa ideophones (1974: 51–60).

Questions still remain as to the diachronic behavior of ideophones. The extent of variability suggests that ideophones constitute a relatively unstable set of words. At the same time ideophones show an imperviousness to phonological rules. The expectation would be that ideophones remain unaffected by regular processes of sound change (cf. Mithun 1982). Their extensive variability, however, prevents the establishment of cross-linguistic correspondences. The situation raises questions as to the limits of variation and variability. Dialect surveys have shown considerable variation. Even in a highly cohesive "micro-population" (a mother and her fourteen-year-old son), agreement reached only 66% (83% when adjusted for "word clusters", i.e. partially homophonous forms) on the appropriate ideophone in a given sentence (Samarin 1991).

How ideophones are learned and transmitted has not been studied. Ideophones have persisted into pidgins and creoles used on the African continent; as a linguistic feature they are found widely across Africa in genetically unrelated languages. Furthermore, ideophones from speakers' first languages are used in their second and third languages. These words thus seem likely candidates for transmission by contact in the multilingual situations common to Africa. Counter-evidence comes from the fact that ideophones in Liberian English and Crioulo (Guinée Bissau) have no apparent link to any of the substrate languages (Childs 1994).

Another important issue revolves around the decomposability of ideophones. Not all languages will feature the extensive inventory of phonesthemes found by, e.g. Awoyale 1988 and Maduka 1988a. Not all languages will feature the extensive inventory of phonesthemes they find, but cross-linguistic comparisons should extend this approach and propose an explanation for this structuring.

Experimental studies should be undertaken. For example, laboratory testing of reset, as discussed above, will reveal whether ideophones are separated by the same prosodic features as separate clauses. Investigations comparable to Wissemann's with onomatopoeia should be extended to synesthesia to see whether or not ideophones can be created *ex nihilo*. The experimental procedure is relatively straightforward; subjects are asked to produce sounds after hearing a stimulus, e.g. chains rattling, movement of water in a bottle, smashing of a bottle (Wissemann 1954, as reported in Brown 1958: 115–118; cf. Samarin 1970a). Such experiments might investigate what intuitions beyond, e.g., size–sound symbolism speakers use in the creation of new ideophones. Are there other universal associations, or even language-specific associations, that would guide them in creating ideophones?

Formal theoreticians need to examine the place of ideophones in a rule-ordered treatment. Because of their intractability to easy analysis, ideophones have been ignored in such treatments, e.g. Schachter and Fromkin 1968. Promising work has already been done in this line with respect to expressive rules (Woodbury 1987), but virtually none with respect to ideophones, except to note their exceptionality and ignore them. Ideophones are unique in being lexically expressive as well as being extremely receptive to expressive processes, such as lengthening and repetition, and thus provide a challenge to any treatment.

Although I have not discussed the importance of ideophones to literary discourse, how ideophones are used in this medium can inform us further as to pragmatic conditions on their appearance. Bible translators have confronted this issue many times, and the responses of native speakers as to the appropriateness of ideophones have been varied; see e.g. Noss 1985a.

In summary, the work that needs to be done should have two major thrusts to be carried out simultaneously in any empirical investigation. The first is simply to adequately describe and document the phenomenon, using the framework developed above. The second focus must be on integrating ideophones into the mainstream of linguistic inquiry, treating ideophones as a legitimate object of inquiry and squarely confronting the problems they pose.

13.4. Conclusion

If our approach is confined to the referential function of language (and an idealized subset of the data accomplishing that function), ideophones will necessarily lurk on the periphery of language. They will have been defined out of existence. Any honest approach requires their inclusion. In this paper I have demonstrated to what extent ideophones stand outside language proper, while advancing a claim for including them within. If linguistic theory is unable to cope with the problems posed by ideophones, there is something wrong with the theory.

My hope is that this brief presentation will establish the scientific respectability of ideophones as well as stimulate the investigation of ideophones in African and other languages. In fact, African ideophones (and ideophones in some Asian languages, e.g. Japanese: Amanuma 1974; Ono 1984) have received a fair amount of attention, but not the sort of explanatory attention that is needed. If indeed linguists integrate ideophones into their descriptions, there will be a greater respect for variation and for language as a part of human interaction.

NOTES

*Conventions used in the paper are:

D = [ɾ] alveolar flap
c = [tʃ] alveo-palatal affricate
. (a dot under a vowel) = the [−ATR] variant of the vowel under which the symbol appears (used in the orthography of several Nigerian languages)

1 I will ignore the position that completely denies them linguistic status, as in Voorhoeve 1965: 197, "Ideophones are not considered to be lexical morphemes and cannot be generated by the grammar" (as quoted in Samarin 1971: 135).
2 Samarin refers to the language as "Gbeya," a local pronunciation (Samarin 1989: 1).

3 This is the opposite of the situation in Shona, where ideophones do not have tone and the rest of the language does (Fortune 1971: 224).
4 What I call a pause here can be construed as an audible prosodic discontinuity, which probably correlates with some kind of syntactic boundary. The phenomenon of pause needs phonological and phonetic study, but for present purposes can be taken as an identifiable and regular prosodic element.
5 These examples come from Mahamad Sabo, a native speaker from Niger.
6 In one text this ideophone was repeated five times.
7 In at least one language with serial verbs (Yoruba), ideophones remain structurally associated with each verb in a serial construction (A. Laniran, personal communication 1989).
8 This verb is a likely cognate with Zulu -*thi* "do," used for the same purpose.
9 I owe this example to Vicki Carstens, who heard it in a Yoruba play to refer (metaphorically) to the sound of someone breathing.
10 The symbol "v̂" represents the labio-dental flap, which occurs only in ideophones.
11 The latter investigation has been begun by Robert Hsu of the University of Hawaii.

REFERENCES

Abraham, R. C. 1962. *Dictionary of the Hausa Language*. London: University of London Press Ltd.
Alexandre, P. 1966. Préliminaire à une présentation des idéophones bulu. In J. Lukas (ed.) *Neue afrikanistische Studien*. Hamburger Beiträge zur Afrika-Kunde, 5. Hamburg: Deutsches Institut für Afrika-Forschung, 9–28.
Amanuma, Y. 1974. *Giongo Gitaigo Jiten* ("A Dictionary of Onomatopoeic and Ideophonic Expressions"). Tokyo: Tokyodo. (In Japanese.)
Andersen, T. 1987. An outline of Lulubo phonology. *Studies in African Linguistics* 18(1): 39–65.
Awoyale, Y. 1981. Nominal compound formation in Yoruba ideophones. *Journal of African Languages and Linguistics* 3: 139–157.
    1983–1984. On the semantic fields of Yoruba ideophones. *Journal of the Linguistic Association of Nigeria* 2: 11–22.
    On the non-concatenative morphology of Yoruba ideophones. Paper given at the Nineteenth African Linguistics Conference, Boston University, April 14–16, 1988.
Bearth, T. 1971. L'énonce Toura. PhD dissertation, Norman, Oklahoma: Summer Institute of Linguistics.
Billings, D. K. 1987. Expressive style and culture: individualism and group orientation contrasted. *Language in Society* 16: 475–497.
Boadi, L. A. 1988. Problems of palatalization in Akan. *Journal of West African Languages* 18(1): 3–16.
Bohnhoff, L. E. 1982. Yag Dii (Duru) ideophones. *Cahier du Département des Langues et Linguistiques*, Université de Yaoundé, 2: 1–14.
    1989. Yag Dii ideophones from a syntactic perspective. ms.
Bolinger, D. L. 1949. The sign is not arbitrary. *Boletín del Instituto Caro y Cuervo* 5: 52–62. Reprinted in Bolinger 1965: 231–240.

1965. *Forms of English*. Cambridge, MA: Harvard University Press.
Brown, R. W. 1958. *Words and Things*. Glencoe, Illinois: Free Press.
Carr, D. 1966. Homorganicity in Malay/Indonesian expressives and quasi expressives. *Language* 42(2): 370–377.
Childs, G. T. 1988. The phonology of Kisi ideophones. *Journal of African Languages and Linguistics* 10: 165–90.
  1989. Where do ideophones come from? *Studies in the Linguistic Sciences* 19(2): 57–78.
  1994. Expressiveness in contact situations: the fate of African ideophones. *Journal of Pidgin and Creole Languages* 9(1). In press.
Courtenay, K. 1974. On the nature of the Bambara tone system. *Studies in African Linguistics*. 5: 303–323.
  1976. Ideophones defined as a phonological class: the case of Yoruba. *Studies in African Linguistics*, Supplement 6: 13–26.
DeCamp, D. 1974. Neutralizations, iteratives, and ideophones: the locus of language in Jamaica. In D. DeCamp and I. F. Hancock (eds.) *Pidgins and Creoles: Current Trends and Prospects*. Washington, DC: Georgetown University Press, 46–60.
Doke, C. M. 1935. *Bantu Linguistics Terminology*. London: Longmans, Green.
  1954. *The Southern Bantu Languages*. London and New York: Oxford University Press.
Durand, M. 1961. Les impressifs en viêtnamien, étude préliminaire. *Bulletin de la Société des Études Indo-chinoises* 36(1): 5–51.
Durbin, M. 1973. Sound symbolism in the Mayan language family. In M. S. Edmonson (ed.) *Meaning in Mayan Languages: Ethnolinguistic Studies*. The Hague: Mouton, 23–49.
Ekere, M. E. 1988a. *Ideophones in Serial Verb Constructions: A Case Study of Ibibio*. Department of Languages, The Polytechnic, Calabar, Cross River State, Nigeria.
  1988b. *Nominal Ideophones in Ibibio*. Department of Languages, The Polytechnic, Calabar, Cross River State, Nigeria.
Emenanjo, E. 1978. *Elements of Modern Igbo Grammar*. Ibadan: Oxford University Press.
Fischer-Jørgensen, E. 1978. On the universal character of phonetic symbolism with special reference to vowels. *Studia Linguistica* 32(1–2): 80–90.
Fivaz, D. 1963. *Some Aspects of the Ideophone in Zulu*. Hartford, Connecticut: Hartford Seminary.
Fordyce, J. F. 1983. The ideophone as a phonosemantic class: the case of Yoruba. In I. Dihoff (ed.) *Current Approaches to African Linguistics*, vol. 1. Dordrecht and Cinnaminson, NJ: Foris, 263–278.
Fortune, G. 1962. *Ideophones in Shona*. London: Oxford University Press.
  1971. Some notes on ideophones and ideophonic constructions in Shona. *African Studies* 30(3–4): 237–257.
Frei, H. 1970. Cinquante onomatopées japonaises. In D. Cohen (ed.) *Mélanges Marcel Cohen*. Janua Linguarum, Series Maior 27. The Hague: Mouton.
Greenberg, S. and J. D. Sapir. 1978. Acoustic correlates of "big" and "thin" in Kujamutay. *Proceedings of the Fourth Annual Meeting of the Berkeley Linguistics Society*. Berkeley: CA: Berkeley Linguistics Society, 293–310.
Haacke, W. and E. Eiseb. To appear. *A Nama Dictionary*. Windhoek: Nama Dictionary Project, University of Namibia.
Hutchison, J. P. 1981. Kanuri word formation and the structure of the lexicon. In M. L.

Bender and T. C. Schadeberg (eds.) Nilo-Saharan Proceedings. Cinnaminson, NJ: Foris, 217–237.

Hutchison, J. P. 1989. The Kanuri ideophone. Paper presented at the Colloquium on Ideophones, Twentieth Conference on African Linguistics, University of Illinois at Urbana Champaign, April 19–22, 1989.

Innes, G. 1964. Some features of theme and style in Mende folktales. *Sierre Leone Language Review* 3: 6–19.

Jakobson, R. and L. R. Waugh. 1979. *The Sound Shape of Language*. Bloomington, In: Indiana University Press. (2nd edn 1987, Berlin, New York, Amsterdam: Mouton/de Gruyter.)

Jaques, A. A. 1941. Shangaan-Tsonga ideophones and their tones. *Bantu Studies* 15(3): 205–244.

Kapinga, M. C. 1983. *Sarufi Maumbo ya Kiswahili Sanifu*. Dar es Salaam: Taasisi ya Uchunguzi wa Kiswahili, Chuo Kikuu cha Dar es Salaam.

Kiparsky, P. 1982. Lexical morphology and phonology. In I.-S. Wang (ed.) *Linguistics in the Morning Calm*. Seoul: Hanshin.

Kita, S. 1992. Speaking processes in balanced and unbalanced Japanese bilinguals: evidence for spontaneous gestures that accompany speech. PhD dissertation, University of Chicago.

Kunene, D. P. 1965. The ideophone in Southern Sotho. *Journal of African Languages* 4: 19–39.

Labov, W. 1972. *Sociolinguistic Patterns*. Philadelphia, PA: University of Pennsylvania Press.

Ladd, D. R. 1988. Declination "reset" and the hierarchical organization of utterances. *Journal of the Acoustical Society of America* 84(2): 530–544.

Ladefoged, P. 1985. Interview with Peter Ladefoged. Introduction to V. Fromkin (ed.). *Phonetic Linguistics: Essays in Honor of Peter Ladefoged*. Orlando, FL: Academic Press, 1–14.

Lanham, L. W. 1960. The comparative phonology of Nguni. PhD thesis, University of the Witwatersrand, Johannesburg.

Louw, J. A. 1965. The consonant phonemes of the lexical root in Zulu. *Afrika und Übersee* 48(2): 127–152.

1974. the influence of Khoe on the Xhosa language. *Limi* 2(2): 45–62.

Lyons, J. 1968. *Introduction to Theoretical Linguistics*. Cambridge: University Press.

Maafi, L. 1990. Tzeltal Maya affect verbs: psychological salience and expressive functions of language. *Proceedings of the 1990 Meeting of the Berkeley Linguistics Society*.

McNeill, D. 1992. *Hand and Mind*. Chicago: University of Chicago Press.

Maduka, O. N. 1983–1984. Igbo ideophones and the lexicon. *Journal of the Linguistic Association of Nigeria* 2: 23–29.

1988a. The K_m critical psychomorph in Igbo. Paper presented at the Ninth Annual Conference of the Linguistic Association of Nigeria, Obafemi Awolowo University, Ile-Ife, Nigeria, July 31–August 4, 1988).

1988b. Size and shape ideophones in Nembe. *Studies in African Linguistics*, 19(2): 93–113.

Mamphwe, C. T. 1987. The ideophone in Venda. Honours dissertation, University of South Africa, Pretoria.

Marivate, C. T. D. 1985. The ideophone as a syntactic category in the Southern Bantu languages. *Studies in African Linguistics*, Supplement 9: 210–214.

Matisoff, J. A. This volume. Tone, intonation, and sound symbolism in Lahu: loading the syllable canon.
Mithun, M. 1982. The synchronic and diachronic behavior of plops, squeaks, croaks, sighs, and moans. *International Journal of American Linguistics* 48: 49–58.
Mohanan, K. P. 1986. *The Theory of Lexical Phonology.* Dordrecht: Reidel.
Moore, M. Jo. 1968. The ideophone in Hausa. M.A. thesis. E. Lansing, MI: Michigan State University.
Moshi, L. 1993. Towards a universal definition of ideophone: evidence from Kivunjo Chaga. To appear in *Linguistic Anthropology* 3(1).
Mphande, L. and C. Rice. 1989. Towards a phonological definition of the ideophone in ChiTumbuka. Paper presented at the Colloquium on Ideophones, Twentieth Conference on African Linguistics, University of Illinois at Urbana Champaign, April 19–22, 1989.
Myers, A. 1974. The phonology of Kikuyu. ms, MIT.
Newman, P. 1968. Ideophones from a syntactic point of view. *Journal of West African Languages* 5: 107–118.
  1989. Reduplication and tone in Hausa ideophones. *Proceedings of the Fifteenth Annual Meeting of the Berkeley Linguistics Society, February 18–20, 1989.*
Newman, P. and P. J. Jaggar. 1989. Low tone raising in Hausa: a critical assessment. *Studies in African Linguistics* 20(3): 227–251.
Noss, P. A. 1975. The ideophone: a linguistic and literary device in Gbaya and Sango with reference to Zande. In S. H. Hurreiz and H. Bell (eds.) *Directions in Sudanese Linguistics and Folklore.* Khartoum: University Press, 142–152.
  1985a. The ideophone in Bible translation: child or stepchild? *The Bible Translator (Practical Papers)* 36(2): 423–430.
  1985b. The ideophone in Gbaya syntax. In G. J. Dimmendaal (ed.) *Current Approaches to African Linguistics* 3. Dordrecht and Cinnaminson, NJ: Foris, 241–255.
Ohala, J. J. 1983. Cross-language use of pitch: an ethological view. *Phonetica* 40: 1–18.
  1984. An ethological perspective on common cross-language utilization of F_0 of voice. *Phonetica* 41: 1–16.
Okonkwo, M. N. 1974. *A Complete Course in Igbo Grammar.* Macmillan Nigeria.
Ono, H. 1984. *Nichiei Gion Gitaigo Katsuyo Jiten* ("A Practical Guide to Japanese–English Onomatopoeia and Mimesis"). Tokyo: Hokuseido Press. (In Japanese.)
Ottenheimer, H. and H. Primrose. 1989. ShiNzwani ideophones. *Studies in the Linguistic Sciences* 19(2): 77–87.
Pulleyblank, D. 1986. *Tone in Lexical Phonology.* Dordrecht: Reidel.
Rice, C. 1987. The ideophone in ChiTumbuka. ms, University of Texas at Austin.
Saidi, M. 1976. *Fani mbali mbali.* Nairobi: Longman Kenya Limited.
Samarin, W. J. 1965. Perspective on African ideophones. *African Studies* 24: 117–121.
  1967. Determining the meanings of ideophones. *Journal of West African Linguistics* 4(2): 35–41.
  1970a. Field procedures in ideophone research. *Journal of African Languages* 9(1): 27–30.
  1970b. Inventory and choice in expressive language. *Word* 26(2): 153–169.
  1971. Survey of Bantu ideophones. *African Language Studies* 12: 130–168.
  1979. Simplification, pidginization, and language change. In I. F. Hancock (ed.) *Readings in Creole Studies.* Ghent, Belgium: E. Story-Scientia, P.V.B.A, 55–68.

1991. Intersubjective and intradialectal variation in Gbeya ideophones. *Journal of Linguistic Anthropology* 1(1): 52–62.

Sapir, E. 1915. Abnormal types of speech in Nootka. Reprinted in D. G. Mandelbaum (ed.) *Selected Writings of Edward Sapir*. Berkeley, CA: University of California Press, 179–196.

Sapir, E. 1929. A study in phonetic symbolism. *Journal of Experimental Psychology* 12: 225–239. (Reprinted in D. G. Mandelbaum (ed.) *Selected Writings of Edward Sapir*. Berkeley: University of California Press, 61–72.)

Saussure, F. de. 1915. *A Course in General Linguistics*. Reprinted 1966. New York: McGraw Hill.

Schachter, P. and V. Fromkin. 1968. *A Phonology of Akan: Akuapem, Asante and Fante*. Working Papers in Phonetics 9. University of California, Los Angeles.

Selkirk, E. O. 1980. Prosodic domains in phonology: Sanskrit revisited. In M. Aronoff and M.-L. Kean (eds.) *Juncture, A Collection of Original Essays*, Studia Linguistica et Philologica 7. Saratoga, CA: Anima Libra.

Smithers, C. V. 1954. Some English ideophones. *Archivum Linguisticum* 6: 73–111.

Steriade, D. 1988. Reduplication and syllable transfer in Sanskrit and elsewhere. *Phonology* 5(1): 73–155.

Van Rooyne, C. S., P. C. Taljaard, and A. S. Davey. 1976. *The Sounds of Zulu*. Pretoria: University of South Africa.

Vandame, C. 1963. *Le Ngambay-Moundou: phonologie, grammaire et textes*. Mémoires de l'Institut français d'Afrique Noire 69. Dakar: IFAN.

Von Staden, P. M. S. 1974. Die Ideofoon in Zulu. PhD thesis. Rand Afrikaans University, Johannesburg.

Voorhoeve, J. 1965. The structure of the morpheme in Bamileke (Bengangté dialect). *Lingua* 13: 319–334.

Welmers, W. E. 1973. *African Language Structures*. Berkeley and Los Angeles: University of California Press.

1976. *A Grammar of Vai*. University of California Publications in Linguistics 84. Berkeley and Los Angeles: University of California Press.

Wescott, R. W. 1973. Tonal icons in Bini. *Studies in African Linguistics* 4: 197–205.

Westermann, D. 1937. Laut und Sinn in einigen westafrikanischen Sudan-Sprachen. *Archiv für vergleichende Phonetik* 1: 154–172, 193–211.

Williamson, K. 1965. *A Grammar of the Kolokuma Dialect of Ijo*. West African Language Monograph Series, 2. Cambridge: University Press.

Wilson, W. A. A. 1961. *An Outline of the Temne language*. University of London, School of Oriental and African Studies.

Wissemann, H. 1954. *Untersuchungen zur Onomatopoiie: 1 Teil, die sprachpsychologischen Versuche*. Heidelberg: Carl Winter Universitätsverlag.

Woodbury, A. C. 1987. Meaningful phonological processes: a consideration of Central Alaskan Yupik Eskimo prosody. *Language* 63(4): 685–740.

PART V

Europe

14
Regular sound development, phonosymbolic orchestration, disambiguation of homonyms

YAKOV MALKIEL

14.1. Introduction

By way of prelude let me clarify a few terminological preferences. For the purpose of this inquiry I shall assume that "phonosymbolism" and "sound symbolism" are two interchangeable labels for the same concept, as are indeed the correlated adjectives "phonosymbolic" and "sound-symbolic." I further propose to take it for granted, on the basis of my readings, that "expressivity" (allegedly patterned on German *Expressivität*[1] conveys virtually the same message as "phonosymbolism," except that it tends to invite discussion in a psychological key rather than in purely linguistic terms. The clearest proof of their fundamental identity is the well-established fact that tone-setting scholars, *chefs d'école*, if addicted to the use of "expressivity," have hesitated, not to say studiously avoided, having recourse to the rival term "sound symbolism."[2] On the other hand, German *Affekt*, a latinism meaning literally "emotional state of disturbance," and its offshoots *affektiv* and, particularly, *affektisch*,[3] despite various significant overlaps with the realm of phonosymbolism here under scrutiny, pertain basically to the province of psychology rather than involving a straight approach to the study of language; the same holds for most uses of "emphatic."

Finally, sporadic attempts have been made in the recent past to set aside the adjacent, but discrete, territory of "morphosymbolism."[4] If phonosymbolism, as is yet to be shown, has a semantic dimension, morphosymbolism, conversely, has a grammatical dimension. Thus, with a single exception (which happens to involve a word borrowed from a different, if genetically related, language),[5] all qualifying adjectives in modern Spanish turn out to be incompatible with monosyllabicity, even though in the Middle Ages the situation was radically different.[6]

Before taking up the issue of definition, we can, by way of characterization, lay down the principle that so-called "concrete" languages (e.g. Old French as well as

Spanish at all times, also English and German) have tended to overindulge in the use of phonosymbolic effects, whereas predominantly "abstract" languages – none more clearly so than Modern French – have given the impression of shying away from them.[7]

14.2. Sound development and phonosymbolism

Once we refuse to confine our attention to the one small murky corner of downright noise imitation, and begin to pay heightened attention to diachrony, we must confront the key issue of the ultimate reconcilability, in that temporal perspective, of the so-called regular sound development – for generations the staple food of students of historical grammar, boasting its traditional emphasis on phonology – with the, often dramatically deviant, separate development of lexical items suspected of being subject to a phonosymbolic bent. In so doing we must, of course, be prepared, indeed eager, to yank ourselves loose from the prevailing assumption that we are here dealing with exceptions. In this our search for a smoother solution of a notorious difficulty we can perhaps appeal for help to Antoine Meillet.

In reviewing in his journal a brilliant but polemically calibrated and highly controversial monograph by Ernst G. Wahlgren, a Swedish scholar sadly known as a "loner,"[8] Meillet remarked that the incompatibility of certain semi-learned words in Old French with the mainstream of the sound development, the so-called regular sound correspondences, need not be credited to morphological interference, as Wahlgren had stubbornly maintained,[9] but could just as smoothly be explained away on the assumption that side by side with the basic phonological structure, which presided over the growth of the bulk of the – orally transmitted – lexis, in its gradual transition from the ancestral to one daughter language, there could perfectly well have existed a sort of separate phonic minisystem valid for those exceptional lexical units handed down, not entirely by word of mouth, from one generation to another. However, once that kind of semi-autonomous coexistence has been admitted, at least in principle, the possibility of the rise and temporary survival of other such minisystems must be allowed for, again at least in theory. Additional categories of exceptional words clamoring for recognition of their concomitant status are primarily, of course, (a) divers borrowings from neighboring languages, whether cognate or not, and from the parental language(s) as well; (b) lexical units affected by such processes as metathesis, haplology, dissimilation in contact or at a distance, which can be distinguished from changes affecting specific phonemic systems over limited periods of time; plus (c), of greater relevance to us, words advancing along the axis of time while being loaded with phonosymbolic effectiveness.[10]

Europe

14.3. An example: claudĕre and its substitutes

Let me now leave behind Wahlgren and Meillet and briefly offer you one concrete illustration of what I have in mind, using for this purpose certain games played in the past by Folk Latin, Arabic, and Old Spanish. You are herewith invited to examine at close range certain substitutes, in medieval and modern Romance, made for the Latin word for "closing, shutting, locking," namely *claudō, -ĕre*. For several reasons that verb turned out to be a weak candidate for survival, starting with Late Antiquity and the Middle Ages.[11]

In French, to be brief, one is privileged to observe step by step the gradual obsolescence of *clore*, to the advantage of an aggressive replacement word, namely *fermer*, which perpetuates ancestral *firmāre* "to make firm, strengthen," presumably with additional support drawn from *ferrum* "iron."[12] In Tuscan *chiudere*, one witnesses the substitution of *clūdere* (extracted from such compounds as *ex-*, *in-*, *oc-*, *re-clūdere*) for Classical *claudere*.[13] In the Iberian Peninsula, to be sure, the Latin verb for a while went on leaving a number of isolated traces in archaic medieval texts, such as *cho-er*, *ir* in the west and *lloír* in the center, but before long was by and large dislodged by two rival innovations: *fechar* in Portuguese and *cerrar* in Spanish. As has been elsewhere demonstrated in painstaking detail, with the help of more readily transparent dialect forms (e.g. Asturian *pechar ~ pesllar*), *fechar*, originally "to bolt," involves another instance of interference of *ferro* "iron" with *pechar* < *pessulāre* "to bolt," from the more familiar noun *pessulum*.[14] These subtractions leave only *cerrar* unexplained; its vicissitudes will form the kernel of the present paper.

There is, practically, unanimity of opinion as concerns the extraction, primarily, of *cerrar* – sometimes spelled *çerrar* and invariably pronounced /ˈseRar/ in the Middle Ages – and, secondarily, of a galaxy of suffixal derivatives[15] from parental *serō, -āre* "to bar, bolt," a verb which, despite its fairly late attestation (in Venantius Fortunatus), could perfectly well have sprung into existence, colloquially, at a distinctly earlier date, and in any event represents an offshoot of the better-documented noun *sera* "latch, bar, bolt," initially designating a crude one made of wood, at a later stage one manufactured in more sophisticated fashion, increasingly of iron, as a lock or padlock.[16] The copious record that *sera* has left in Roman literature – including its peak period, the Augustan Age[17] – confirms this hypothesis, and the transmutation of *(op)pessulāre* "to latch" (Petronius) into synonymous Asturian *pechar* offers a tempting semantic parallel.[18]

Unfortunately, any advocate of this conjecture, however suggestive, must account for two major irregularities, both weighing heavily on the side of phonology and both apparently tolerated by the speech community on a sweeping scale:[19] (a) the lengthening of medial, intervocalic -*r*- and (b) the substitution, word-initially, of *ç*- /ˈts/, a voiceless affricate, for unaffricated *s*-. These two instances of striking abnormality invite interpretations set in radically divergent keys. Compared to them, a third, sporadically surfacing peculiarity, namely the occasional shifting of the low front vowel before /r/ or /R/ in the direction of /a/, deserves qualification as minor, despite its remarkable chronological spread.

Isolated examples, e.g. in monolingual or bilingual glosses, of the capricious graphies *serra* and even *sarra* are traceable to Late Antiquity. Classicists report having encountered in two such texts *serrāculum* "rudder" explained by "clāvis nāvis," in Latin, or translated by *pēdalion*, into Greek (Meillet and Ernout, 1959–1960: 616b). A glance at the abundant inventory of Romance reflexes discloses that the use of lengthened *r* /R/ has been so overwhelming in several branches as to have prompted Meyer-Lübke to list the base as **serrāre* (19[30]–1935: §7867), with appropriate references to It. *serrāre*, Fr. *serrer*, Old Provençal *serrar*, etc. Conversely, the transition from the word-initial simple sibilant to the corresponding affricate apparently has not been observed outside the Iberian peninsula. Consequently it represents, for sure, if not a narrowly local, then at least a provincial, innovation, and also by implication, in all likelihood a measurably more recent phenomenon.

The lengthening of word-medial -*r*- in this isolated instance has, again and again, provoked surprise, being labeled "unexplained" (Meyer-Lübke, 19[11]–1920: §7867) or "obscure" (Meillet and Ernout, 1959–1960: 616b). Not a few authorities have tacitly operated with **serrāre* without bothering to justify this departure from tradition (Real Academia 1984: 309b), or have dared to make a leap across a millennium by noncommittally tracing *cerrar* to *serāre* (García de Diego, [1957]: 163 and §6072). Certain scholars have wondered whether the baffling shift could possibly be attributed to phonosymbolism or traced to the imagerial influence of *serra* "saw," citing archeological evidence to that effect (ibid.), "en raison de la forme dentelée de certaines pièces de serrure ou de cadenas".[20] Meyer-Lübke, upon abandoning his earlier agnosticism in this respect, in the end opted for the influence of *ferrum* "iron" as the relevant factor in the process of deflection (19[30]–1935: §7867), a decision which in retrospect indeed makes good sense, inasmuch as certain words semantically akin show effects of the very same pressure of the name of the newly introduced, highly prestigious metal. Thus, the record of *veruculum* "bolt," from the simplex *veru* or *verum* "spit, broach, dart," likewise displays traces, in various daughter languages, of having adopted, from the very same *ferrum*, first its -*rr*- /R/ and, in addition, here and there, its salient word-initial *f*- as a substitute for ancestral /w/: Witness OFr. *verroil* /veRoλ/, modern *verrou* alongside the verb *verrouiller*; Prov. *verrolh*, Sp. *berrojo*, Tusc. (Lucchese) *verrocchio*, etc., and even Ptg. *ferrolho* (Meyer-Lübke, 19[30]–1935: §9260).[21] Add the aforementioned case of *pechar* > - *fechar* in the West.

Europe

14.4. Development of word-initial *s-*

Yet, it is the second, geographically less extensive, departure from the familiar norm, namely the affrication of word-initial *s-*, that must henceforth hold our attention. The norm clearly demands that Latin *s* in this position, regardless of any such co-occurrent conditions as form class, channel of transmission, heaviness of stress in the syllable involved, and the like, be rendered by *s* in Hispano-Romance (including Galician-Portuguese), whatever the differences in finer phonetic detail between starting point and end point,[22] thus:

saeculu "lifetime, age" > OSp. *sieglo*; *sagitta* "arrow" > *saeta*; *sēcrētu* "out of the way, remote," "solitude, secrecy" > Ptg. *segredo*; *sedēre* "to sit" > OSp. *seer* "to sit, be"; *septe* (m) "seven" > *siete*; *sĭtĭ* (m) "thirst" > *sed*; *sībilō* "to hiss, whistle" > *silbo*; *sōle* "sun" > *sol*; *solu* "ground" > *suelo*; *soc(e)ru* "father-in-law" > *suegro*; *solēre* "to use, be wont" > *soler*; *super* "above" > *sobre*; *sūdat* "he perspires" > *su(d)a*.

With comparable frequency one comes across word-initial *c* /ᵗs/, overwhelmingly before the front vowels *e* and *i*, plus the diphthong *ie*, in Old Spanish; but its source is by no means ancestral *s*, but /kᵉ˒ⁱ/, subject to gradual assibilation in the environment just described, including the contiguity of the falling diphthong *ae*, which gravitated toward monophthongal pronunciation in Late Latin, thus:

caecu "blind" > OSp. *ciego*; *caelu* "sky, heaven" > *cielo*; *cēra* "wax" > *cera*; *certu* "certain" > *cierto*; *cīvitāte* "citizenry" > *cibdad* "city, town"; *cĭtō* "quickly, soon" > *cedo*.

The post-medieval history of this /ᵗs/, which in part developed into a voiceless interdental /θ/, as in Castile, in part into /s/, as in most of Andalusia and in the New World, will be of no further concern to us here.[23]

The rules so far laid down are not ironclad; in three special categories of exceptional cases the /ᵗs/ trespasses, with varying consistency, on the territory of the /s/, while the reverse deviation seems not to occur, at least not in the chosen position:

(1) First, if the word has a medial affricate, either voiced /ᵈz/ or voiceless /ᵗs/, word-initial *s-*, through anticipatory assimilation, tends to yield ground to /ᵗs/, thus: from *saeta* "bristle," "thick, stiff hair" the Romans extracted two adjectives, well-documented *saetōsus* as against *sae-*, *sē-tāceus*, recorded only in glosses, but apparently by no means marginal in actual usage. The latter, eventually pronounced /seːtaːkju/, gave rise to OSp. *cedazo* "sieve," with *ç* (sometimes spelled *c-*) in lieu of expected *s-* making its appearance by way of anticipation of the *-z-* /ᵈz/. There is a wealth of parallel examples.[24]

(2) Second, in Arabisms. Maghrebi Arabic *sīn* must have sounded not unlike modern Polish *ś*, and the closest approximation the speakers of medieval Hispano-Romance hit upon in lexical borrowings was, of all imaginable possibilities, their

/ˢs/ — originally arrived at, we recall, from an entirely different sector of their language's Latin foundation. Hence the appearance, in Old Spanish orthographic garb, of the following Orientalisms:

çafarí "shelf for water jugs," *çaga* "rear," *çahinas* "sorghum," *çanahoria* (= Ptg. *cen-oura, -oira*) "carrot," *çaquiçami* "garret, attic"; "hovel, pig pen," *çaranda* "sieve, screen," *çaratán* "cancer of the breast"

with the segments *çe-*, *çi-*, *ço-*, and *çu-* being also represented, if not quite so liberally as *ça-*, and with Arabic /ṣ/ and the cluster /st/ likewise serving, on occasion, to produce *ç-* in Old Spanish.[25]

(3) Third, and conceivably most relevant in the context of this volume, *ç-* emerges as a surprise substitute for otherwise foreseeable *s-* in words of Latin stock which, on semantic grounds, can be — hazily — suspected of pertaining to the domain subject to phonosymbolic interferences, with the hard core of this particularly troublesome group comprising lexical items associated with acoustic effects, sometimes but not invariably musical. Interestingly, in this third group, in contrast to what has happened in the preceding two, another affricate, namely /č/, spelled *ch*, alternated with *ç* in conveying the same acoustic message, namely the presence of a phonosymbolizable event. From a distinctly more elaborate study (Malkiel, forthcoming) let me select a few illustrations.

The Greek word that underlies our own Hellenism *symphony* must have been pronounced on its native ground, in Antiquity, as *sumpōnía* and, upon its adoption by the artistically less talented Romans, as **sumpónia* with the expected accent shift, as in the case of Gr. *ekklēsía* "assembly" > L. *ec(c)lēsia* "church." **Sŭmpónia* is the direct predecessor or prototype of Sp. *zampoña*, originally *çampoña*, "shepherd's flute," the predictable vowel dissimilation *o – ó > a – ó* having coincided with the transmutation of *s-* into *ç-*. Descending from the heavenly heights of music to the snakepit of ugly noises, we can adduce the two examples of *sepelīre* "to bury" transformed into *ça-* or *çam-bollir* (mod. *zambullir*) "to dive," literally "to bury oneself (in water)," via OSp. *se-*, somewhat later *so-bollir*. Once more, the vowel dissimilation *o – ó* to *a – ó* in, e.g., most of the paradigms of the present tense coincides here with the change of *s-* into *ç*, and the nasal is an expressive intercalation (*ça- > çam-*).

For stronger orchestration, speakers have the option of switching to *ch-* /č/ rather than to *ç-* /ˢs/. Thus, from *sībilāre* "to hiss" Spanish has extracted three rival verbs, each accompanied by a retinue of its own: *silbar* "to whistle," beside *chiflar* "to whistle, mock, jest, tipple," and, even more radically syncopated, *chillar* "to scream, squeak, shriek, screech, mewl, crackle, creak, hiss, imitate the notes of birds, sizzle in a frying pan," with such semantically advanced derivatives as *chifladura* "craziness" and *chillón* "bawler, screamer." Beyond the realm of sound we find all sorts of tags suggestive of violent reactions: contempt, disgust, restlessness, with *s-* moving in the direction of *ç*, and *ç-*, in turn, aiming at advance to *ch-*, as when *cīmice* "bedbug," metamorphosed into OSp. *cīmze*, is allowed to become *chinche*; *stra(m)bu* "squinting," through a dazzlingly bold transposition of imagery, becomes *zambo* "knock-kneed"; and a word of obscure parentage, still *secrano* or *siclano* in older Portuguese, is allowed by older Spanish to adopt such fancy forms as *cicrano*, *cit(r)ano*, and finally *cutano*, as it was gradually fitted into the contemptuous formula *Fulano, Mengano y Zutano* "Mr. X, Y, and Z." Among the stealthy, nerve-wrecking activities qualifying for such a label one may include *acechar* "to ambush," from older *assechar* > *assectārī* "to follow (secretly)" and several other words of comparable semantic contour.[26]

With much of the etymological marshland involving otherwise unexplained OSp. *ç-* from Lat. *s-* probably falling under the rubric of phonosymbolic coloring,[27] it begins to look as if an explanation for that classic crux OSp. *cerrar* were at long last gradually coming into view.[28]

Let me recapitulate the essentials so far established. Step 1: As classical *claudere* "to close, shut" in certain provincial varieties of colloquial Latin shows symptoms of obsolescence, substitutes start arising here and there, among them an easily reconstructible **serāre*, from well-documented *sera* "bolt." Step 2: **serāre* gains in local appeal by giving way to **serrāre*, both through closer association with that magic word *ferrum* "iron," notoriously contagious, and for the sake of avoiding any homonymic conflict with other verbs revolving around the *ser-* stem.[29] Step 3: To suggest the loud banging of the door, preferably one equipped with an iron lock, or simply the noisy clicking of that lock, *serrar* is endowed with an acoustically suggestive *ç-* /'s/. *Cerrar*, if this analysis is correct, at the outset must have meant not just "to shut," but "to lock in, lock off, lock out" and the like; cf. the parallel use of the musical verb *fistulāre* for "bolting." An added benefit that speakers reaped by switching to *cerrar* was that, by so doing, they avoided any ludicrous homonymic conflict with *serrar* "to saw" and *sierra* "saw," figuratively "mountain range," the outgrowth of Class. *serra*. After all, no one declaring: "I've locked the (wooden) door" would want to be misunderstood as saying: "I've sawed the (wooden) door in two."

Without denying the existence of a few weak alternatives to this explanation,[30] I venture to hope that it is less far-fetched than any rival conjecture and, in addition, conducive to a firmer grasp of how phonosymbolism actually works in language growth.

NOTES

1 This, at least, is the opinion of *Webster's Third* (1961: 803c). C. T. Onions does not cite the derivative at all, but credits the underlying adj. "expressive" (in the late Middle Ages, "tending to expel"; later "full of expression" and, in the end, "serving to express") to French or Medieval Latin influence (Onions *et al.* 1966: 338b). The editors of the

American Heritage Dictionary (revised edn., 1982: 478b) single out for mention the use of "expressivity" as a technical term of genetics rather than of linguistics, and allow for the neologism "expressiveness" as a by-form.

2 Thus, R. Jakobson, throughout most of his long career, leaned toward use of "expressivity" and its counterparts in related languages, in the company of most Continental scholars (1962: 18, 219–220, 289ff., 295, 297–298, 378, 451, 469ff., 476, 617, 626, 647). Only in his concluding years (e.g., in the book he wrote jointly with Linda R. Waugh) did he reveal a preference for "emotive (features)," while allowing for the qualifier "expressive" by way of variation (1979: 39ff., 43ff., 46, 49–50, 72, 132, 163, 180, 195–196, 198, 231); the term "emphatics" by then had acquired new relevance in the context of the contrast "flat" ~ "non-flat."

3 These must, of course, be sharply distinguished from *affektiert* "affected, mannered." Strictly speaking, the latest academic usage demands that only *affektisch* serve as a technical term of linguistics "durch Affekte hervorgerufen, auf Grund von Affekten gebildet" (favored, e.g., as a qualifier of hypocoristic forms of proper names or of intimate forms of address), whereas *affektiv*, interchangeable with *emotional*, pertains to the vocabulary of psychology ("affekt-, gefühlsbetont, durch Affekte gekennzeichnet"). *Affektuos, -ös* seem to be Gallicisms ("mit Wärme und Gefühl zum Ausdruck bringend"). The numerous compounds involving *Affekt-* as the opening ingredient (the second can be *-stauung, -steigerung, -störung, -verdrängung, -verlagerung*) have remained strictly psychological key concepts (see Duden 1976–1981: 1.88b).

4 See my own experiment in this direction offered before a forum of LACUS members (1978: 511–529).

5 The exceptional word is *gris* "gray," an early Gallicism, which initially served to qualify certain varieties of imported furs. To *gris* one might want to add *beige*, as used of late increasingly, especially in the sector of fashion, even though *beige*, not least on account of its hospitality to the exotic phoneme /ž/, continues to smack of a foreignism, even to uninitiated ears. Fr. *gris*, in turn, is a word of Frankish provenance. Native to Spain, in contrast, has been *ceniciento* "ash-gray," cf. Ptg. *cinzento*.

6 This point has been the topic of a fairly recent inquiry (Malkiel 1984: 5–27).

7 On these polar concepts of prevalent "concreteness" vs. "abstractness" see Viggo Brøndal's celebrated pamphlet (1936); also, in retrospect, Veikko Väänänen (1981: 417–427; originally published in 1979), with references to earlier literature (A. Meillet, C. Bally, W. von Wartburg, etc.). For consistently adverse criticism see Albrecht 1970.

8 See my two papers, mutually complementary (1976: 757–778 and 1977: 69–85).

9 The point under heated discussion was the transmutation of Latin intervocalic *d* into *r* in Old French (e.g. *mĕdicu* "physician" > *mire*), rather than its total loss, as in *cauda/cōda* "tail", Fr. *queue* (Wahlgren 1930; Meillet 1931: 113–114).

10 Observe, however, that Rebecca Posner (1961) refused to allow such a wedge to be driven between consonant dissimilation in Romance (i.e. the topic consecrated by Grammont 1895) and the structurally underpinned regular sound changes. For the keenest appreciation of Posner's monograph see Togeby 1964: 642–667. Also, Alf Sommerfelt, in a talk – apparently left unpublished – which he gave shortly before his death at Stanford, used Celtic evidence to drive home the point that so-called sporadic or saltatory sound changes, far from being wholly unpredictable, were closely co-conditioned by regular changes. As is well known, Bloomfield was near despair in trying

Europe

to fit these changes, recalcitrant to easy classification, into his rigid system: "Changes like these are very different from those which are covered by the assumption of sound-change" (1933: 391). That scholar's misgivings about the wisdom of operating with sound symbolism beyond the narrow strip of onomatopoeic territory require no documentation.

11 Its points of vulnerability were: (a) the wavering between nuclear *au* and *u* (with the former tending to be monophthongized to *o*); (b) the instability of intervocalic *-d-*, especially in the Western varieties of spoken Latin; (c) the dialectal split of *cl-* into [č], later [š], and [kλ], later [λ]. It has been customary, in Romance quarters, to adduce Gilliéron's suspicion (1915) that the near-homonymy of the outgrowths of *claudere* and *clāvāre* "to nail" was responsible for the gradual replacement of *clore* by *fermer*. The situation in Luso- and Hispano-Romance proves that Gilliéron recognized only one out of several strands. For a bird's-eye view of the situation in Latin see Meillet and Ernout (1959–1960: 125b, 126a), who explain the relation of *claudere* to *clavis* "key" and *clāvus* "nail." For a panoramic view of *claudere*'s status in Romance see Meyer-Lübke 19[30]–1935: §1967.

12 The details of the rivalry between *fer-* and *ferm-* in composition (e.g. ONorm. *ferlier* beside (OWall. *ferm-lier*) have been laid bare by Klingebiel (1985: 25–26, 91, 103, 110, 118, etc.). On the general stratification of rival verbs in Gallo-Romance see Dauzat *et al.* 1982: 174a, 301b, and Gamillscheg 1969: 237b, 238a, and 421b, with clues to researches conducted by Meuser (1929) and Bambeck (1959: 20).

13 In Italian *fermare* has not transcended the semantic stage of "to stop, halt" (= Fr. *arrêter*) and thus does not qualify as a competitor of *chiudere*, whose etymology poses no problem and which is surrounded by a number of compounds, involving the simple and composite prefixes *ac-*, *dis-*, *rac-*, *ri-*, *rin-*, *s-*, *soc-* (Migliorini and Duro 1964: 106b, 502b). There also exists a short learnèd branch: *escludere*. For a guide to relevant dialectal formations see Jaberg and Jud 1960: 119a.

14 On Asturian *pechar/pesllar* and the prehistory of Ptg. *fechar* I can cite my own circumstantial account (1952: 299–338), which, however, casts scant light on the vicissitudes of *cho(uv)ir*, *choer*. The Old Spanish counterpart(s) might have been *lloer* or *lloír*; if at all extant, these forms could have been used, at best, residually, judging from the silence of Oelschläger (1940) and, previously, from Hanssen's inattention (1913) to the entire family of *claudere*; Alvar and Pottier's recently published treatise on morphology (1983) is equally discreet.

It is more accurate to argue that, of the entire edifice of the verb under study, only the substantivated past ptc. *clausu*, *-a* was allowed to survive for a while in fossilized form, as *llosa* (Menéndez Pidal 1941: §39) < *clausa*, originally – as Meillet and Ernout remind us – the plural of *clausum* "enclosed place"; cf. the archaic hypercorrections *flausa/flosa*, Old Leon. *xosa*, and mod. dial. *josa* (Menendez Pidal 1950: §43). In the Portuguese-Galician area both the finite verb and the past ptc., in nominalized forms beside derivatives from these, were still in use until the end of the Middle Ages. For Portugal proper see Viterbo (1798: 2.273ab) on *chous-o*, *-a*, *-al*, and *-ura* "small hedged-in property," and Huber (1933: §295) on *chouvir*, var. *choivir*; and on Galician usage, old and modern, consult Carré Alvarellos 1933: 250b and Crespo Pozo 1963: 177, 180, with mention of *chous-a*, *-o*, *choer* "to close (a door, a window)," and *chouvir* "to surround a small property with a hedge" (from older *choír*, no doubt like *oír* ~ *ouvir*/ < *audíre* "to hear"). The absence of *cho(uv)ir* from the fourteenth-century verb glossary (Carter, 1952–1953: 71–103) points to its early obsolescence, under pressure from the near-homonym *chover* "to rain" < *plŭere*.

15 A full history of the growth of the family cannot be offered here. Such obvious guides as García de Diego ([1957]: 162a, 164a, 167a, plus §§6069–6070) and the Academy (Real Academia 1984: 309b, 314b, 1412c, etc.) offer a profusion of suffixal derivatives (also back formations) and a few compounds. Several points of light contact with the family of *cercar* < *circāre* "to ring, circle" can be observed here at close range, a state of affairs which prompted Ford (1911: 197b) to interpret *cerrar* as *serrāre/circāre*. Of the derivatives here cited, *cerradura*, *cerrajà*, *cerrajero*, and *cerrojo* were not uncommon in medieval texts; Castro (1936: s.vv.) offers examples and exegetic comments.

16 See Meillet and Ernout (1959–1960: 616b). The authors provide a graphic definition ("serrure constituée à l'origine par une barre de bois qu'on glissait derrière la porte"); refer the readers to an archeological dictionary; and record the survival of *sera* borrowed into Welsh as *ser*; they resolutely separate Varro's *serāre* "to open," which they declare a ghost word, from the authentic history of this word family. Unfortunately, in mentioning the genesis of *serrāre*, they neglect to point out the fact that the semantic space of verbal *ser-* had been blocked by the previous expansion of *serō, -ĕre*₁ "to sew" as well as of *serō, -ĕre*₂ "to join, entwine, interweave." For details see later. The var. *serra* appears in a late-antique gloss.

17 Examples can be cited from Tibullus, Propertius, Ovid; among their predecessors, from Plautus; and among their followers, from Juvenal, who all used *sera* in the singular or the plural, not infrequently with an allusion to the private quarters of the beloved woman.

18 As regards what is here held to have been the further change, in Portuguese, of *pechar* into *fechar*, some scholars, including Spitzer (1911: 159–160) and, later and in much greater detail, Tilander (1959–1950: 1–13) have short-circuited the development, reckoning with the possibility of spontaneous facetious allusion to *fistula* "pipe, tube," esp. "water pipe, reed pipe, shepherd's pipe," via the verb *fistulāre* familiar from the subsoil of Italo-Romance. In his effort to eliminate any need for operating with the shift *p-* > *f-*, difficult of explanation, the Swedish scholar went to the extreme of denying any causal connection between *pessulāre* > Asturian and Galician *pechar* (and vars.) and *fistulāre* > Ptg. *fechar*, citing both acoustic and visual analogs between the primitive lock and the archaic flute. One is tempted to ask: Could this jocose way of looking at things (or, rather, of listening to the noises they make) have really constituted more than a secondary influence, presumably weaker than the pressure exerted by *ferrum* "iron"? For further details and bibliography, see Malkiel 1952: 313–317.

19 True, scattered traces of the old *s-* entering into *ser(r)āre* are likely to have lingered on in sheltered dialect speech, but even there, for the most part, indirectly, namely in derivatives, as when García de Diego ([1957]: s.vv.) so analyzed Galician, Aragonese *serralla*, Pyrenean *serala* (a datum he owed to A. Badia Margarit's fieldwork), Galician and Ribagorzan *sarralla* (a by-form for which he was indebted to Ferraz y Castán 1934), and Galician *sorralla*.

20 Lexicologists can here fall back on the iconography supplied by the British Museum's guide to an exhibition illustrating ancient Greek and Roman life.

21 Actually, Spanish has also tended to transcend the stage of *berrojo* by using instead *cerrojo* (its *c-* borrowed from *cerrar*).

Europe

22 A dimension of the problem made even more complicated by the fact that, say, Andalusian *s-* [s] falls short of coinciding with Castilian *s-* [ś]. I am omitting from consideration the fact that word-initial *s* + Consonant clusters requires a prothetic vowel, as in *spērāre* "to hope" > Sp. *esperar*.

23 We owe the most circumstantial – perhaps too detailed – account of these vicissitudes to Alonso's posthumous study (1955: 93–450), which, in its second edition (1967), underwent typographic cleaning, chiefly in light of my extended review (1955: 237–252).

24 An abundant collection of material, assembled by myself, was presented, with a few architectural flaws, in 1949 (183–232, especially 210–222: Vacillation between [s] and [ts] in Ancient Hispano-Romance). One encounters, side by side, true examples of the change *s-* > *ç*, undergone in deference to a following *-ç-*, i.e. of exact parallels of *cedaço*: *siccīna* > *cecina* "hung beef" (and its congener *cecial* "fish cured and dried in the air"), *si-* ~ *çi-mencera* (related to *simiente* "seed," *-ze* "seed time"), *ço-* ~ *ça-lloçar* alongside *solloçar* "to sob" (cf. *singultīre*, Fr. *sangloter*); and variants of learnèd words similarly shifted: *çaçardote* ~ *sacerdote* "priest," *cervicio* ~ *servicio* "service," *reçucitar* ~ *resuš(c)itar* "to arouse again, revive." But one also finds, as a reaction to protracted wavering, traces of primary, etymologically legitimate *ç-* before *-ç-* sporadically transformed into secondary *s-*, as with *Çaragoça* (mod. *Zaragoza*) ~ *Saragoça* (from *Caesar Augustea*), *çarcillo* ~ *-sarcillo* "earring, tendril" < *circellu* "little ring" (as distinct from *carcillo* ~ *sarcillo* "weeding hook," based on *sarc -ulu*, *-ellu*); also, if Wagner was right (1934: 225–228) in tracing *çaraça* "meatball filled with glass (to kill dogs)" via *ceraça* to *cērācea*, this rare word turns out to have been normally developed. Where the etymological problem remains in abeyance, as with *çarça* ~ *sarça* "common bramble, blackberry bush," there is no way of firmly assigning the forms to any subdivision. The earlier paper also documented the offshoots *cedaçero* or *zero* and dimin. *cedaçuelo*.

25 Arabic /ṣ/ underlies older Spanish *ç* in *çafariche* "shelf for holding water vessels," *çara* "(Muslim) religious adoration, prayer with various ceremonies," *çanefa* (var. *cenefa*) "frame (of a picture)"; "border, list, fringes, trimming." Arabic /st/ is the source of *ç* in *çaguán* "porch, entrance hall" and in the proper name *Çúñiga*. This information was offered by Cuervo (1895: 19, cf. 1954: 259), who added a fourth Arabic consonant to his inventory of sources, supporting this contention with a single capsulized word history, namely that of *çafio* "coarse," for which he offered an unreliable etymology. In the revised version, prepared ca. 1910–1911 but published posthumously (1954: 363), Cuervo elaborated on this statement, tossing in a few additional examples of OSp. *ç* < Ar. [ś], e.g. *çalea* "undressed sheepskin"; and of OSp. *ç* < Ar. [ṣ], e.g. *çahareño* "intractable, haughty" and *çurrón* "shepherd's provisions bag, game bag." For further details and a more modern approach see Steiger 1932: 136–143, 166–169, and Neuvonen 1941: 278–293; 1951: 290–352.

26 My earlier attempt to account for *assechar* > *acechar* by selecting the abstract *assechança* "(devil's) trap," with its characteristic suffix *-ança*, as the starting point, suffers from the fact that the only abstract endowed with real vitality has, of late, been the post-verbal *acecho*. *Çoçobrar* "to founder, sink, capsize"; "to grieve, be in pain" beside *çoçobra* "uneasiness, anguish, anxiety" was, originally, a nautical term borrowed from Catalan and suggestive of the up-and-down (literally, the down-and-up) movement of waves in stormy weather. The word-medial *ç* here involves the aggregate of Cat. *t* + *s* (*sots*, *sobre*), while the word-initial *c* merely anticipates the medial affricate.

27 It is hardly an exaggeration to affirm that these mystifying instances of Lat. *s-* > OSp. *ç-*, especially where no effect of consonant assimilation at a distance was inferable, proved to be one of the most recalcitrant slices of the material that puzzled the pioneering explorers of the "sibilants problem" (Cuervo, Ford, Saroïhandy, Tallgren-Tuulio, and others of their ilk).

28 Aside from the semantic affinity and phonic proximity of *cercar*, already cited as Ford's favorite argument in 1911, one may refer to Meyer-Lübke's strange, if hesitantly proffered, hypothesis (19[30]–1935: §7867) to the effect that between the dental nasal of the prefix *en-* and the opening consonant of **serrar* there developed a *-t-* by way of transitional (or buffer) consonant, giving rise to *ençerrar*, and that this compound in turn exerted sufficient pressure on the simplex **serrar* to have transmuted it into *çerrar*! To lend credibility to this far-fetched conjecture, its proponent should have offered massive evidence (a) of simplicia ushered in by *s-* with counterparts heralded by the prefix *en* exhibiting a *ç* in lieu of the *s*; and (b) of high-frequency simplicia falling, on a sweeping scale, under the influence of corresponding lower-frequency compounds.

29 A less than benevolent critic could at this juncture raise the question: What was the point in speakers shifting **serrar$_1$* to *cerrar* in recoil from a homonymic clash with *serrar$_2$* "to saw" if the newly arrived-at *cerrar*, in turn, threatened to block clarity of communication through its own collision with *cerro* "hill, neck (of an animal), backbone" from parental *cĭrru* "lock, curl, ringlet, tuft of hair, crest (of birds), hair on a horse's forehead, arm of a polyp, filament of plants, fringe on a tunic"? The two-pronged answer to any such skeptic's query must be: (1) The center of the *cĭrr-* family was a noun, not a verb, with the consequence that entirely different derivational suffixes were attracted into its orbit; and (2) the *ĭ* of *cĭrru* yielded in Spanish the monophthong *e* under heavy stress, while the *ĕ* of *sĕra*, etc., under comparable prosodic conditions, produced the diphthong *ie*.

The unimpaired strength of *cerro* shows in the rise of a plethora of derivatives and compounds surrounding it, among them: *cerrajón* "steep hill," *cerrazon$_2$* "steep hill"; (Columbia) "abutment of a mountain chain," *cerrejón*, "hillock," *cerrero* "running wild" (lit. "mountain-hopping") flanked by *cerrería* "lack of manners," *cerril* "mountainous, uneven"; "boorish, unpolished" (accompanied by abstracts in *-idad* and *-ismo*), *cerrillo* "small protuberance," pl. "dies for milling coined metal" beside *cerrilla* "die for milling coins" and *cerrillar* "to mill coined metal, mark it at the edge," (Salamanca) *cerristopa* "Sunday or holiday bedding" (*cerro* + *estopa*), etc.; add the toponym *El Cerrito*. A few words clustering around a *cerr-* nucleus seem to belong to neither family: *cerraja* "common sow-thistle" < *serrālia*; obs. *cerraje* = mod. *serallo* "seraglio" (a word of Turkish provenance) < *serāy*; *cerrateño* "inhabitant of *Cerrato*" (Palencia); *cerrebojar* = *rebojar* "to glean," *cerretano* "inhabitant of *Cerdaña*," Ast. *cerrica* "diminutive bird" < onomat. *cerri, cerrión* "icicle" < *stiria* "frozen drop," etc.. With the prominence accruing to *cer(r)-*, a few isolated formations drifting through the local lexical space could not help being attracted to it, sometimes exchanging, in the process, their etymological *se-* for *ce-*.

30 One might, e.g., argue that, as the fluid cases previously considered under such rubrics of wavering as consonant assimilation and phonosymbolism shifted *s-* to *ç-*, speakers, availing themselves of that momentum, also disambiguated **serrar* "to close"/*serrar* "to saw" by changing the *se-* segment to *çe-* in the former, but not in the latter.

Europe

REFERENCES

Albrecht, J. 1970. *Le français, langue abstraite?* Tübinger Beiträge zur Linguistik 10.
Alonso, A. 1955. *De la pronunciación medieval a la moderna en español*, rev. by Rafael Lapesa, vol. 1, 2nd edn. Biblioteca románica hispánica (dir. D. Alonso). Madrid: Gredos.
Alvar, M. and B. Pottier. 1983. *Morfología histórica del español*. Madrid: Gredos.
American Heritage Dictionary (college edn). 1982. Ed. William Morris. Boston: Houghton Mifflin. (Orig. edn. of the revised version: 1976.)
Bambeck, M. 1959. *Lateinisch-romanische Wortstudien*. Wiesbaden: Steiner.
Bloomfield, L. 1933. *Language*. New York: Holt.
Brøndal, V. 1936. *Le français, langue abstraite*. Copenhagen: Levin & Munksgaard.
Carré Alvarellos, L. 1933. *Diccionario galego-castelán e vocabulario castelán-galego*. 2nd edn. A. Cruña [= Corunna]: Zincke Hermanos.
Carter, H. H., ed. 1952–1953. A fourteenth-century Latin–Old Portuguese verb dictionary. *Romance Philology* 6 (2–3): 71–103.
Castro, A. 1936. *Glosarios latino-españoles de la Edad Media*. Suppl. to *Revista de filología española*. Madrid: Centro de Estudios Históricos.
Crespo Pozo, J. S. 1963. *Contribución a un vocabulario castellano-gallego, con indicación de fuentes*. Madrid: Revista "Estudios."
Cuervo, R. J. 1895. Disquisiciones sobre antigua ortografía y pronunciación castellanas (Part 1). *Revue hispanique* 2: 1–69.
    1954. Disquisiones sobre antigua ortografía y pronunciación castellanas, 1^a y 2^a versiones. In *Obras*, vol. 2: 240–476. Bogotá: Instituto Caro y Cuervo.
Dauzat, A., J. Dubois, and H. Mitterand. 1982 (1964). *Nouveau dictionnaire étymologique et historique*. Rev. 4th edn. Paris: Larousse.
Duden: *Das groß e Wörterbuch der deutschen Sprache in sechs Bänden* (gen. ed.: G. Drosdowski). 1976–1981. Mannheim/Vienna/Zürich: Bibliographisches Institut.
Ferraz y Castán, V. 1934. *Vocabulario del dialecto que se habla en la Alta Ribagorza*. Madrid: Tipografía de archivos.
Ford, J. D. M. 1911. *Old Spanish Readings, Selected on the Basis of Critically Edited Texts* Boston, etc.: Ginn & Cie.
Gamillscheg, E. 19[66]–1969. *Etymologisches Wörterbuch der französischen Sprache*. Rev. 2nd edn. Heidelberg: Winter.
García de Diego, V. [1957.] *Diccionario etimológico español e hispánico*. Madrid: SAETA.
Gilliéron, J. 1915. *Pathologie et thérapeutique verbales*. In: *Résumé de conférences faites à l'École pratique des hautes études*. Neuveville: Beerstecher.
Grammont, M. 1895. *La dissimilation consonantique dans les langues indo-européennes et dans les langues romanes*. Dijon: no publ.
Hanssen, F. *Gramática histórica de la lengua castellana*. Halle a.S.: Niemeyer.
Huber, J. 1933. *Altportugiesisches Elementarbuch*. Heidelberg: Winter.
Jaberg, K. and J. Jud. 1960. *Index zum Sprach- und Sachatlas Italiens und der Südschweiz*. Bern: Verlag Stämpfli & Cie.
Jakobson, R. 1962. *Selected Writings 1: Phonological Studies*. The Hague: Mouton.
Jakobson, R. and L. R. Waugh (with M. Taylor). 1979. *The Sound Shape of Language*. Bloomington and London: Indiana University Press.

Klingebiel, K. 1985. Romance reflexes of the Latin type *manūtĕnēre*. PhD dissertation, University of California at Berkeley.

Malkiel, Y. 1949. Old Spanish *assechar* and its variants. *Hispanic Review* 17: 183–232.

    1950. The hypothetical base in Romance etymology. *Word* 6: 42–69.

    1952. Studies in Hispano-Latin homonymics: *pessulus, pāctus, pectus, dēspectus, suspectus, fistula. Language* 28: 299–338.

    1955. Review of Alonso 1955. *Romance Philology* 9(2): 237–252. (William A. Nitze Testimonial)

    1976. Multi-conditioned sound-change and the impact of morphology on phonology. *Language* 52: 757–778.

    1977. Ernst G. Wahlgren – et les perspectives de la réhabilitation de la morphologie. *Studia Neophilologica* 42: 69–85.

    1978. From phonosymbolism to morphosymbolism. *LACUS Forum* 4: 511–529.

    1984. La aversión al monosilabismo en los adjetivos del español antiguo y moderno. *Lingüística española actual* 6(1): 5–27.

    Forthcoming. Integration of phonosymbolism with other categories of language change. Paper presented in September 1985 at the Seventh International Conference on Hispanic Languages (Pavia) and to appear in its proceedings.

Meillet, A. 1931. Review of Wahlgren, 1930. *Bulletin de la Société de linguistique de Paris* 31(2): 113–114.

Meillet, A. and A. Ernout. 1959–1960 (1932). *Dictionnaire étymologique de la langue latine*. Rev. 4th edn. Paris: Klincksieck.

Menéndez Pidal, R. 1941. *Manual de gramática histórica española*. Rev. 6th edn. Madrid: Espasa-Calpe, SA (numerous reprints).

    1950. *Orígenes del español*. Rev. 3rd edn. Madrid: Espasa-Calpe, SA. (= *Obras completas*, vol. 8).

Meuser, H. 1929. *Lateinisch CLAUDERE*. Giessener Beiträge zur romanischen Philologie 22.

Meyer-Lübke, W. 19[11]–1920. *Romanisches etymologisches Wörterbuch*. Heidelberg: Winter.

    19[30]–1935. *Romanisches etymologisches Wörterbuch*. Rev. 3rd edn. Heidelberg: Winter.

Migliorini, B. and A. Duro. 1964 (1950). *Prontuario etimologico della lingua italiana*. Turin, etc.: Paravia.

Neuvonen, E. K. 1941. *Los arabismos del español en el siglo XIII*. Helsinki.

    1951. Los arabismos de las *Cantigas de Santa Maria*. *Boletim de Filologia* (Lisbon) 12: 290–352.

Oelschläger, V. R. B. [1940.] *A Medieval Spanish Word-List*. Madison: The University of Wisconsin Press.

Onions, C. T., *et al.* 1966. *The Oxford Dictionary of English Etymology*. Oxford: Clarendon.

Posner, R. R. 1961. *Consonant Dissimilation in the Romance Languages*. Publications of the Philological Society 19. Oxford: Blackwell.

Real Academia Española. 1984. *Diccionario de la lengua española*. 2 vols. (continuous paging). Madrid: Editorial Espasa-Calpe, SA.

Spitzer, L. 1911. Etymologische Miszelle ... *Archiv für das Studium der neuren Sprachen* 127: 153–161.

Steiger, A. 1932. *Contribución a la fonética del hispano-árabe y de los arabismos en el ibero-románico y el siciliano*. Suppl. 17 to *Revista de filología española*. Madrid: Centro de Estudios Históricos.

Tilander, G. 1949–1950. L'étymologie de portugais *fecho, fechar* élucidée par la construction des serrures primitives. *Studia Neophilologica* 22: 1–13.
Togeby, K. 1964. Qu'est-ce que la dissimilation? *Romance Philology* 17(3): 642–667.
Väänänen, V. 1981. *Recherches et récréations latino-romanes*. Biblioteca Enrico Damiani 4 (dir. Nullo Minissi). Naples: Bibliopolis (Istituto Universitario Orientale).
Viterbo, J. de Santa Rosa de. 1798. *Elucidário das palavras, termos e frases que em Portugal antigamente se usárão* . . . 2 vols. Lisbon: S. T. Ferreira.
Wagner, M. L. 1934. Etimologías españolas y arábigo-hispánicas. *Revista de filología española* 21: 225–247.
Wahlgren, E. G. 1930. *Un problème de phonétique romane: le développement* d > r. Skrifter utgivna av Kungl. Humanistika Vetenskapssamfundet 26(4). Lund: Gleerup.
Webster's Third New International Dictionary of the English Language, Unabridged, ed. Philip Babcock Gove. 1961. Springfield, MA: G. & C. Merriam Co., Publishers.
Williams, E. B. 1955. *Spanish and English Dictionary/Diccionario inglés y español*. New York: Holt.

15
Modern Greek ts *: beyond sound symbolism*[1]

BRIAN D. JOSEPH

15.1. Introductory remarks

The phenomenon of sound symbolism in language in general and in individual languages is undeniably noteworthy and of interest in its own right. However, it is often the case that sound symbolism is but one facet of a more comprehensive and extensive set of expressive linguistic domains. It therefore turns out that in order to fully understand this phenomenon, one must view it within such a broader context.

In this paper, a detailed case study from Modern Greek is presented in order to document the complexity of the interaction between a language's sound-symbolic elements and its other exponents of expressivity. This complexity is apparent not only in the synchronic intertwining of various expressive elements but also in the nature of the diachronic developments that give rise to the synchronic state. The lesson to be learned from this is that the identification of a given element as a sound symbol generally yields just the tip of the phonosemantic iceberg, a point of departure for an investigation of the workings and origins of the more iconic and expressive realms in a language.

It is useful at this point to introduce some terminology for referring collectively to the various aspects of a language which contribute to a language's expressivity through the iconicity, the colour, the connotative value, and the like that they display. Following Wescott (1975: 497), the expressive domains in a language can be lumped together as "allolanguage," and characterized as those aspects "that [are] alienated from conventionally structured speech," so-called "microlanguage."[2] Allolanguage includes non-human communication systems, child language, interjections, language play, and the like, and is expressive, affective, connotative, colorful, and iconic, while microlanguage has none of these properties. Although nothing in the discussion of Greek to follow hinges crucially on the terminology just introduced, it does provide a convenient labeling for the lexical domains beyond mere sound symbolism in which the Greek phonological elements to be considered here range and are to be found.

Europe

The particular elements in Greek in question are the voiceless dental affricate [ts] and, to a somewhat lesser extent, its voiced counterpart [dz]. As far as the standard language is concerned, at least, these sounds can be shown to be sound-symbolic elements, occurring in a wide-ranging and well-represented set of sound symbols. However, as noted above, they are also much more than that. In particular, the basic hypothesis to be developed here is that [ts] and [dz] are the primary phonic exponents of Greek allolanguage. The main evidence to support this contention is the fact that the vast majority of lexical occurrences of [ts]/[dz] falls into word classes which fit Wescott's criteria for allolanguage. Under the assumption that this distribution is not just accidental, it becomes apparent that [ts]/[dz] occupy a special place in the overall system of phonic expressivity in Greek.

As the survey of the relevant evidence concerning the role of [ts]/[dz] in Modern Greek phonology and phonosemantics begins, two important points must be borne in mind. First, while it might seem that the preponderance of allolinguistic occurrences of [ts]/[dz] is simply the result of selectivity of presentation, it turns out that no other sounds in the language have the same lexical distribution as [ts]/[dz] and that, moreover, the frequency of [ts]/[dz] in these expressive lexical domains is greater than that of any other sound that might happen to occur in them and also greater than the frequency of [ts]/[dz] in non-allolinguistic domains (Greek "microlanguage"). Thus, even though the sounds [ts]/[dz] do occur in non-expressive lexical items, such as the borrowings *tsiménto* "cement" and *dzáz* "jazz" or the native word *vutsí* "cask," their disproportionate representation in expressive domains is striking and reveals something significant about their status in the phonological system. Second, while it is usually the case that only one of the two sounds occurs in a particular word or group of words cited here in support of the basic hypothesis, in some of them both [ts] and [dz] are to be found, with one and the same word occasionally showing a fluctuation between a [ts]-pronunciation and a [dz]-pronunciation; because of this, [ts]/[dz] can be considered together as a unit in terms of their functional status.

15.2. [ts]/[dz] as a sound symbol (in Standard Modern Greek)

The evidence for sound-symbolic value for [ts]/[dz] in Standard Modern Greek comes from the existence of groups of words which share a formal element – in this case [ts] or [dz], with or without some additional material – and are related in meaning. Three such groups can be identified.[3]

The first group shows a clustering of words and morphemes with the general meaning of "small; narrow"[4] and the formal characteristic of an initial sequence #*tsi*-. Relevant forms are given in (1), with the sound-symbolic portion in italics:

(1) *tsí*tóno   "I stretch"
     *tsí*ta-*tsí*ta   "just, barely" (said of a tight fit)
     *tsí*ma-*tsí*ma   "right up to the edge; close"
     *tsí*xla   "thin, woman" (primary meaning: "thrush")
     *tsí*livíθra   "thin woman" (primary meaning: "wagtail")
     *tsí*ros   "thin person" (primary meaning: "dried mackerel").

Also possibly belonging with this group is *dzudzés* "dwarf," which, however, shows the voiced [dz] instead of [ts] and a high back vowel instead of the high front vowel found in (1). A related subgroup is the cluster of morphemes and forms with diminutive value, i.e. indicating that an object or epithet is "small" along some dimension.[5] This includes two types of forms: a set of suffixes used in the derivation of diminutive nouns and adjectives, given in (2a) with some examples, and several independent diminutives and hypocoristics, as in (2b):[6]

(2) a. Diminutive suffixes (with affective value, for the adjectives):
   -*íts*a, e.g. *fuskítsa* "little bubble," *lemonítsa* "little lemon-tree," *voltítsa* "a little walk"
   -*íts*i, e.g. *korítsi* "(little) girl," *lemonítsi* "little lemon"
   -*úts*ikos, e.g. *kalútsikos* "goodish" (cf. *kalós* "good"), *ɣlikútsikos* "cute" (cf. *ɣlikós* "sweet")
   -*dzí*kos, e.g. *maskaradzíkos* "scoundrel-like" (cf. *maskarás* "scoundrel"), *kavɣadzíkos* "quarrelsome" (cf. *kavɣás* "quarrel")

   b. Independent diminutives:
   Kó*ts*os (from *Konstandínos*)
   Mí*ts*os (from *Dimítrios*)
   Mí*ts*is (from *Dimítrios*, dialectally).

If, as suggested above, *dzudzes* "dwarf" is included in the "small" group in (1), then both subgroups illustrated here show both [ts] and [dz] (cf. -*dzíkos* in 2a) and also show both [i] and [u] vocalism (cf. -*útsikos* in 2a).

The second group shows forms with #*tsV*-, with the general meaning "sting; bite; tease; burn." Some examples of members of this group are given in (3), with the sound-symbolic sequence in italics:

(3) *tsú*zo   "sting" (and derivatives *tsuxterós* "stinging," *tsúxtra*
                     "jellyfish")
     *tsu*kníða   "nettle"
     *tsi*mbó   "pinch"
     *tsi*m(b)úri   "tick" (biting insect)
     *tsi*víki   "tick"
     *tsi*ngló   "goad"
     *tsa*tízo   "tease"
     *tsa*tsára   "comb"

*ts*ungrána "rake" (and derivative *tsungranízo* "I rake")
*tsitsi*rízo "sizzle; torment slowly"
*tsi*γarízo "fry lightly; brown"
*tsu*ruflízo "singe; burn"
*tsi*kna "smell of meat or hair burning" (and derivative *tsiknízo* "I burn (e.g. in cooking)."

The third group of words is characterized by reference to some sort of deformity or deficiency and by the occurrence of [ts] or [dz] in the word.[7] Some examples of members of this group are given in (4), with the sound-symbolic sequence in italics:

(4) *tse*vϑós "lisping" (and derivatives *tsevϑízo* "I lisp," *tsévϑizma* "lisp")
  *tsá*tra-pátra "after a fashion; stumblingly (especially of speech)" (so Pring 1975: 196)
  *tsi*mbliáris "bleary-eyed" (and cf. base word *tsímbla* "eye-mucus")
  *dzudzé*s "dwarf."

Though the examples with initial [ts] or [dz] are few, the group in general is expanded by the inclusion of a subgroup having the shape [kVts-], exemplified in (5):

(5) Deficiency/deformity subgroup with #kV*ts*-
  ku*ts*ós "lame" (and derivatives *kútsa* "limp," *kútsa kútsa* "limpingly")
  ku*ts*o- "(prefix indicating) deficiency"
  ka*ts*o- "wrinkledy-"
  ka*tsí*ϑa "balding, scurvy head"
  ka*ts*ipoϑjá "bad luck" (dialectal),

which itself overlaps with a group characterized formally by #*kuC-ó-*:

(6) ku*ts*-ós "lame"
  kut-ós "stupid"
  kuf-ós "deaf"
  kul-ós "one-armed."

The sound-symbolic effect displayed by [ts] and [dz] in these groups is most evident in the standard language, but there are relevant dialectal forms, a few of which have already been mentioned, that fit into the above groups and thus are deserving of mention here. A small sampling of these forms is given in (7):

(7) a. West Crete (cf. Xanthoudides 1918):
  *dz*íngra "eye-mucus" (cf. Std. *tsímbla*, in (4))
  *dz*úngra "claw" (cf. Std. *tsungrána*, in (3))
  *dz*íngu-*dz*íngu "drop-by-drop" (cf. SMALL group in (1))
  *dz*íngazo "flow out in drops" (cf. SMALL group in (1))

b. Cypriot:
   ka*tsu*rízo "sting; burn" (cf. STING group in (3)).

These words become especially important in section 15.3, where other relevant dialectal forms are also mentioned.

15.3. Interrelatedness of sound-symbolic groups

That [ts] and [dz] should function in three such well-defined and well-represented sound-symbolic groups is certainly significant regarding the status of these sounds in Greek phonology, but even more remarkable and striking is the fact that these three groups seem to be interrelated subgroups of a more all-encompassing sound symbol. There are several lines of evidence attesting to the connections among these groups.

First, there is the semantic evidence of words which arguably could be assigned to more than one group, based on their meaning. For example, as already given in the data above, *dzudzés* "dwarf" fits in with the SMALL group (cf. (1)), based on the criterion of size, but also with the DEFORMITY group (cf. (4)). Similarly, *tsímbla* "eye-mucus" can be seen as belonging both to the DEFORMITY group (cf. especially the derivative *tsimbliáris* "bleary-eyed") and, when viewed as an irritant in the eye, to the STING group (as in (3)) as well. An additional example is provided by two words for "miser; stingy," *tsingúnis* and *tsifútis*, both of which, based on possible metaphors in which the notion of "miserliness; stinginess" can participate cross-linguistically, are assignable to both the STING group (cf. the derivation of Eng. *stingy* from *sting*) and the SMALL group (cf. Eng. *tightwad, tightfisted, closefisted*, etc.).

Such words provide links between the various groups, but at the same time clearly show that the boundaries between any of these groups are not rigid. This lack of semantic discreteness plays a role too in the second piece of evidence for interrelatedness, namely the fluidity shown by members of these groups from an etymological standpoint. That is, based on some reasonable etymological conjectures,[8] it seems that words of one group can move rather readily into others of other groups. One example is *kutsós* "lame," in the DEFORMITY group, which plausibly derives from *kopsós* "cut" via an irregular change of -*ps*- to -*ts*- (an etymology accepted by Andriotis 1983: 173), and so is literally "cut short" and therefore connected (originally) with the SMALL group. A somewhat more interesting – but also more controversial – example in terms of interconnectedness is the West Cretan from *dzíngra*, noted in (7) above as the equivalent of standard *tsímbla* "eye-mucus." Based on its meaning and its form, it belongs in the DEFORMITY group, but it seems to be connected etymologically with an adverb, *dzíngu-dzíngu* "drop-by-drop," which can be assigned to the SMALL group; moreover, this adverb is (supposedly) the source of *tsingúnis* "stingy; miserly," which, as noted above, belongs in both the SMALL and the STING group.[9]

A third piece of evidence relating these three groups to one another is the existence of formal links, in which a word has the form of one group but the meaning of another. For example, Cypriot *katsurízo* "burn," noted in (7) above, has the form of the #kVts- DEFORMITY subgroup (cf. (5) above) but the meaning of the STING/BURN group (of (3)). More widely ranging is the initial sequence *kuts-*, which, while figuring in the DEFORMITY subgroup (through *kutsós* "lame" and prefix *kutso-*), is also the basis for the dialectal *kútsikos* "little" (cf. Verveniotis 1976: 66), with a meaning appropriate for the SMALL group, and for the dialectal *kutsníða* "nettle" (from Imbros, cf. Favis 1939), a metathesized variant of *tsukníða*, from the STING group (with initial #tsV-). It therefore provides an especially important formal link connecting three groups.

Finally, the various interconnections evident from the above considerations can be put together into what may be termed a "relatedness network," in which the paths uniting the various groups and subgroups are laid out together:

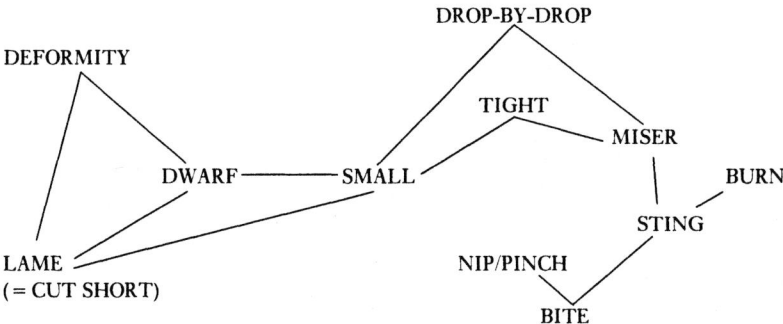

Conceptually, such a network is akin to the radial view of the meaning of a category espoused by Lakoff (1986), and while "small" has been put at the hub of the network, it need not be taken to be the basic meaning of the whole unit defined by the network (see also note 4).[10] It does, however, demonstrate clearly how the various sound-symbolic groups enumerated here can be taken to represent different facets of the same gem.

The extensiveness of this network of sound symbolism involving [ts] and [dz] indicates that they are not just elements that happen to participate in a few sound-symbolic sequences, but much more. In particular, since what all these related groups have in common from a formal standpoint is the occurrence of [ts] or [dz], these sounds can be identified as the primary carriers of the sound-symbolic function by which the groups are united. As such, they are the primary exponents of phonic symbolism in Modern Greek.

15.4. ts/dz in other expressive domains

The interrelatedness of the various sound symbols involving [ts] and [dz] shows that these sounds are the sound symbols *par excellence* in Greek. However, their special role in Greek expressivity goes far beyond this sound-symbolic value, for they are to be found in the full range of expressive lexical domains, i.e. in all the categories which would be allolinguistic, in Wescott's terms. To be sure, sounds other than [ts] and [dz] occur in these categories, just as [ts] and [dz] themselves occur in non-expressive lexical items (see above, section 15.2), but no sounds other than [ts] and [dz] occur with so great a frequency in expressive categories, and no other sounds show the overall somewhat restricted lexical distribution that [ts] and [dz] do, occurring primarily in these expressive categories.

One such class of words is interjections. Some of the interjectional elements of Greek containing [ts] or [dz] are given in (8):

(8)   prí*ts*   "no way; oh yeah?!" (also onomatope for breaking wind)
     ts   NEGATION (actually an apico-dental click, but conventionally represented in this way; cf. also *tsuk* as conventionalization of this noise)
     *dz*á   "noise used in peek-a-boo game" (with variant *tsá*).

A subclass of interjections is the set of calls to animals, those noises used in a situation – talking to non-humans – that by its very nature is outside the realm of microlanguage;[11] here, too, [ts] and [dz] are well represented:

(9)   gú*ts*   "call to pigs"
     *ts*ús   "call to donkeys"
     *ts*únks   "call to donkeys" (cf. Kalojeras 1975)
     ó*ts*   "whoa!"
     í*ts*   "whoa!"

Another class of expressive words belonging to allolanguage by virtue of their iconicity is the onomatopoeic words of the language and their derivatives. Again, one finds [ts] and [dz] well in evidence in this group:

(10)   *ts*ák   "crack!" (cf. *tsakízo* "I break")
      krí*ts*-krí*ts*   "crunch" (cf. *kritsanízo* "I crunch")
      má*ts*-mú*ts*   "kissing noise"
      *ts*iú-*ts*iú   "bird's chirp"
      plí*ts*-plá*ts*   "splish-splash!"
      γrá*ts*   scratching sound (with variants *xráts*, *kráts*, and *kráts krúts*, and derivative *γratsunízo* "I scratch")
      *dz*í-*dz*í   "noise of a cicada" (cf. *dzídzikas* "cicada").

Another relevant class of lexical items is the set of forms that are not expressive of a definite, easily characterizable meaning so much as expressive of an attitude (understood in its broadest sense). These attitudinal expressions tend to be more or less integrated into the syntax of a sentence, and correspond to what have been called ideophones in other languages. By virtue of their perceived non-arbitrary connection between form and meaning, ideophonic expressions in general are allolinguistic in nature. Among the ideophones of Greek are the following containing [ts] or [dz]:

(11)   *ts*áka-*ts*áka   "immediate quick action; straightaway; directly"
      *ts*úku-*ts*úku   "steadily and surely, with a hint of secretive activity"
      *ts*áf-*ts*úf   "in an instant."

Yet another lexical realm in which [ts] and [dz] occur and which is also, by dint of its very nature, expressive and part of allolanguage is the set of conventionalized child-language forms (see note 11). By this is meant those forms which children use but do not necessarily create themselves; rather they arise from adults' expectations of children's usage. A sampling of forms with [ts] or [dz] in this group is given in (12):

(12)   *ts*a*ts*á   "aunty" (cf. Andriotis 1983: 380, where a variant *tsátsa* is also given; note meaning of "madam [in a brothel]" in adult slang)
      *ts*i*ts*í   "meat" (also "breast" in adult slang)
      *ts*ís(i)a   "peepee" (with variants *dzís(i)a*)
      pí*ts*i-pí*ts*i   "(act of) washing" (cf. Kalojeras 1975)
      *dz*á   "noise used in peek-a-boo game" (with variant *tsá*).

A final group of lexical items relevant to the hypothesis concerning [ts] and [dz] is a miscellaneous group, composed of the words which are themselves highly expressive, iconic, privatized, connotative, and playful – in short, words with "allolinguistic" properties, which add color to the language, but which do not have any common thread beyond that to unite them. The sounds [ts] and [dz] are well represented here, although, as in all the other groups, other sounds occur as well. Some examples include:

(13)   *ts*ambunó   "whimper; prate; bullshit"
      *ts*alavutó   "do a slovenly job; splash around in shallow, muddy water"
      *ts*apa*ts*úlis   "slovenly in one's work"
      *ts*urápi   "vulgar woman" (primary meaning: "woolen sock")
      *ts*ókaro   "vulgar woman" (primary meaning: "wooden shoe")
      *ts*irízo   "screech"
      *ts*ilimburðó   "gallivant; fart about; whore around"
      *ts*i*ts*íði   "(stark) naked"

pi*ts*ilízo	"sprinkle, especially with dirty water"
*dz*ámba	"for free"
*dz*iri*dz*án*dz*ules	"evasiveness; coquettish airs"
*dz*án*dz*ala-mán*dz*ala	"this and that."[12]

This completes the survey of expressive lexical groups that contain [ts] and [dz]. One of the main points, as noted earlier, concerning the occurrence of these sounds in such words is the strikingly high frequency with which [ts] and [dz] occur in these and only these types of lexical items. Although it is hard to develop meaningful statistics on such a frequency, so that the claims on that score that have been made are largely impressionistically based, two rudimentary measures can be cited here. A count was made of the occurrence of these sounds in a corpus that is inherently allolinguistic in nature – the set of interjections and onomatopes given in one standard description of Modern Greek (Householder et al. 1964). Tokens of [ts] were taken together with those of [dz] – a reasonable step, considering the interchange often found between these two sounds in expressive words – and a frequency of occurrence of 4.1% for these sounds was found. What is striking about this result is that it is so much more than the percentage reported in Householder et al. 1964 for a count they made, together with one made by Mirambel (1959); based on a "normal" corpus of lengthy passages of connected prose, they reported a frequency of occurrence of 0.07% for [ts] and [dz] combined, lower than any other sounds in Greek. Similarly, a count of the initial segments of entries in a listing of nicknames from Kefallonia (Lorendzatos 1923) – a corpus of inherently allolinguistic items – yielded a frequency of 6.4% for [ts] and [dz] combined. Though there are some inherent difficulties with such counts,[13] the results here are suggestive and are what would be expected, given the basic hypothesis under consideration here about the special allolinguistic status of [ts] and [dz] in Greek.

At the end of the previous section, it was stated that the evidence of the interrelatedness of the various sound-symbolic groups leads to the conclusion that [ts] and [dz] are the primary phonosemantic exponents in Greek. Given the evidence cited in this section concerning the overall lexical distribution of [ts] and [dz], it seems that this conclusion can be expanded: [ts] and [dz] are the primary exponents of phonic expressivity in general in Greek.

15.5. Diachronic perspectives on [ts] and [dz]

Further evidence of the special status of [ts] and [dz] comes from the diachronic developments which have given rise to them in the standard language. As would be expected for sounds that function primarily in highly iconic and expressive ways, the paths by which [ts] and [dz] have entered Greek are generally irregular types of changes.

For example, a number of sporadic and irregular sound changes[14] have yielded allolinguistic occurrences of [ts] and [dz]. A sampling of these, with some relevant examples, is given in (14):

(14) a. ps → ts, e.g. *kopsós* "cut" → *kutsós* "lame" (DEFORMITY group), *psevðós* "lisping" → *tsevðós* "idem" (DEFORMITY group)

b. s → ts, e.g. (AGk) *sízo:* "hiss" → *tsúzo* "sting" (STING group), (AGk) *syrízo:* "whistle" → *tsirízo* "screech" (cf. 13)), (AGk) *sile:pordõ:* "behave with vulgar arrogance" → *tsilimburðó* "gallivant; fart about" (cf. (13))

c. t → ts, e.g. (AGk) *pitylízo:* "dart about with oars" → *pitsilízo* "sprinkle, especially with dirty water" (cf. (13))

d. k → ts, e.g. (Hell.Gk [Hesychius]) *kímmyros* "counting trifles" → (via diminutive *kimmyrion) *tsim(b)úri* "tick" (STING group); (AGk) *kimbíks* "skinflint" → (via diminutive *kimbíkion) *tsivíki* "tick" (STING group).

Similarly, there have been morphological reshapings in the direction of an allolinguistic form. For example, Ancient Greek *kni:sa* "savor of burnt offerings" yielded Modern Greek *tsíkna* "(pungent) smell of meat or hair burning" (STING/BURN group), where the changes are so drastic (multiple metatheses as well as creation of [ts]) as to suggest morphological processes rather than purely phonological ones. Also, Ancient Greek *knide:* "nettle" yielded Modern Greek *tsuknída* "nettle" (STING/BURN group) via the "prefixation" of *tsu-*, bringing it in line formally with the sting group (cf. *tsúzo* "sting").[15]

Also, many instances of expressive [ts] and [dz] occur in loanwords, especially loans from Turkish, as in (15), but also neighboring Slavic languages and Italian:

(15) *dzámba* "for free" ← Turkish *caba*
dzudzés "dwarf" ← Turkish *cüce*
tsifútis "miser" ← Turkish *çıfıt* "Jew"
kútsikos "little" ← Turkish *küçük*.

The fact that many of these loanwords are marked stylistically by being expressive and are also marked by the occurrence of [ts] or [dz] seems not to be accidental; this semiologico-stylistic dimension of [ts] and [dz] is taken up in the next section.

15.6. The semiologico-stylistic dimension of [ts] and [dz]

Based on the view of the role of [ts] and [dz] in Greek expressivity that has emerged here, it is fair to say that words with these sounds in general have a marked stylistic status, in that they are (generally) expressive while words without these sounds are (generally) not. This becomes especially clear when synonyms which differ formally in the presence or absence of [ts]/[dz] are compared with one another. For example, when confronted by a synonymous pair such as *kritsanízo* and *trayanízo*, both meaning "I crunch," native speakers of Greek typically label the former more "lively" or "vivid"; this result is not unexpected, for *kritsanízo* is derived from the sound-word *kríts* for a crunchy noise (see (10) above), and as such is more iconic and more expressive in nature. The existence of synonyms with one member marked stylistically in some way has come about in other ways as well, so that, internal to Greek, there are other stylistic dimensions – at least three more – by which a word can be opposed to a synonymous word; moreover, they all interact with the stylistic dimension defined by the presence of [ts] or [dz] in a word.

First, there is the distinction of (roughly) high style versus low style – usually referred to as *Katharevousa* (i.e. "puristic") versus *Dhimotiki* (i.e. "colloquial") – brought on by years of diglossia in Greek. This has led to the coexistence of stylistic doublets – pairs of synonymous words of quite different stylistic values – e.g. *líθos* (of Katharevousa origin) vs. *pétra* (of Dhimotiki origin), both meaning "stone." Another stylistic distinction within Greek is native versus foreign, and again there are stylistic doublets, e.g. native *tíxos* vs. *duvári* (of Turkish origin), both meaning "wall." Last, there is the dimension of Standard forms versus (regional) dialectal, evident in a pair such as Standard *ótan* versus dialectal *óndas*, both meaning "when."

The [ts]/[dz] stylistic dimension is relevant here in two ways. First, within any given dimension, the [ts]/[dz] dimension can serve to distinguish members and, as might be expected given the nature of [ts] and [dz] argued for here, generally yields a more marked form. This is evident in the native pair *kritsanízo* and *trayanízo* given above, and also in pairs of synonymous non-native words, e.g. *vólta* (of Italian origin) versus *tsárka* (of Turkish origin), where both words mean "walk; stroll," but the one with [ts] is felt by Greek speakers to be "slangier." Another pair involving words which are both of native origin is *yimnós* versus *tsitsíði*, where both mean "naked," but the *ts*-word is felt to be more evocative (e.g. "stark-naked" versus merely "without clothing").

Second, the [ts]/[dz] stylistic dimension cuts across the other three, thereby adding an extra stylistic distinction to the ways in which members of stylistic doublets can differ from one another. In most cases, as expected and as with the examples *kritsanízo/trayanízo* and *vólta/tsárka* mentioned above, the word containing [ds] or [dz] is the marked member of the doublet. These doublets with multiple stylistic distinctions can involve non-allolinguistic occurrences of [ts] or [dz], as in (16):

(16) a. [Katharevousa vs. Dhimotiki] and [− ts vs. + ts]: *astráyalos* vs. *kótsi* "ankle"

b. [Native vs. Foreign] and [− ts vs. + ts]: *flúði* vs. *tsófli* "skin; peel"

c. [Standard vs. Dialectal] and [− ts vs. + ts]: *kóskino* vs. *tsíta* "sieve,"

or allolinguistic occurrences of [ts] or [dz], as in (17):

(17) a. [Katharevousa vs. Dhimotiki] and [− ts vs. + ts]: *xolós* vs. *kutsós* "lame" (cf. (5))

b. [Native vs. Foreign] and [− ts vs. + ts]: *nanós* vs. *dzudzés* "dwarf" (from Turkish; cf. (4))

c. [Native vs. Foreign] and [− ts vs. + ts]: *ðoreán* vs. *dzámba* "free" (from Turkish; cf. (13))

d. [Standard vs. Dialectal] and [− ts vs. + ts]: *mikrós* vs. *mitsós* "small" (cf. (1) and (2)).

In some of these doublets, there are added dimensions of a non-oppositional nature as well; for example, in (17c), the Greek word *ðoreán*, while in common use and really only high-style when opposed to the non-native *dzámba*, is actually of Katharevousa origin (a fact evident in the presence of a final -*n*, which generally does not occur in words of Dhimotiki origin).

The sounds [ts] and [dz], therefore, make a contribution to the stylistic oppositions otherwise present in the language. This contribution complements their overall role in Greek expressivity.

15.7. Conclusion

The facts presented here give a very detailed look at the multiple parameters of expressivity that are relevant for two sounds, [ts] and [dz], in Greek. In order to fully understand the ways in which these sounds function in the phonosemantics of Greek, one must go beyond their functions as sound symbols and examine them in the full range of affective and stylistic domains in the language. Although just one language has been investigated here, it is safe to suggest that this situation is likely to be typical of expressive phonological units cross-linguistically, and therefore investigators must be sensitive to the broader expressive context into which sound symbols in any language may fit.

NOTES

1 This paper draws on findings concerning Greek [ts]/[dz] reported on in Joseph 1982 [1985], 1983, 1984a, 1984b, 1987, 1991, and 1992, and in Joseph and Philippaki-Warburton 1987:

Chapter 4). At the same time, though, those findings are expanded upon here, with additional supporting data and argumentation given that was not discussed in these earlier works. There is even more yet to be said, and all relevant material is being collected in a monograph in preparation on Greek [ts] and [dz] from a synchronic and dischronic perspective.

2 See Wescott 1975 for a discussion of the terminology and details on the properties of allolanguage beyond those mentioned here.

3 In citing these and other Greek forms, I follow standard transcription conventions; note though that [ð] is used for the voiced interdental fricative and [j] is used in its IPA value of a palatal glide. Also, the realization of nasal-plus-stop clusters is subject to socially and regionally conditioned variation between nasal-less pronunciations and pronunciations with the nasal; in representing them here with the nasal (e.g. in *tsimbó*), I mean only to indicate that the nasal is possible for at least some speakers with this word. Increasingly, one encounters only the nasal-less pronunciation within lexical items, and the absence of the nasal is categorical for younger Athenian speakers (see Arvaniti and Joseph 1993 for some discussion). In citations, AGk = Ancient Greek; Hell.Gk = Hellenistic Greek.

4 As George Lakoff has pointed out to me, it may be misleading to refer – here and elsewhere in the discussion – to a single, basic meaning for any given sound symbol, for each category might best be characterized as a whole defined by the interrelations of meaning and metaphorical extensions that its members exhibit. An approach similar to that is taken below for unifying the various sound-symbolic groups under consideration, though at this point, reference to *the* meaning of an element is made for convenience.

5 This includes the focusing – i.e. narrowing – of attention along the emotional dimension, in order to account for the affectionate or endearing use of many diminutives, possible in Greek, as in many languages.

6 There are listed separately from (2a) because they may well involve the independent "deformation" of part of a name in a hypocoristic formation process, not unlike the creation in English of *Betsy* out of *Elizabeth* (with $\theta \rightarrow ts$). Georgacas 1982 has an extensive discussion of the diachronic development of the diminutive suffixes and other related formations.

7 The Northeast Caucasian languages Chechen and Ingush, as discussed by Nichols 1986, provide a typological parallel to the existence of a sound-symbolic group centering on such a meaning, for one of the word groups characterized by "adventitious" (i.e. unexpected, from an etymological standpoint) pharangealization is a set of human nouns denoting some deformity or deficiency (typical meanings include "klutz," "hulk," "giant").

8 The wording is cautious here because not all linguists accept these etymologies and because of the general difficulties with proving proposed etymologies to be correct; often, the evaluation of etymological proposals comes down to a matter of taste.

9 The derivation of *tsingúnis* from the West Cretan form is the proposal of Xanthoudides 1918. It has not met with much approval, being characterized by Andriotis (1983: 381) as "unlikely," though there seem to be no actual phonological or semantic problems with the etymology; the more widely accepted derivation has *tsingúnis* as a borrowing from Turkish *çingene* "gypsy" (despite the need for some phonological and semantic adjustments in the borrowing).

10 A similar type of schema has been employed by Matisoff 1978 for showing the semantic relations among body-part words.

11 Note that Wescott, following Trager 1955, places animal communication, along with child language, into "prelanguage," as a subdomain of allolanguage.
12 Note also that this form shows the highly marked and affective reduplication (of Turkish origin as far as Greek is concerned) with #m- in second member.
13 For example, as Charles Fillmore has pointed out to me, the "normal" corpus would certainly have contained expressive words and differs in character from the word list used in my own count of allolinguistic terms. Also, the existence of polysemous words such as *tsurápi*, which is not expressive in its meaning "woolen sock" but is expressive in its meaning "vulgar woman," could skew the count somewhat. A more controlled frequency count, comparing, for example, the percentage of [ts] and [dz] obtained from a conventional dictionary with that obtained from a slang dictionary, is clearly needed here (and is planned).
14 Some of these changes may actually have been regular in dialects other than those of the Peloponnese which underlie the modern Standard language, and the appearance of irregularity or sporadicity may be simply the result of dialect borrowing into Standard Greek.
15 This is tantamount to calling *tsuknída* a blend, as first proposed by Filindas 1905 (cited in Andriotis 1983: 383).

REFERENCES

Andriotis, N. 1983. *Etimolojikó leksikó tis kinís neoelinikís*. Thessaloniki: Institute of Modern Greek Studies, Aristotelian University of Thessaloniki. (In Greek.)

Arvaniti, A. and B. D. Joseph. 1993. The sociophonetics of nasal suppression in Modern Greek: sound change in progress. Paper read at Annual Meeting of the Linguistic Society of America (Los Angeles), January 1993.

Favis, V. 1939. Metáθesis ke andimetáθesis fθóngon en ti neotéra eliniki γlósa met' anaforás is tin arxéan, *Leksikoγrafikón δeltíon* 1: 89–142 (Athens: Academy of Athens.) (In Greek.)

Filindas, G. 1905. *Posoγnosía ke γlosoγrafía elinkí*. Athens. (In Greek.)

Georgacas, D. 1982. *A Graeco-Slavic Controversial Problem Reexamined: The -ITS- Suffixes in Byzantine, Medieval, and Modern Greek: Their Origin and Ethnological Implications*. Pragmatie tis Akadimías Aθinon 47. Athens: Academy of Athens.

Householder, F., K. Kazazis, and A. Koutsoudas. 1964. *Reference Grammar of Literary Dhimotiki*. Indiana University Research Center in Anthropology, Folklore, and Linguistics Publications 31, and vol. 30(2) of *International Journal of American Linguistics*. Bloomington: Indiana University.

Joseph, B. D. 1983 [1985]. Ja tin iδiéteri θési tu [ts]/[dz] stin elinikí fonolojía. In *Studies in Greek Linguistics. Proceedings of the Third Annual Meeting of the Department of Linguistics, Faculty of Philosophy, Aristotelian University of Thessaloniki, 26–28 April 1982*. Thessaloniki: Publication Service of the Aristotelian University, 227–235. (In Greek with English résumé; actually published in 1985.)

1983. Language use in the Balkans: the contributions of historical linguistics. *Anthropological Linguistics* 25: 275–287.

1984a. Balkan expressive and affective phonology – the case of Greek *ts/dz*. In K. Shangriladze and E. Townsend (eds.) *Papers for the V. Congress of Southeast European Studies, Belgrade, September 1984*. Colombus, OH: Slavica Publishers, 227–237.

1984b. The Appropriateness of [ts] in certain Greek suffixes. *Onomata. Revue Onomastique* 9: 21–25.

1987. On the use of iconic elements in etymological investigation. Some case studies from Greek. *Diachronica. International Journal for Historical Linguistics* 4(1/2): 1–26.

1991. A Greek perspective on the question of the arbitrariness of linguistic signs. *Modern Greek Studies Yearbook* 7: 335–352.

1992. Interlectal awareness as a reflex of linguistic dimensions of power: evidence from Greek. *Journal of Modern Greek Studies* 10(1): 71–85. (Special Issue, *Language and Power, Language and Freedom in Greek Society*, edited by B. Joseph.)

Joseph, B. D. and I. Philippaki-Warburton. 1987. *Modern Greek*. London: Croom Helm.

Kalojeras, V. 1975. *Ixopiités léksis ke rízes stin elinikí*. Thessaloniki: Altindzi Brothers. (In Greek.)

Lakoff, G. 1986. Systematic sound symbolism: the semantic side. Paper presented at the Berkeley Conference on Sound Symbolism, January 1986.

Lorendzatos, P. 1923. Simbolí is ta neoeliniká paronímia. *Leksikoγrafikón arxíon tis mésis ke néas elinikís* 6: 40–71. (In Greek.)

Matisoff, J. 1978. *Variational Semantics in Tibeto-Burman. The "Organic" Approach to Linguistic Comparison*. Occasional Papers of the Wolfenden Society on Tibeto-Burman Linguistics 6. Philadelphia: Institute for the Study of Human Issues.

Mirambel, A. 1959. *La langue grècque moderne. Description et analyse*. Collection Linguistique Publiée par la Société Linguistique de Paris. Paris: Librairie Klincksieck.

Nichols, J. 1986. The semantics of pharyngealization in Chechen and Ingush. Paper given at the Conference on Sound Symbolism, University of California at Berkeley.

Pring, J. T. 1975. *The Oxford Dictionary of Modern Greek (Greek–English)*. Oxford: Clarendon.

Trager, G. 1955. Language. Article in *Encyclopedia Britannica*. Chicago: Encyclopedia Britannica.

Verveniotis, A. 1976. *Etimolojikón leksikón ton ksénon lékseon en xrísi is tin néan elinikin*. Athens. (In Greek.)

Xanthoudides, S. 1918. Glosiké ekloγé. *Leksikoγrafikón arxíon tis mésis ke néas elinikís* 5: 92–116. (In Greek.)

Wescott, R. 1975. Allolinguistics: exploring the peripheries of speech. In P. Reich (ed.) *The Second LACUS Forum*. Columbia, SC: The Hornbeam Press, 497–513.

16
On levels of analysis of sound symbolism in poetry, with an application to Russian poetry

TOM M. S. PRIESTLY

16.1 Introduction

With respect to sound symbolism, I accept as a premise the position which appears to me self-evident, and in any case proved in psycholinguistic experiments: that both synesthetic (or: universal) sound symbolism and conventional (or: local) sound symbolism coexist in every language.[1] I suggest that this coexistence is precisely what should be suspected: it is surely natural that the direct links between sound and meaning should be based both on phonetics and on the lexicon.

This is very probably a simplification of the real state of affairs. I suggest, however, that it is worth following this simplified hypothesis to its conclusion: namely, that it is to be expected that different languages will have synesthetic and universal sound symbolism in differing amounts. Over time, the sound changes and the semantic changes that occur may bring the two closer together, or, conversely, may force them further apart,[2] and hence some languages may be expected to have richer overall sound-symbolic associations than others: thus, reputedly, Korean, and some West African languages.[3]

I think that there are more factors at work than this stark dichotomy suggests; in particular, it seems that there are cultural factors that may or may not emphasize the use of certain kinds of sound symbolism for certain purposes. Nevertheless, I suggest that the disparities between the scope of sound symbolism in different languages may be explained at least in part by the "coalition-or-conflict" theory I have outlined. A theory of this kind is also the most likely basis for an explanation of apparent anomalies such as the following: the reports by Žuravlev (1974) and Levickij (1973) (both based on psycholinguistic testing procedures that are difficult to assess) that Russian /a/ = [FAST] for Russians, whereas Ukrainian /a/ = [SLOW] for speakers of closely related Ukrainian;[4] or that /e/ = [WARM] and /o/ = [LARGE] for Russians, while /e/ = [COLD] and /o/ = [SMALL] for Ukrainians.

My forays into the vast literature make me suspect that inattention to the probable coexistence of (at least) the two kinds of associations outlined above has bedevilled most of the discussions of sound symbolism. This seems particularly true with reference to poetry; for most analyses of this phenomenon in the poetic context have not allowed for both conventional and synesthetic sound symbolism.

Sound symbolism is particularly appropriate in certain types of poetic context, those where the medium simultaneously conveys and embodies the message. This context is especially exemplified in some kinds of poetry, but the simultaneous carrying and manifesting of the semantic content may occur in texts that are not normally called "poetry," such as prose written for children and the verbiage written for advertising. Texts of this nature will provide a window into the nature of sound symbolism, and their analyses should be of supreme interest to linguists; who, in turn, should do all they can to ensure that those analyses are carried out properly. If it is true that both synesthetic and conventional sound symbolism occur in languages, and that they differ in their scope, in their level of operation and in their relationship to the language structure, this fact must be the foundation for approaches to the analysis of sound symbolism in poetry.

Given a theory of sound symbolism of this kind, it follows that two levels of analysis of poetry will be required; and, if this theory is oversimplified, then more than two levels of analysis will be necessary. I will restrict myself here, however, to just the two levels of analysis that appear to fit this theory, emphasizing that this is already more complex than virtually all analyses of sound symbolism in poetry made hitherto.

If synesthetic sound symbolism exists and operates at an immediate phonetic level, then surely the sounds should be investigated at this level, and the meanings associated with them must be investigated at a similarly "superficial" level. If, on the other hand, conventional sound symbolism (being specific to each linguistic community) derives from and operates at the lexical level, then the sound–meaning associations should be analyzed at the language-specific phonemic level and the level of meaning corresponding thereto. And while the synesthetic associations are necessarily "more-or-less," the conventional associations are "either-or": in other words, synesthetic associations should be analyzed on phonetic and semantic scales, while conventional associations should be analyzed in terms of distinctions between the phonemes, or (better, I suggest) in terms of the presence or absence of the distinctive features that compose them, and, similarly, in terms of "plus-or-minus" semantic distinctive features.

In the literature on sound symbolism in poetry, there are occasional comments which appear to hint at the position I have just outlined.[5] In the main, however, my readings in the analysis of poetic "instrumentation" show a flat, uninterrupted vista: all the linguistic analyses are performed at a single level, viz. they deal with phonemes (either as such, or in terms of their distinctive features.)[6] None that I know of have been what might be called "split-level" analyses.[7]

As a complement to the many "either-or," phonemic/sememic distinctive feature analyses of Russian and other poetry that have been made, I therefore urge some kind of analysis of the associations between "more-or-less," phonetic and semantic scales. Of these two, the former may, in some instances at least, be made instrumentally. For example: to parallel the popular "emic" analysis of the parameter [± grave] = [± DARK/SAD/BAD] (see below) could one not devise an "etic" way of measuring the height of the relevant formant, and correlating this with psycholinguistically tested impressions of "darkness" or "sadness" that use, say, seven-point scales?

It is also worth recalling that among the approaches to the analysis of verse are those (the vast majority) which study the sound structure without any reference to sound symbolism, sometimes flatly denying its existence. This is not the place to go into these polemics. Clearly, I accept the relevance of sound symbolism in poetry: since it is known, from psycholinguistic experiments and the preponderance of comparative evidence, that synesthetic and conventional sound symbolism both exist in language generally, then I assume that these associations are present in poetry, *along with everything else.* Many of the analyses made by distinguished scholars of poetry provide insights into verse which analyses of sound symbolism can only supplement, but even supplementary approaches have their value; and when a poet makes use of sound instrumentation, it is clearly useful, perhaps essential, to know to what extent the associations derive from "Universal" or "Local" sound symbolism, and/or to what extent (as very often happens) they are derived from and limited to the context of the actual poem.[8]

It should be added that "non-unique" analyses do not have to be restricted to the two levels outlined above. We should also probably allow for analysis at the morphophonemic level. This is especially important for the analysis of poetry in languages where the orthography is (as in Russian) more or less morphophonemic: at least the visual (the printed) aspect plays a role in poetry; and the analysis of "underlying" forms should not be excluded.

16.2 Tentative approach

I have not attempted any kind of instrumental analysis; what I have tried, as a kind of preliminary experiment, is an impressionistic analysis of the subphonemic structure. This is meant to be a supplement, not only to traditional structuralist analyses of poetry, but also to analyses of sound symbolism on the phonemic, i.e. distinctive feature, level.

For this purpose, I have on the formal side worked with syllables in some Russian poems. My reasons for deciding on syllables are threefold: (1) The importance of the syllabic unit in many aspects of phonological investigation has been amply demonstrated, and I propose that whenever syllables, rather than individual vowels or consonants, lend themselves to being used as units of analysis, that this should be preferred; (2) attention to syllables allows us to ignore a very awkward question in the analysis of poetry, namely, the weighting of consonants vs. vowels.[9] In my analysis, each syllable is weighted as a separate unit; and (3) the choice of a phonetic transcription is not prevented: one can be as "narrow" as one wishes.

As for the semantic side: the most frequently quoted sound-symbolic association in analyses of Russian poetry has been what may be labeled the "gravity–sadness" association, which I represent (for brevity) as

$$[\pm \text{grave}] = [\pm \text{SAD}]$$

for its application at the phonemic (conventional) level. For illustrative purposes, I will assume that there is a "gravity–sadness" association operative at the phonetic (synesthetic) level also.[10] Since we are now dealing with "more-or-less" and no longer with "either-or," I use two-headed arrows (representing n-ary scales), thus:

$$[\text{grave} \leftrightarrow \text{acute}] \pm [\text{SADNESS} \leftrightarrow \text{HAPPINESS}]$$

16.3 Procedure

My procedure is as follows:
1. The ideal situation is for the analysis of sound symbolism to be preceded by a thorough structuralist analysis of everything *except* sound symbolism – all the poetic devices and the whole of the semantic import. Let us assume this as a given, which will assist in the analysis of sound symbolism. (It helps if the poems have been analyzed by recognized authorities, of course, as was the poem which forms my starting point.)
2. The text is transcribed phonetically, and segmented into syllables (as it happens, this involves only occasional arbitrary decisions).
3. All of the syllables are allotted strengths relative to one another. This is done in two stages:
    3.1 First, strengths are allotted according to stress. Ideally, this should be done instrumentally, from recordings of the poet reading his/her own poetry; but the metre is normally a sufficient guide;
    3.2 Second, additional strengths are allotted to syllables which, as is revealed by the already-analyzed sound structure of the poem (alliteration, assonances, instrumentation and various other kinds of repetition) – and its orthographic and grammatical structure also, when relevant – are foregrounded by the poet.
4. The occurrent syllables are given weights on the selected phonetic scale (here: grave–acute), preferably by instrumental measurements, or by estimate.
5. Totals (weights × strengths) are computed for relevant portions of text; relevance is derived from clues provided by the poet (the visual, phonological, grammatical, and semantic clues.) Relevant portions may be as short as individual phrases or as long as the complete poem.

Europe

6. The total scalar weight (here: gravity) of each portion of text is assumed (for this experiment) to reflect its position on the semantic scale (here: SADNESS), and may now be related to a reading of the semantic content of that portion of text.
7. This completed analysis of sound symbolism in a poem must be controlled by reference to the relevance of this phenomenon in other poems by the same poet, other poems of the same period or movement, other poems in the same language, indeed whatever makes for informative comparisons.
8. Finally, any complete "etic" analysis of the synesthetic sound symbolism in a poem or poems must be correlated (compared or contrasted, as necessary) with an "emic" analysis of conventional sound symbolism in the same poem(s).

16.4 Example

As a trial run for this approach, I attempted a *phonetic scale/semantic scale* analysis of four poems by the modern Russian poet Andrej Voznesenskij:[11] "Goya," which has been the object of analysis by both Jurij Lotman (1964: 101–106), who denies the force of sound symbolism, and Dennis Ward (1974), who accepts its relevance; and three other poems, chosen so that they (a) were of about the same length as "Goya," (b) were replete with the sound instrumentation for which Voznesenskij is so well known, and (c) seemed to embody the feeling of [DARK/SAD/BAD] to different degrees. "Goya" is a stark and grim denunciation of the horrors of war; "Sidiš, beremennaja" is also bitter, but on a much less emotive level; "Pervyj lěd" is at most rather sad; and "Velosipedy," while not really "happy," is better described as gently whimsical.

I present the first seven lines of "Goya" in example (1),
(a) in the original;
(b) in my translation;[12]
(c) transcribed phonetically;[13]
(d) with each syllable allotted strengths, first, from the stress which each syllable bears, on a scale of 1 (least) – 3 (most);[14]
(e) with each syllable allotted additional strengths, deriving in my estimation (and, more importantly, that of the authorities quoted above) from various kinds of foregrounding effects chosen by the poet. Note: for the total strength, I chose an arbitrary upper limit of 5;
(f) "weights" on a seven-point [grave ↔ acute] scale are allotted to the occurrent syllables: from the least grave (+ 3) through (+ 2), (+ 1), (0), (− 1), (− 2) to the most grave (− 3).
(g) the "weight" of each syllable is multiplied by its aggregate strength.
(h) As an illustration, every line is totalled separately, and the average darkness/lightness per syllable computed (see final column). This figure I refer to as the "chiaroscuro coefficient."[15]

(1) Analysis of first seven lines of Voznesenskij's *Goya*
a. 1. Й – Лщ й!
   2. Лшфкпьег ищзщпщо дпу игошуифш ищзщл,
   3.   Цшуыфй пф сщшу пфлщу.
   4. Й – лщзу.
   5. Й – лщшщщ
   6. Ищ   пг, лщзщ'щи лщшщипь
   7.   Пф цпулр цщзщо сузищлщ лщ'ф.

b. 1. I am Goya!
   2. The enemy swooped on the desolate field
   3.   and blinded me, pecking out craters.
   4. I am grief.
   5. I am the grumble
   6. Of battle, charred logs from the towns
   7.   engulfed in the 'forty-one snows.

c. 1. já gɔ́ja
   2. glʌzɲítsi vʌrɔ́nək mɲe víkl̡ival vɔrək
   3. s̡l̡etája napɔ́l̡a nʌgɔ́ja
   4. já gɔ́r̡ɛ
   5. já gɔ́ləs
   6. vʌjni gərʌdɔ́v gəlʌvɲí
   7. nəs̡ɲɪgú sɔ́rak pɛ́rv:ə gɔ́da

d. 1. ja² gɔ³ ja²
   2. glʌ² zɲi³ tsi¹ vʌ² rɔ³ nək² mɲɛ² vi³ kl̡ɪ¹ val² vɔ³ rək²
   3. s̡l̡ɛ² ta³ ja¹ na¹ pɔ³ l̡a² nʌ² gɔ³ ja²
   4. ja² gɔ³ r̡ɛ²
   5. ja² gɔ³ ləs¹
   6. vʌj² ni³ gə¹ rʌ² dɔv³ gə¹ lʌ² vɲi³
   7. nə² s̡ɲɪ² gu³ sʌ² rak² pɛr³ v:¹ ə¹ gɔ³ da²

e. 1. ja⁴ gɔ⁵ ja⁴
   2. glʌ⁴ zɲi⁴ tsi³ vʌ⁴ rɔ⁵ nək⁴ mɲɛ² vi⁴ kl̡ɪ² val⁴ vɔ⁵ rək⁴
   3. s̡l̡ɛ² ta⁴ ja¹ na² pɔ⁵ l̡a³ nʌ⁴ gɔ⁵ ja⁴
   4. ja⁴ gɔ⁵ r̡ɛ²
   5. ja⁴ gɔ⁵ ləs³
   6. vʌj³ ni⁴ gə³ rʌ³ dʌv⁴ gə³ lʌ³ vɲi⁴
   7. nə³ s̡ɲɪ³ gu⁴ sɔ³ rak³ pɛr³ v:² ə¹ gɔ⁵ da⁴

f. – 3:   pɔ   vɔ   v: gɔ   gu
   – 2:   vʌ   val dɔv nək rək rak gə   glʌ

Europe

```
− 1:   vi    vʌj   sʌ    rək
  0:   ta    da    na    nʌ    nə    rʌ    lʌ    ə
+ 1:   tsi   ni    ləs   l̦a    ja
+ 2:   pɛr   vɲi   mɲɛ   kl̦ɪ
+ 3:   zɲi   șɲɪ   șl̦e   r̦e
```

g. 1. $(+1 \times 4)(-3 \times 5)(+1 \times 4)$
   2. $(-1 \times 4)(+3 \times 4)(+1 \times 3)(-2 \times 4)(-1 \times 5)(-2 \times 4)(+2 \times 2)$
      $(-1 \times 4)(+2 \times 2)(-2 \times 4)(-3 \times 5)(-2 \times 4)$
   3. $(+3 \times 2)(0 \times 4)(+1 \times 1)(0 \times 2)(-3 \times 5)(+1 \times 3)(0 \times 4)(-3 \times 5)$
      $(+1 \times 4)$
   4. $(+1 \times 4)(-3 \times 5)(+3 \times 2)$
   5. $(+1 \times 4)(-3 \times 5)(+1 \times 3)$
   6. $(-1 \times 3)(+1 \times 4)(-2 \times 3)(0 \times 3)(-2 \times 4)(-2 \times 3)(0 \times 3)(+2 \times 4)$
   7. $(0 \times 3)(+3 \times 3)(-3 \times 4)(-1 \times 2)(-2 \times 3)(+2 \times 3)(-3 \times 2)(0 \times 1)$
      $(-3 \times 5)(0 \times 4)$

		"light"	"dark"		total	mean/syll.
h.	1.	+ 08	− 15	=	− 07	− 2.3
	2.	+ 23	− 60	=	− 37	− 3.1
	3.	+ 14	− 30	=	− 16	− 1.7
	4.	+ 10	− 15	=	− 05	− 1.7
	5.	+ 07	− 15	=	− 08	− 2.7
	6.	+ 12	− 23	=	− 11	− 1.4
	7.	+ 15	− 41	=	− 26	− 2.4

Coefficients of this nature were computed for the four poems as wholes. These are set out in the column headed "mean" in table 16.1. Here I emphasize that these numerals have only the vaguest of values *relative to one another*. It is tempting, for

Table 16.1. *"Chiaroscuro coefficients" in four of Voznesenskij's poems compared with results of two tests*

	Mean "darkness/lightness" per syllable	Klagenfurt	Heidelberg
"Velosipedy"	+ 1.85	5.50	5.00
"Pervyj lëd"	+ 0.91	3.67	4.50
"Sidiš, beremennaja"	+ 0.52	2.83	4.18
"Goya"	− 1.50	2.33	1.50

example, to deduce that "Velosipedy" is twice as "light-and-happy" as "Pervyj lëd'; but the actual quantifications are of course only functions of the scaling system that I arbitrarily chose in the first place. The only valid deduction at this stage is that there is a *rank order* in which these four poems can be placed with respect to the manner and extent to which they utilize the synesthetic association [grave ↔ acute] = [SADNESS ↔ HAPPINESS].

Having made these calculations, I asked two groups of listeners to do a simple task. They first listened to a tape recording of Voznesenskij declaiming each poem; then they ranked each poem that they had heard on a ten-point semantic scale, labeled (since these were two German-speaking universities) [DUNKEL/TRAURIG (0) ↔ (10) HELL/GLÜCKLICH].[16] The results (the mean responses) are displayed under the headings "KLAGENFURT" (University of Klagenfurt, Austria) and "HEIDELBERG" (University of Heidelberg, Germany): it can be seen that the rank ordering of the four poems according to my analysis on the one hand, and according to the perceptions of my two sets of respondents on the other, are *identical*. The two groups of subjects were very small and were all academics with an interest in Russian poetry. Although these statistics are unrefined, and although specialists of this kind are presumably not very representative of a general population, what I am studying is (primarily) a *universal* association. Therefore, the fact that the rank ordering is the same as that which resulted from my own analysis is very encouraging. I hope that this kind of psycholinguistic testing will be performed in more exacting conditions: for validity (as far as synesthetic symbolism is concerned) tests with speakers of very many languages will be needed. Eventually, I suggest, this kind of undertaking will expand our knowledge about the coexistence of synesthetic and conventional sound symbolism in poetry.

16.5 Concluding comments

I have three concluding comments. The first is a short excursus: I suggest that synesthetic associations will differ in at least one important way from conventional ones: namely, they will be *fewer*. Where it may be possible to determine whole series of associations for conventional sound symbolism (as Žuravlev and Levickij have attempted for Russian and Ukrainian respectively), the synesthetic ones may be only two or three in number. Moreover, an immediate, "emotive" association between formant height and a generalized concept such as the "gravity-sadness" one is surely something that is more typically "universal" than "local." It is interesting to compare the scaled results from Žuravlev's psycholinguistic experiments (1974: 46–49): here the "sounds" (more strictly, *zvukobukvy*, i.e. phonographemic units) take up *very* disparate positions on the three scales [GOOD/BAD], [LIGHT/DARK], and [HAPPY/SAD] – positions which are often incompatible with the traditionally accepted association [grave] = [DARK/SAD/BAD]. Two examples, for these three scales, where 1.0 is [GOOD], [LIGHT] and [HAPPY] and 5.0 is the opposite in each instance: the *zvukobukva* "o" stands at 1.6, 2.2, and 2.9 respectively, thus is to be interpreted as "extremely good," "rather light" but "neither happy nor sad"; and the *zvukobukva* "šč" is rated as 3.5, 3.7 and 2.9 respectively, i.e. "on the bad side," "rather dark" and also "neither happy nor sad." Note that "o" here represents the [+ grave] /o/, usually [ʌ], while "šč" represents the [− grave] /šč/, most frequently [ʃ:]. To the extent that the experiment and the choice of *zvukobukvy* as units of analysis are valid, these scales presumably represent what should be considered part of the *accumulation of synesthetic and conventional sound symbolism* in Russian; but in any case, the numerous instances of disagreement with any generalized synesthetic association of the "gravity-sadness" kind must be explained.

Second: I emphasize that this approach to the analysis of instrumentation in verse, with its use of and reliance on syllables, can be adapted to an analysis of distinctive features and/or of phonemes, and even to an analysis of morphophonemes. Also, the weighting system allows an analysis of *unstressed* syllables, a procedure not normally attempted (cf. Ward 1975: 385–386).

Third: I recognize that I have assumed a simple two-way distinction between the levels of application of synesthetic and conventional sound symbolism, and based an approach to the analysis of sound patterns in poetry on a logical extension to that assumption. Any venture into the terrain of sound symbolism involves treading on what Wilhelm von Humboldt called "ein schlüpfriges Pfad"; but the ventures must be attempted, since sound symbolism is of such interest and, especially for poetry, of such importance.

NOTES

1 This is in general agreement with what Brown (1958: 130) apparently wished to assume but was hesitant to accept without proof; and with the views of, e.g., Hymes 1960: 112, Žuravlev 1974: 28, Ohala 1986. See the "Introduction" to this volume, pp. 1–12.
2 This formulation sidesteps the question of the apparent role of sound symbolism in language change – sometimes inhibiting changes from occurring, sometimes enabling them to occur; see Priestly 1978.
3 Respectively, Martin 1962 and Kim 1977; Fischer-Jørgensen 1978 and Wescott 1980: 225–301.
4 In the sound-symbolic equations used here, " = " means "is associated with"; semantic features are in capitals.
5 For example, Taranovski 1965: 116: "one has to deal both with phonological and redundant distinctive features."
6 Thus, the following post-war analysts explicitly use phonemic transcriptions: Lynch 1963 ("I am not concerned with subphonemic distinctions of importance to the phonetician"); Jakobson (e.g. 1960, 1970); Fónagy (e.g. 1965); Ward 1974, 1975; and more

recently Humesky 1983. Many of these analysts use a phonemic transcription and "count" phonemes, but involve distinctive features in their analysis; for a good example, see Ward 1974: 18. For a greater emphasis on distinctive features see Taranovski 1965; Jones 1965, 1983; Waugh 1980. Note that analysts of sounds in verse who treat Russian "*y*" and "*i*" as separate units (thus Taranovski 1968, 1970) are already, in most phonologists' eyes, working at a subphonemic level; note, too, that Žuravlev 1974 also treats these as separate units.

7 And yet *everything* in the poem is considered to have a purpose (or, at least, an effect): "In the poetic text all linguistic elements potentially have autonomous value and may interact with one another in various ways," Jones 1965: 125; see also Ward 1974, Hrushovski 1980. Of course, some poets use sound symbolism less or much less than other poets, and some use it not at all; but in the poetic tradition of Russian and other European languages there is much "instrumentation" that provides material for the analysis of sound symbolism, and few analyses to date attempt to treat *everything* that may be achieved.

8 It is argued (by e.g. Shapiro, Delbouille) that *every* sound-symbolic association in poetry may be explained by reference to its individual poetic context. Though I accept this as a theoretical possibility, I believe it to be both illogical and short-sighted to deny that both synesthetic and conventional sound symbolism can exist in poetry: if we accept the weight of evidence about different kinds of sound symbolism outside poetry, it is inconceivable that their use should be suspended in the poetic context. See Delbouille 1961 and Shapiro 1976: 91–134, 1983: 356 for the negative view; Fónagy 1965, Waugh 1980: 69–71, and Hrushovski 1980 for the positive side; and Melhem 1973 for a good summary of the arguments in both camps.

9 Cf. "Methodologically, investigation of the phonic texture . . . of Russian verse [has] been characterized by an openly atomistic approach which focuses either on the patterning of vowels . . or on that of consonants. I know of no study . . . that even attempts systematically to integrate the organizations of both vocalic and consonantal patterns into a unitary framework," Shapiro 1983: 360. Note that the relative weighting of consonants and vowels at the phonological level involves a specific methodological presupposition in the analysis of Russian, namely that differences in the "frontedness" of syllables depend either on the palatalization of the consonants or on the quality of the vowels concerned; although this feature is normally made dependent on consonants, there have been analyses (especially those that can be termed "polysystemic") assigning the phonological distinction (in certain syllables, at least) to vowels.

10 The label SADNESS is shorthand for what has traditionally been interpreted as "darkness/sadness/negative emotions generally."

11 See Voznesenskij 1983. For the literary and political impact of Voznesenskij in the 1960s, see e.g. Blake and Hayward 1966.

12 I know of seven other translations of this poem into English; my own benefited most from the versions by Markov and Sparks (1966) and by Reavey (1966).

13 The transcription is from two recordings of Voznesenskij reading his own poetry: a private recording, made at the University of Western Ontario in 1971, courteously made available to me by Rudolf Neuhäuser (now of the University of Klagenfurt, Austria); and the commercial Soviet recording *Poèty čitajut svoi stixi. Andrej Voznesenskij*, TU 35/XP 558–563/ZZD–0008523(a). Where the two recordings differ, the version closer to the prescribed norm for Contemporary Standard Russian was the one chosen for analysis.

Note that Voznesenskij, especially while declaiming a poem of the emotional intensity of "Goya," has a very formal, explicit style of pronunciation, with less vowel reduction and less consonant palatalization than is the norm. As a result, what is indeed a phonetic transcription appears to be not far removed from a phonemic one; and there are inconsistencies when this transcription is compared with the Standard Russian norm.

14 Done impressionistically from the recordings, see above. Again in many instances Voznesenskij does not follow prescribed "Standard" norms.

15 One refinement would be to "average" in terms of metrical feet rather than in terms of total syllables; this has not yet been attempted.

16 Meaning, respectively, "dark/sad" and "light/happy."

REFERENCES

Blake, P. and M. Hayward. 1966 (eds.) *Antiworlds and the Fifth Ace. Andrei Voznesenskij. A Bilingual Edition*. New York: Basic Books.

Brown, R. 1958. *Words and Things*. New York: Free Press.

Delbouille, P. 1961. *Poésie et sonorités: la critique contemporaine devant le pouvoir suggestif des sons*. Paris: Les Belles Lettres.

Fischer-Jørgensen, E. 1978. On the universal character of phonetic symbolism with special reference to vowels. *Studia Linguistica* 32: 80–90.

Fónagy, I. 1965. Le langage poétique: forme et fonction. *Diogène* 51: 72–116.

Humesky, A. 1983. Sound expressivity in the poetry of Ivan Franko. *Slavic and East European Journal* 27: 245–255.

Hrushovski, B. 1980. The meaning of sound patterns in poetry. An interaction theory. *Poetics Today* 2: 39–56.

Hymes, D. H. 1960. Phonological aspects of style: some English sonnets. In T. A. Sebeok (ed.) *Style in Language*. Cambridge, MA: MIT Press, 109–131.

Jakobson, R. 1960. Closing statement: linguistics and poetics. In T. A. Sebeok (ed.) *Style in Language*. Cambridge, MA: MIT Press, 350–377.

1970. Subliminal verbal patterning in poetry. In R. Jakobson and S. Kawamoto (eds.) *Studies in General and Oriental Linguistics*. Tokyo: TEC, 302–308.

Jones, L. G. 1965. Tonality structure in Russian verse. *International Journal of Slavic Linguistics and Poetics* 90: 125–131.

1983. Distinctive features and sound tropes in Russian verse. In T. Eekman and D. S. Worth (eds.) *Russian Poetics. Proceedings of the International Colloquium at UCLA, September 22–26, 1975*, Columbus, OH: Slavica, 195–208.

Kim, K-O. 1977. Sound symbolism in Korean. *Journal of Linguistics* 13: 67–75.

Levickij, V. V. 1973. *Semantika i fonetika. Posobie, podgotovlennoe na materiale èksperimental'nyx issledovanij*. Černovcy: Černovickij gosudarstvennyj universitet. (In Russian.)

Lotman, J. M. 1964. *Lekcii po struktural'noj poètike. I. Vvedenie. Teorija stixa*. Učenye zapiski Tartusskogo gos. universiteta 160. Tartu: Tartusskij gosudarstvennyj universitet. (Reprint, Providence, RI: Brown University Press, 1968.) (In Russian.)

Lynch, J. J. 1953. The tonality of lyric poetry: an experiment in method. *Word* 9: 211–224.

Markov, V. and M. Sparks. 1966. *Modern Russian Poetry. An Anthology*. Indianapolis: Bobbs Merrill.

Martin, S. E. 1962. Phonetic symbolism in Korean. In N. Poppe (ed.) *American Studies in Altaic Linguistics*. Bloomington, IN: Indiana University Press, 177–189.

Melhem, D. H. 1973. Ivan Fónagy and Paul Delbouille: sonority structures in poetic language. *Language and Style* 6: 206–215.

Ohala, J. J. 1986. Sound symbolism in an ethological context. Paper given at the Conference on Sound Symbolism, University of California at Berkeley.

Priestly, T. M. S. 1978. Affective sound-change in Early Slavic. In *Canadian Contributions to the Eighth International Congress of Slavists*. Ottawa: Canadian Association of Slavists, 143–166.

Reavey, G. 1966. *The New Russian Poets, 1953–1968. An Anthology*. London: Calder & Boyars.

Shapiro, M. 1976. *Asymmetry. An Inquiry into the Linguistic Structure of Poetry*. Amsterdam: North-Holland.

1983. The evaluative component in a theory of poetic language. In T. Eekman and D. S. Worth (eds.) *Russian Poetics. Proceedings of the International Colloquium at UCLA, September 22–26, 1975*. Columbus, OH: Slavica, 352–372.

Taranovski, K. 1965. The sound-texture of Russian verse in the light of phonemic distinctive features. *International Journal of Slavic Linguistics and Poetics* 9: 114–124.

1968. Certain aspects of Blok's symbolism. In: R. Magidoff *et al.* (eds.) *Studies in Slavic Linguistics and Poetics in Honour of B. O. Unbegaun*. New York: New York University Press, 249–261.

1970. Zvukovaja faktura stixa i ee vosprijatie. In: B. Hála *et al.* (eds.) *Proceedings of the Sixth International Congress of Phonetic Sciences*. Prague: Academia, 883–885. (In Russian.)

Voznesenskij, A. A. 1983. *Sobranie sočinenij v trex tomax*, vol. 1. Moscow: Xudožestvennaja literatura. (In Russian.)

Ward, D. 1974. The functions of tonality and grammar in a Voznesenskij poem. *International Journal of Slavic Linguistics and Poetics* 17: 87–104.

1975. Puškin's Èxo – sound, grammar, meaning. *Studia Slavica Hungarica* 21: 377–386.

Waugh, L. 1980. The poetic function in the theory of Roman Jakobson. *Poetry Today* 2: 57–82.

Wescott, R. 1980. *Sound and Sense. Linguistic Essays on Phonosemic Subjects*. Lake Bluff: Jupiter.

Žuravlev, A. P. 1974. *Fonetičeskoe značenie*. Leningrad: Leningradskij gosudarstvennyj universitet. (In Russian.)

17
Finnish and Gilyak sound symbolism – the interplay between system and history

ROBERT AUSTERLITZ

17.1. Introduction

Some of the citizens in a community of vowels are more equal than others. Thus, of the eight vowels in Finnish, *ö* is the least equal; *y* (a high rounded front vowel, like German *ü*) is better integrated into the lexical and inflectional-derivational system than *ö*, but still not as well as its back counterpart, *u*. This hierarchy among the Finnish vowels can be best observed in Finnish sound symbolism. What is more, it can also be observed in the history of the Finnish vowel system, in that the most recent arrival in this system is *ö*. This *ö* is also the vowel with the highest sound-symbolic index. As in the Finnish vowels, the Finnish consonants are also unequally rooted in the system, but less obviously so. Some Finnish consonants can nevertheless play a role in sound symbolism. All of these facts suggest that the idea that there is a language-specific correlation between recentness and exploitability in sound symbolism.

The main axis in the Finnish vowel system is horizontal (*o:ö, u:y*). The main axis in the Gilyak vowel system is vertical: *e:i, o:u, a:y* (where *y* is a high back unrounded vowel). These pairs of vowels (low vs. high) are exploited in the grammar and in the lexicon, but unequally: *a:y* is exploited in grammar; *e:i* is predictable and productive (vowel harmony); *o:u* is unsystematic, irregular, and highly affective. (The historical dimension – lexical ablaut as it issues from reconstruction – is ignored here.)

Neither Gilyak nor Finnish has reduced vowels. This would suggest that the vowels within each of the two systems are equal. They are not.

A unifying approach to the systems of vowel alternations in Finnish and in Gilyak, plotted against the large North Eurasian linguistic area, is suggested in the conclusion.

Robert Austerlitz

17.2. Finnish[1]

Finnish has the eight vowels *i y u , e ö o, ä a*, where *y* and *ä* stand for IPA [y, æ]. On a more abstract level, one can reckon with five: I E A O U. These five abstract units obviate vowel harmony, which can be relegated to a prosody (fronting). The *y ö ä : u o a* opposition thus becomes redundant.

Traditional scholarship derives the eight vowels from seven:

(1) i   y   u   *i   *ü   *u
     e   ö   o   <   *e   *o
     ä   a   *ä   *a

A more daring and slightly more imaginative view, espoused here, is to assume a proto-sextet,

(2) *i   *u
     *e   *o
     *ä   *a

which summons up the challenge to explain both *y* and *ö*, possibly in one stroke. This challenge is accepted below.

Example (3) illustrates sound symbolism in a unique, prefixed morpheme (Finnish has no prefixation otherwise), the special role of the labial *p* in SS, and the sound-symbolic function of *ö* and *o* in non-first syllable. The rounded mid vowels are secondary in that position.

(3) täysi   full   : *täpö&täysi* chock full
     yks-in   alone   : *ypö&yksin* all alone
     uusi   new   : *upo&uusi* brand new
     suomalainen Finn(-ish)   : *supi&suomalainen* 100% Finnish
     uusi   new   : *upi&uusi* brand new, spick and span
     outo   odd   : *upi&outo* ⎫
     outo   odd   : *uppo&oito* ⎬ perfectly strange

The distinction of quantity among the obstruents is firmly rooted in the language, but affective gemination is obvious both synchronically and diachronically. Note the affective (sound-symbolic) function of the geminate in *sokko* "blind man's buff"//*sokea* "blind" and *Ylppö* (a neologized surname) //*ylpeä* "proud" (with *-ö* in the surname). The paradigm in table 17.1 displays an example from diachrony: *makkara* "sausage," a product of material culture, with a medial geminate (and otherwise sound-symbolic suffix, *-ra*) as against other manifestations of the same root, all from the domain of nature, with single *-k* (or *-k* < ∅).

There follows a digression on short *ö* and its history: see table 17.2. There is no long *öö* in native words. Both *yö* (< *öö) and *öy* are older than short *ö*; in terms of system it is therefore not necessary to reckon with *ö* in order to account for its

Table 17.1 *Development of* makkara

	Term	Analyzed	Reconstructed
"flavor"	maku	mak-u	*make-U
"sweet, tasty"	makea	make-a	*make-δa
"taste" trans.	maista-	ma-i-s-ta-	*make-i-se-ta-
"sausage"	makkara	mak-Qa-ra	*make-QV-ra

Table 17.2 *Short* ö *in sound-symbolic roots*

ö, ö–ö		öy	
möhkäle	"chunk, lump"	möyheä	"loose, spongy"
möhi-	"fumble, bungle"	möyh-i-	"crush, stir up"
mökki	"hut, cottage"	möykky	"lump, clod"
mökä	"hullabaloo"	möyr-i-	"stir up; roar"
mörkö	"bugbear, bogey"	möyryt-	"(g)rumble"
hökkeli	"hovel, shack"	höyhen	"feather"
hölkkä	"trot"	höylä	"plane (tool)"
höll-entä-	"slacken"	höyry	"steam"
höllä	"slack, lax"	höy-stä-	"spice"
hölmö	"fool, idiot"	höytäle-	"flake, tassel"
hölynpöly	"nonsense"		
höperö	"muddled (head)"		
höp-ise-	"mumble"		
hör-istä-	"prick up (ear)"		
nökö-ttä-	"sit moping"	nöyrä	"humble"
		nöyhtä	"fluff, down"

occurrence in *öy* and *yö*. The examples in table 17.2 are adduced to show that short *ö* is extremely frequently found in sound-symbolic roots, in both first and second syllable. Forms with *öy* in the first syllable are less often symbolic, and forms with *yö* never. Some forms with *ö* have analogs with *o*, e.g. *höpö-ttä-* "babble, talk indistinctly"//*hopo-tta-* "prattle," *röykkiö* "heap, pile"//*roukkio* "heap, pile." Others have analogs at a greater distance, e.g. *rökäle*//*rekale*//*riekale*, all of which mean more or less "rag, shred, tatter."

The high front rounded vowel, *y*, also has a sound-symbolic component. This *y* maintains a family relationship with various other members of the repertory. Thus, *tyhmä* "stupid, foolish" is obviously related to *tuhma* "bad, disobedient (child)" and *tylppä* "blunt-ended, obtuse"//*tölppä*//*töllö*//*tollo*, all of which are more or less "dopey, simple-minded, dull-witted." Cf. also *tylmä* "dull," *tylsä* "dull, weak, stupid," *typerä* "silly, stupid" and perhaps *typy-* "bob-tailed" (and *töpö-* "id."). Then, there is something that could be called cross-fertilization, as in the network described by *tupe-htu-* and *type-hty-*, both folksy forms for *tuke-htu-* = *tuk-ahtu-* = *tik-ahtu-* "choke" (intrans.) //*tuke* "plug, stopper, dam, clog." Note also *type* "short and bad hay." All of these forms, for reasons of syllabic structure, have geminate medial stops in their abstract (i.e. underlying) forms. It is therefore interesting to note that when a word for "nitrogen" (German *Stickstoff*, lit. "suffocating substance") was created in the nineteenth century, it emerged as *typpi*.

It is now time to assemble the pieces presented into a coherent whole. The pair *u/o* is old. Some instances of *y* may also be old, but a great many of them are engendered by *u*, just as many instances of *ö* came about by analogy to *o* and sometimes *e*. In this way a new proportion was formed: *u:o* :: *y:ö*. All of this was facilitated by a fact which has not been mentioned up to this point, namely that long *yy* is older than short *y*. Furthermore, *yy* is not sound-symbolic; witness the entire catalogue of monosyllabic forms with this vowel: *myy-* "sell," *pyy* "hazel-grouse," *kyy* "(a kind of) snake," *syy* "tree-ring, fiber; reason for," *hyy* "chill, jell-," *lyy* "(kind of) trajectory, track, trace." Without even referring to *öy* and *yö* mentioned above, we must then assume that *yy* is older than *y* and that it served as a model for the latter's integration into the repertoire.[2]

There is a class of phonesthemic verbs with the shape *CVC-ise-* (and *CVC-inA* for the deverbal noun). They have been discussed by Anttila (1976). See table 17.3. Sample reading, cell 4.1: *U* indicates that the CVC-root exists with both front and back vowels, viz. *pur-ise-* "(sound of a low voice; water)" (= *por-ise-*) and *pyr-ise-* (= *pör-ise-* = *pär-ise-*). Likewise, *O*: *por-ise-* "murmur, bubble, hum," *pör-ise-* "buzz, drone, burr." Small *ä* indicates that there is only *pär-ise-* "buzz, rattle, bray" but no **par-ise-*. Note also that *pir-ise-* "buzz, enliven"//*pirteä* "brisk, vivacious, alert."

If we extract from table 17.3 only those phonesthemic roots which have pendants, i.e. those with U, O, and A, we emerge with what could be an index of productivity. See table 17.4. Thus, O turns out to be the most popular vowel pair (*o:ö*) and *A* occurs once after *k-* and four times after *r-*. Is this popularity of O connected with the assumption, mentioned above, that *ö* is the most recent vowel?

There follows an attempt to enlist sound symbolism in the service of etymology. An innocent form such as *päre* now means primarily "shingle (for roofing)," as in *katto-päre* (*katto* "roof"). Secondarily, it means "splint, splinter," a source of light in a fairly rudimentary dwelling, Germ. *Kienspan*, Russ. *lučin(k)a*. The following phonesthemic words are relevant here: *pär-ise-* "buzz, hum, whirr; noise of frying fat in frying pan or of a fly in the window," *pör-ise-* "buzz, hum," and *pyr-ise-*

Europe

Table 17.3 *CVC-ise-* verbs

-C-	.1 -r-	.2 -p-	.3 -h-	.4 -m-	.5 -l-	.6 -t-	.7 -k-	.8 -n-	.9 -v-
1 h-	U O ä	u ö	u o	U	u i ä	U O e	o		o
2 k-	O ä	*i o a	u i O A	u i	u i o a		u i		
3 r-		i o A		U O A	U O A		U i o A		
4 -p	U i O ä	ö	u i O	o a	u O ä			a	
5 s-	u i o ä	u i ä	u i			o			
6 m-	u ö a			u	ö		u	u	
7 t-	u i ä		u o	ö					
8 n-	u i a	a	i a						
9 j-	ü o		o		ü	ü	ü		
10 v-	ä	a			i		i		a
11 l-		a							
12 ∅-	U ö ä								

253

Table 17.4 *Phonesthemic roots with U, O, and A*

	−r−	−p−	−h−	−m−	−l−	−t−		
h-	hUr- hOr-			hUm-	hOl-	hUt-	U O	3 2
k-	kOr-		kOh- kAh-				O A	2 1
r-		rAp-	rOh- rAh-	rUm- rOm- rAm-		rUt- rAt-	U O A	2 2 4
p-	pUr- pOr-		pOh-		pOl-		U O	1 3
	−r	−p	−h	−m	−l	−t		9 6
	5	1	5	4	2	3		5 UCA

= *pör-ise-* = *pär-ise*. The primary function of *päre* at an earlier stage in Finnish society must have been to denote a splinter for providing light. The object could be of any length, 5–8 cm wide, and ca. 2 mm thick. When shingles for roofing were introduced, *päre* was also summoned to serve as "shingle," probably because of its shape and texture (fatty, resinous, water-repellent). Is *päre* from the verb *pär-ise-*? (The final *e* in *päre* is a noun-forming derivational suffix.) Or is *pär-ise-* from *päre*? In addition to the meanings listed for *pär-ise-* above, the lexicographer also says that *pär-ise-* has a near-synonym, *pärsky-* "spatter (e.g. saliva, during delivery of a sermon)." Now, this "spatter" may have something to do with the noise made by splinters while burning, thus establishing a firmer link between *pär-ise-* and *päre*. If the root **pär* is affective, then it is not too far-fetched to imagine that this *pär-* is attracted first to an *ö*-vocalism, which is also affective (sound-symbolic), and later even to a *y*-vocalism, which is less blatantly affective. This, then, is how the triad *ä–ö–y* may conceivably cohere. The *ö* in *pör-ise-* may also be the result of the *playful raising* of *ä*. It has been noted[3] that Finnish long *ää*, when affectively sung, is sometimes slightly raised *and rounded* in the direction of an open [œ:].

17.2.1. Broadening the background and sharpening the focus

In languages which have front rounded vowels, these issue from four preconditions: vowel rotation (Attic, French); umlaut (Germanic); adjacency (Mandarin *ü*, which comes from the sequence [iu] or [ⁱu], in which the palatility of *i* spills over into *u*); and sound symbolism, as in some of the examples from Finnish enumerated above.

In the case of Finnish, there is a further precondition: the earlier existence (i.e. before the birth of Finnish short *y*) of long *yy* and of the sequences *öy* and *yö*. These three (note that they are all long) all arose from the precondition of adjacency. It is also very likely that in the case of Finnish, contact with coterritorial Germanic (and therefore umlauting) languages helped to bring about the birth of Finnish short *y* and perhaps even of long *yy*.

It is important to remember that we are discussing the *fronting of already rounded vowels*. It is well known that rounding (lip pursing) and labials can have affective roles in many cultures and languages. Once an item contains a rounded vowel to begin with, what feature can be added to such rounding so as to make the word still more affective? Answer: fronting, i.e. palatalization. Palatalization and its congener, the affrication of coronals, as devices for affect – i.e. sound symbolism – are well known.

This may also be the place to make a plea for the *neural* and the *visual* sides of the question. Should we not try to learn more about the neurology of palatalizing, of lip pursing, of lip rounding? What is involved in the neural command? How is the neural command transmitted? What possible other commands and what other final gestures are connected with these original commands? Furthermore, too little attention seems to be paid to the obvious fact that very little children not only hear what is being said to them but also watch and see what facial gestures the speaker is making while speaking. The child – even the very small child – then imitates and thus associates muscular events with acoustic-articulatory ones. There is already a field called neurolinguistics. Let it also handle neurophonetics.

On p. 252–253 above it was suggested that a process connected with sound symbolism – the birth of *y* and *ö* – gathers momentum as it proceeds. A similar idea suggests itself as we turn to the consonants. In table 17.5 initial and medial consonants, as they occur in the phonesthemic verbs (tables 17.3 and 17.4) are quantified. The most frequent initials are *h*-, *k*-, *r*-, and *p*-. The most frequent medials are -*r*-, -*h*-, -*l*-, and -*p*-. Of these, *k*, *p*, and *l* are old. Both initial *h*- and medial -*h*- have multiple origins (*č, *š, *ć, *-s-). While initial *r*- is rare in the normal (non sound-symbolic) vocabulary, it ranks third as favored initial in phonesthemic verbs. The working hypothesis proposed here is: *New or rare members of the repertoire are more thoroughly exploited in sound symbolism.* Interestingly enough, *s*- (from *s, *š, and *ć) ranks fifth as favored *initial* but is completely absent from *medial* position in this class of verbs. The reasons for this are unclear. Could it be connected with the fact that -*s*- occurs in the very suffix (derivational -*ise*-) which marks this class of verbs? Or is medial sound-symbolic -*h*- also from *-s-?

Table 17.5 *Initial and medial consonants in phonesthemic words*

	-r-	-h-	-l-	-p-	-m-	-t-	-k-	-n-	-v-	
h-	5	2	6	2	2	3		1		21
k-	3	6	4	3	2	2				20
r-		4		4	6	6				20
p-	6	4	4	1	2		1			18
s-	4	3	1	2						10
m-	3		1		1	1	1			7
t-	3	2			1					6
n-	3	2	1							6
j-	2	1	1		1	1				6
v-	1		1	1					1	4
l-				1						1
Sum	30	24	18	15	15	13	2	1	1	Sum

Table 17.6 *Gilyak vowels and obstruents*

	i y u e a o					
1	p	t	c	k	q	voiceless aspirated
2	b	d	¢	g	ġ	voiceless unaspirated
3	f	ř	s	x	ẍ	voiceless
4	v	r	z	γ	ÿ	voiced

17.3. Gilyak

Gilyak is a Paleosiberian language spoken by about 4,400 persons along the lower Amur and on the island of Sakhalin. It is an isolate; its traditional neighbors are principally South-Tungus languages and Ainu. The data used here are from the author's fieldwork, carried out in Japan in 1954 and 1956–1957.

Three main sound-symbolic processes will be singled out here: (1) vowel length/lengthening, (2) stem reduplication, (3) high/low vowel alternations. The last of these will be given the most attention.

Table 17.6 displays the vowels and obstruents. *y* is a high, back unrounded vowel, higher and tenser than what is called "barred *i*."

Row 1 alternates with row 3 and row 2 with row 4 under grammatically and

Europe

phonologically specifiable conditions. *c* and *ɟ* are hushing, palatalized affricates; *q* and the column under it: post-velars, "uvulars"; *ř* is an alveolar fricative with a preceding tap. Non-obstruents: *m n ñ ŋ, w l j h* (*ñ* as in Spanish; *j* as in German). There is no stress, i.e. stress is on the first syllable, except for certain morphemes, which appropriate it (conditional, imperative, vocative). Some reduplicated items have stress on the reduplicated syllable, e.g. *oj&òj* (name of a plant); the reasons for this are not clear.

In the category of numerals, of which there are over 20 classes (with classifiers), there is V-lengthening, as dictated by class. In some numerals these long Vs can be etymologically justified; in others not.

Some isolated root morphemes have long Vs which do *not* alternate with short Vs. In these, sound symbolism is obvious and dictated by cultural values. E.g. *tīřiy* "bat" (a semi-divine animal), **ti&ři-*, a form which also violates the phonological canon in another respect: the sequence *-iy* (? *-ijy*). There are similar long root vowels in the words for "rot, pus" and "splash" and in the enclitic *-ī* "n'est-ce pas?".

There is banal sound symbolism in the lengthening and lowering of the V in the inflectional morpheme *-fki* "(while) . . . -ing" to *-fkē*, generally in story-telling and almost always accompanied by some theatrical effect; *-fkē* is therefore textually more frequent in narratives than *-fki*. Similarly: *ŋuli-* "smile" / (affective) *ŋulē-*. Raising and lengthening: (normal) *ajru-r-à* / (affective) *ajru-r-ỳ* (especially in story-telling, emotional reporting, and singing) "and cursing."

Some animal names are in fact reduplicated stems which have no corresponding simplices: *maw&maw* "geometer, loper"; *viz&vis* "grasshopper" (also uncanonic in that this noun begins with a fricative); *gy&gy-k* "swan" (final *-k* is playful); *kyv&ɣyf* "spider" (irregular; more likely: **gyv&ɣyf*), another animal with divine properties. Bird names: *laɣ̂&laẍ, qaz&ẍas, ṭew&zew*. Also: *pso&fzo* "dolphin" (but cf. Orok [Tungus] *picɔ&picɔ* "id."). There are seemingly no reduplicated fish names. Why not?

Expressive verbal stems which have no corresponding simplices: *paki&faki-* "with all one's might," *pla&fla-* sound-symbolic/synesthesic for "shine," *ply&fly-* "shine," *vat&vat-u-* "walk quietly," *kuj&xuj-* and *lym&lym-* "walk in sand," *bař&bar-* "lightning," *toq&řoq-* glossed by the informant as "walk without using one's feet" (= ? "without lifting feet to take steps").

The same, but *with* corresponding simplices or crypto-simplices: *tam&řam-* "quiet (of persons)," cf. *tam-la-* "id."; *nanq&nanq* "id.," ? cf. *nenq* "doll," *nonq* "sister"; *da mif xmy&xmy-ř* "land animals other than mammals and insects" (*da* [folkloristic] "this," *mif* "land, earth") and *dol xmy&xmy-ř* "maritime *xmy&xmy-ř* (= molluscs, shells)," cf. *kmy-* in *kmy-ju-* on p. 259 below.

There follows the most important part of the Gilyak segment of this paper. The high Vs *i y u* alternate with their low counterparts, *e a o*, under different sets of conditions.

Table 17.7 *Suggested correlation between increased markedness and sound-symbolic function*

		Vowels	Number of features	Meaning
a	pure morphonology, i.e. V harmony	FRONT	1	*none*
b	lexical exploitation: -*ly*-/-*la*-, with SS, cf. also pl_y^a & fl_y^a-	back − ROUNDED	1	*playful/creative*
c	phonesthemic exploitation, sound symbolism; governance: V-harmony	back + ROUNDED	2	*visceral*

The two front vowels, *i/e*, alternate under conditions dictated by V-harmony and only in preposed pronominal morphemes (which are ñi "I," ci "thou," pi "own, self-" in their free forms). The quality (low vs. high) of the first root vowel determines the choice of *i* or *e*, e.g. *tla* "harpoon," *ñe-ŕla* "my harpoon" (low *a* in the stem requires a low vowel, *e*, in the pronoun) vs. *tly* "thimble," *ñi-ŕly* "my thimble" (high *y* in stem, high *i* in pronoun). This alternation, *i/e*, is automatic before stems with initial consonant clusters. (When a pronominal element precedes a *verbal* stem it indicates the object.) *i/e* is restricted to mere vowel harmony.

The unrounded back vowels *y* and *a* alternate in the morphemes -*ly*-/-*la*-. The second of these, -*la*-, follows verbal stems which mark qualities (our adjectives), much as in a certain subclass of the so-called Japanese "adjectives": *do*- "thick, fat" = *do-la*- "thick, fat" (attrib.). The simplex (*do*-) also exists, but occurs more rarely. -*ly*- has the same function as -*la*-, but with the additional meaning-feature "a little, somewhat": *do-ly*- "a little fat, a little thick (= ? chubby)." The process is productive.

Occasionally, *y/a* is also found elsewhere, e.g. in *ply*&*fly*- and *pla*&*fla*- (both) "shiny." An informant uses the former as in "shiny" for "light/lumière" and the latter as in "shiny" for the sun or the moon. The informant rendered the former in Japanese as *pika*&*pika* (which exists in Japanese) and the latter as **bika*&*bika* (which does not exist). This may be a creative adumbration of Japanese *pera*&*pera* "yackata-yack" (of chatter) and *bera*&*bera* "id.," both of which exist in Japanese and are synonymous. *y/a* also alternate dialectally and unsystematically (sound change in progress). There seems to have been lexical ablaut in Proto-Gilyak: *y/a*, ∅/*a*.

The *u/o* alternation is restricted to the derivational morphemes -*ju*-/-*jo*-, e.g.

třiv-ju- "cool (as in the shade of a tree)," *fo-jo-* "foggy, misty rain" (Japan. *kiriame*), *tol-jo-ÿar-* "sulk" (*-ÿar-* is an intensive), *kmy-ju-* "creep" (a zoological term, see *xmy&xmy-ř*, p. 257 above). The examples adduced here are regular in terms of vowel harmony: a high stem-V dictates *-ju-* and a low stem-V dictates *-jo-*. However, the alternation is defective. First of all, the *o* of *-jo-* is often so high (after *j*) that it is difficult to distinguish it from the *u* of *-ju-*, e.g. *lol-ju-* = *lol-jo-* "has a secretion in the eyes." Second, there are blatant violations of vowel harmony: *gifr-jo-* (expected: **gifr-ju-*) = *fo-jo-* "misty rain" (as above). Also: *la* "wind": *la-ju-* (**la-jo-*) "weather is bad."

A correlation *between* an increasing scale of markedness among the vowels *and* an increasing scale of sound-symbolic function (from zero to fully sound-symbolic) will now be proposed. The plain front vowels *i* and *e* have no sound-symbolic function; they serve merely as the substance for the automatic implementation of vowel harmony. The plain back vowels *y* and *a* serve the lexicon in a secondary – playful, creative, improvisatory – fashion; see above, pp. 257, 258, for *-la-/-ly-*, *pla&fla-/ply&fly-*, etc. the most patently marked vowels are *u* and *o*: they are both back and rounded. In this case, *markedness* also means: (1) visibility – one can see rounding better than any other comparable feature, just as one can see labial consonants better than other consonants. "One" here means especially the mother and the child learning to speak. (2) Presumably the greatest muscular effort, or a special route of conveying the command for the labial gesture. (3) Perhaps the greatest amount of effort in terms of neural command, transmission, and processing.

(In the case of Finnish we saw that the back rounded vowels were fronted for affect – *u* and *o* were fronted to *y* [ü] and *ö*. In the light of Gilyak markedness this means that an already marked set, *u* and *o*, is further marked by fronting, i.e. primary vowels are made secondary.)

The role of *u* and *o* in Gilyak *-ju-/-jo-* will be called *visceral* here because of the elusive, difficult-to-articulate meaning of this suffix.

Table 17.7 displays the suggested correlation between increasing markedness and sound-symbolic function.

17.4. Conclusion

Finnish and Gilyak belong to the same North Eurasian typological zone. Finnish has three degrees of height (*u:o:a, y:ö;ä* plus *i:e*), while Gilyak has two degrees of height (*i:e, u:o, y:a*). Finnish has two front rounded vowels, *y* and *ö*. The latter, *ö*, is found east of Finland (in the aforementioned typological area) only in Mari (Cheremis), Turkic languages and Mongolic languages. In Finnish, *ö* is recent. An effort was made in section 17.2 above to show that Finnish *y* (*ü*) is also recent, but older than *ö*. It is important to note that Finnish *y* is, in Daniel Jones's terms, a secondary vowel: the roundness of the exit (the buccal aperture) is at odds with the place of the articulatory chamber (posterior) of this vowel. If Finnish *y* is a secondary vowel, then Finnish *ö* ought to be called a tertiary vowel: roundedness and non-height, when they do co-exist, are also at odds with each other. Nevertheless, or precisely because of these facts, Finnish *ö* is the vowel which is most intensely exploited for purposes of sound symbolism. It is also the most recent vowel in the language. Note the connection.

Gilyak has no front rounded vowels, but it has one secondary vowel, *y* (high back unrounded; *i*). This vowel is secondary because it has an unrounded exit but an anterior articulatory chamber. This is also the vowel which has the highest lexical specification. It occurs in the suffix *-ly-* "somewhat X, a little X" and stands in opposition to *-la-*. However, the most emotional pair of vowels in Gilyak is the pair of rounded vowels *u:o* in the phonesthemic suffixes *-ju-:-jo-*. The occurrence of these suffixes is governed by vowel harmony, albeit defectively and imperfectly. Again, rounding seems to correlate strongly with affect.

Are the Finnish and Gilyak scenarios rooted in the nature of human phonation or, more specifically, in the cultural make-up of the North Eurasian area?

NOTES

1 Abbreviations and symbols: V = vowel, C = consonant; / = alternation; // = is paradigmatically, lexically, or historically related to; & = reduplication.

Thanks are due to my colleague Aili Flint, who has clarified many of the glosses and provided essential help in treating Finnish sound-symbolic forms in general.

The two principal lexica used were *Nykysuomen sanakirja* and Alanne 1962. It goes without saying that glossing sound-symbolic forms is close to impossible.

2 Note the meanings of the monosyllables with *-yy*. The meanings clearly reflect a hunting-and-gathering culture.
3 By Alfredo Quintero, personal communication, autumn 1985.

REFERENCES

Alanne, V. S. 1962. *Finnish-English Dictionary*. Porvoo and Helsinki: Söderström.
Anttila, R. 1976. Meaning and structure of the Finnish descriptive vocabulary. *Texas Linguistic Forum* 5: 1–12. (*Papers from the Transatlantic Finnish Conference*, ed. R. T. Harms and F. Karttunen.)
Nykysuomen sanakirja [Dictionary of Modern Standard Finnish]. 1953–1962. Six volumes. Porvoo and Helsinki: Söderström.

PART VI
English

18
*Phonosyntactics**

JOAN A. SERENO

18.1. Introduction

Although the search for linguistic universals has been successful in discovering a wide variety of similarities among the languages of the world (Greenberg 1966, 1978), few generalities about the semantic properties of languages have been uncovered (Weinreich 1963). Some of the most striking examples of a structured semantic domain are to be found in the connection between sound and meaning. In principle, resemblances between meaning and sound should not exist. As Greenberg (1957) notes, the connection between sound and meaning is essentially arbitrary. A meaning can theoretically be represented by almost any set of sounds in a language.

Despite claims that this principle applies to all languages, the articles in this volume show that connections between the meanings and the sounds of language do exist. Two universal and well-documented cases of sound symbolism are relevant to the present study. First, Ultan (1978) found evidence for distance symbolism. The notion of distance symbolism must be considered within the broader framework of deixis. Deixis refers to those features of the language which reflect the spatio-temporal coordinates of the relative situation of the utterance. Distinctions are made between things that are near in space and/or time versus things that are far in space and/or time. In an analysis of 136 languages, Ultan found that 33.1% of the sample exhibited distance (spatial) symbolism in their demonstrative system. More importantly, the languages that overtly symbolized distance relationships predominantly used front or high front vowels to represent proximity to the speaker. Ultan also found universal correspondences for size symbolism in language. Some languages overtly mark words expressing diminution by changing the phonological features of the sound in the root. Ultan found that 27.3% of the 136 languages he sampled had diminutive marking. In almost 90% of these languages, the diminutive was symbolized by high front vowels. The widespread distribution of these consistently recurring patterns of sound symbolism suggests that the relation between sound and meaning in language is not completely arbitrary.

Taking these universal semantic–sound correspondences as a model, a different type of sound symbolism is suggested here. Correspondences between *sound* and the clearly delineated and linguistically salient categories of syntactic class are analyzed. Specifically, the syntactic classes of "noun and "verb" are compared in terms of the phonological classification of their vowels. The data to be presented in this chapter suggest that there exists a peripheral type of sound symbolism in which specified phonological features are associated with different syntactic categories.

A preliminary lexical database analysis was undertaken to carefully examine the sound–syntactic class relationship. The reference set of words was the list usually referred to as the Brown Corpus compiled by Francis and Kučera (1982). Francis and Kučera categorized over one million American English words, recording both lexical and grammatical information. The frequency of occurrence as well as the grammatical category of every word is listed.

Francis and Kučera rank-order the words in the Brown Corpus in terms of lemmata. They define the term "lemma" as a set of words belonging to the same major word class. For example, the base form of the word "comment" consists of two separate lemmata – a noun lemma with a frequency of 64 per million and a verb lemma with a frequency of 31 per million. A noun lemma includes singular or mass nouns, possessive singular nouns, plural nouns, possessive plural nouns, and singular proper nouns. A verb lemma includes verbs in the base form and inflected verbs, such as third-person singular forms, past tense forms, past participles, present participles, and gerunds. The modals ("can," "may," "shall," "will") and the non-standard verbs "be," "have," and "do" are categorized separately and are not included in the verb lemmata.

In the present study, the first 1000 noun and verb lemmata in the rank list (a descending order of lemmata by frequency) were first classified according to the phonological category of their stressed vowel (front vowel [i, ɪ, e, ɛ, æ] vs. back vowel [ɚ, ɑ, ʌ, ɔ, o, ʊ, u, aɪ, aʊ, ɔɪ].[1] This division into front and back vowels was motivated by previous universal sound-symbolism research in which front or high front vowels are implicated. In the present analysis, the base form of each word was used. Diphthongs were classified on the basis of the more prominent first vowel sound (Ladefoged 1993). A previous analysis (Sereno 1983), using the Lorge (1949) frequency word list, had shown that the exclusion of all possible controversial cases did not affect the categorization results. In that analysis, multisyllabic words, words containing diphthongs, and words that change the categorization of the stressed vowel (e.g. strong verbs with alternative forms, such as "see/saw") were excluded. This restricted sample of words nevertheless showed identical associations in the comparison of syntactic class membership and phonological categorization of the

English

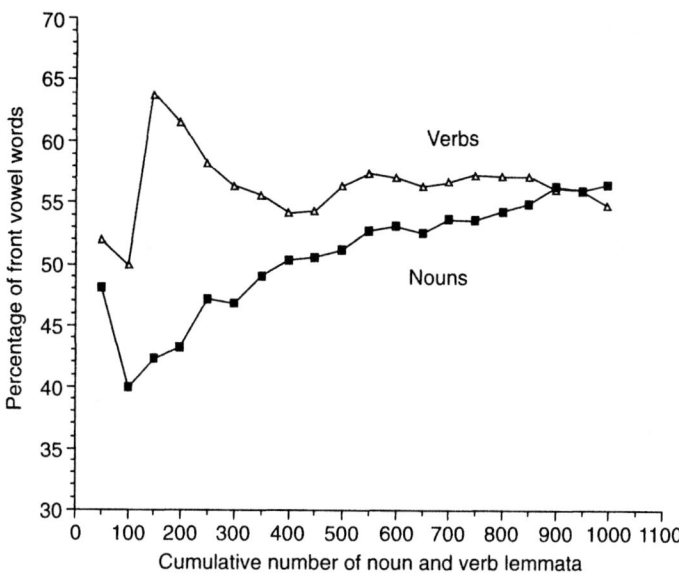

Figure 18.1. Percentage of nouns and verbs in English with front vowels as tabulated from the rank list of the Brown Corpus.

stressed vowel. The present analysis of the Brown Corpus used the broader sample of words.

The phonological analysis of nouns and verbs in the Brown Corpus revealed a systematic, skewed distribution. In general, nouns were more likely to have back vowels rather than front vowels, while verbs were more likely to have front vowels compared to back vowels. However, this distribution was frequency-dependent, occurring only in high-frequency words. The dichotomy between high-frequency nouns and verbs and their low-frequency counterparts with regard to the phonological category of their stressed vowel shows up clearly in figure 18.1. Figure 18.1 represents a cumulative listing (calculated every fifty lemmata) of the first thousand nouns and verbs categorized in terms of the front/back quality of the stressed vowel. A greater number of high-frequency nouns have back vowels, while high-frequency verbs have a greater number of front vowels. However, this pattern does not occur in lower-frequency words. As lower frequency words are included, an equal number of front and back vowels is found in nouns and verbs.

To quantify and evaluate this pattern, two sets of 200 stimuli (a high-frequency set and a low-frequency set) were analyzed in terms of vowel quality. For the high-frequency set, the first 200 nouns and verbs in the rank list representing words with frequencies greater than 250 per million were analyzed. In these high-frequency words, nouns were more likely to have back vowels rather than

Table 18.1 *Vowel categorization of the first 200 high-frequency nouns and verbs (frequency greater than 250 per million). Percentages represent the proportion of a single form class (i.e. noun or verb) having front or back vowels.*

	Front vowels					
	i	I	e	ɛ	æ	Total
Nouns	9	9	12	15	10	55 (43%)
Verbs	17	8	7	7	6	45 (62%)

	Back vowels									
	ə	ɑ	ʌ	ɔ	o	ʊ	u	aI	aʊ	ɔI	Total
Nouns	8	12	10	3	4	10	5	13	4	3	72 (57%)
Verbs	3	3	3	3	1	5	3	7	0	0	28 (38%)

Table 18.2 *Vowel categorization of the first 200 low-frequency nouns and verbs (frequency less than 50 per million) in the rank list of the Brown Corpus. Percentages represent the proportion of a single form class having front or back vowels.*

	Front vowels					
	i	I	e	ɛ	æ	Total
Nouns	4	20	25	17	9	75 (54%)
Verbs	3	5	8	7	6	30 (48%)

	Back vowels									
	ɚ	ɑ	ʌ	ɔ	o	ʊ	u	aI	aʊ	ɔI	Total
Nouns	9	12	6	0	8	1	11	11	3	2	63 (46%)
Verbs	3	5	4	2	5	1	2	7	2	1	32 (52%)

front vowels in their stressed syllable, while verbs were more likely to have front vowels than back vowels (see table 18.1). Only 43% of nouns have front vowels, while 57% have back vowels. This pattern is reversed for the verbs, of which 62% have front vowels while only 38% have back vowels. A Chi-Square test for the high-frequency words showed that there is indeed a significant relationship between the syntactic category of the word and the front/back quality of the stressed vowel of the word ($\chi^2 = 6.23$, $p < 0.025$). There is a significantly greater number of nouns with back vowels and verbs with front vowels.

English

A similar distribution, however, was not maintained for low-frequency nouns and verbs. For the low-frequency set, the first 200 nouns and verbs in the rank list having a frequency less than 50 per million were analyzed. In this set of words, the proportion of front and back vowels for nouns and verbs is virtually identical (see table 18.2): 54% of nouns have front vowels and 46% have back vowels, while 48% of verbs have front vowels and 52% have back vowels. A Chi-Square test for these low-frequency words showed that there was no significant relationship between the syntactic category of the word and the vowel quality of the stressed vowel ($\chi^2 = 0.61$, $p > 0.50$, n.s.).

To summarize, then: for high-frequency words, there is a significantly greater number of nouns with back vowels and verbs with front vowels, but this pattern does not hold for low-frequency nouns and verbs in English. The sound-symbolic correspondences found in studying linguistic universals suggest the possibility that languages of the world do not represent completely arbitrary symbolic systems. As shown above, an analysis of high-frequency words occurring in modern American English reveals a definite relationship between syntactic category and the front/back quality of the stressed vowel. To further investigate these correspondences, a psycholinguistic experiment was conducted to determine whether this relationship is effective in the processing of language.

In this experiment, a series of words was presented to subjects. Their task was to categorize the stimulus word as a noun or verb. Stimulus words were divided into separate groups: a high-frequency set and a low-frequency set. If it is the case that a systematic relationship obtains between syntactic class and phonological features of the language, it may be expected that nouns with back vowels and verbs with front vowels will be processed faster. In addition, a comparison of the high-frequency set to the low-frequency set might clarify whether such an effect (i.e. speeded response latencies for back vowel nouns and front vowel verbs) is simply a distributional artifact of the language (response latency differences present only in high frequency words) or a general processing strategy.

18.2. Methods

18.2.1. Subjects

Twelve students (eight male, four female) attending Brown University volunteered to participate in the experiment. All were native speakers of American English with normal or corrected-to-normal visual acuity.

18.2.2. Stimuli

A total of 64 nouns and verbs was selected from the Brown Corpus. The stimuli are shown in appendix 18.1. The first set consisted of 32 high-frequency words (occurring more than 250 times per million) and the second set consisted of 32 low-frequency words (occurring between 30 and 50 times per million).

Within each set of words, all groups (front-vowel nouns, back-vowel nouns, front-vowel verbs, and back-vowel verbs) were matched for word frequency (Francis and Kučera 1982). In the high-frequency set, mean frequency of occurrence for front-vowel nouns, back-vowel nouns, front-vowel verbs, and back-vowel verbs was 452, 443, 442, and 437, respectively, with standard deviations of 179, 164, 153, 133, respectively. Low-frequency words were similarly matched. Mean frequency of occurrence was 42, 41, 39, and 44, respectively, with standard deviations of 5, 4, 10, 6, respectively.

Only monosyllabic, consonant-initial words were used (see Spoehr and Smith 1973). Mean letter frequency of initial consonants (Baddeley et al. 1960) and word length (Forster and Chambers 1973) were matched among all groups. Finally, only orthographically regular words (see Parkin 1982) were used in the experiment.

18.2.3. Procedure

All subjects were tested individually. They were told to respond as quickly and accurately as possible to each stimulus item. One half of the subjects were first given the High-Frequency List followed by the Low-Frequency List. The other half of the subjects were first given the Low-Frequency List followed by the High-Frequency List. After a short interval, the entire test procedure was repeated.

Following instructions, subjects were given a set of 20 practice items to introduce them to the procedure. A separate practice set accompanied each test set of words (High Frequency and Low Frequency). Practice items were not used in the experiment. For the test, each list (High Frequency, Low Frequency) consisted of 32 words – 16 nouns and 16 verbs. One half of each List contained front vowels and the remaining half contained back vowels. The 32 words were presented in a random order to each subject.

The experiment was controlled and presented on an Apple IIe computer. The stimuli, all in upper case letters, subtended a visual angle of approximately 2° horizontally and 0.5° vertically. Subjects were seated two feet in front of the display. All responses to the stimuli were made by pressing one of two clearly marked buttons on a control box placed in front of the subject. The entire experiment lasted approximately 20 minutes.

Subjects were instructed to identify each stimulus either as a noun or a verb. Each trial was completed when a subject moved the index finger of the preferred hand from a neutral location and pressed one of two equidistantly placed response buttons labeled "noun" or "verb."

Subjects were told that the stimuli were all familiar English words. They were further informed that, although some of the words could occur both as a noun and a verb, each stimulus was to be categorized on the basis of its more frequent usage.

English

Table 18.3 *Mean response latencies (in milliseconds) for each presentation of the test. Total number of errors is given in parentheses.*

First presentation							
High-frequency words				*Low-frequency words*			
Noun		Verb		Noun		Verb	
Front vowel	Back vowel	Front vowel	Back vowel	Front vowel	Back vowel	Front vowel	Back vowel
784	714	740	762	808	745	844	846
(3)	(1)	(10)	(5)	(3)	(5)	(7)	(9)
Second presentation							
High-frequency words				*Low-frequency words*			
Noun		Verb		Noun		Verb	
Front vowel	Back vowel	Front vowel	Back vowel	Front vowel	Back vowel	Front vowel	Back vowel
743	687	737	720	769	717	785	803
(5)	(3)	(5)	(2)	(3)	(3)	(7)	(8)

The stimuli were presented at a fixed rate. Initially, a fixation pattern "****" appeared at the center of the display screen. This pattern disappeared after 1.0 second, followed by a blank screen for 0.25 seconds. The stimulus word then appeared on the display screen and remained there until the subject responded. Reaction times were measured from the appearance of the stimulus on the screen until a key press was made. Following a response, the stimulus word disappeared, leaving a blank screen for three seconds until the next fixation pattern appeared. This entire sequence was repeated for every stimulus item.

18.3. Results

The mean latencies of noun/verb classifications are given in table 18.3. No errors were included in these averages, and all reaction times more than three standard deviations from the individual's mean were discarded. A four-way repeated measures ANOVA (Frequency List × Syntactic Class × Vowel Category × Trial) revealed a main effect for Frequency List (high frequency versus low frequency), $[F_{(1,11)} = 7.33, p < 0.02]$, and Vowel Category (front vowel versus back vowel),

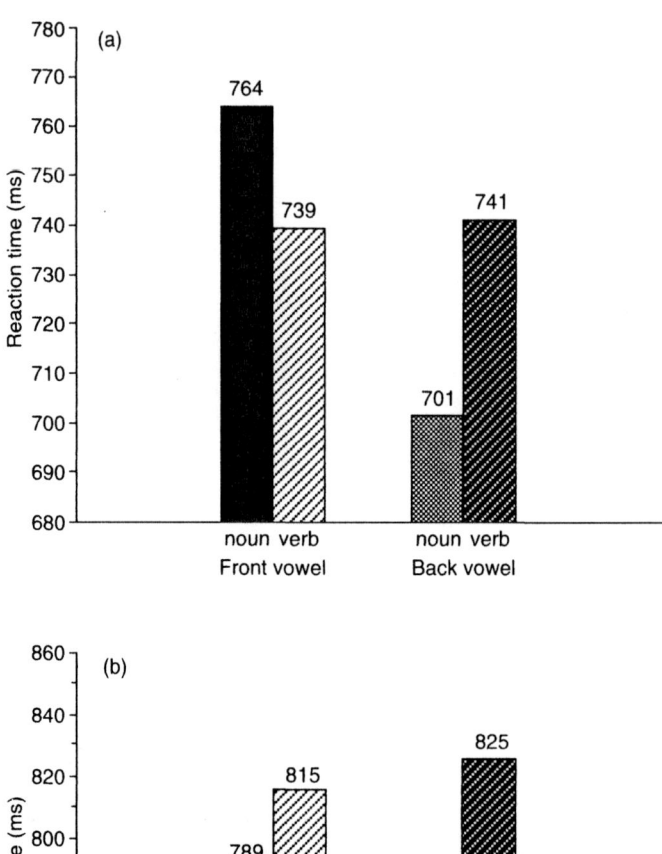

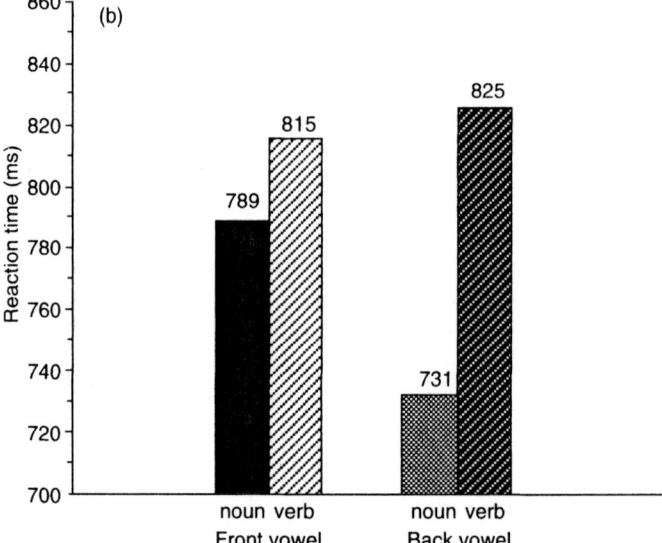

Figure 18.2. Response latencies (in milliseconds) for the classification of nouns and verbs as a function of vowel quality (front vowels vs. back vowels) in (a) high-frequency stimuli and (b) low-frequency stimuli.

English

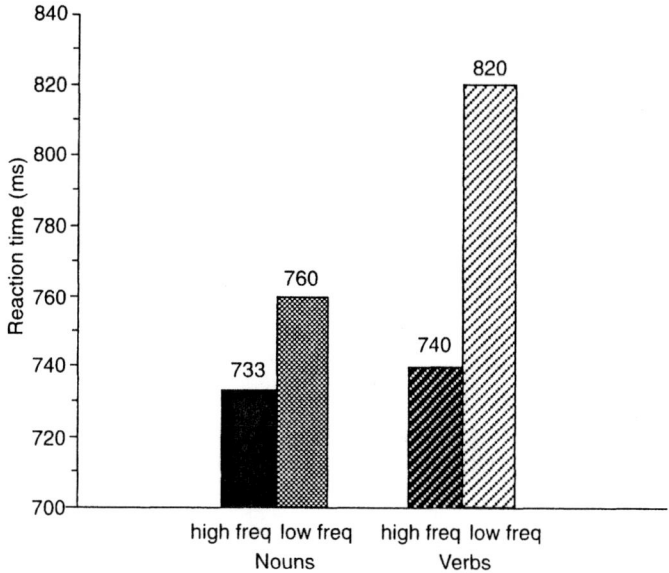

Figure 18.3. Response latencies (in milliseconds) for the classification of nouns and verbs as a function of frequency (high frequency vs. low frequency).

$[F_{(1,11)} = 24.49$, $p < 0.0004]$. High-frequency words (736 ms) were categorized faster than low frequency words (790 ms), and back-vowel words (750 ms) faster than front-vowel words (777 ms).

There was also a significant main effect for Trial, $[F_{(1,11)} = 26.06$, $p < 0.0003]$. Total mean response latencies were 780 ms on initial tests and 745 ms on repetition tests.

More importantly, however, only one significant interaction between factors was found. Specifically, there was a significant interaction between Syntactic Class (noun versus verb) and Vowel Category (front vowel versus back vowel), $[F_{(1,11)} = 11.54$, $p < 0.006]$. Nouns with back vowels (716 ms) were categorized significantly faster than nouns with front vowels (777 ms), and verbs with front vowels (776 ms) faster than verbs with back vowels (783 ms). This effect, moreover, was found for both high-frequency and low-frequency stimuli (see figures 18.2a and 18.2b).

Two interesting trends were also present in the data. Noun categorization (747 ms) was slightly faster than verb classification (780 ms), $[F_{(1,11)} = 3.40$, $p < 0.09$ (n.s.)]. In addition, a slight interaction was found between Frequency List (high frequency vs. low frequency) and Syntactic Class (noun vs. verb), $[F_{(1,11)} = 4.34$, $p < 0.06$ (n.s.)] (see figure 18.3). It seems that categorization latencies for frequency-matched nouns and verbs are approximately equal (733 ms and

740 ms, respectively) in commonly used, high-frequency words, but differ in low-frequency words where response latencies to verbs (820 ms) are slower than to nouns (760 ms).

The mean number of errors is shown in table 18.3. These totals include both mistakes in categorization (i.e. making a noun decision for a verb stimulus or vice versa) and trials in which latencies exceed three standard deviations of the subject's mean. A total of 79 errors were made, representing less than 5% of all responses. A four-way repeated measures ANOVA of errors (Frequency List × Syntactic Class × Vowel Category × Trial) revealed a main effect for Syntactic Class, [$F_{(1,11)} = 7.26$, $p < 0.02$]. There were significantly more errors for verbs (53) compared to nouns (26). In addition, there was a significant interaction of Frequency List × Syntactic Class × Trial, [$F_{(1,11)} = 9.16$, $p < 0.01$]. There were fewer mistakes for low-frequency nouns on the second trial. The error analysis is consistent with the analysis of mean response latencies in that both show that categorization of verbs, particularly low-frequency verbs, is more difficult (i.e. takes more time and results in more errors).

18.4. Discussion

The present study examines a form of sound symbolism in which syntactic form classes are distinguished in terms of the phonological classification of their vowels. A lexical search of American English revealed a striking pattern involving nouns and verbs and front and back vowels. In English, nouns were more likely to have back vowels rather than front vowels while verbs were more likely to have front vowels compared to back vowels.

The results of the psycholinguistic experiment showed that, in a noun/verb categorization task, significant processing differences exist between nouns and verbs depending on the front/back quality of the stressed vowel. Nouns with back vowels were categorized faster than nouns with front vowels. Conversely, verbs with front vowels were categorized faster than verbs with back vowels. These results are in accord with similar experiments run in the auditory modality investigating these phonological and syntactic class interactions. In both an auditory noun/verb categorization task and an auditory lexical decision task, Sereno and Jongman (1990) found that noun stimuli containing back vowels were processed faster than nouns with front vowels while verb stimuli containing front vowels were processed faster than verbs with back vowels.

A further result of the present study is that the facilitation of nouns with back vowels and verbs with front vowels occur for both high-frequency and low-frequency words. Recall that the lexical analysis of English showed that the phonological and syntactic class correspondences existed only in the high-frequency words. Low-frequency words in English, on the other hand, showed equivalent distributions of front and back vowels in nouns and verbs. The psycholinguistic data, however, do not directly reflect this pattern. The present results show that processing differences exist for both high and low-frequency words. These psycholinguistic effects suggest the presence of a general processing strategy for both high and low-frequency words. This frequency-independent nature of the phonosyntactic correspondences was not found in the auditory tasks mentioned above. Sereno and Jongman (1990) found that in these auditory tasks the processing effects directly mimic the lexical distribution of nouns and verbs with front and back vowels in the language. The present data, however, seem to suggest the operation of a general processing strategy. Two tentative explanations are possible. First, the blocked presentation of the high and low-frequency stimuli in the present experiment may have encouraged the use of a general processing strategy. Second, the present experiment was presented visually. The visual presentation of the stimuli may have contributed some additional variance that may be affecting the pattern of results. One possible contributing factor may be the use of words with orthographic/phonological vowel clash, such as "wife," which is categorized phonologically as a back vowel but orthographically as a front vowel. However, it is not apparent how inclusion of such words could result in significant sound–syntax correspondences in both high and low-frequency stimuli. Further experimentation is clearly needed to resolve these issues.

Nevertheless, the present lexical and psycholinguistic data suggest that syntactic class membership and phonological information regarding the stressed vowel are important and influential variables in processing. It should be noted that the divisions between nouns and verbs and between front and back vowels are highly salient distinctions in language. The syntactic categories of noun and verb are universal categories in languages of the world (Hockett 1968; Sapir 1944). Moreover, the division between front and back vowels is a basic phonological contrast (e.g. Chomsky and Halle 1968; Jakobson *et al.* 1963), which can be easily characterized in terms of formant frequencies (e.g., Ladefoged 1993; Lieberman and Blumstein 1988). Specifically, front vowels have high second-formant frequencies which approximate third-formant levels, resulting in a concentration of energy in relatively higher frequencies. Back vowels, on the other hand, have low second-formant frequencies. The close proximity of the second and first formants, in this case, emphasizes lower frequencies of the spectrum. The perception of vowels has been shown, for the most part, to be based on the location of formant frequencies, especially the first and second formants (e.g. Carlson *et al.* 1975). Clearly, the categories of nouns and verbs and front and back vowels could be plausible candidates in perception.

The present data suggest that syntactic-form-class membership as well as phonological classification of vowels is explicitly coded in the lexicon. The interaction between syntactic class and phonological categorization of the stressed vowel suggests that this information may be used to structure the lexicon. Noun/verb categories and front/back vowel classification seem to be possible organizing principles of the lexicon.

In conclusion, a lexical search revealed that high-frequency words participate in a systematic skewed distribution in English. This distribution showed up clearly in terms of differences in processing times for both high and low-frequency words. In a noun/verb classification task, subjects were able to exploit differences that exist in commonly used words. It seems that a general processing strategy is used to access nouns and verbs in the lexicon based on vowel categorization.

Although the noun/verb classification task is rarely used in traditional psycholinguistic experiments, this task may be more appropriate for the analysis of linguistic processing. In contrast, the widely used lexical decision task, in which subjects are to decide whether a stimulus is a word or not, requires a decision which is not commonly made by a listener in normal sentence processing. Noun/verb classification data, therefore, may better reflect lexical orgaization. The present results suggest that there is a robust interaction between syntactic class and vowel categorization and that the lexicon may be organized on this basis.

Appendix 18.1. *Stimuli used in the experiment*

High-Frequency stimuli			
Front-vowel Nouns	Back-vowel Nouns	Front-vowel Verbs	Back-vowel Verbs
hand	school	leave	want
thing	house	feel	write
fact	group	keep	put
week	church	let	try
field	door	meet	move
street	month	reach	grow
friend	book	sit	serve
death	wife	wait	lose

Low-Frequency stimuli			
Front-vowel Nouns	Back-vowel Nouns	Front-vowel Verbs	Back-vowel Verbs
milk	clerk	mix	bind
fence	porch	swim	shut
gift	dirt	snap	pour
cat	bus	beg	quote
bench	bride	seize	hunt
prince	tongue	weigh	stir
sand	corn	melt	crawl
leaf	barn	cease	wipe

English

NOTES

* This research was conducted at Brown University while the author was supported by a National Science Foundation Graduate Fellowship.

1 The term "back vowel" in this paper refers to both back vowels and central vowels as defined in the phonetics literature (e.g. Ladefoged 1993).

REFERENCES

Baddeley, A., R. Conrad, and W. Thomson. 1960. Letter structure of the English language. *Nature* 186: 414–416.

Carlson, R., G. Fant, and B. Granström. 1975. Two-formant models, pitch, and vowel perception. In G. Fant and M. A. A. Tatham (eds.) *Auditory Analysis and the Perception of Speech*. London: Academic Press.

Chomsky, N. and M. Halle. 1968. *The Sound Pattern of English*. New York: Harper & Row.

Forster, K. and S. Chambers. 1973. Lexical access and naming time. *Journal of Verbal Learning and Verbal Behavior* 12: 627–635.

Francis, W. N. and H. Kučera. 1982. *Frequency Analysis of English Usage: Lexicon and Grammar*. Boston: Houghton Mifflin.

Greenberg, J. 1957. *Essays in Linguistics*. Chicago: University of Chicago Press.

1966. *Language Universals*. The Hague: Mouton.

1978. *Universals of Human Language*. Stanford: University Press.

Hockett, C. F. 1968. *The State of the Art*. The Hague: Mouton.

Jacobson, R., G. Fant and M. Halle. 1963. *Preliminaries to Speech Analysis*. Cambridge, MA: MIT Press.

Ladefoged, P. 1993. *A Course in Phonetics*. New York: Harcourt Brace Jovanovich.

Lieberman, P. and S. Blumstein. 1988. *Speech Physiology, Speech Perception, and Acoustic Phonetics*. Cambridge: University Press.

Lorge, I. 1949. *The Semantic Count of the 570 Commonest English Words*. New York: Bureau of Publications, Teachers' College at Columbia University.

Parkin, A. 1982. Phonological recoding in lexical decision: effects of spelling-to-sound regularity depend on how regularity is defined. *Memory and Cognition* 10(1): 43–53.

Sapir, E. 1944. *Language*. New York: Harcourt, Brace and World.

Sereno, J. A. 1983. Phonosyntactics: sound-syntax correspondences. MA thesis, Brown University.

Sereno, J. A. and A. Jongman. 1990. Phonological and form class relations in the lexicon. *Journal of Psycholinguistic Research* 19(6): 387–404.

Spoehr, K. and E. E. Smith. 1973. The role of syllables in perceptual processing. *Cognitive Psychology* 5: 71–89.

Ultan, R. 1978. Size–sound symbolism. In J. Greenberg (ed.) *Universals of Human Language*, vol. 2 – *Phonology*. Stanford: University Press, 525–568.

Weinreich, U. 1963. On the semantic structure of language. In J. Greenberg (ed.) *Universals of Language*. Cambridge, MA: MIT Press, 142–216.

19
Aural images

RICHARD RHODES

19.1. Introduction

In Rhodes and Lawler 1981 (henceforth R&L) we sketched an analysis of English monosyllables which involved dividing them into initial consonant(s) versus the vowel nucleus plus final consonant(s). Following one of the traditional terminologies of syllable analysis, we called the initial consonant(s) the *assonance* and the remainder of the syllable the *rime* (cf. Bolinger 1950). We argued that the resulting parts fall into systems which are sound-symbolic in the sense that they participate in sound–meaning correspondences even though they are, by traditional analysis, submorphemic entities.

Many of the entities that we concentrated on in R&L have semantics that are based on vision. For example, we proposed that there is a rudimentary classifier system like that in (1) and a system of path shapes like that in (2) both of which primarily depend on the shape of objects or paths referred to.

(1) Classifiers
st- [1 dimensional] (*stick, staff, stem*, etc.)
str- [1 dimensional, flexible] (*string, strand, strip*, etc.)
fl- [2 dimensional] (*flap, flat, floor*, etc.)
š-/sk- [2 dimensional, flexible] *sheet, scarf, skin*, etc.)
n- [3 dimensional] (*knob, knot, node, nut*, etc.)
sp- [cylindrical] (*spool, spine, spike*, etc.)
dr-/tr- [liquid] (*drink, drain, trickle, trough*, etc.)
et al.

(2) Paths
tr-/dr- [simple] (*track, trip, drive, drag*, etc.)
p-/b- ["anchored"] (*push, pop, bump, bounce*, etc.)
j-/č- [short] (*jerk, jiggle, jagged, chop*, etc.)
w- [back and forth] (*wag, wiggle, wobble*, etc.)
et al.

In this paper we will refer to the mental entities which these assonances label as *image schemata* or, for the sake of brevity, *images*.[1] Single perceptions are both image schemata in their own right and analyzable into subordinate image schemata, and some of those schemata are analyzable into subordinate schemata, and so on. The words we use to label perceptions often do not refer to the perceptions as wholes, but refer rather to a subset of the image schemata that make them up. This view is similar to the one Langacker (1987) takes in his cognitive grammar. It also parallels Whorf's (1940) gestalt approach, in which his term *figure* corresponds to our *image (schema)*. There is, however, one crucial way in which we disagree with Whorf. He was so taken by the discovery of the figure-ground aspect of visual perception that, following the psychologists of his day, he dumped all other perceptions into a single catch-all "egoic field."[2] In our approach, single perceptions may be comprised of images from all modes of perception – visual, aural, tactile, taste, and/or smell. I will discuss some implications of this below.

What is important to the immediate discussion is that there is also a set of forms with meanings based in aural images which are also susceptible to submorphemic analysis. The assonances in (3) were identified in R&L.[3]

(3) *p-* [abrupt onset] (*pop, ping, peep*, etc.)
    b- [abrupt, loud onset] (*boom, bang, beep*, etc.)
    bl- [loud, air-induced sound] (*blat, blast, blab*, etc.)
    kl- [abrupt onset] (*clank, click, clip clop*, etc.)
    r- [irregular onset] (*rip, roar, roll*, etc.)
    y- [loud, vocal tract noise] (*yell, yap, yak*, etc.), and so on.

That visual and aural images are of two separate kinds can be seen most clearly in the existence of forms which are ambiguous between the two.

(4) crack visual — *A crack appeared in the wall.*
           aural — *He heard the crack of a whip.*
    pop   visual — *He suddenly popped up.*
           aural — *It popped loudly.*
    rip   visual — *There is a rip in his coat.*
           aural — *The fabric split with a loud rip.*

In this paper I will explore the range of English simplex words[4] referring to aural images. This represents a piece of groundwork which is necessary to build a full theory on which to base submorphemic analysis. Forms labeling aural images are mapping sound onto sound. An analysis of them should circumvent the unknowns of synesthesia. Therefore a thorough examination of words which label aural images should, we expect, allow us to see in relatively direct ways what sorts of transformations (in the intuitive sense) take place in reducing an image to a string of phonemes. Of particular interest are the linearization of simultaneously perceived events, and the imposition of discreteness on analog phenomena.

English (and probably most other languages) distinguish two types of aural images: those which are produced in mammalian vocal tracts (both human and non-human) and those which are produced elsewhere.

(5)   vocal tract images   non-vocal tract images
      yell, growl, hum,   *click, bang, plop,*
      murmur, roar,   *crack, ping*
      et al.   *et al.*

In this paper I will concentrate on words labeling aural images of the second sort.

It should of course be noted that labels for vocal tract aural images are frequently transferred to label images to the other sort, on the basis of the similarity of some of the latter images to images evoked by the sounds produced in mammalian vocal tracts.

(6)   *roar*
      simple   *the roar of a lion, the roar of a crowd*
      transferred *the roar of the ocean, the roar of the traffic*

  murmur
      simple   *a murmur of approval, a murmur of acquiescence*
      transferred *a heart murmur, the murmur of the waves*

  hum
      simple   *to hum a tune*
      transferred *the hum of the engine*

Again I will not be concerned with these cases.

The analysis in this paper is intended (1) to help decide whether pitch is the sole determinant of sound-symbolic character in the labels of aural images, and (2) to provide an initial step in the direction of working out the mappings between linguistically structured sound and naturally occurring sound as a basis for a better understanding of the nature of other types of mappings involving linguistically structured sound. In the first section I will deal primarily with types of form–meaning correspondence found in the vocabulary in question. In the second section I will deal with a preliminary analysis of the submorphemic entities involved. In the final section I will deal with some theoretical issues.

19.2.   Form–meaning correspondence

There are three general types of form–meaning relationships appearing in the vocabulary referring to sound: true onomatopoeia, sound symbolism, and arbitrary naming.

English

19.2.1. Onomatopoeia

In true onomatopoeia, the word is directly shaped by the sound it represents. That is to say, there is some fairly direct mapping between the acoustic features of the sound itself and the phonological features of the word that labels that sound. The largest class of this sort of English is found among those words which represent the sounds made by animals.

(7) *arf, meow, moo, tweet, baa, hoot*

In fact a relatively large number of bird names arise by onomatopoeia, the second-formant pattern of the bird name mimicking in a fairly direct way the call of the bird. This is true of other languages as well as English, as can be seen in (8).

(8) English
bobwhite, whippoorwill, killdeer, chickadee

Ojibwa (Ottawa dialect)[5]
pichi "robin," *waahoonwenh* "whippoorwill,"
jigjigaaneshiinh "chickadee,"
baaghaakwaanh "chicken"

Chiapas Zoque[6]
pichu "robin," *quiyuquiyu,* "sp. swallow," *pijiji* "sp. sparrow"

This definition of onomatopoeia is, however, too loose to be of much use to us. But in order to tighten it up we will need to recognize that the class of words we want to treat as onomatopoeic is quite diverse phonetically in that such words fit on an analog scale, ranging from the very precise imitations of the impressionist to words such as those in (8). Let me call the ends of this scale *wild* and *tame*. At the extreme wild end the possibilities of the human vocal tract are utilized to their fullest to imitate sounds of other than human origin. At the tame end the imitated sound is simply approximated by an acoustically close phoneme or phonemic combination.

(9) | wild | tame |
| --- | --- |
| [ʔẅæ̰ʔ·ẅæ̰ʔ][7] | *quack, quack* |
| [u⊥:³²³u⊥:³²³] | *hoo/hoot* |
| [bæ̰ʔæ̰ʔæ̰ʔæ̰ʔ] | *baa* |
| [ʔm̰ɨ:⁵⁴⁵] | *moo* |

Of course, there is a full range from wild to tame, and it can be argued that some of what I treat as sound-symbolic in aural image labels is simply very tame onomatopoeia, except for one factor, sound symbolism.

19.2.2. Sound symbolism

Sound symbolism in aural image labels is different from true onomatopoeia in that the submorphemic pieces in question have some measure of paradigmatic support, i.e. they occur in groups sharing a correlation between structural parts and acoustic reference, as in (10), and occasionally even in minimally contrasting pairs, as in (11).

(10) a. assonances
   r- [irregular]
      *r*attle, *r*oll [of thunder], *r*ip, *r*acket
   θ- [low pitch, slow onset]
      *th*ump, *th*wack, *th*unk, *th*ud
   b- [abrupt, (relatively) loud onset]
      *b*ang, *b*eep, *b*oing, *b*ellow
   p- [abrupt onset]
      *p*op, *p*eep, *p*ing, *p*ow, *p*itter, *p*atter, *p*eal

   b. rimes
   -æk [abrupt decay]
      cl*ack*, cr*ack*, wh*ack*, sm*ack*
   -ıŋ [extended decay]
      r*ing*, d*ing*, p*ing*, bo*ing*

(11) high pitch vs. unmarked pitch
      click vs. *clack*
   (relatively) loud vs. unmarked
      beep vs. *peep*
   abrupt irregular onset vs. abrupt smooth onset
      crack vs. *clack*

I will call the type of sound symbolism found in aural image labels *structured sound symbolism*.

19.2.3. Arbitrary forms

There also exist some words used to refer to sounds that have no basis in acoustics, at least not synchronically. These all appear to be generic terms as, for example, the forms in (12).

(12) *noise, sound, din*

One might also argue that adjectives such as *loud* and *quiet* should be in this set.

Occasionally a cartoonist like Johnny Hart (*B.C.*) will even use the labels for actions based on visual images to express the sound associated with those action(s).

English

(13) *clamp, nab, bump, squeeze, munch, suck* (all from J. Hart)

Of necessity these must be classified as arbitrary names for sounds when they are used in this manner.

19.3. Structured sound symbolism

Now let us turn to a preliminary analysis of the words involved in structured sound symbolism. In R&L we divided words into assonances and rimes, splitting the form between the initial consonant(s) and the vowel. While that approach works quite well for visual images, the words labeling aural images are immediately susceptible to a different though related analysis, one in which every phoneme has its own individual role. As shown in the preceding sections, the class of words that could be taken to refer in some way to aural images constitutes a rather diverse set. For the first level of analysis here I will concentrate on forms that can appear in the syntactic context "*go*____(locative adverbial)," like those in (14).

(14) a. *go*____
    It goes ping.
    It went ping.
    It goes creak, creak.

   b. *go*____ + locative adverbial
    It went smack against the wall.
    It went wham on the floor.
    It went zip through the window.

I choose this set because it allows only wild forms, cf. the weirdness of *go rattle, *go groan, *?*go smash*. This means that if we restrict ourselves to forms that consist of tame phonology, they will be at the wild end of tame as forms, the fewest possible other conventions will apply, and we are less likely to run into competing pressures. I will call these forms *semi-wild*.

19.3.1. Semi-wild words

The most important set of distinctions made in the semi-wild segment of the vocabulary of aural images relates to aspects of the amplitude of the sound represented. We will treat the amplitude as consisting of an *onset*, a *decay*, and sometimes a *shoulder*. The onset is the initial rise in amplitude. The decay is the final fall in amplitude. Some sounds have as the final part of their initial rise a transition of some length between the onset and the decay that has a different slope from either. This distinct part of the amplitude rise I will call the shoulder. A sample graphic representation is laid out in (15). In the semi-wild forms, the phonological parts of words correspond to the amplitude envelope iconically. The initial consonant represents the onset. If there is a resonant clustered with the initial consonant, it represents the shoulder. The final consonant represents the decay.

(15)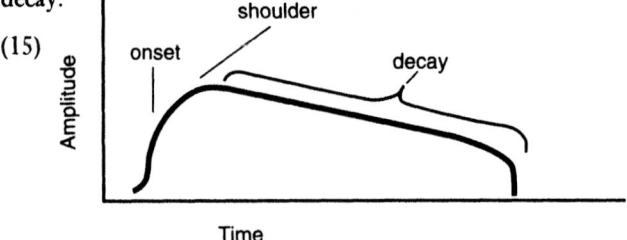

19.3.1.1. Onsets in semi-wild worlds

The assonances most widely used in the semi-wild sound vocabulary are exemplified in (16).

(16) a. abrupt onsets
    p-   *p*eep, *p*ing, *p*itter *p*atter, *p*op, *p*ow
    b-   *b*eep, *b*ang, *b*oing
    pl-   *pl*ink, *pl*op, *pl*unk
    kl-   *cl*ick, *cl*ank, *cl*ang, *cl*unk
    kr-   *cr*eak, *cr*ack, *cr*unch

b. irregular onset
    č-   *ch*irp, *ch*eep, *ch*itter *ch*atter

c. poorly resolvable onsets
    θ-   *th*wack, *th*ump, *th*unk, *th*ud
    W-   *wh*iz, *wh*ack, *wh*am, *wh*ap, *wh*osh
    z-   *z*ip, *z*ing, *z*ap, *z*ak, *z*ot, *z*oom

The assonances referring to images with abrupt onsets distinguish instantaneous-onset types, *p-*, *b-*, and *pl-*, from steep-onset types, *kl-* and *kr-*.[8] The single-consonant assonances, *p-* and *b-*, both representing instantaneous onsets, differ in that *b-* represents (relatively) loud sounds, while *p-* represents (relatively) small sounds, cf. *bang*, *beep* with *pop*, *peep*. *pl-* represents sounds which are both (relatively) small and have an instantaneous onset with a following shoulder, e.g. *plop*, *plink*. *kl-* and *kr-* are distinguished in that *kr-* has an irregular shoulder, cf. *clack* with *crack*. These distinctions are sketched in (17), where the amplitude curves are gross representations of the amplitude rise in the signified sounds. The *kl-* and *kr-* exist without a corresponding *k-* precisely because the angle of the onsets they represent entails the existence of a shoulder. On the other hand the vertical onsets that *p-* and *b-* represent may or may not have a shoulder, hence the contrast of *p-* vs. *pl-*.

(17)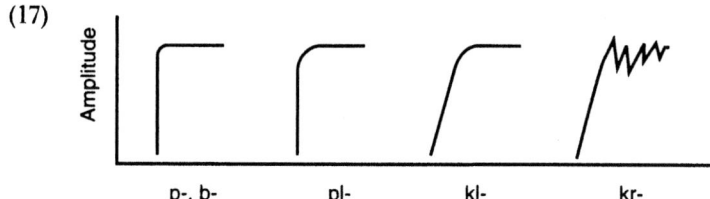

Signified sounds with onsets that are not monotonically increasing in amplitude we call *irregular*. *č-* represents sounds with irregular onsets, e.g. *chirp*.

The poorly resolvable onsets are hard to describe precisely because they are not readily resolvable by our aural apparatus. They are best described individually. *ð-* represents sounds with a class of slowly increasing onsets involving a burst of white noise, e.g. *thump*. Such sounds are generally described as "dull." *w-* or *ʍ-* (spelled *wh-*) represents sounds which arise through air turbulence, e.g. *whiz*. *z-* represents sounds which are, for want of a better term, the sound of speed; most frequently this includes both air turbulence and some additional component which is resolvable by the human aural apparatus, giving the impression of a white noise overlaid on a periodic component, i.e. a pitch, e.g. *zoom*.

There are a few additional onsets which have a preceding *s-*, *spl-*, *spr-*, *skr-*, and *sw-*. These all seem to refer to sounds that are acoustically complex, with a white noise component at onset, or have an initial small amplitude before the big jump.

(18)   *slash, splat, sproing, screech, scrunch, swish*

19.3.1.2. Vowels in semi-wild words

Vocalic nuclei mark several distinctions in the resonance of aural images. The neutral vowel seems to be *-æ-*. Forms containing *-æ-* are not semantically marked as referring to aural images that have high or low pitch, except by virtue of an opposition, as in (19b). Nor do they represent images that are either marked as loud or soft, except as other parts of these words entail loudness as in (19c).

(19)   a. *crack, smack, jangle, snap*
       b. (i) *clack* (cf. *click*)
          (ii) *clank* (cf. *clink* and *clunk*)
       c. *whap, bang*

Examples of *-æ-* stand as the unmarked member in sets which differ only in the nucleus. Forms with *-æ-* contrast with forms with *-ɪ-* on the one hand and with *-ən-* on the other.

(20)   a. *clink, clank, clunk*
       b. *jingle, jangle*
       c. *click, clack*

Forms with -ɪ- signify high-pitched and/or low-amplitude sounds. Generally they have a diminutive sense.

(21) a. *clink*   (from *clank* or *clunk*)
     b. *jingle* (from *jangle*)
     c. *click*   (from *clack*)
     d. *plink*   (from *plunk*)
     and possibly also
     e. *bing*   (from *bang*)

Forms with -*i*- signify high-pitched sounds unmarked for loudness.

(22) *peep, beep, creak, squeak, tweet, screech*

Forms with -ǝN-, as in (23), signify distinctively low-pitched sounds, while the few forms in -*a*- (Brit. -ɔ-), listed in (24), signify sounds that are distinctively not high-pitched.

(23) *clunk, plunk, thunk, thump, whump, (s)crunch*

(24) *pop, plop, whomp, bong, tick, tock, clip clip, ding dong*

What the difference is between the simple forms in -*a*- (Brit. -ɔ-) and those containing -*æ*- I do not know at the present time. In reduplications it looks like there are factors relating to the degree of wildness governing the choice. Comparing *jingle jangle*, *chitter chatter*, and *pitter patter* with *tick tock*, *clip clop*, and *ding dong*, the distinction seems to be that reduplications in -*a*- (Brit. -ɔ-) are semi-wild but reduplications in -*æ*- are tame. Unfortunately there are not sufficient numbers of forms to be able to tell for sure that this is not just a coincidence.

19.3.1.3. Decays in semi-wild words

The remaining part of the syllable is the final consonant. Final consonants refer to the decay of a sound. The final consonants of primary concern are -*p*, -*t*, -*č*, -*š*, -*k*, and -*ŋ*. They mark whether or not the decay is extended, and if it is irregular.

(25) a. extended decays
     -ŋ   di*ng*, cla*ng*, bo*ng*, ba*ng*
     -m   boo*m*, wha*m*, bla*m*
     -č   cru*nch*, scree*ch*
     -š   cra*sh*, spla*sh*, whoo*sh*

   b. abrupt decays
     -p   po*p*, plo*p*, thum*p*, wha*p*
     -t   twee*t*, zo*t*, spla*t*
     -k   cla*ck*, thwa*ck*, thun*k*, za*k*

284

English

The easiest of these to characterize is -ŋ. It represents an image with an extended decay. In contrast, -*m* represents an image with a slow, generally muffled decay. Of this pair -*m* is the marked form. It is associated with a relatively low-pitched sound, cf. *bang* vs. *boom*.

(26) a. pi*ng*, bi*ng*, di*ng*, ba*ng*, cla*ng*, boi*ng*, sproi*ng*, bo*ng*
    b. bla*m*, wha*m*, boo*m*, ka-ba*m*

This use of -*m* is probably also related to the tame initial *m*-, which has aural meanings of indistinctness and low pitch (27a) and visual meanings of indistinctness (27b).

(27) a. *m*umble, *m*utter, *m*urmur, *m*oan, *m*uffle
    b. *m*urk, *m*ist, *m*ess, *m*uddle

The -č and -š represents images with an extended irregular decay. The difference between -č and -š appears to be that the extension of the decay is greater with -š.

(28) a. crun*ch*, scrun*ch*, scree*ch*
    b. cra*sh*, sla*sh*, whoo*sh*

Final -*t* represents images that have a steep but not precipitous decay.

(29) twee*t*, zo*t*, spla*t*, bla*t*

Final -*p* and -*k* refer to images that have an instantaneous decay. As a first approximation, they differ in that -*p* is associated with "hollow" sounds, while -*k* is unmarked. This hollowness is probably associated with the pitch drop in the second formant that labials induce.

(30) a. wha*p*, thum*p*, po*p*
    b. wha*ck*, thun*k*, cla*ck*

After *i* or *ɪ* it is less clear what the difference is between -*p* and -*k*.

(31) a. chee*p*, bee*p*, zi*p*
    b. crea*k*, squea*k*, cli*ck*

19.3.2. Tame words

Let me conclude this preliminary overview of the vocabulary of aural images by taking a brief digression into some tamer forms. Because these forms are tamer, they are more difficult to explain completely, and have weirdnesses associated with them. For example, -*r*- is used as part of the assonance to represent an irregular shoulder, as we noted above. It also appears post-vocalically in an analogous meaning in at least one small group of semi-wild forms, *chirp* and its variants.

However, it appears initially in a number of tame forms which cannot be used semi-wildly with essentially the same meaning.

(32)　roar, roll, rumble, rattle

Furthermore the syllabic *-er* occurs in a number of tame forms in a meaning of irregularly varying amplitude over a (relatively) extended period of time. Of these there are a few referring to inanimately produced sounds, basically nouns, (33a) and a sizable group referring to vocal tract sounds, all verbs and all very tame, (33b).

(33)　a. clatter, chatter, patter
　　　b. chatter, twitter, stutter, blither, blubber, jabber, stammer, yammer

The syllabic *-er* contrasts in its representation of irregularly varying amplitude over time with the syllabic *-le*, which occurs in tame forms indicating a more or less constant amplitude over a (relatively) extended period of time.

(34)　jangle, jingle, rattle, sizzle, whistle, tinkle, etc.

These syllabic resonants, *-er* and *-le*, also occur in non-aural image vocabulary with distinct but probably related meanings. Both refer to actions or events which have some inherent plurality, either multiple actors or actions with multiple parts as exemplified in (35).

(35)　a. straggle, huddle, tumble, waddle
　　　b. hammer, flutter, tinker, putter (around), fritter (away)

This plurality is probably related to the continuous/extended part of the meaning of these syllables in the aural image vocabulary.

There is also a number of tame forms which seem only to have partial explanations in terms of aural images. Among the most interesting are those which consist of both visual and aural images, as in (36).

(36)　a. *bleep*　　(cf. *bl*oat, *bl*ob; b*eep*, ch*eep*)
　　　b. *drizzle*　(cf. *dr*ip, *dr*ain; s*izzle*, f*izzle*)
　　　c. *smack*　(cf. *sm*ash, *sm*ite; cr*ack*, wh*ack*)

While the rimes in the forms in (36) are aurally based, the assonances are visually based. The assonance *bl-* refers to things that are (over)full, *dr-* is a classifier for liquids, and *sm-* is one of a set of classifiers that refer to surfaces.

19.4.　Assonance-rime analysis

A comparison of the type of assonance-rime analysis proposed here and in R&L raises an interesting question in regard to the matter of sound symbolism. In this type of analysis based on some aspect of the sound-symbolic character of language,

English

or is it morphology, or is it something else again? There are proponents of all three positions. Most others who have concerned themselves with assonance-rime types of analysis have shied away from calling their analyses morphology and used other terms for their analytic units, like *phonestheme* (Bolinger 1950) and *submorpheme* (McCune 1985), suggesting that such approaches are neither sound symbolism nor morphology. In R&L we took the position that assonance-rime analysis is, in effect, derivational morphology. But with regard to the question of whether assonance-rime analysis is sound symbolism we have to distinguish two general lines of research the findings of which have been called sound symbolism.

One line of inquiry called sound symbolism treats the question of whether there exist iconic relations between the meanings of forms and phonological and/or articulatory aspects of those forms. The other line of inquiry called sound symbolism deals with regularities of relationships between forms and meanings that do not readily appear in traditional morphological analysis – what we are calling structured sound symbolism here.[9]

Given our current state of knowledge, most assonance-rime analysis is sound symbolism only in the sense of structured sound symbolism. While some (G. Lakoff, personal communication) hold out hope that there may ultimately be an articulatory basis for some of the semantic aspects of assonances and rimes, our current understanding of the material does not give us enough to go on yet. For example, the classifiers laid out in R&L are arbitrary in phonological content, at least synchronically. So the four classifiers for liquids, *dr-*, *sl-*, *fl-*, and *m-*, exemplified in (37), are distinct in many ways. They represent two of the three possible assonance types – single consonant and two-member cluster. They belong to two of the three major articulatory classes, sonorant and obstruent; they represent two of the four possible points of articulation, labial and apical; etc., etc.

(37) a. *dr-* (e.g. *dr*ip, *dr*ain, *dr*op, *dr*izzle)
 b. *sl-* (e.g. *sl*op, *sl*ush, *sl*urry, *sl*uice)
 c. *fl-* (e.g. *fl*ow, *fl*ush, *fl*ood, *fl*uid)
 d. *m-* (e.g. *m*ud, *m*ush, *m*ire, *m*arsh)

From these differences we conclude that there is no common phonetic feature which we can associate with the meaning of liquidness. Furthermore, *dr-* and *fl-* refer to motion properties of liquids, whereas *sl-* and *m-* refer to the consequences of the shapelessness of liquids, especially that they can be messy. Again there are no uniting phonetic features. And lastly there are no general acoustic properties associated with liquids that are reflected in any of these assonances.

It is only in the aural-image vocabulary that there is any provable iconicity in assonance-rime analysis, and I would argue that its iconicity is of a special type. The aural-image vocabulary refers to sound by using sounds. All other vocabulary refers to other classes of images – visually based, tactilely based, taste-based, and smell-based – synesthetically. In the aural-image vocabulary the iconic relationships are between acoustic events; the articulations required to achieve the acoustic events on the linguistic side are in some very important sense merely incidental. On the other hand to the extent that it exists, the iconicity in assonance-time analysis of non-aural vocabulary may be based on articulation or, more accurately, on the proprioception of articulation or in acoustics, but either way the iconic connection is synesthetic.

19.4.1. *The morphology question*

But what light does the vocabulary of aural images shed on the question of whether assonance-rime analysis is morphology or not? There are three kinds of evidence in this vocabulary that assonance-rime analysis is morphology. First there is evidence of a taxis in these words, second the evidence of combinability of assonances with rimes, and lastly the existence of morphologic processes operating on both assonances and rimes.

19.4.1.1. *Tactics*

There is no argument that English monosyllables are organized in accordance with a set of phonotactic constraints. But in R&L we argued that there were also semantico-syntactic constraints, such that rimes are the heads of constructions and assonances are subordinate, representing either modifiers or modifiers of arguments. In the aural-image vocabulary there is some evidence that this is true. The phonotactic constraints of English frequently require that forms referring to aural images of complex acoustic structure have the phonological material representing simultaneous parts of such aural images linearized. When this happens the "basic" part of the aural image is represented in the rime, while the "attendant" properties appear in the assonance. The basic part of a sound consists of the part which is most salient, often by virtue of its relative duration and/or amplitude. Attendant properties include onset, less salient properties, and decay. Of these attendant properties only decay is represented in the assonance, and that only for iconic reasons. Thus in forms like *buzz* the white noise represented by the *z* in the rime is the most salient part of the naturally occurring sound. In contrast, the *Star Wars* light saber, which has a complex acoustic structure consisting of a hum with white noise only when it moves, is represented in the *Star Wars* comics by forms like *zzzwit*. Here the attendant white noise over the hum is represented by a *z* in the assonance while the salient hum is represented by the vowel of the rime.[10] A similar kind of argument for a modifier-head taxis can be made for the forms with prefix extensions in (39) below.

The existence of a taxis is what is important. Since a taxis is a requirement for morphology, and is in fact the one most often pointed to as the reason why assonance-rime analysis cannot be morphology, the existence of a taxis governing forms of both the simple assonance-rime type and this semi-wild aural-image type constitutes a strong argument in favor of the position that assonance-rime analysis should simply be considered a special case of morphology.

19.4.1.2. Productivity

The next argument that assonance-rime analysis is morphology concerns the fact that assonances and rime never combine productively. Although we sometimes recognize that productivity is scalar, it is more generally treated as a matter of two extremes. Either a process is productive or it isn't. There is, however, a discernible midpoint on the scale – an intermediate level of combinatory possibility between productive and non-productive. Let me use the term *active*. A construction is productive if all or nearly all combinations of relevant morphemic units can combine up to the limits of semantic compatibility. In contrast, a construction is active if, of all the possible combinations of relevant morphemes, only a few are grammatical, but new instances of the construction can be formed. For example verb–object compounding was productive, particularly in the sixteenth century. Now it is active, giving rise to only occasional new forms, as suggested in (38).

(38) Surviving forms from   Forms of more recent origin
      the productive period

   cutthroat (1535)   *tattletale* (unlisted, *OED*;
   pickpocket (1591)   no date, *Webster's Third*)
   scarecrow (1592)   *killjoy* (1776)
   etc.

The point is that just because a construction is not productive doesn't mean that it is frozen. The assonance-rime combination never reaches the level of productivity. The most it can be is active. A quick glance through the etymologies of English monosyllables, most of which read "origin uncertain," "prob. akin to...," and the like, should convince one that monosyllables must be being innovated continuously, but at a slow rate. This is active combination. The reality of this is further underscored by the reinterpretation of forms of varied historical sources as new instances of assonances, e.g. the largely Germanic *sl-* liquid classifier (*sl*op, *sl*ush, *sl*urry, etc.) also includes the *sl-* in Latinate *sluice* (< Vulgar Latin *exclusa) and the largely Germanic *fl-* liquid classifier (*fl*ow, *fl*ush, *fl*ood, etc.) also includes the *fl-* in Latinate *fluid* (< L. fluidus). These assonances have the meanings they now do as part of a convention of modern English, regardless of the original source. The semi-wild aural image forms come as close to being productive as anything among monosyllables. Aural-image forms are made up quite freely by some speakers, although such forms generally enjoy only limited success. A small sample from Johnny Hart's *B.C.* is given in (39).

(39) *spl*ang "the sound of a type of forceful collision"
            (cf. *spl*at, *spl*ash; b*ang*, cl*ang*)
    *gr*onk   "the sound a dinosaur makes"
            (cf. *gr*owl, *gr*oan; h*onk*, b*onk*)
    *b*oink[11] "the sound of a small collision (with a rebound)"
            (cf. *b*ounce, *b*ump; spr*oing*; cl*ink*)

19.4.1.3. Process morphology

The last argument that assonance-rime analysis is morphology is that there exist processes which operate on the morphological units that appear in such analyses. Processes are substitutions for, or additions to, those units, or parts of those units, carrying a corresponding and systematic adjustment in meaning. The forms in (21) (repeated here as (40)) reflect a substitution of an *ɪ* for the vowel of the basic form with a corresponding adjustment of meaning.[12]

(40) a. *clink*   (from *clank* or *clunk*)
     b. *jingle* (from *jangle*)
     c. *click*   (from *clack*)
     d. *plink*   (from *plunk*)
     and possibly also
     e. *bing*   (from *bang*)

There is also a process on semi-wild forms that expands them with an initial *ka-* (or *ker-* before *s*, *pl*, and for some speakers, before *W*), meaning (approximately) "extra loud and/or acoustically complex."

(41) a. *pow*   *ka-pow*
        bang   *ka-bang*
        thump   *ka-thump*
     b. *splash* *ker-splash*
        smack   *ker-smack*
        plop   *ker-plop*

Thus it seems this type of sound symbolism, also known as phonesthematic or submorphemic analysis, while interesting in its own right, is really just a special case of derivational morphology.

NOTES

1 Note that these image schemata are *not* Peircean images. Images, in the sense that we are using the term here, are not only hierarchical but also recursive.

English

2 Treating visual perception as specially privileged is a mistake of the same sort as the assumption that writing is "real" language, i.e. what can be reduced to a tangible form is more real than what can't. What is missed by treating visual perception as specially privileged is that there is just as much figure and ground in the other modes of perception as there is in the visual (cf. Langacker 1987). For example, consider the background noise of daily life in an urban setting, or the crickets of a rural spring evening. When we talk over these noises they are one layer of ground against which our speech is a figure. And even within speech itself, voice quality stands as a perceptual ground against which contrastive material is a figure. And similarly for the other senses. Clothing provides the most common tactile ground. Brushing against something or stepping on something is commonly a tactile figure contrasting with this normally unperceived ground.

3 The analysis that lies behind (3) is a significant improvement over that presented in R&L for assonances referring to aural images.

4 Following the practice in R&L, I will treat disyllables with primary stress on the initial syllable and an unstressed final syllable as belonging to the same class as monosyllables, a class I will call *simplex words*. This is warranted for English because the only process known that distinguishes monosyllables from polysyllables, the comparative *-er* vs. *more*, treats this class of disyllables with the monosyllables, e.g. *happier*, *simpler*, *yellower*, but **naiver*, **inepter*, **chartreuser*.

5 Ojibwa is spelled with *h* representing /ʔ/ except in the combinations *ch*, *sh*, and *zh*, which are palatals, and in word final *nh* which represents nasalization of the preceding vowel.

6 Zoque is spelled in a system with Spanish conventions. *J* represents /h/; *qu* represents /k/ before /i/ or /e/; and ' represents /ʔ/.

7 The unusual symbols used here are $\overset{\vee}{v}$ to represent a laryngealized vocoid, $\underset{\vee}{v}$ to represent a pharyngealized vocoid or sonorant, $v\bot$ to represent a raised vocoid, and superscript numbers to represent pitch contours with 5 representing a low pitch ca. in the middle of the second octave below middle C and 1 representing a high pitch ca. middle C.

8 It may not be immediately obvious why *pl-* differs from *kl-* and *kr-* in the rate of increase in amplitude. But consider that *k-* in aspirated positions is regularly a near affricate [k^{xh}] while *p-* in the same positions is always a simple aspirate [p^h].

9 It is completely possible, and even likely, that the question is not black and white, but rather that there are degrees of iconicity between the articulatory content of a form and its meaning. In the synchronic analysis of single languages the degree of this type of iconicity is generally very low. But it is likely that there do exist quite subtle iconic pressures toward associating certain types of images with certain types of articulations – pressures of a strength that can easily be washed out by sound change, borrowing, or other incidental factors. If this is the case that these factors can only be seen as statistical tendencies over large bodies of data extending over time and across unrelated languages. Attempts to explore very remote relationships among languages must take into account the possibility of such a factor.

10 Cf. the discussion of the onset *z-* in (16c) above.

11 Of course, this word has now been taken over in another meaning due to its use in the recently popular TV series *Moonlighting* as a euphemism for the *f*-word. Although I don't want to be too explicit here, I would not rule out the possibility that this word was chosen for this euphemistic use on sound-symbolic grounds.

12 The same process operates on forms based on visual images yielding diminutives (R&L, p. 335). There are other processes operating in visual image forms (but only rarely in aural image forms) that were not noticed in R&L. For example, there is a process that flips the voicing of obstruents in assonances, yielding a semantically specialized version of the assonance. This is the reason why some of the assonances in (1) and (2) are given in voicing pairs. Consider the path classifier *p-/b-*. The voiceless version (*p*ush, *p*ull, *p*op [in/out/up], *p*ounce, *p*oke, *et al.*) refers to paths with respect to one end-point. The voiced variant (*b*ump, *b*ound, *b*ounce, *b*ob, *et al.*) refers to paths that are (or appear to be) rebounding.

REFERENCES

Bolinger, D. 1950. Rime, assonance, and morpheme analysis. *Word* 6: 117–136.
Langacker, R. 1987. *The Foundations of Cognitive Grammar*, Vol. 1. Stanford: University Press.
McCune, K. 1985. *The Internal Structure of Indonesian Roots*. Badan Penyelenggara Seri Nusa, Universitas Katolik Indonesia Atma Jaya.
Reddy, M. 1979. The conduit metaphor. In A. Ortony (ed.) *Metaphor and Thought*. Cambridge: University Press.
Rhodes, R. A. and J. M. Lawler. 1981. Athematic metaphors. *Chicago Linguistic Society* 17: 318–342.
Whorf, B. L. 1940. Gestalt technique of stem composition in Shawnee. In Carl F. Voeglin (ed.) *Shawnee stems and the Jacob P. Dunn Miami Dictionary*. Indiana Historical Society Prehistory Research Series 1: 393–406. Indianapolis.

20
Inanimate imitatives in English

ROBERT L. OSWALT

20.1. Introduction

There is in English an indistinctly delineated class of words described variously as onomatopoeic, echoic, and imitative. As used here, an *imitative* is a word based on an approximation of some non-linguistic sound but adapted to the phonemic system of the language. If the modeled sound is one produced vocally by an animate creature – human, mammal, bird – the adapted form, as a working procedure, is classified as an *animate imitative* (abbreviated AI); if the sound is emitted by an inanimate object (although often through manipulation by some animate creature) then it is an *inanimate imitative* (abbreviated II). A third related class, concerned mainly with the expression of emotional states and attitudes, is the *exclamation* (abbreviated EI for *exclamatory interjection*). In certain of their syntactically detached uses, dictionaries refer to all three of these semantic classes as *interjections*.

20.1.1. *Sources of data*

Comic strips. Examples of IIs, AIs, and EIs have been systematically clipped from comic strips on a daily basis, out of from one to three different newspapers, over the period 1978–1990. What is found from these sources is a mixture of words in different stages of acceptance: idiosyncratic innovations used only by their individual creators; innovations whose use has spread to several comic strips; forms which may be common in colloquial speech but which are not in standard dictionaries; and standard words contained in standard dictionaries. The meanings of these comic-strip occurrences have been inferred from the situations in which they are pictured.

Dictionaries. Each form discussed in this paper has been checked in the Oxford English Dictionary (OED) for citation therein, for definition, and for history. Since the first draft of this paper was written in 1986, the second edition of the Oxford

English Dictionary (OED2) has appeared, with expanded coverage of imitatives, and revisions have been made herein to include the new citations most germane to the present discussion (especially in sections 20.9.1–20.9.3). These and other dictionaries also contain a mixture of named types – standard, colloquial, dialectal, archaic, obsolete – including many pertinent forms other than those which show up in the comic strips.

Miscellaneous sources. Less intensively collected are forms from a wide variety of other sources, written and spoken (radio, TV, conversations).

20.1.2. Scope

There is no way a short article could account for all the facts in such a large and diverse mass of data; consequently, the coverage here is focused on the class II and, within that, on monosyllables adapted to the phonological system of English. The distinction is the same as that imparted by Rhodes's metaphors "wild" and "tame" (this volume). Thus vowelless forms like *phzz*, *hmm*, and *bzz* are too wild for present consideration, but related forms like *fizz*, *hum*, and *buzz* are tamed enough; semi-wild *pting*, with an unEnglish cluster, sometimes appears tamed as *piting* or *pating* (accent undoubtedly to be read onto the second syllable) "sound of a ricocheting bullet," in which form it is classifiable as a disyllable and given only passing mention herein. Polysyllables, whether arising by vowel insertion, as with *pating*, or by some other process – *splish splash*, *splishety splash*, *ka-* (or *ker-*) *splash* – are excluded from systematic treatment herein, although deserving of more comprehensive treatment in some other exposition. If it were not for these restrictions on the scope, the number of forms to be accounted for would be unmanageable for the present, being limited only by the imaginations of the most imaginative writers.

As for the monosyllables, the various descriptive statements – phonological, semantic, grammatical, and historical – are not meant to be complete and airtight; they are a sampling of salient features of the II system revealed by the data. Although the analysis has been influenced by forms of all types, examples are in general restricted to dictionary standards and comic-strip forms that I judge to be in very wide colloquial use. Occasionally idiosyncratic creations or obsolete or dialectal forms are used to illustrate special points (such as exceptions to the general statements).

20.2. Phonology

Although the separation of the class II from the classes AI and EI has been made on semantic grounds, that separation has helped reveal several striking phonological correlates. In the IIs, there is a notable differentiation in the distribution of two classes of consonants: *obstruents* (stops, affricates, fricatives) and *resonants* (nasals *m*, *n*, *ng*; liquids *l*, *r*; glides *w*, *y*).

English

Transcription. In the main, ordinary English orthography is employed and it is assumed that most readers will recognize that, for example, *ph, th, ch,* and *sh* and syllable-final *tch, ck, ff, ss, zz,* and *ng* represent single consonants; *wh-* is to be taken as a sequence of fricative *h-* plus *-w-*; and that English vowel graphemes may have different values depending upon the graphemic environment. When the orthography is inadequate for the discussion, there will be a phonemic or phonetic representation (based on my own pronunciation but in accord, I believe, with that of the majority of American English speakers).

20.2.1. Canon

In general, the minimum canon for monosyllabic IIs appears to be C_1VC_2, that is, a single vowel bounded fore and aft by single consonants: *tap, tick, pop, buzz*. In contrast, some of the commonest EIs are lone vowels or vowels accompanied by one consonant: *ah, oh, eh, ugh, bah*. AIs with one consonant are also common: *baa, caw*.

As for the IIs, the corpus contains none consisting of a vowel alone, and extremely few missing C_1 or C_2.

The maximum canon is $(s)C_1(R_1)V(V)(R_2)C_2$, where R stands for Resonant and parentheses indicate that a particular slot need not be filled. Two modifications can be made to a comparison with the overall phonotactic system of English. First, the great bulk of the IIs are actually confined to a subset of the overall system, and these will be discussed in sections 20.2.2 to 20.2.4. Second, there are widely used colloquial IIs containing limited extensions of the permissible sequences beyond what occur in the regular vocabulary, and these, as they yield derivative nouns and verbs, bring about adjustments in the system (discussed in sections 20.6 and 20.9.1–20.9.3).

20.2.2. Prevocalic canon, $(s)C_1(R_1)$-.

C_1 is an obstruent, not normally a resonant: *pop, tap, tick, thump, zing*. This distribution contrasts with the EIs and AIs of creatures with a vocal apparatus, which often begin with a resonant. EI: *rah, wow, yi;* AI: *meow, moo, rowr, woof, yip*. Occasionally aberrant IIs with the resonant *w-* in the C_1 position have developed from a sound change, in the speech of many, by which the fricative *h* is lost from the initial *wh-: whack > wack, whoosh > woosh*. Other exceptions are quite rare and idiosyncratic; for example, in animated cartoons, the Roadrunner's rendition of *beep* "short sound from a small (automobile) horn" is *meep*. In this case, the use of the resonant *m-* rather than *b-* may be an attempt, conscious or unconscious, to indicate that the sound is made by an animate character.

R_1 is a resonant that may show up between C_1 and V; it is commonly *w, l,* or *r*: *wham, clack, creak*. There are no examples with *y* and nasals are rare, occurring only after *s-*: *smack*, *snap*. The one consonant to precede an obstruent C_1 is *s-*, and then only when C_1 is a stop. Three-consonant clusters are restricted to those beginning with *s-*: *splash*, *sproing*, *screech*, *squeak*.

20.2.3. Postvocalic canon, -(R_2)C_2.

In contrast to the limitation on C_1, C_2 can be either an obstruent or a resonant, although there are certain restrictions. Obstruents are common: *bop*, *splat*, *whiff*, *whiz*. The resonants *n* and *l* do not occur as C_2, but *m*, *ng*, and *r* are common: *bam*, *bang*, *whirr*.

Whether the glides, *w* and *y*, occur as C_2 depends on the analysis. For example, an uncommon form like *fwee* "sound produced with a whistle" could be analyzed as [*fwiy*], ending in *-y*. (Cf. section 20.2.4.) Otherwise *fwee* stands as one of the rare examples with missing C_2. For whistles that tail off, without a sudden cessation, the unstopped imitative *fwee* would seem more iconic; for whistles with a sudden termination, the following, more widespread, IIs are more suitable: *fweet*, *fweep*, *tweet*. Such sounds produced by musical instruments lie in some ways on a fuzzy borderline between animate and inanimate.

R_2 usually appears only when C_2 is a stop or affricate, and then it is commonly a nasal which must be homorganic with C_2: *thump*, *crunch*, *thunk* (with the orthographic *n* representing nasals homorganic to the following consonants, palatal and velar). Interestingly, there are no IIs in this corpus with an ending containing an alveolar nasal, either *-nt* or *-n*.

An alternative representation of the post-vocalic segment could be -C_2(S_2), where S_2 is a stop that can appear only when C_2 is a resonant, most commonly a nasal, and then nasal and S_2 must be homorganic. The choice between these two analyses, -(R_2)C_2 or -C_2(S_2) is the same as the choice of deriving *clank* from *clack* by infixing the nasal or deriving *clank* from *clang* by suffixing *-k*. I do not favor one interpretation over the other for all situations.

In R_2 position, *r* is much less common: *splork*.

20.2.4. Vocalic nucleus, -V(V)-.

The vocalic nucleus can be simple, symbolized with a single V, and consist of one vowel (traditionally called short); or be complex, with the second slot of V(V) filled, and consist of a vowel cluster or diphthong. The full range of English vowels does not appear in IIs. For the simple vocalic nuclei there is a definite proclivity (not apparent in EIs and AIs) toward a small contrasting set of only four vowels, which are charted in (1) with orthographic symbols accompanied in square brackets by other representations. Examples are *clink*, *clank*, *clunk*, *bop*.

English

(1) *Simple V*

i[I]	u[ə]
a[æ]	o[a]

(2) *Complex VV*

ee	oo
[i, ii, iː, iy]	[u, uu, uː, uw]
oi	
[oi, oy]	

Noteworthy is the absence of the mid front vowel [e]. The mid back rounded vowel [ɔ] is also absent, with certain qualifications. When R_1 is [w], orthographic *a* and *o* may vary dialectally between [a] and [ɔ]: *whap* = *whop* = [hwap] ~ [hwɔp]. Before the velar nasal, *o* is also somewhat raised and rounded by many speakers: *bong* [bɔŋ]. In Britain, short orthographic *o* is quite generally pronounced [ɔ], retaining a rounded vowel from the past in those situations in which North American dialects have shifted the pronunciation to [a]. However, whatever these dialectal variations, there is no contrast within the II system between [a] and [ɔ], although there may be such a contrast in the non-II vocabulary.

There is also a definite proclivity toward a small number of complex nuclei, or diphthongs, each neatly represented orthographically by two letters (see (2)). Only *ee* (or *ea*) and *oo* are common in standard dictionary IIs: *beep, creak, boom*. A nucleus *oi* is becoming common colloquially in an expanding number of forms, but has not yet been accepted into most dictionaries: *boing, boink, poit* (see sections 20.9.1–20.9.3). A fourth diphthongal possibility is of quite restricted use: *pow*.

There are a number of possible analyses of the complex nuclei, each with certain consequences for the statements on the canon. Orthographic *-ee-, -oo-*, and *-oi-* can be taken as clusters of two vowels *-ii-, -uu-, -oi-*; or as nuclei consisting of a vowel plus a glide *-iy-, -uw-, -oy-*; or as simple nuclei with glides as consonants in either R_2 or C_2 positions *-i-y, -u-w, -o-y*. No one analysis fits all IIs best; the various pros and cons will not be gone into here (cf. section 20.9.1) and henceforth most examples will be cited in the perfectly adequate orthographic system, which, it might be noted, is essentially the vowel-cluster analysis.

20.3. Symbolism of the obstruents

20.3.1. Stops

Being themselves short abrupt sounds, stops represent, when they appear in C_1 and C_2 positions, short abrupt sounds and actions: *bop, pop, tap, tick*.

20.3.2. Fricatives

Being sounds produced by friction or air turbulence in the vocal tract, fricatives represent similar sounds of abrasion or air turbulence produced in or out of that tract.

Certain words have the form hVC_2. These words have the h symbolic meaning carried entirely by C_2 and have been created with h as C_1 (evidently because h has no strongly marked symbolic meaning) plus a vowel (all examples are with orthographic *i* or *u*), both arising solely to bring the word into the minimum form C_1VC_2. As nouns they basically mean the "sound of C_2"; as verbs, "to emit, or cause to emit, the sound C_2." However, several of the C_2s exemplified below are also prominent as EIs, and their meanings as such may dominate in the derivatives. Some designate sounds made by animate beings, but also similar sounds emitted by inanimate objects:

Hiss is a word for "the sound *s*," or "a sound like *s*, from gas or vapor forced through a constriction (tongue and alveolar ridge, throat of goose or snake, nozzle), or from hot iron plunged into water." And, since a long *s*, as an EI, is an expression of disapproval, *hiss* is a noun and a verb for the expression of disapproval by such means.

Hush is a word for "the sound *sh*"; since *sh* is an EI calling for silence, *hush* easily becomes a transitive verb "make quiet" or intransitive "become quiet." As a noun, by such a route, it ends up at a pole opposite from the denotation of a specific sound, namely no sound at all, "silence."

Hum can be noted here to show that this type of formation is not restricted to fricatives in C_2 position. *Hum* is basically a word for "the sound *m*," but as an AI it is expanded to include "using the voice, or singing, with the mouth closed" and, as an II, a similar "sound of a wire vibrating in the wind" or "sound of machinery running quietly and smoothly."

Other words of this shape are *huff* and the obsolete or dialectal *hish, hizz, huss, huzz* (cited and defined in the OED).

There also are related forms of similar meaning with $C_1 = C_2$: *shush* is nearly synonymous with *hush* but is more closely restricted in meaning to "to call for silence with a *sh*," without the semantic extensions of *hush*. Other similar constructions are *siss, sussing, shish* (definitions are in the OED).

With other fricatives, there are *fizz* "sound of small gas bubbles escaping through a liquid" and *sizz* (related to *sizzle*) and a number of forms with *-w-* as R_1 (see 20.4.1 below).

These two types of symbols, stops and fricatives, can be mixed in a single II, one as C_1, the other as C_2. If the stop is at the beginning, the sound and action have an abrupt beginning and a frictional end: *puff* (cf. *huff*), *poof, plash*. If the fricative is at the beginning, then the sound and action have a frictional onset and abrupt end (illustrated in section 20.5.).

20.4. Symbolism of R_1

In general, one might say that continuants represent continuing sounds. As for resonants representing resonance, that appears clearly true only for nasals after the nucleus (sections 20.9.1–20.9.2), not before. In R_1 position it is difficult to find a

English

meaning for most resonants isolable from their combinations with specific accompanying obstruents. One possibility is -*w*- after fricatives (to be distinguished from -*w*- after stops, section 20.9.1).

20.4.1. *w*

As R₁, -*w*- appears to intensify the meaning of a preceding fricative so that, instead of a sound of simple movement of air, the interpretation often shifts to the sound of strong swift movement through air.

The effect can be illustrated by the pair *hizz* and *whiz(z)*. One might say that *whiz* [hwɪz] has been derived from *hizz* by the infixation of -*w*-, but the evidence is not totally clearcut. Both have a history (OED) of 400 years of application to approximately the same set and variety of situations. Both, starting in the sixteenth century, have been employed for the sound of bullets and shot, *hizz*ing and *whizz*ing. More recently *hizz* has faded from contention and one might postulate that the triumph of *whiz* is due to its being symbolically more potent. In other applications, *hizz* has succumbed to *hiss*. Homophony with the common pronoun *his* might also have inhibited the use of *hizz*, although the effect could not have been strong, because of the quite different syntactic roles. (A similar possible derivation of *thwack* from *thack* is discussed in section 20.5 below.) Other forms of the shape F*w*V(V)F also symbolize the sound and action of rapid movement through air (along with various semantic developments): *swish, swoosh, whish, whoosh*.

One explanation for the augmenting value of -*w*- is that, in addition to the constriction at the point of articulation of the fricative, the pursing of the lips for the -*w*- creates an additional constriction to the airflow, increasing the velocity and thus the turbulence of the stream of air and giving thereby a stronger representation of the sound (Ohala 1983). Though *wh*- [hw], *thw*-, *sw*-, *shw*-, and *fw*- are written as sequences, the pursing of the lip for the -*w*- actually overlaps with the constriction for the voiceless fricative.

A second explanation is that the insertion of the -*w*- creates a transition between the fricative, with its sound of low frequency and low amplitude, and the following vowel with its sound of higher frequency and amplitude. This transition could represent the rapidly increasing amplitude in the sound of an arrow approaching the ear or the rising frequency of the sound from an accelerating swing of a stick.[1]

20.5. Mixed obstruents

I shall now present and discuss in more detail a set with two different types of obstruents in C_1 and C_2 positions:

Fricative + *w* + Vowel + Stop.
whack = *thwack* = *swack* = *shwack* = *fwack*

To me each of these forms denotes, as an imitative, substantially the same sound, one that follows directly from its constituent symbolic elements:

(3) C_1 Fricative Sound of movement of air, or of some object through air (or of friction between two objects in some other cases).
R_1 -w- Intensifies the effect of the fricative by increasing the velocity of the airstream and by providing a transitional glide between fricative and vowel.
V -a- Has no salient meaning, but since -i- would tend to indicate smaller or lighter, -a- is less small. There is some evidence that -a- favors an interpretation of the sound of a musical instrument as flat.
C_2 Stop Abrupt termination of the sound and movement.

Together the elements represent two sounds: an object moving swiftly and forcefully through the air, and that movement stopped abruptly and loudly by striking something; hence the sum meaning "the sound of a resounding blow."

Forms with each of the five initial fricatives occur in comic strips many times and with many different authors; only the first three are included in the OED. The words are arranged in an impressionistic order of frequency of occurrence – impressionistic because actual counts would not be completely meaningful; *whack* shows up so often, several times as frequently as the other four combined, that I quit collecting samples of it. Connotational differences arise from these differences in frequency, and from differences in the usage of derivative nouns and verbs.

The ages of the three forms in the OED are in inverse order to their present-day frequency: *swack* with first citation in 1375, *thwack* 1530, *whack* 1719. There is more substantiation than with the pair *hizz-whiz(z)* (section 20.4.1) for a hypothesis that *thwack* is derived from *thack*. The simpler form is much the older, with citations going all the way back to 897 AD as *thaccian* "to clap, slap" and continuing through Chaucer up to the present. The two, *thack* and *thwack*, have coexisted for centuries, with *thwack* gaining ascendancy in the meaning "sound of a resounding blow," for the reason, one would surmise, that the sound of the word is more appropriate to its meaning. The entry in the OED for *thwack* suggests in fact that it "may have been altered from the earlier *thack* ... the initial *thw*- expressing more forcible effort than *th*-." And the OED entry for *whack* suggests that it, in turn, was perhaps created as an alteration of *thwack*. One might add to the latter speculation that the existence of the verb *hack* "to chop or cut crudely" could also have contributed to the rise of *whack*.

20.6. Expansion of the canon

Of interest also are the two recent creations *shwack* and *fwack* because they participate in filling what is close to being a "hole" in the pattern of initial fricatives plus *-w-*. *Shw-* itself is already somewhat accepted into the language through the loanword *schwa* and family names from German: *Schwab, Schwartz*, etc. Innovations like *shwack* and *shwoosh*, as they become widely accepted as nouns and verbs, will help solidify the new cluster in everyday vocabulary.

Labials plus *-w-* seem rarer than the above, but with them too there is a sprinkling of words, mainly proper nouns, beginning so: *Fuentes, Puerto Rico, pueblo, bwana*. An additional impetus to the inclusion of all voiceless fricatives plus *-w-* as permissible initial clusters would here again appear to be coming from IIs with the development of the forms with *fw-*: *fwack, fwop, fwoosh*.

A possible explanation of a "need" for such innovations is the following. In many English speech communities, *wh-* has lost the *h*, so that common IIs like *whack* and *whoosh* have come to be pronounced *wack* and *woosh*. Some users of these forms without an initial fricative may feel the weakening in symbolic force so much that they create, perhaps unconsciously, a new form with an initial fricative, *f-*; one might almost say recreate, as *fw-* is so similar acoustically to *wh-*: *whack* > *wack* > *fwack*.

In order to check this hypothesis, I wrote to twelve of the comic strip creators who use forms beginning *fw-*, and received eleven replies. The question, "Do you pronounce *which* and *witch* the same?" and "*whale* and *wail* the same?" revealed that to ten of the eleven these were in fact pairs of homophones and pronounced without the *h*. A question such as, "Why did you use *fwack* instead of *whack* in [a specific strip and scene]?" typically led to such unspecific answers as, "Because it is more like the sound I had in mind." The eleventh reply was the most revealing. Although Bruce Hammond, the creator of "Duffy" and "Orbit," distinguishes *wh-* and *w-* in his own speech, when he had used *WHOP* in the ideophonic way of comic strips, he had received many complaints that he was employing an ethnic slur for Italians. That is, a substantial body of readers not only say and hear *whop* as *wop*, they also see the two forms as the same. Consequently, the author consciously avoids *whop*, substituting *fwop* (or *phwop*) as its equivalent in sound symbolism but without the racial associations.

On occasion a form from a dialect with *w-* derived from *wh-* might be borrowed into a dialect preserving the distinction. This explains the doublets *whacky* and *wacky* in the meaning "eccentric, irrational," and *whacko* and *wacko* "irrational person." The variants without the *h* can exist as the favored forms, even in the speech of those retaining the *h*, as the meaning is so divergent from the source in "sound of a blow" that there is no motivation to restore the fricative. But for meanings closer to the imitative origin, the spelling *whack* is overwhelmingly more common than *wack*.

20.7. Syntactic uses of IIs

The most elemental use of an II appears to be as a representation of a sound. As such it appears in certain syntactic contexts; even the wilder unadapted onomatopoeic forms can appear in the first three situations below (1, 2, 3). The tamed English IIs can also always be employed, unchanged in form by any affix or derivational process, as nouns and verbs (4, 5).

(1) One elemental use is as the object of a verb of saying, marking a direct quotation. In modern English the verb is usually *go*: "The cork went *pop*." The OED calls this use "adverbial," taking *pop* as descriptive of the manner in which the cork was going. In older periods of the language, *cry* was also common: "The cork cried *pop*." A less assimilated form is "The cork went *p'*" (substituting a glottalized *p'* or other close imitation of a popping sound).

(2) Related to this use is one that the OED classifies as interjectional or adverbial, but *ideophonic* would be more indicative: it is similar to the use of ideophones in African languages in that it portrays an idea by sound: "Our eyes met. *Zing!* Cupid!" (from a 1985 radio commercial). Here, the noun "Cupid" is pulled out of its normal syntactic trappings, but is the agent of an implied verb "cause to fall in love." *Zing!* is an ideophone, which one might take to represent the sound of Cupid's arrow through the air, or of the plucked bowstring, or perhaps one of the speaker's heartstrings – whichever case, love comes quick as a shot.

(3) We might also consider *graphic ideophones*. In comic strips, the most common practice of all is the printing of IIs (and other forms to be taken ideophonically), across or between frames of pictures. Thus one frame can depict a woman holding a club overhead and a snake on the ground in front of her; the next, the snake mashed. In between, in bold vertically stacked letters, the word *SWACK*. The size of the letters expresses the loudness of the sound and the force of the blow.

(4) An II may always be used as a noun designating the sound: "The *whack* at the door woke me up".

(5) An II may also always be used as a verb, either intransitive "to emit the sound," or transitive "to cause some object to emit the sound," or both: "The bell is *clang*ing. Someone is *clang*ing the bell."

Some IIs tend to yield mainly transitive verbs or mainly intransitive verbs, but no firm class distinction can be made. Thus members of the *whack* series seem, to me, principally transitive: "He *whack*ed the board against the house." But intransitive uses are possible: "The shutters were *whack*ing in the wind."

20.8. Semantic expansion

Once the basic noun and verb derivatives have come into existence, it is very easy for them to undergo semantic extensions and shifts, often in unpredictable leaps.

The first extension, and one taken by most noun IIs, is as a designation of an action that may produce the sound, but the sound is not central to the meaning: "The *whack* set the child to crying." (It was the blow and not the sound that hurt

English

the child.) The corresponding extension for a verb would be "to do the action that causes the sound": "The mother *whack*ed the child."

This usage grades into actions taken as similar to the above, although not necessarily involving any sound at all; and there is a tendency, not totally carried through, for IIs of similar canon to assume the same semantic amplifications. Thus there are many words beginning with a fricative and ending with a stop that mean "give a resounding blow to" and, derivatively, "defeat decisively (in a serious struggle, or in a casual game)," and many of these have been attested in English for centuries: *whack, thwack, swack, whap, whop, thump, whump, whomp*, etc. A similar extension also occurs with forms more separated from any II origin: *whip, slap, smack, swat*; as well as with the more general verb *beat* "hit repeatedly; defeat; etc."

Perhaps originating in the above are verbal derivatives implying a verb meaning "to be huge or abnormally large." ("To defeat" involves being "stronger" or "bigger.") Thus *whack*ing, *thwack*ing, *thump*ing, and *whopp*ing mean "huge"; and *whack*er, *thwack*er, *thump*er, and *whopp*er mean "something huge." As a further extension in this direction, probably as a reduction from phrases like *thump*ing lie, *whack*er, *thwack*er, *thump*er, and *whopp*er also mean "a big lie, a tall tale" (and this too has been true for centuries).

In another direction, *whack* and *thwack*, as verbs (often with the particle *up*) mean "to divide into portions"; and as nouns, "portion" (and again this use is centuries old). A nominal derivative *whack*-up means "the event where a division was made (of booty, etc.)."

There may be leaps into more distant semantic fields: to have a *whack* at "to have a try at," out of *whack* "out of order," *whack* off "masturbate," *whack*ed "exhausted," and *whack*y "irrational" (see the discussion at the end of section 20.6).

20.9. Resonance and *-oi-*

In C₂ position, nasals often symbolize resonance. In this position, alveolar *n* is not used, *m* tends to represent loud sounds that may reverberate, and *-ng* is the commonest choice for ringing sounds: *boom, bam, bong, clang, ding*. In contrast to the more ancient developments set forth for the *whack*-series, I shall now describe a development of the present.

20.9.1. The velar nasal

The velar nasal provides one setting for a nucleus *-oi-* in a rapidly proliferating set of forms. The first creation with the specific termination *-oing* appears to be *boing*, prototypically "sound of a compressed spring suddenly expanding and oscillating with gradual diminution of the sound and movement." Semantic extensions include "bounding around (on a pogo stick)" and "hopping (like a rabbit)." Animated cartoons have had a lot to do with the popularization of *boing*. Its use was perhaps solidified by the production in 1951 of the first of a series of animated cartoons featuring a boy, Gerald Mc*Boing-Boing* (a Dr. Seuss cartoon). who could speak only in sound effects like *boing boing*.

When spoken, there can be shifts in the prominence given the two parts of the vocalic nucleus between *bóing* and *boíng* and all the way to *bwang*. In comic strips, many intermediate written forms are attested (accents are supplied): *bóing ~ boíng ~ bawíng ~ bawáng ~ bwáng*. Note that the *-w-* of *bwang*, although it is in R_1 position, behaves like part of a complex vocalic nucleus with an oscillating peak, in contrast to the *-w-* that follows a fricative (sections 20.4, 20.5). A concept of continued vibration is brought out iconically in wilder forms by lengthening the nasal or repeating parts of the vocalic nucleus: *boinnnng, boiiiing, boioioing, bawawawawang*. And a gradual diminution of the vibration is often indicated by pronouncing these stretched forms decrescendo.

The termination *-oing* appears with many different initials, with the full forms having symbolic meanings of "resonance, vibration, oscillation, undulation, pulsation, elasticity, recoil, spring, bounce." Attested in comic strips and colloquial writings and speech are *boing, bloing, choing, doing, foing, poing, shtoing, skoing, sproing, toing,* and *zoing*. Of these, none is in the OED, and only *boing* makes an appearance in OED2, with an earliest date of 1952 in the wilder stretched form *boi-i-ing*.

Certain of the forms with different initial consonants tend to specialize semantically. While forms in *b-* (and the less common *d-*) are more concerned with longitudinal vibrations, those in *t- – toing ~ tawing ~ tawang ~ twang* – are more concerned with transverse vibrations (of a plucked string, or vibrating fork) and this is especially true of its very common, everyday alternant *twang*, which has a long history (earliest attestation 1553) with many semantic developments (see under *twang* in the OED).

20.9.2. *Velar nasal plus homorganic voiceless stop*

This symbolizes a resonating sound cut short: *bonk, clank, clunk, clink*. Attested forms terminating in *-oink* are *boink, doink, foink, goink, koink, poink, sproink,* and *toink*. The meaning of "dampened or shortened oscillation" converts easily to "act of shortened duration" and "act of lessened importance," and *boink* can thus refer to a single bounce rather a series.

Boink also provides an example of how quickly new semantic applications can arise and spread. In the winter of 1985–1986, on two different TV shows (*Moonlighting* and *Cheers*), the word was used in a sense that never appears in comic strips: "perform the sex act in a quick and casual manner." The meaning development is easily understood, and there was in fact a rather lengthy discussion

English

on the show *Moonlighting* in which the woman decries the man's reducing the act of human procreation to a mere *boink*.

In the meantime, there has been in Great Britain a comparable development in which the term *bonk* (a shortened *bong*) takes on, in addition to its other meanings – a frequent one is "blow to the head" – the new meaning "have sexual intercourse (with)," of common use in British tabloids in the 1980s (with earliest attestation in OED2 of 1975). *Boink* and *Bonk* themselves join earlier crude slang uses of IIs ending in nasals for the sex act: *bang* (OED2 1937) and *wham-bam* (OED2 1956).

20.9.3. Phonotactic constraints

Whether *-oink* (and *-oing*) really break old phonotactic limits depends upon how tightly those limits are defined. If the permissible sequence is presented as *oi* + Nasal + Stop (homorganic) then it can be seen to have been well established in the language for many centuries for the alveolar position (*point, joint, anoint*), although the sequence *-oint* does not appear in IIs (the absence of -nt and -n was commented on in section 20.2.3). The velar sequence *-oink* was little used until the past few decades, but would not be felt by native speakers to be strongly prohibited or "impossible to pronounce." In fact, for generations most English speakers have learned *oink* "sound of a pig" as very young children from nursery tales and rimes and are thus predisposed to accept unhesitatingly words with *-oink*. Curiously, in spite of this, the AI *oink* is not in the OED, appearing first in OED2 with an earliest data of only 1969. The parallel labial sequence *-oimp* would have a little harder time in gaining acceptance because there does not now exist a predisposing word, nursery or otherwise.

20.10. Summary

This exposition has dealt with a sampling of the Inanimate Imitatives of English, some arising in the distant past, some coming into being now. In the process of becoming established as IIs, they tend strongly to be confined within certain unexpected phonotactic limits and yet, on occasion, can help bring about a realignment of these boundaries and those of the language as a whole. As nouns and verbs, they often undergo semantic extensions and leaps, resulting in the enrichment of the wordstock of the language.

NOTE

1 I am indebted to an anonymous reviewer for elaborating this second explanation and providing spectrographic support: "Wideband spectrograms of two 'whooshes' of the

cane through the air in my study reveal a low-amplitude energy peak around 400–500 Hz at noise onset, gliding to a higher amplitude peak around 700 Hz at the noise's maximum amplitude. In other words, something not unlike the transition from a /w/ into a following vowel."

REFERENCES

Ohala, J. J. 1983. The origin of sound patterns in vocal tract constraints. In P. F. MacNeilage (ed.) *The Production of Speech*. New York: Springer-Verlag, 189–216.

OED. *The Compact Edition of the Oxford English Dictionary*, 1971. First Edition. Oxford Unviersity Press.

The Oxford English Dictionary. 1989. 2nd edn. Prepared by J. A. Simpson and E. S. C. Weiner. Oxford: Clarendon Press; New York: Oxford University Press.

PART VII
The biological bases of sound symbolism

21
Some observations on the function of sound in clinical work

PETER F. OSTWALD, M.D.

21.1. Introduction

People who request medical attention usually produce various sounds, including physiological noises, vocal expressions, and spoken language. Physiological noises are meaningful in that they may point directly to a malfunctioning organ. Vocal expressions indicate the emotions experienced by a patient. Speech communicates the patient's observations, thoughts, and beliefs about disease.

The study of so vast an array of sonic behaviors requires a number of different approaches, including acoustic methods (Ostwald 1963) and semiotic analysis (Ostwald 1973). The study of language has always been important for clinical research, particularly in psychiatry, which is the branch of medicine most closely connected to the exploration of psychological and social issues in human behavior (Kaplan 1974). In recent years, there has also been a considerable amount of psycholinguistic investigation of human soundmaking (Andreasen and Hurtig 1980). The present paper will (1) define what is meant by clinical work, (2) describe certain disease states that manifest themselves sonically, and (3) discuss some of the processes involved in communication about disease, specifically those concerning language and emotion.

21.2. What do we mean by "clinical work"?

Clinical work is conducted within a social network consisting of patients who seek relief from diseases, clinicians capable of diagnosing and treating them, and cultural expectation about the nature and course of these diseases. This work is action-oriented: clinicians must respond immediately to the needs of their subject – a living, suffering, or dying patient. Interactions and interventions predominate, not the contemplative analysis of phenomena, or the abstract pursuit of knowledge. What kinds of interventions are made depends, of course, on the clinician's specialty, be it pediatrics, surgery, radiology, psychiatry, internal medicine, or some other. Yet all clinical work entails, first and foremost, *communication* (Ruesch 1975). The predominating strategy is to collect all kinds of information about the patient so that a working hypothesis about his/her *state of body and mind* may be formulated. *Time and duration* are critical issues in the evaluation and resolution of all clinical states (Doob 1971). Some can be very brief: states of emergency, crisis, etc. Others are more long-lasting, but still reversible: mood states, acute illnesses, etc. Finally there are enduring states which may or may not be reversible: chronic diseases, terminal conditions, etc.

The initial phases of communication do not differ greatly from ordinary conversations, except that the patient is expected to be completely self-revealing and clinicians are allowed to ask highly personal questions pertaining to "the history" of the disease. Problems are posed by the limits of self-awareness: many disease processes occur unconsciously. Nevertheless, patients as well as clinicians develop certain intuitive diagnostic hunches. In the course of the physical examination, this basically *interpretative* aspect of clinical work includes also the *semiotic* functions: inspection, palpation, percussion, auscultation, and olfaction (Ostwald 1964). Today it is possible to augment all of this by technical means, including chemical tests on the patient's body fluids, x-ray and electro-magnetic visualizations, endoscopic examinations, and surgical explorations.

21.3. Diseased bodies make sounds

Although a "state of the art" synopsis about speech and language evaluation has recently been published (Darby 1981, 1985), there is as yet no compendium of the clinically relevant physiological noises, including heart (Semlow *et al.* 1983), respiration (Fenton *et al.* 1985), striated muscles (Oster 1984), joints (Watt *et al.* 1983), abdominal organs, or the pregnant uterus to which the reader can refer. Thus it will be necessary to give specific examples here.

Wheezing alerts the clinician to the possible presence of bronchial obstruction, or he may be made aware of the possibility of a tumor of the larynx when a peculiar rasping sound is heard during phonation (Yoon 1984). Pulmonary emphysema, weakness of the chest muscles, and vocal cord paralysis are some other audible physical conditions. Although phonation will be affected primarily, one may also be aware of syntactic and semantic changes. With shortness of breath, for example, a patient will often reduce the length of sentences, be unable to complete them, or try to avoid words that are difficult to pronounce (Darby 1981). Speech being a complex process organized by the brain, one must always be alert to motor speech signs that provide clues to neurological impairment (Aronson 1981). Multiple sclerosis, for example, can produce a characteristic disturbance in articulation and intonation called "scanning" speech.

Brain lesions, particularly those located in the left hemisphere, may produce severe disturbances of soundmaking (Mueller and Fields 1984). When Broca's area (in the left frontal cortex) is disrupted, the effect is called *motor aphasia* because the patient can no longer encode language into the necessary muscle movements for speech. What is produced sounds labored and dysfluent; words are incorrectly articulated; many items are left out of sentences, producing a "telegraphic" or agrammatical style. Often there is a concomitant paralysis of the right arm and face, further interfering with communication, and the patient appears frustrated and angry.

Sensory aphasia is a disorder produced by lesions of Wernicke's area (in the left temporal cortex), where the input analyzer for language is located. These patients have lost the ability to decode language. Thus they have no difficulty in speaking, but what they say is a confused, senseless, and frequently unintelligible jargon. Also their comprehension of speech is impaired. In terms of their emotional displays, these patients often seem to be indifferent, euphoric, agitated, or suspicious.

Disruption of the pathways linking the motor area and the sensory areas of the brain results in what is called *conduction aphasia*. These patients are able to speak spontaneously, and they can comprehend language. But when asked to repeat something, they cannot do so because information from the auditory detection apparatus can no longer be transferred to the motor output center. There are many other forms of aphasia, depending on where the lesions are located. *Global aphasia*, resulting from destruction of the entire neurological system serving speech, including Broca's area, Wernicke's area, and the interconnecting pathway, is the total inability to produce, to comprehend, and to repeat language sounds.

It should be mentioned that the emotional and paralinguistic properties (called "prosody" by neurologists) of speech, including its melodiousness, intonation, rhythm, and stress patterning, are frequently altered in cases of aphasia. Thus patients, when addressed, may be unable to tell the difference between a question and a statement, or between an angry and a friendly tone of voice. Similarly, when speaking, they cannot produce emotional nuances or vocal qualifiers. Lesions of the right side of the brain seem to be especially important in producing these so-called *dysprosodies* (Weintraub et al. 1981).

Unusual sounds can also be produced by patients suffering from convulsive disorders. A unique, high-pitched scream, the so-called "cry of epilepsy," may be heard at the beginning of a major seizure, while in its aftermath there may be temporary aphasias of various types ("Todd's paralysis"). Speech disorders may also be associated with *petit mal* and temporal-lobe forms of epilepsy.

A developmental perspective is often helpful, since many forms of disturbed soundmaking begin in infancy, childhood, or adolescence. Some of the most striking examples are newborn babies afflicted with chromosomal deficiencies. The trisomy 13/15 disorder, for example, is characterized by abnormal cries, excessively long or short in duration, lacking in intonation, and with an F_0 that is too high or too low (Ostwald et al. 1970). Another congenital anomaly has been called *Cri du Chat* disorder because of a distinctive mewling sound emitted by these infants. Metabolic diseases such as hypothyroidism, cardiac conditions, asphyxia, and various other diseases of the newborn are often signaled by disturbed patterns of crying (Ostwald and Murry 1985).

Infantile autism, characterized by bizarre reactions to the environment and lack of social responsiveness, has its onset usually before age three. These children may remain mute, but if they speak one hears peculiar intonation and rhythm patterns, a tendency to "echolalia" (repeating back in a rote fashion what they have heard), and semantic errors such as pronoun reversals and idiosyncratic word usage (Baltaxe and Simons 1981). *Gilles de la Tourette* Disease (named for the French neurologist who described most of its manifestations) begins usually between age two and fifteen. These patients cannot suppress certain body movements. There are sudden involuntary "tics" of the head, neck, tongue, arms, or legs. Voice and speech are often affected as well, so that one hears explosive utterances, noises, animal-like sounds, and obscenities (Shapiro et al. 1978).

Stuttering should also be mentioned here, since many of the "functional" forms of this disorder (i.e. those cases wherein no clearly "organic" basis can be proven) begin in childhood. Speech tends to be dysfluent or overproductive, and there may be sudden blocking, with forceful repetition of phonemes, syllables, words, or entire phrases (Ostwald 1970).

Schizophrenic disorders tend to have an early onset as well, usually in adolescence, although cases have also been reported in childhood and beginning in the third to fourth (rarely fifth) decades. Typically, there is disorganization of sequential and logical thinking, often with intrusive auditory hallucinations, and speech is blocked, disorganized, or overproductive. Emotional expression may be absent or blunted ("flat affect"), or inappropriate to the social realities (for example, grinning while a tragic theme is being discussed). Behavior can become chaotic and overactive, or subdued to the point of stupor. Communication obviously poses an enormous problem. Some patients become isolative and talk mainly to themselves. Others develop bizarre speech patterns, make up new words, and even invent language systems all their own. Still others use expressions that are highly metaphorical, almost poetic, with strange, unexpected associations and unusual references. Vocal parameters are also affected in different ways, including vocal monotony, stereotyped shouting, ranting, or whispering, imitation of animals, peculiar noises, or strange foreign accents (Ostwald 1978).

Affective (mood) disorders can occur at any age. Along with the other dimensions of behavior, speech slows down and loses its intensity when the patient is severely depressed. The range of vocabulary is reduced, with words about sadness, guilt, self-blame, suicide and other negative, unpleasant themes predominating (Bucci 1982). Errors of perception and judgment occur, and condemnatory voices may be hallucinated. When the mood swings upward, toward elation and euphoria, ideas rush quickly into consciousness, speech becomes unduly rapid, the voice grows louder and more animated. In severe cases ("mania"), there is a torrent of aggressive behavior, incessant speech, clang-association, punning, rhyming, and often some disorganization not unlike that observed in acute schizophrenia (Andreasen 1979).

Anxiety disorders are conditions of extreme fearfulness. Some patients are under increased pressure to talk, while others experience much difficulty in communication. Often there is substantial physical discomfort, and numerous bodily complaints may be articulated, especially in chronic cases complicated by depression (Oxman et al. 1985). In acute cases, respiration may be excessive, so that speech is disrupted by panting, sighing, or breathlessness. The voice sounds jittery and agitated, the pitch rises, and crying sounds may accompany the speech or replace it altogether. Rarely, in cases of conversion disorder (formerly called "hysterical neurosis"), there may be partial or complete loss of voice (aphonia), or peculiar, falsetto-like vocalizations. A more chronic disorder called spastic dysphonia is characterized by a tremulous, breathy, over-pressured vocal sound which some people liken to inhibited sobbing (Izdebski and Dedo 1981).

Personality disorders belong to a category of diseases in which interactions with the social environment are judged to be deviant, destructive, or otherwise significantly impaired. These patients tend to be unduly self-centered ("narcissistic"), overly dependent, or inept and unreliable in their behavior. Speech and voice manifestations may provide some diagnostic clues. For example, histrionic personalities tend to speak in a theatrical manner that seems artificial or contrived. On the other hand, these patients may also display a dramatic absence of feeling, a kind of pseudo-blandness called *la belle indifférence*. Anti-social personalities may be so adroit in concealing or disguising their feelings that their "body language" (including vocal behavior) becomes highly deceptive (Diamond 1981). Whether vocal analysis can be used for lie-detection in such cases remains a moot point; experiments with the "Psychological Stress Evaluator," an instrument designed to measure frequency modulations in the voice, have not been reliable even in detecting anxiety and hostility (Grantham et al. 1981). Patients with the rare condition called multiple personality disorder are able, at different times, to externalize various contrasting or split-off aspects of the self, each with its own unique way of speaking (Bliss 1980).

21.4. The process of disease communication

The eminent Russian physiologist Ivan Pavlov once asked "Does not the eternal sorrow of life consist in the fact that human beings cannot understand one another, that one person cannot enter into the internal state of another?" (Pavlov 1928: 50). A clinician would have to say "Yes, there surely are limits to human understanding, but one must try, no matter how clumsily and imperfectly, to allow a patient's 'internal state' to flow into one's own inner self." Let me speculate about the process involved.

Self-awareness and introspection can give an individual partial access to his/her personal experiences, memories, motives, bodily sensations, thoughts, perceptions of external reality, images, and feelings. This conglomerate of mental material is organized by the brain according to rules derived from two sources: (1) innate programs, and (2) social plans. The innate programs seem to be encoded within the genes; they derive from biological evolution and are transmissible only in one direction, from parents to children. Included among the innate programs are, presumably:

(1) designs for the physical formation, growth, maturation, involution, and death of a human organism;
(2) capacities for movement, breathing, and other self-preservative actions;
(3) readiness to acquire cognitive, linguistic, and other "communication" skills;
(4) abilities to feel, emote, and socialize with others;
(5) willingness to produce and to reproduce in the service of species-preservation.

At the time of conception, information from the paternal genes conjoins with information from the maternal genes, resulting in a new, one-of-a-kind innate program for that particular member of the species. Societal plans also begin to operate at a very early stage of development, probably during gestation. It seems that some signals from the outer world manage to impinge upon the embryo. Certain toxic messages, for example, are able to cross the uterine barriers if mothers ingest excessive amounts of alcohol, nicotine, or other chemical substances obtained from the environment. A social system that fails to provide sufficient nourishment for the mother will also hamper a growing fetus in terms of its physical growth and cognitive development. And then there is the influence of the acoustical environment on the unborn child: loud noises, music, speech, and other sounds are transmitted not only directly, via the aqueous medium of the uterus, but also indirectly through the mother's movements, her vocalizations, and inner vibrations. Birth itself is as much a social event as it is a biological process. (Consider the drugs given to enhance or reduce the labor contractions; the presence of doctor or midwife, family members, or friends; the proffered positions of lying or squatting; pushing, manipulating, or instrumentally extracting the fetus.)

Societal plans become much more influential once the baby is born. Information flowing to his/her brain is patterned by separation from the mother, feeding experience, cuddling and play, punishment, and by the availability of oxygen and nutrients. Crucial in terms of social adaptation are the rules regarding waste material – the elimination of vomitus, urine, and feces.

Innate programs governing human development call for a period of substantial dependency on the parents or other caretakers. At first the dependency is almost total, and it is during this period, when the neonate cannot as yet crawl away from danger or cling to another person for protection, that an important survival mechanism is activated – language (Lenneberg 1967). Recognition of the human voice, phoneme discrimination, and other important auditory developments occur within the first few weeks of life, along with cooing, babbling, and other expressive developments. The vocabulary expands and sentences become more complex, all part of a developmental sequence, innately determined, that parallels the development of cognitive and motor skills. Soon schooling and the process of formal education can begin. For the next ten years or so, a person's body and brain structures remain sufficiently plastic for numerous communicative skills to be acquired sequentially or simultaneously. Thus some children readily become multilingual, while others develop, along with language, astonishing mathematical, musical, or visual–spatial abilities. Still others become youthful athletes, fighters, or workers.

Fundamental to success in all of these endeavors is *emotion*, a set of biologically determined behaviour patterns designed to deal swiftly and effectively with the potentially lethal problems of hunger, abandonment, and social isolation. The infant's cry is probably its first "expression" of emotion. The survival value of this signal becomes apparent when we consider that crying can indicate pain, distress, hunger, cold, and other states of displeasure, just as cooing, another early (and presumably innate) emotional expression, can indicate satisfaction, contentment, warmth, and other states of pleasure (Ostwald 1972). Such emotional signals (or "expressions") make immediate and powerful impacts (or "impressions") on the social environment. And the fact that these are vocal expressions and auditory impressions should alert us to the close affinity between emotion and speech, the other communicative modality requiring vocal–auditory information processing. The human repertory of emotion sounds (humming, whistling, singing, music, etc.) grows along with the linguistic structures (phonemes, morphemes, phrases, etc.), so that by the time we reach adulthood it is difficult to know what the upper limits might be.[1]

How many emotions can be felt? How many can be expressed? How many perceived? What are their acoustical correlates? A useful approach to these questions lies in the field of musicology. For example, Friederich Marpurg (1718–1795) thought he could identify nineteen emotional states in terms of their acoustical patterns, i.e. the rhythms, tonal progressions, harmonies, embellishments, and other devices used by composers of the eighteenth century (see Table 21.1). Certain of his observations, for example that "slow melody and dissonance" signals a state of sorrow, seem convincing and consistent with the results of modern psycho-acoustical research. Associations have also been proposed between specific emotions and musical keys. C major is the key of "innocence, the language of children"; B-flat major is the key of "happy love, easy conscience, hope, and visions of a better world"; B-flat minor is the key of "terror, raging doubts, and darkest

Table 21.1 *Acoustic expression of emotional states. According to Friederich Marpurg*

Emotion	Expression
Sorrow	Slow, languid melody; sighing; caressing of single words with exquisite tonal material; prevailing dissonant harmony
Happiness	Fast movement; animated and triumphant melody; warm tone color; more consonant harmony
Contentment	A more steady and tranquil melody than with happiness
Repentance	The elements of sorrow, except that a turbulent, lamenting melody is used
Hopefulness	A proud and exultant melody
Fear	Tumbling downward progressions, mainly in the lower register
Laughter	Drawn out, languid tones
Fickleness	Alternating expressions of fear and hope
Timidity	Similar to fear, but often intensified by an expression of impatience
Love	Consonant harmony; soft, flattering melody in broad movements
Hate	Rough harmony and melody
Envy	Growling and annoying tones
Compassion	Soft, smooth, lamenting melody; slow movement; repeated figures in the bass
Jealousy	Introduced by a soft, wavering tone; then an intense, scolding tone; finally a moving and sighing tone; alternating slow and quick movement
Wrath	Expression of hate combined with running notes; frequent sudden changes in the bass; sharp violent movements; shrieking dissonances
Modesty	Wavering, hesitating melody; short, quick stops
Daring	Defiant, rushing melody
Innocence	A pastoral style
Impatience	Rapidly changing, annoying modulations

From Ostwald, *Soundmaking: The Acoustic Communication of Emotion*, 1963 melancholy."[2] The structural elements of music – rising and falling melodies, changing harmonic progressions, major and minor modes, rhythmic patterns – all serve to delineate emotion in sound (Cooke 1959), and thus may provide clues for the interpretation of emotion from paralinguistic aspects of spoken language. Finally, it should be mentioned that interesting relationships have been demonstrated between the acoustical elements of songs (e.g. vocal width, embellishments, nasality, glottal effects, rhythm), and the cultural determinants of emotionality (e.g. child care, the role of women, intimacy, punitiveness) (Lomax 1968).

Several dozen emotional states have been described by psychologists (see Table 21.2), but some of these are probably blends or derivatives of more basic (instinctual, or biologically determined) emotions. (Psychoanalysis postulates as few as three basic emotions: love, aggression, and fear.) Cross-cultural studies focusing on visual cues have revealed seven basic emotions: happiness, surprise, fear, sadness, anger, disgust/contempt, and interest (Ekman 1982), Scherer (see Table 21.3) found that he could be "reasonably certain" about the vocal correlates of two of the eleven emotions he studied: *anger* (high pitch level and wide range, loud voice and fast tempo) and *grief* or *sadness* (low pitch and narrow range, downward pitch contour, soft voice, and slow tempo: Scherer 1979).

The importance of F_0 in signaling emotional states has been emphasized repeatedly. For example, from acoustical science:

Vocal utterances obtained in anger, fear, and sorrow situations tend to produce characteristic differences in contour of fundamental frequency, temporal characteristics, average speech spectrum, precision of articulation, and waveform regularity of successive glottal pulses.
(Williams and Stevens 1981: 238.)

From many other sources, including cross-linguistic and anatomical studies, John Ohala has compiled evidence to support the notion of an "innately specified frequency code" that carries information about behavioral attitudes such as submissiveness vs. dominance, passivity vs. aggressivity, and threat vs. non-threat, all having important emotional implications (Ohala 1984).

The clinician or receiver of all this sonic information is of course the bearer of emotions as well. Indeed, everything that has been said above about the innate programs and social plans governing patient/sender behavior could be repeated for the clinician/receiver. The input side of sound-communication systems, however, has been much more difficult to study than the output side. What seems clear is that the ear is not simply a transformational device for converting acoustical energy from the environment into neuronal signals, but an extremely sophisticated analytical instrument which controls and modulates its own input at every level, from the tympanic membrane, through the middle-ear bones and muscles, and at several way stations within the cochlea and the auditory nuclei of the brain (Dallos 1985). Clinicians have described eloquently the "art of listening," but its scientific understanding is still rudimentary (Barbara 1958).

Table 21.2 *Emotion categories proposed by five investigators*

Woodworth (1938)	Plutchik (1962)	Tomkins and McCarter (1964)	Osgood (1966)[a]	Frijda (1968)[b]	proposed
Love Mirth Happiness	Coyness Happiness Joy	Enjoyment Joy	Complacency Quiet pleasure Joy Glee Worried laughter	Happy	Happiness
Surprise	Surprise Amazement Astonishment	Surprise Startle	Surprise Amazement Bewilderment Awe	Surprise	Surprise
Fear	Apprehension Fear Terror	Fear Terror	Fear Horror	Fear	Fear
Suffering	Pensiveness Sorrow Grief	Distress Anguish	Despair Boredom Dreamy sadness Acute sorrow Despair	Sad	Sadness

Anger			Annoyance	Anger	Sullen anger	Anger	Anger
Determination			Anger	Rage	Rage		
			Rage		Stubbornness		
					Determination		
Disgust			Tiresomeness	Disgust	Annoyance	Disgust	Disgust/
———			Disgust	Contempt	Disgust		Contempt
Contempt			Loathing		Contempt		
					Scorn		
					Loathing		
			Attentiveness	Interest	Expectancy	Attention	Interest
			Expectancy	Excitement	Interest		
			Anticipation				
			Acceptance	Shame	Pity	Calm	
			Incorporation	Humiliation	Distrust	Bitter	
					Anxiety	Pride	
						Irony	
						Insecure	
						Skepticism	

Source: Ekman (ed.) 1982

[a] All categories found in at least two of Osgood's three types of data analyses were listed.
[b] All categories that emerged in the analysis of judgments of both stimulus persons were listed.

Table 21.3 *Summary of results on vocal indicators of emotional states*

Emotion	Pitch level	Pitch range	Pitch variability	Loudness	Tempo
Happiness/joy	High	?	Large	Loud	Fast
Confidence	High	?	?	Loud	Fast
Anger	High	Wide	Large	Loud	Fast
Fear	High	Wide	Large	?	Fast
Indifference	Low	Narrow	Small	?	Fast
Contempt	Low	Wide	?	Loud	Slow
Boredom	Low	Narrow	?	Soft	Slow
Grief/sadness	Low	Narrow	Small	Soft	Slow
Evaluation	?	?	?	Loud	?
Activation	High	Wide	?	Loud	Fast
Potency	?	?	?	Loud	?

Source: Scherer 1979: 206

Perhaps what we would like to call "symbolism" in clinical soundmaking is nothing more (or less) than a transaction between the patient and the clinician, an intuitive agreement to simplify their discourse by setting limits to what may be talked about, so there can be a mutual focusing on the disease state. Giving names to the state, expressing emotions about it, and finding ways to change it (hopefully for the better) seem to be some of the expectations encompassed within the focus of clinical work. It should be emphasized that these are human transactions. Machines may be used for collecting, recording, transcribing, and analyzing sounds, but only people can have diseases and make symbols.

21.5. Conclusion

Suppose one were to pursue the goal of an automated, computer-assisted technology for recognition of the sonic characteristics which systematically accompany certain states of disease. (The investigation of *Type A behavior*, an intense, rapid, and "aggressive" way of talking that may be predictive for the development and severity of myocardial disease, suggests that such a goal would be desirable (Hecker *et al.* 1981). High-risk cases may be recognized earlier, and treatment could be monitored over the telephone. Other practical applications of a sound-diagnostic technology are (1) the early detection of neurological diseases and mental disorders, (2) cry-diagnosis in infancy, and (3) monitoring and evaluation of drug effects (Feldstein and Weingarten 1981).

Methodological problems are legion. All one can do at this point is to list some of the output, input, and situational variables involved.

21.5.1. Output (speaker) variables

21.5.1.1. Idiosyncracy of speakers

Every person's voice seems to be unique, like fingerprints. Even identical twins differ in regard to their vocal attributes. A "normal" baseline would have to be established for any prospective patient, perhaps at the time of routine physical examination, before changes in his/her voice-speech pattern could be considered diagnostic.

21.5.1.2. Vocal aging

Along with the distinctiveness of each patient's own voice, one would have to take into account any age-related maturational change. These occur very rapidly during childhood, are very significant during the adolescent period with gender differentiation of vocal behavior, stabilize to a certain degree in adult life, and again become noticeable with old age.

21.5.1.3. Coexistence and suppression of emotion

It is possible for speakers to hold more than one emotion internally, e.g. fear and anger, while externalizing only one (say anger). Neutrality of emotional display, overdramatization, and deception of emotion have already been mentioned. Undoubtedly there are blends of emotional states which will be very difficult to distinguish on the basis of voice alone.

21.5.1.4. Motivation and status

People (even very sick patients eager to be helped) do not necessarily say what they mean (Bittner 1977). Patterns of vocal self-presentation are influenced by education, family attitudes, sexual identity, and a host of other psychosocial factors.

21.5.2. Input (listener) variables

21.5.2.1. Auditory sensitivity

What we hear is just as much a function of individual identity, age, maturation, motivation, etc. as what we say.

21.5.2.2. Intolerance

The auditory system may be blocked to the reception of conflicting messages and emotions, for example vocal expressions of hostility from a friend or love from an enemy.

21.5.2.3. Relative attention/inattention

Meaning to language, as contrasted with non-linguistic information in the voice.

21.5.2.4. Time duration

Perception of the voice and what meanings are conveyed may vary over seconds, minutes, hours, days, and longer. Distinctions between "immediate" reactions to acoustical stimuli and more "long lasting" judgments would have to be built into a disease-detection system.

21.5.3. Situational (interactional) variables

21.5.3.1. The nature of the relationship

Vocal behavior and listening patterns are adjusted to the specific needs of couples, groups, parent–child situations, client–helper situations, adversarial relationships, etc.

21.5.3.2. The task at hand

Allowances would have to be made for observations in experimental conditions, during bedside or "client-centered" interviews, high-stress situations such as automobile accidents, and under medico-legal constraints about confidentiality.

21.5.3.3. Instrumentation

What kinds of recording devices are being used? Where are they placed in relation to speaker and listener? What is the ambient sound level? etc.

21.5.3.4. Type of analysis employed

Spectrographic, sonagraphic, phonetic, musical, verbal? Statistical methods, spectrum averaging, single-vs.-cohort analysis, stochastic process changes? etc.

NOTES

1 As Paul Ekman points out in the preface to his book (Ekman 1982), more than a thousand appearances can be produced by the muscles of the face.
2 These statements are from an influential treatise of the nineteenth century, *Ideen zu einer Ästhetik der Tonkunst* by Christian Schubart (see Ostwald 1985: 145–146).

REFERENCES

Andreasen, N. C. 1979. Thought, language, and communication disorders – II. Diagnostic significance. *Archives of General Psychiatry* 36: 1325–1330.
Andreasen, N. C. and R. R. Hurtig. 1980. Psycholinguistics. In H. I. Kaplan, *et al.* (eds.) *Comprehensive Textbook of Psychiatry* (3rd edn), vol. 1. Baltimore and London: Williams & Wilkins, 458–463.
Aronson, A.É. 1981. Motor speech signs of neurological disease. In Darby 1981, II:159–180.
Baltaxe, C. A. M. and J. Q. Simons. 1981. Disorders of language in childhood psychosis. In Darby 1981, I: 285–328.
Barbara, D. 1958. *The Art of Listening*. Springfield, IL: C. C. Thomas.
Bittner, E. 1977. Must we say what we mean? In P. F. Ostwald (ed.) *Communication and Social Interaction*. New York: Grune & Stratton, 83–97.
Bliss, E. L. 1980. Multiple personalities. *Archives of General Psychiatry* 37: 1388–1397.
Bucci, W. 1982. The vocalization of painful affect. *Jnl of Communication Disorders* 15: 415–440.
Cooke, D., 1959. *The Language of Music*. New York and Toronto: Oxford University Press.
Dallos, P. 1985. Lecture on auditory physiology. Given at the UCSF Conference, 23 Sept.
Darby, J. K. (ed.) 1981. *Speech Evaluation*. Volume 1: *Speech Evaluation in Psychiatry*; volume 2: *Speech Evaluation in Medicine*; volume 3: *Speech and Language Evaluation in Neurology – Childhood Disorders*; volume 4: *Speech and Language Evaluation in Neurology – Adult Disorders*. New York: Grune & Stratton.
Darby, J. K. 1981. The interaction of speech and disease. In Darby 1981, II: 3–43.
Diamond B. L. 1981. The relevance of voice in forensic psychiatry. In Darby 1981, I: 243–250.
Doob, L. W. 1971. *Patterning of time*. New Haven and London: Yale University Press.
Ekman, P. 1982. *Emotions in the Human Face*. Cambridge: University Press.
Feldstein, S. and H. Weingarten. 1981. Speech and psychopharmacology. In Darby 1981, I: 369–396.
Fenton, J. R. *et al.* 1985. Automated spectral characteristics of wheezing in asthmatic children. *IEEE Trans. Biomed. Eng.* 32: 50–55.
Grantham, C. D. *et al.* 1981. The psychological stress evaluator as a clinical assessment instrument. *Journal of Nervous and Mental Disease* 169: 283–288.
Hecker, M. H. L. *et al.* 1981. "Speech analysis of type A behavior." In Darby 1981, II: 385–397.
Izdebski, K. and H. H. Dedo. Spastic dysphonia. In Darby 1981, II: 105–127.
Kaplan, B. 1974. The study of language in psychiatry. In S. Arieti (ed.) *American Handbook of Psychiatry* (revised edition), vol. 1. New York: Basic Books, 1046–1073.

Lenneberg, E. 1967. *The Biological Foundations of Language*. New York: Wiley.
Lomax, A. 1968. *Folk Song Style and Culture*. Washington, DC: AAAS Publication no. 88.
Mueller, J. and H. Fields. 1984. Brain and behavior. In H. H. Goldman (ed.) *Review of General Psychiatry* Los Altos, CA: Lange Medical Publications, 93–124.
Ohala, J. J. 1984. An ethological perspective on common cross-language utilization of F_0 of voice. *Phonetica* 41: 1–16.
Oster, G. 1984. Muscle sounds. *Scientific American* 250(3): 108–114.
Ostwald, P. F. 1963. *Soundmaking, the Acoustic Communication of Emotion*. Springfield, IL: C. C. Thomas.
  1964. How the patient communicates about disease with the doctor. In T. A. Sebeok, A. S. Hayes, and M. C. Bateson (eds.) *Approaches to Semiotics*. The Hague: Mouton, 11–34.
  1970. The psychiatrist and the patient who stutters. *Journal of Nervous and Mental Diseases* 150: 317–324.
  1972. The sounds of infancy. *Developmental Medicine and Child Neurology* 14: 350–361.
  1973. *The Semiotics of Human Sound*. The Hague: Mouton.
  1978. Language and communication problems with schizophrenic patients – a review, commentary, and synthesis. In W. E. Fann et al. (eds.) *Phenomenology and Treatment of Schizophrenia*. New York: Spectrum, 163–191.
  1983. *Soundmaking, the Acoustic Communication of Emotion*. Springfield, IL: C. C. Thomas.
  1985. *Schumann – The Inner Voices of a Musical Genius*. Boston: Northeastern University Press.
Ostwald, P. F. et al. 1970. Cries of a trisomy 13/15 infant. *Developmental Medicine and Child Neurology* 12: 472–477.
  Ostwald, P. F. and T. Murry. 1985. The communicative and diagnostic significance of infant sounds. In B. H. Lester and C. F. Z. Boukidis (eds.), *Infant Crying*. New York: Plenum, 139–158.
Oxman, T. E. et al. 1985. Linguistic dimensions of affect and thought in somatization disorder. *American Journal of Psychiatry* 142: 1150–1155.
Pavlov, I. P., 1928. Translated by W. Horsley Gantt. *Lectures on Conditioned Reflexes*, vol. 1. New York: International Publishers.
Ruesch, J. 1975. *Knowledge in Action*. New York: Jason Aronson.
Scherer, K. L. 1979. Nonlinguistic vocal indicators of emotion and psychopathology. In C. E. Izard (ed.) *Emotion in Personality and Psychopathology*. New York: Plenum, 495–529.
Semlow, J. et al. 1983. Coronary artery disease – correlates between diastolic auditory characteristics and coronary artery stenosis. *IEEE Trans. Biomed. Eng.* 30: 136–139.
Shapiro, A. K. et al. 1978. *Gilles de la Tourette's Disease*. New York: Raven Press.
Watt, D. M. et al. 1983. An analysis of temporomandibular joint sounds. *Jnl. Dentistry* 11: 346–355.
Weintraub, S. et al. 1981. Disturbances in prosody, a right-hemisphere contribution to language. *Archive of Neurology* 38: 742–744.
Williams, C. E. and K. N. Stevens. 1981. Vocal correlates of emotional states. In Darby 1981, 1985, vol. 1: 238.
Yoon, K. M. et al. 1984. Sound spectrographic analysis of the voice of patients with glottic carcinona. *Folia Phoniatrica* 36: 24–30.

22
The frequency code underlies the sound-symbolic use of voice pitch[1]

JOHN J. OHALA

22.1. Introduction

In this paper I propose that certain global uses of intonation across languages exhibit sound symbolism, i.e. they show a motivated link between the shape of an intonation pattern and its meaning or function. This is not a new claim (Hermann 1942) and, in general, there is a very large literature claiming the existence of sound symbolism in other, usually segmental or lexical, domains. But there are several good reasons for being sceptical of such claims, including those I make here.

First, it runs counter to the dominant Saussurian dictum that "the sign is arbitrary," i.e. that the link between sound and meaning is conventional, not natural. This has been a productive working principle and we should not weaken its application to language without good reason. Actually, some amount of acoustic iconism or onomatopoeia in language has always been acknowledged, but it was usually held to represent a negligible fraction of the entire language.

Second, there has typically been no convincing theory offered as to why sound symbolism should exist in languages, nor for the most part has anyone offered a motivation for linkage between particular phonetic features and semantic features. Notable exceptions to this can be found in the work of Paget (1930) and Fonagy (1983), among others, although none of these can be said to have had widespread influence. None of the phonetically based theories of sound symbolism that do exist has been able to unify the various claims about sound symbolism in consonants, vowels, tones, and intonation; e.g. Paget's theory that speech originated as audible gestures made with the mouth would fail to encompass systematic cross-language use of fundamental frequency (F_0) in intonation.

Third, most of the evidence offered for sound symbolism lacks the rigor found in linguistic argumentation at its best, e.g. as demonstrated in linguistic reconstruction via the comparative method. Though immensely fascinating, most of the literature claiming cross-language sound symbolism is anecdotal (e.g. Jespersen 1933) and, a sceptic might legitimately charge, exhibits selectivity in the gathering of data. (Even so, there have been numerous fairly well-controlled experimental and statistical studies, to be cited below, which cannot be ignored.)

The most I can hope to do in this paper is to reduce the level of scepticism surrounding sound symbolism by proposing a unifying, ethologically based and phonetically plausible theory of aspects of sound symbolism. I will not only attempt to identify the motivation for a sound–meaning connection but will also suggest a link between sound symbolism in vowels, consonants, tones, and intonation. My basic strategy is to argue that sound symbolism is a manifestation of a much larger ethological phenomenon that is also seen in the vocal communication and certain facial expressions of other species. Furthermore, the theory will also account for sexual dimorphism of the vocal anatomy in humans and other species, since phonatory mechanisms have evolved to exploit a specific sound–meaning correlation. To the extent possible I will cite experimental results in support of my claims although, admittedly, much more empirical work needs to be done.

22.2. F_0 in speech

I will assume that most of the facts about how speech prosody is used for the expression of certain basic meanings are well known and have been adequately documented in the literature. I will therefore give most attention to establishing *connections* between these facts and facts about other forms of communication.

22.2.1. *Universal tendencies for fundamental frequency (F_0) and sentence type*

It has been frequently noted that languages use high and/or rising F_0 to mark questions – and low and/or falling F_0 to mark statements (Hermann 1942; Bolinger 1964, 1978; Ultan 1969; Cruttenden 1981). Although there are exceptions to this pattern, notably when questions are marked by special words or word order, the high cross-language incidence of this particular sound–meaning correlation makes it quite unlike the typically arbitrary sound–meaning correlation that exists for most lexical and grammatical entities. For example, consider the word *cup* in various languages: English /k ʌ p/, Spanish /taza/, Hindi /pjala/ – and these are languages that are genetically related! Moreover, the pattern found in intonation is too widespread to be explained by borrowing, descent from a common linguistic source, or chance. It follows that there is something common to all human speakers, at all stages in history, which creates this phenomenon. Nevertheless, attempts to explain it by reference to universal physiological constraints (Lieberman 1967) have so far not been convincing (Ohala 1970, 1977, 1978, 1982a, 1983, 1990).

22.2.2. F_0 and affect

Anecdotal and experimental evidence are in general agreement that there are cross-culturally similar uses of F_0 to signal affect, intention, or emotion. There are numerous terminologial, conceptual, and methodological problems in this area, however. What are the non-linguistic messages which can be conveyed by the voice? Are these signals under voluntary control? How can one obtain natural samples of them? What labels for these messages should one use when instructing listeners to judge how well a given speech sample embodies them? Nevertheless, although the evidence is not as extensive as that concerned with the use of F_0 to mark sentence types, it seems safe to conclude that such "social" messages as deference, politeness, submission, lack of confidence, are signaled by high and/or rising F_0 whereas assertiveness, authority, aggression, confidence, threat, are conveyed by low/or falling F_0 (Bolinger 1964, 1978).

In so-called "assertiveness training," the trainees are told explicitly to use as low a pitch of voice as they are comfortable with in order to enhance their assertiveness or image of self-confidence. Radio and television announcers tend to have a low pitch of voice (in comparison to the general population), so that they may sound authoritative. Actors and actresses are generally "locked into" certain types of roles as a function of their voice pitch, e.g. it would seem ludicrous to have Macbeth or Falstaff played by actors with high-pitched voices.

Some of the exceptions to the generalization that rising F_0 is associated with questions and falling F_0 with statements involve an overlay of emotional or socially dictated attitudes (see Ching 1982).

The experimental literature reveals some apparent conflict on the F_0 correlates of affect, however. Whereas Apple *et al*. (1979) found that a higher F_0 of voice made a speaker sound "less truthful, less emphatic, and less 'potent' (smaller) and more nervous" (cf. comparable results, but with different labels, by Fairbanks and Pronovost 1939; Williams and Stevens 1972; Brown *et al*. 1974; Uldall 1960, 1964). Scherer *et al*. (1973) found higher maximum F_0 of voice associated with *greater* confidence in some cases. The conflict may be only superficial due to different experimental and measurement procedures. Apple *et al*. (1979) obtained listeners' evaluations of natural speech samples, which were resynthesized with an overall upshifted, downshifted, or unaltered F_0 with all other parameters left unchanged (except duration, in one condition). Scherer *et al*. (1973) presented listeners with unaltered samples of speech which were allowed to vary naturally in a variety of acoustic parameters from one token to the next. Under these circumstances they found peak F_0 to show an occasional correlation with listeners' perception of greater confidence.

To attempt to resolve this conflict I conducted the following study (Ohala 1982b). Short samples (4 sec) of spontaneous speech produced by two male and two female adult speakers of American English were digitally processed in such a

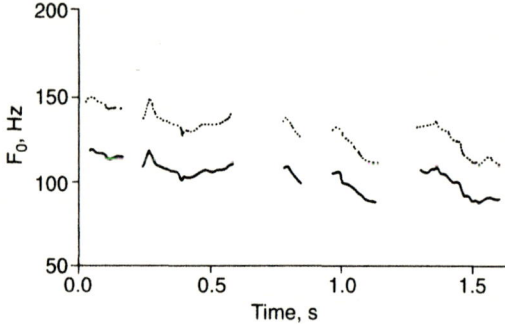

Figure 22.1. The F_0 contours of two samples of "stripped speech" (see text) presented as a pair to listeners to determine which sounded "more dominant, more self-confident." The contour depicted as a dotted line was identical to that depicted by the solid line except that it was upshifted in frequency by a factor of 1.25. The latter, with lower frequency, was judged "more dominant" in 92% of the judgments.

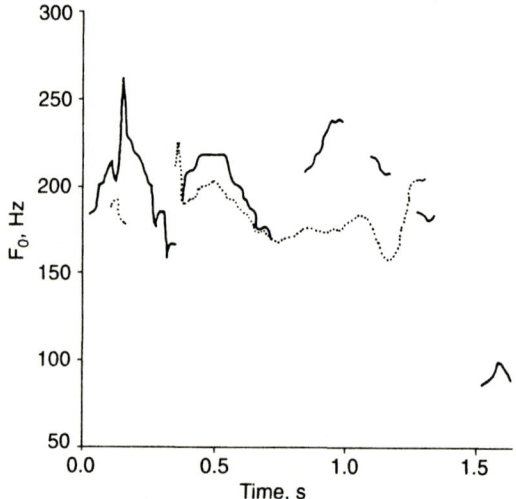

Figure 22.2. The F_0 contours of two samples of "stripped speech" (see text) presented as a pair to listeners to determine which sounded "more dominant, more self-confident." The contour depicted by the solid line was judged "more dominant" in 92% of the judgments.

way as to remove all spectral details but to retain the original amplitude and F_0 contour, the latter of which was either linearly upshifted or downshifted by varying amounts or left unchanged. In this way the sex of the speakers and the actual linguistic content of the sentences were completely masked. These samples of "stripped speech" were presented in pairs to American English-speaking listeners who were asked to judge which voice of each pair sounded more dominant or self-confident. The results indicate that, other things being equal, lower F_0 does make a voice sound more dominant. This agrees with the results of Apple et al. (1979). This is evident, for example, in the judgments for the two samples presented graphically in figure 22.1, which are derived from the same speech sample but with one of them upshifted from the original by a factor of 1.25 (when F_0 is expressed in Hertz). The sample with the lower F_0 was judged as sounding more dominant than the sample with the higher F_0 by 92% of the listeners. However, when "other things" were not equal, the one feature which contributed most to making a voice dominant was a steep terminal fall in F_0. This is shown in Figure 22.2, where the sample shown as a solid line, even though it has a higher peak F_0, was judged as sounding more dominant (92% of all judgments) than the sample shown as a dotted line, even though the latter is lower in F_0 during most of its duration. The sharp F_0 terminal fall, lacking in the other sample, seemed to be the determining factor in listeners' evaluations. This result is compatible with those of Scherer et al. (1973), but it suggests that the occasionally higher peak F_0 in the voices exhibiting greater confidence is there in order to make the terminal fall seem to be even steeper, i.e. by virtue of having fallen from a greater height.

22.2.3. Tone in sound symbolism

The documentation is not extensive, but there is an apparent cross-language tendency in certain tone languages to use tone systematically in a "sound-symbolic" way (Westermann 1927; Chao 1947; Whitaker, 1955–1956; Welmers 1973). This observation was made earlier by Bolinger (1978) and Liberman (1978: 92). High tone tends to be associated with words denoting or connoting SMALL (and related concepts such as DIMINUTIVE, FAMILIAR, NEAR, or NARROW), whereas low tone is associated with the notion LARGE, etc. Some examples are given in table 22.1.

22.3. F_0 in non-human vocalizations

A systematic F_0–meaning correlation is also found in the vocal signals of other species. Morton (1977) documented the existence of a remarkable cross-species similarity in the form–function relationship of the acoustic component of "close-contact agonistic displays" (i.e. the signals given during face-to-face competitive encounters). The sounds made by a confident aggressor (or one who wanted to appear so) are typically rough and have a low F_0; submissive or non-threatening individuals' cries are typically tone-like and have a high F_0. The dog's threatening growl and submissive whine or yelp are familiar examples of this. The same pattern is found in vocalizing species as diverse as the chickadee, the Indian rhinoceros,

Table 22.1 *Examples of the "sound-symbolic" use of tone*

Language	"Small" and high tone	"Large" and low tone
Ewe	[kitsíkitsí] "small"	[gbàgbàgbà]
Yoruba	[bírí] "be small"	[bìrì] "be large"
Cantonese	[to 21] "terrace, stage"	[to 215] "table"

and the frog (Davies and Halliday 1978; Ryan 1980). Morton (1977) provided the following explanation for this sound–function correlation.

Animals in competition for some resource attempt to intimidate their opponent by, among other things, trying to appear as large as possible (because the larger individuals would have an advantage if, as a last resort, the matter had to be settled by actual combat). Size (or apparent size) is primarily conveyed by visual means, e.g. erecting the hair or feathers and other appendages (ears, tail feathers, wings), so that the signaler subtends a larger angle in the receiver's visual field. There are many familiar examples of this: threatening dogs erect the hair on their backs and raise their ears and tails, cats arch their backs, birds extend their wings and fan out their tail feathers. Some animals have even developed permanent (i.e. non-plastic) size markers, e.g. the bison's and gnu's hump, the mane of the male lion, and the growth of hair around the perimeter of the face in so many primate species, including male humans (Guthrie 1970). As Morton (1977) points out, however, *the F_0 of voice can also indirectly convey an impression of the size of the signaler*, since F_0, other things being equal, is inversely related to the mass of the vibrating membrane (vocal cords in mammals, syrinx in birds), which, in turn, is correlated with overall body mass. Also, the more massive the vibrating membrane, the more likely it is that secondary vibrations could arise, thus giving rise to an irregular or "rough" voice quality. To give the impression of being large and dangerous, then, an antagonist should produce a vocalization as rough and as low in F_0 as possible. On the other hand, to seem small and non-threatening a vocalization which is tone-like and high in F_0 is called for. It is also possible in some cases that this latter behavior represents a form of infant mimicry (Ewer 1968: 211, 215, 232ff.; Tembrock 1968). If so, this is a particularly effective way of pacifying a would-be aggressor since, for obvious reasons, natural selection has left most species with a very strong inhibition against harming conspecific infants.

Morton's (1977) analysis, then, has the advantage that it provides the same motivational basis for the form of these vocalizations as had previously been given to elements of visual displays, i.e. that they convey an impression of the *size* of the signaler. I will henceforth call this cross-species F_0–function correlation "the frequency code."

The frequency code in non-human vocalizations suggests an explanation for the three phenomena mentioned above. Its application to the affective use of F_0 of voice to communicate aggression, assertiveness, dominance, etc. and high F_0 to convey social subordinacy, politeness, non-threat, etc. parallels almost exactly the function of F_0 in the non-human cries. In the case of the typical F_0 contours for question and statement, one need only allow that the person asking a question is, from an informational standpoint, in need of the goodwill and co-operation of the receiver. The questioner, as it were, is appealing to the addressee for help. The high-pitched whine of the loser (or anticipated loser) of a battle has much the same meaning. The person making a statement is self-sufficient – again, from an information standpoint. Thus the F_0 used should be, and *is*, just the opposite to that found in questions. The F_0 of voice is used, as it were, as a *gesture* which *accompanies* or is *superimposed* on the linguistic message in order to enhance, elaborate, or even, in some cases, to contradict its meaning. In much the same way we use kinesic signals ('body language') to modify the meaning of our verbal messages. In fact, the rise and fall of F_0 during speech often parallels, both literally and functionally, the rise and fall of some speakers' eyebrows. (See note 2 below.)

The explanation for the systematic use of F_0 in the choice of tones in sound symbolism is somewhat more problematic. The Yoruba speaker who utters the words /bìrì/ and /bírí/ is presumably not trying to appear large and small, respectively, or even dominant or submissive. Rather it is the size of the referent of the word which is symbolized by the tone. But there is still this common element: F_0 is used to make the receiver *react* as if something in the environment were large (or small, as the case may be). If the purpose of communication is to effect a change in the receiver – one might say a change in the "cognitive map" of the receiver (MacKay 1969) – then the use of different extremes of frequency in the signal is quite an effective way to accomplish this, whether with an emotive or denotative intent.

I think the amazing cross-language and cross-cultural similarity of these uses of F_0 represent by *themselves* a strong argument for their being innately determined. I do not think that the consistency we find in the shape and meaning of these signals could result from a culturally maintained template. To see why this is so, consider that the phonetic shape of the bulk of any language's vocabulary is maintained by a cultural template, but since the sound–meaning correlation is arbitrary, this template is subject to gradual distortion with the passage of time; thus, sound change gives rise to such radically different pronunciations as English /kaŭ/ 'cow' and French /bøf/ "boeuf," both of which had a common pronunciation a few millennia ago. In contrast, the sound–meaning correlation found in intonation and in sound-symbolic vocabulary seems to be less subject to deviations.

John J. Ohala

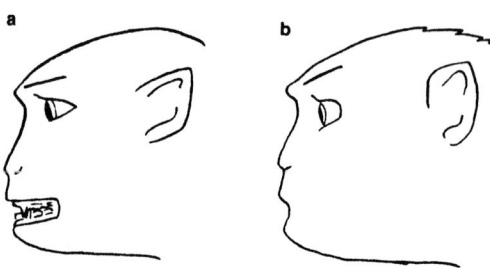

Figure 22.3. Two facial expressions of monkeys. (a) Expression of submission. (b) Expression of aggression (redrawn from van Hooff 1962).

22.4. The frequency code in other communicative domains

In the remaining sections I will attempt to reinforce my argument that an innate frequency code links the above-mentioned use of F_0 in human communication by integrating a few more communicative phenomena into it (although they will not concern prosody *per se*).

22.4.1. Facial expressions

It is an old observation – in fact, at least since Darwin's 1872 work, *The Expression of Emotions in Man and Animals* – that humans and non-humans show certain similarities in their facial expressions. Although Darwin's evidence was extensive, it was largely of an anecdotal sort. Now, however, careful ethological surveys and, in some cases, experimental work have verified Darwin's claims (Ekman *et al*. 1969; Andrew 1963; Van Hooff 1962, 1967, 1972). The smile or lip-corner retraction, one of these cross-cultural and cross-species facial displays, is used to express attitudes or emotions variously characterized as "submissive," "content," "desirous of the goodwill of the viewer," etc. Another one is the facial expression that is the opposite of the smile but which does not have a convenient name: it involves drawing the corners of the mouth forward, even to a protrusion of the lips. For the sake of convenient reference, I call this the "o-face." It is used to express aggression, disapproval, the desire for the viewer to leave the signaler's presence, etc. (figure 22.3).

On the face of it, the shape of the smile and o-face are not well matched to the meaning or functions assigned to them. Why, during a non-threatening display, should the teeth, potential weapons, be exposed (Izard 1971)? And why, during a threatening display (that is, the o-face), should the teeth be partially hidden?

A variety of imaginative accounts has been given for the origin of these two facial expressions. Some have suggested that the smile arose in primates as a play bite or an invitation to grooming (Bolwig 1964; Eibl-Eibesfeldt 1971). Andrew (1963) argues that it was part of a generalized protective response; specifically, the gesture used to dislodge something noxious from the mouth. Erasmus Darwin (1803: 77) suggested that the smile arose in infants as a reflex relaxation of the muscles used in suckling and thus became associated with the state of contentment and pleasure. Charles Darwin speculated that the o-face arose as a way to augment the resistance to the increased expiratory airflow that accompanies great emotion. Zajonc (1985) suggests that many facial expressions, the smile included, serve as "ligatures on facial blood vessels and thereby regulate cerebral blood flow, which, in turn, influences subjective feelings." All of these suggestions are worthy of serious consideration, but all, I think, have drawbacks. They either apply only to primates in general or humans in particular (whereas I think that they should work for canids, too) (Schenkl 1947; Fox 1970); they do not provide an account that applies equally well to the smile *and* the o-face; or they fail to integrate these facial displays with other known aggressive/submissive displays. I offer what I believe is a better hypothesis on the origin of these displays, an account which avoids these defects.

One is struck by the fact that the meanings or functions of the smile and o-face parallel those of F_0 that were discussed above. Could they have the same motivational basis, that is, serve to convey an impression of the size of the signaler? The answer I propose (Ohala, 1980) is *yes*, if we make two simple and not implausible assumptions. One, that we extend Morton's (1977) account so that the size of the vocalizer may be conveyed not only by the F_0 of vocalizations but also by their resonances (those spectral details of the vocalization contributed by the air space between the sound generator and the point where the sound radiates to the atmosphere). Second, we must assume that the smile and the o-face originally served to modify the resonances of accompanying vocalizations. High resonances are typical of short vocal tracts which, in turn, are indicative of a small vocalizer; and conversely, low resonances of a larger vocalizer. Retracting the mouth corners in effect shortens the vocal tract and raises its resonances (this is particularly true in species with a snout where fully retracting the mouth corners can reduce the effective length of the resonator by some 40% or more). This resonance shift can be demonstrated by the use of Plasticine models with and without a simulated mouth-corner retraction, as shown in Figure 22.4. Cylindrical models of vocal tracts with the dimensions indicated were coupled to horn drivers and excited by low frequency (50 Hz) pulse trains. The resulting sound was sampled by a high-quality microphone placed 10 cm from the opposite end and then fed to a spectrum analyzer. As can be seen the resonance peaks shift upwards in the model with simulated mouth-corner retraction, e.g. the second resonance increases from 1,700 to 1,970 Hz. (The spectrum of a shorter resonator is also shown for comparison; the effect of the simulated mouth-corner retraction is thus to shift the resonances towards those of the shorter resonator.)

It is true that in humans and some primates the smile is often done soundlessly and even with the mouth closed, so that in these cases it could not serve to modify

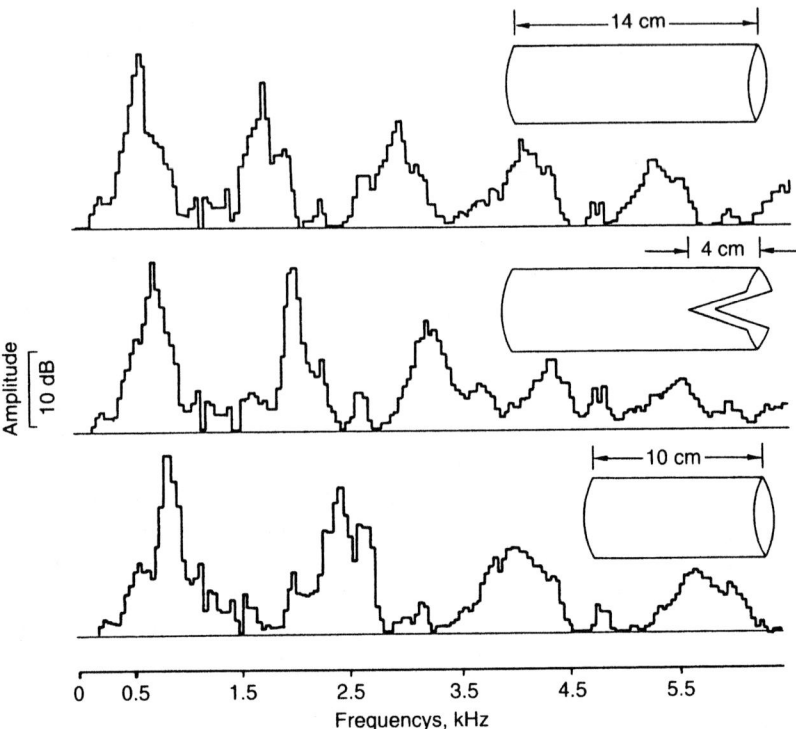

Figure 22.4. The transfer functions of three simulated vocal tracts. Top: a uniform tract 14 cm long. Middle: the same tract with simulated mouth-corner retraction. Bottom: a uniform tract 10 cm long. The effect of the "mouth-corner retraction" is to raise the resonant frequencies towards those characteristic of a shorter tract.

the acoustic shape of a vocalization. However, it has been noted that the high-F_0 submissive screams of many primates are almost invariably accompanied by mouth-corner retraction (if not the other way around), and the low-F_0 cries are typically accompanied by lip corners brought forward (Andrew 1963). It is plausible to assume that through what ethologists call *ritualization* this peculiar mouth shape (which I claim originally served an acoustic purpose) became reinterpreted as an independent visual display having the same meaning or function as the original vocalization.

This account avoids what I believe has been the mistake of some of the earlier speculations on the origin of the smile and o-face, namely to posit that their shapes were originally functional for certain vegetative activities, e.g. eating, biting, regurgitating, respiration, and then to construct quite complex and dubious scenarios whereby these functions could become integrated into agonistic displays.

One can legitimately challenge these theories with this question: when face to face with a competitor, what survival value is there for an animal to give a non-functional enactment of these vegetative behaviors, e.g. regurgitation? The answer is that any animal exhibiting behavior that doesn't deal effectively with a threat probably will not survive long enough to pass on its non-functional behavior to the next generation. It makes much more sense to view the smile and the o-face as signals which attempt to influence the behavior of competitors by either scaring them or inhibiting aggression. The account I give also has the advantage over previous accounts of (1) providing a principled relationship between the smile and o-face, (2) accounting for the presence of these expressions in the many diverse species it has been observed in, and (3) like Morton's (1977) analysis of F_0, it brings these displays under the same explanatory umbrella as has previously been provided for the visual components of agonistic displays, i.e. *that they convey (or originally conveyed) an impression of the size and therefore the degree of threat posed by the signaler.*[2]

Bauer (1987) has recently provided support for the claim that the frequency code underlies the vocal aspect of agonistic facial displays in chimpanzees by showing a correlation between the mouth dimensions and simultaneous F_0. There is no plausible physiological motivation for such a correlation; it is reasonable to assume then that both high F_0 and mouth-corner retraction go together to mutually enhance the acoustics of a submissive display.

22.4.2. *Consonants and vowels in sound symbolism*

There is extensive documentation of a cross-language similarity in the use of certain consonants and vowels in sound symbolism. The evidence is stronger than in the case of tone because although not all languages have tones, all languages have consonants and vowels. Words denoting or connoting SMALL or SMALLNESS (and related notions) tend to exhibit a disproportionate incidence of vowels and/or consonants characterized by high acoustic frequency. Words denoting or connoting LARGE use segments with low acoustic frequency. In consonants, voiceless obstruents have higher frequency than voiced because of the higher velocity of the airflow, ejectives higher than plain stops (for the same reason) and dental, alveolar, palatal and front velars higher frequencies (of bursts, frication noise and/or formant transitions) than labials and back velars. In the case of vowels, high front vowels have higher F_2 and low back vowels the lowest F_2 (Fischer-Jørgensen 1978 gives evidence that the relevant dimension for vowels is F_2–F_1). Table 22.2 presents a few examples of this type of vocabulary (see also other papers in this volume).

To be sure, there are exceptions to this pattern. The English words *small* and *big* are examples. In spite of such exceptions, subjects of various language backgrounds have, in numerous psycholinguistic tests, shown a clear preference for associating

Table 22.2 *Examples of sound-symbolic words in which choice of consonants and/or vowels show a systematic correlation with concepts of size*

Language	"Small"	"Large"
English	*teeny, wee, itsy-bitsy*	*humongous*
Spanish	*chico*	*gordo*
French	*petit*	*grand*
Greek	/mikros/	/makros/
Japanese	/tʃiisai/	/ookii/

the high-frequency segments with things SMALL and low frequency ones with LARGE. For example, Edward Sapir in 1929 did a test in which he required subjects to assign nonsense words like [gil] and [gɔl] as names for smaller or larger versions of objects. There was a significant tendency for forms like [gil] to be assigned to the smaller object and [gɔl] to the larger. (Other tests, both statistical and psychological, of the systematicity of the segment–meaning correlation in languages have been reported by, among others, Usnadze 1924; Newman 1933; Thorndike 1945; Chastaing 1958, 1964a, 1964b, 1965; Fischer-Jørgensen 1967, 1968, 1978; Ultan 1978; Woodworth 1991; see also the review of this literature by Jakobson and Waugh, 1979.)

If we assume that the resonances (spectral shapes) of vocalizations can carry an impression of size as discussed above, then the pattern of segment utilization in this way is explained in the same way as was the use of tone in sound symbolism, i.e. higher frequencies are associated with smallness, lower frequencies with largeness, because these are the frequencies characteristically emitted by respectively small and large things.

22.4.3. *Sexual dimorphism of the vocal anatomy*

I discuss now the piece of evidence which, more than any other, suggests that the frequency code is innate,[3] i.e. part of humans' (and other species') genetic makeup.

Establishing the innate character of a given form of behavior is very difficult. One might think that sensitivity to the special qualities of music is innate since it is a behavior so widely distributed among humans of all cultures. Nevertheless, it has not yet been possible to prove the innate character of such behavior (Roederer 1982). Two-legged walking is another interesting case. One might want to argue that we walk on our two lower limbs because we learn to do so. There are even anecdotes that feral children – so-called "wolf children" – left on their own or "adopted" by wild animals, walk on "all fours," not as "civilized" humans do. There is, however, conclusive anatomical evidence in favor of an innate disposition

The biological bases of sound symbolism

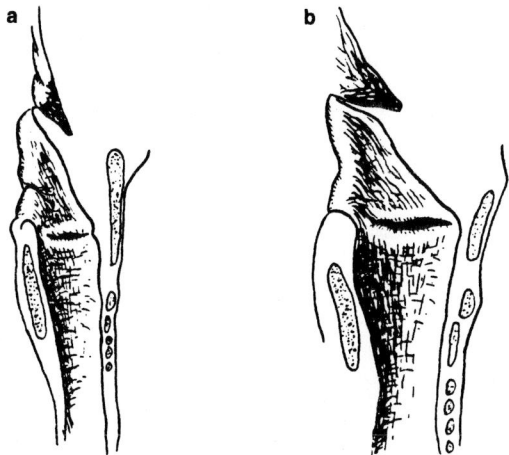

Figure 22.5. Sagittal sections of the larynges of a 15-year-old female (a) and a 19-year-old male (b). The vocal cords of a 19-year-old female (were such available for more precise comparison) would be only approximately 15% longer than those shown here (redrawn from Negus 1949).

for two-legged walking, namely, not only the anatomical structure of our legs and hip joints (in contrast to those of the arms and shoulders and wrists) but also the fact that the skin on the soles of the feet is thicker than the skin on the palms of the hands – even several weeks before birth.

Is there comparable anatomical evidence in favor of the frequency code being innate? I suggest that there is. As such, it does not manifest itself in the womb, but it is still quite clearly genetically determined. This is the evidence of dimorphism in the vocal anatomy of adult males and females.

The facts are well known, but I do not think their significance has been fully appreciated. The adult male larynx is approximately 50% larger than the adult female's in the anterior-posterior dimension (Negus 1949; Kahane 1978; see figure 22.5). The difference is less marked in the lateral dimension. In other words, it is larger precisely in a way that would give the male longer vocal cords and thus a lower F_0. The male larynx is also lower in the throat than the female's, thus making the vocal tract about 15–20% longer. This gives the male voice lower resonances.[4] Now, what is the significance of these facts? They have been widely noted, but I know of only one attempt to give a functional interpretation to them: Negus (1949) speculated that the larger larynx of the male is necessitated by his having to engage in more vigorous physical activity than the female and therefore needing, as it were, a larger intake valve to his lungs. However, this would not explain why the male larynx is disproportionately larger only in the anterior-posterior dimension and not

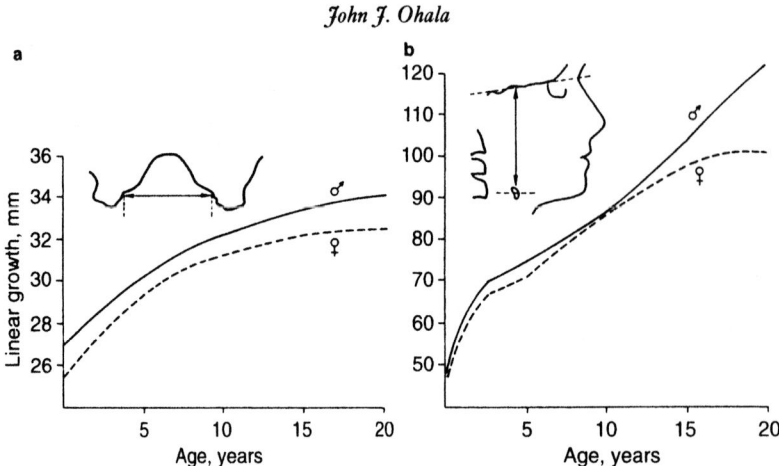

Figure 22.6. The lineal growth of two features of the vocal anatomy as a function of age. (a) The palatal width. (b) The distance between the sella-nasion line and the hyoid bone. The solid line gives the function for males, the dotted line that for females (redrawn from Goldstein 1980).

the lateral dimension, and it would not explain why the male larynx is lower in the throat.

Although the reasons for the sexual dimorphism have not been adequately studied, the low larynx position in the human vis-a-vis other primate species *has* been the subject of much discussion and speculation. It will be useful to discuss these two phenomena together. It has been claimed that the low larynx in humans is a special adaptation to (a) erect posture, (b) lack of a snout, and/or (c) the ability to speak (Negus 1949; Lieberman 1972; DuBrul 1976). All of these characteristics are indeed found only in or predominantly in humans, not in apes or monkeys. Nevertheless I believe these hypotheses lack plausibility.

First of all, as mentioned, the larynx is *not* remarkably low in adult females. To maintain these previously mentioned hypotheses one would also have to assert, implausibly, that women were less well adapted to erect posture, lack of a snout, or the ability to speak.

Second, it is important to note *when* this sexual dimorphism occurs developmentally. It occurs at puberty. Prior to that both sexes have virtually identical vocal anatomy. This can be illustrated in Figure 22.6, which presents data collated by Goldstein (1980). This figure shows average growth curves for, on the left, palatal width and, on the right, the distance between the sella-nasion line and the hyoid bone. Age is the horizontal axis. The palatal width data exhibit rather typical growth curves: rapid initial growth which starts to taper off during the teens. There is a slight difference between the sexes, but the difference is small and fairly constant. A similar pattern of growth has been reported for the velum (Subtelny 1957).

Differential or sexually dimorphic growth in these parts of the vocal anatomy would not significantly affect the resonant frequencies of the voice. The growth curve of the distance between the hyoid bone and the sella-nasion line in the female, on the right, shows a pattern roughly similar to that of the palatal width. In contrast, the growth curve of the male for this anatomic feature is quite different. It starts to deviate from the normal curve at puberty and continues in this way until approximately age 20. (It is clear from other data that it is the lowering of the hyoid, not the raising of the roof of the nasal cavity, which is the primary source of the increase in the nasal cavity-to-hyoid distance. Furthermore, this is not the only section of the vocal tract which shows such a large between-sex difference; Goldstein [1980] demonstrated that the growth curve of the hyoid–vocal cord distance is similar in shape to that of the nasal cavity–hyoid distance, i.e. that it also shows rapid growth in the male at puberty.) This feature of the vocal anatomy, the length of the pharynx, has a major impact on the resonant frequencies of the voice, namely, to lower them.

Generally such sex and age dimorphism occurs at the time it is needed. The male deer, for example, grows full antlers only by the time he is ready to compete for a mate. It should be obvious that the conditions of erect posture, lack of snout, and onset of speech come long before puberty. We can therefore rule out these factors as having anything to do with the low larynx of human males. On the other hand, a number of other secondary sexual characteristics show up in the male at puberty, e.g. the growth of facial hair. We might usefully entertain the idea, then, that whatever the reason is for the growth of facial hair, the same reason may apply to the enlargement of the vocal anatomy. I will elaborate on this below.

Third, many other species besides humans show an anatomical enlargement of the vocal anatomy – and often not in a way that could be explained as an adaptation to erect posture, lack of a snout, speech, special respiratory requirements, or, for that matter, any other purely vegetative needs. Among the many species which have this trait are the gorilla, the howler monkey (Schön 1971), many species of ducks, swans, and geese, the whooping (and other) cranes (Roberts 1880), and the elephant seal (Shipley *et al.* 1981). In the case of the elephant seal, the male but not the female has a rather long proboscis which is used in phonation: the trunk-like snout is inserted into the mouth and may function like the fist of the French-horn player to modulate and lower the frequencies of the emitted sound. Equally, the size of the snout itself may influence the acoustic output: there is evidence that the length of the proboscis correlates inversely with the dominant frequency of the phonation and correlates directly with the success of maintaining a harem in the face of competition from other males (Bartholomew and Collias 1962; Shipley, personal communication, 1981). One of the most extreme cases of enhancement of the vocal apparatus is the bird of paradise *Phonygammus* which, although only about 25 cm long itself, has a trachea over 80 cm long (Clench 1978). The extra length is coiled up between the

Table 22.3 Summary of the relationship between the phenomena discussed in the text

Meaning		Shape of signal				
		visual		acoustic		
primary	secondary	nonplastic	plastic	nonplastic	plastic I (nonlinguistic)	plastic II (linguistic)
To appear large	threat, intention to prevail in a contest, dominance, self-sufficiency	e.g.: bison's, gnu's hump; male lion's mane; growth of hair on perimeter of face of many primates, including human male	e.g.: piloerection, extension of tail, ears in mammals; extension of wings and tail feathers in birds; arching of back in cats; wearing top hats, epaulets, elevator shoes in humans	e.g.: longer tracheae of geese, cranes, *Phonygammus*; bulla in male of some water fowl, e.g., mergansers, wood duck; proboscis in male elephant seal; human male's longer vocal cords, longer vocal tract	vocalizations with low F_0 and low resonances (implemented by reducing tension on vibrating membrane – vocal cords or syringeal membrane – and by lengthening vocal tract, including protrusion of lips [= "o'face"])	in intonation, low and/or falling F_0 for statements; in sound symbolism, concept LARGE conveyed by use of low tone, vowels with low F_2, e.g., [ɑ, ɔ, u], consonants with low acoustic frequency, e.g., [grave] (labial and back velar), [flat] (labialized, retroflexed, velarized, or pharyngealized), voiced

To appear small	nonthreat, submission, appeasement, desirous of goodwill and cooperation of receiver	e.g.: opposite of above, including retraction of ears, tail; infant mimicry; cowering	vocalizations with high F_0 and high resonances (implemented by increasing tension on vibrating membrane and by shortening vocal tract, including retracting mouth corners [= "smile"])	in intonation, high and/or rising F_0 for questions; in sound symbolism, concept SMALL conveyed by use of high tone, vowels with high F_2, e.g., [i, ɪ, y, e], consonants with high acoustic frequency, e.g., [acute] (apical and palatal), [sharp] (palatalized) voiceless, ejectives

the visual component of the smile ⟶ via ritualization ⟶

sternum and the external skin. This bird, like the cranes, which also have unusually long tracheae, has a very loud call.

In all the cases I have mentioned there is evidence of some sexual dimorphism of the vocal anatomy such that the male has the larger vocal cavity (Winn and Schneider 1977: 822). It goes without saying that these cases cannot be explained as special adaptations to erect posture, lack of a snout, or a speech. Therefore I see little reason to invoke these factors in explaining the same phenomenon in humans and human males in particular.

But now we come to the question of why these vocal enlargements do occur, why there is sexual dimorphism evident, why this crops up only at puberty, and what this has to do with males' beards.

As for the beards, a very plausible case has been made by Guthrie (1970) that facial hair is present to enhance the visual aspect of aggressive displays. Other primate species – and male lions, of course, – also exhibit peculiar hair growth around the perimeter of the face. As alluded to above, all of these enlarge the angle which the head subtends in the viewers' eyes, thus making the individual appear larger and more awesome. The humps on bisons and gnus, mentioned above, probably also function in a similar way. I think it is also the case that *the enlargement of the vocal apparatus occurs to enhance the acoustic component of aggressive displays*. Males, by their role in the family unit and the fact that they compete for the favors of the female – i.e. they are subject to what Darwin called sexual selection – would more often be the ones to develop such deviations from the "norm." However, they would only need these aggressive decorations when they are ready to compete for and retain the favors of a female, that is, at the time of sexual maturity.

There would obviously have to be an innate predisposition for these anatomical developments even if the actual triggering of the growth is regulated by hormonal secretions, the intensity of which might be influenced by environmental factors. There would be no "payoff" for the evolution of such an elaborate anatomical pattern if there was not an innate predisposition in the receiver – the listener – to recognize the "meaning" of its acoustic consequences in vocalizations. Ergo, the frequency code must be innate.

Table 22.3 summarizes many of the points I have argued for in this paper and depicts more clearly the connections I have tried to establish between different phenomena.

22.5. Conclusion

I have argued that uses of voice F_0 in speech where the sound–meaning correlation shows cross-language consistency, e.g. in intonation, the communication of "affect," and in sound-symbolic vocabulary, can be explained by reference to the factors which have influenced the shape of the acoustic component of agonistic displays in virtually all vocalizing species. The sound–meaning correlations found in these cases adhere to the "frequency code," which also governs the vocalizations of other species, namely, where high F_0 signifies (broadly) smallness, non-threatening attitude, desire for the goodwill of the receiver, etc., and low F_0 conveys largeness, threat, self-confidence and self-sufficiency. In support of this hypothesis I have reviewed data from other domains which, I claim, can also be explained by the frequency code: (a) the shape of certain facial expressions involving specific mouth shapes, e.g. the smile, (b) the cross-linguistic similarities in choice of consonants and vowels in sound symbolism, and (c) the existence of sexual dimorphism in the vocal anatomy of humans and other species.

I do not mean to imply that acoustic frequency is the *only* phonetic feature that can figure in imparting inherent meaning or function to vocal sounds. Other features are also plausible candidates for this, including repetition (reduplication) and such "amplitude envelope" features such as continuancy and rate of onset or decay of sound. These deserve further research as they operate both in human speech and in other species' vocalizations.

NOTES

1 This is a revised version of Ohala 1984, and incorporates material from Ohala 1983. These two articles used with permission of S. Karger AG, Basel. The first-cited publication was based on a paper presented at the meeting "Prosody, Normal and Abnormal: An Interdisciplinary Symposium on Suprasegmentals of Speech," Zurich, April 6–8, 1983, organized by Dr. D. Weniger under the auspices of the Association Européene de Psycholinguistique and funded by the Schweizerischer Nationalfonds. Measuring the transfer function of the Plasticine vocal-tract models was done with the assistance of S. Pearson. I am grateful to P. Marler, E. Morton, T. Priestly, and J. Wheatley for advice and bibliographic tips. I also gratefully acknowledge the support of the Harry Frank Guggenheim Foundation for the research reported here.

2 As was noted above, speakers occasionally raise and lower their eyebrows along with rises and falls in F_0. There may be a principled reason for this. The raising and lowering of eyebrows in facial expressions may, like the smile and the o-face, help to convey an impression of the size of the signaler (with all the accompanying significance of apparent size). I would speculate that the eyebrows function as a kind of pseudo-boundary to the eyes: raised eyebrows enhance an impression that the eyes are large, lowered brows that they are small. We probably have an innate reaction to relative eye diameter, since the ratio of eye diameter to head diameter is otherwise a good cue to the age and thus the size of the individual: this ratio is far higher in infants than in adults. See Eibl-Eibesfeldt (1971: 21ff.) on the innate appeal of infantile body dimensions and imitations of them.

3 I accept and do not wish to fall afoul of the legitimate criticisms leveled at the simplistic labeling of behaviors as "innate" or "learned." Innate behavior usually has some "learned" or postnatal component, e.g. some amount of practice or "triggering" by appropriate environmental stimuli, and every learned or acquired behavior must have an

innate component, e.g. the anatomical organs or the sensory mechanisms needed in the execution of the behavior. I use "innate" in the sense "having a genetic predisposition which, however, may require extensive post-natal stimulation for its full development and implementation."

4 There is some evidence, however, that the difference in male and female formants is greater than could be explained solely by anatomical differences, and that some of the observed differences may be learned (Fant 1975; Sachs 1975; Kahn 1975). This suggests that speakers are aware of the sex-determined differences in speech and that they may choose to emphasize their masculinity or femininity by producing speech which exaggerates these differences.

REFERENCES

Andrew, R. J. 1963. The origin and evolution of the calls and facial expressions of the primates. *Behaviour* 20: 1–109.

Apple, W., L. A. Streeter, and R. M. Krauss. 1979. Effects of pitch and speech rate on personal attributions. *Journal of Personality and Social Psychology* 37: 715–727.

Bartholomew, G. A. and N. E. Collias. 1962. The role of vocalization in the social behavior of the elephant seal. *Animal Behavior* 10: 7–14.

Bauer, H. R. 1987. The frequency code: oral-facial correlates of fundamental frequency. *Phonetica* 44: 173–191.

Bolinger, D. L. 1964. Intonation as a universal. In H. G. Lunt (ed.) *Proceedings of the Ninth International Congress of Linguists, 1962*. The Hague: Mouton, 833–844.

Bolinger, D. L. 1978. Intonation across languages. In J. H. Greenberg, C. A. Ferguson, and E. A. Moravcsik (eds.) *Universals of Human Language*, vol. 2: *Phonology*. Stanford: University Press, 471–524.

Bolwig, N. 1964. Facial expressions in primates with remarks on a parallel development in certain carnivores (a preliminary report on work in progress). *Behaviour* 22: 167–192.

Brown, B. L., W. J. Strong, and A. C. Rencher. 1974. Fifty-four voices from two: the effects of simultaneous manipulations of rate, mean fundamental frequency, and variance of fundamental frequency on ratings of personality from speech. *Journal of the Acoustical Society of America* 55: 313–318.

Chao, Y. R. 1947. *Cantonese Primer*. Cambridge, MA: Harvard University Press.

Chastaing, M. 1958. Le symbolisme des voyelles: significations des "i". I and II. *Journal de Psychologie* 55: 403–423; 461–481.

1964a. L'opposition des consonnes sourdes aux consonnes sonores et muettes: a-t-elle une valeur symbolique? *Vie et Langage* 147: 367–370.

1964b. Nouvelles recherches sur le symbolisme des voyelles. *Journal de Psychologie* 61: 75–88.

1965. Dernières recherches sur le symbolisme vocalique de la petitesse. *Revue Philosophique* 155: 41–56.

Ching, M. K. L. 1982. The question intonation in assertions. *American Speech* 57: 95–107.

Clench, M. H. 1978. Tracheal elongation in birds-of-paradise. *Condor* 80: 423–430.

Cruttenden, A. 1981. Falls and rises: meanings and universals. *Journal of Linguistics* 17: 77–91.

Darwin, C. 1872. *The Expression of the Emotions in Man and Animals*. London: Murray.
Darwin, E. 1803. *The Temple of Nature; Or, the Origin of Society: A Poem with Philosophical Notes*. London: Johnson.
Davies, N. B. and T. R. Halliday. 1978. Deep croaks and fighting assessment in toads *Bufo bufo. Nature* 274: 683–685.
DuBrul, E. L. 1976. Biomechanics of speech sounds. In S. R. Harnad, H. Steklis, and J. Lancaster (eds.) *Origin and Evolution of Language and Speech*. Annals of the New York Academy of Sciences 280: 631–642.
Eibl-Eibesfeldt, I. 1971. *Love and Hate. The Natural History of Behavior Patterns*. New York: Holt, Rinehart & Winston.
Ekman, P., R. E. Sorenson, and W. V. Friesen. 1969. Pan-cultural elements in facial displays of emotion. *Science* 164: 86–88.
Ewer, R. F. 1968. *Ethology of Mammals*. New York: Plenum.
Fairbanks, G. and W. Pronovost. 1939. An experimental study of the pitch characteristics of the voice during the expression of emotions. *Speech Monographs* 6: 87–104.
Fant, G. 1975. Non-uniform vowel normalization. *Quarterly Progress and Status Reports*, Speech Transmission Laboratory, Royal Institute of Technology, Stockholm, no. 2/3: 1–19.
Fischer-Jørgensen, E. 1967. Perceptual dimensions of vowels. In *To Honor Roman Jakobson*, vol. 1. The Hague: Mouton, 667–671.
  1968. Perceptual dimensions of vowels. *Zeitschrift für Phonetik, Sprachwissenschaft und Kommunikationsforschung* 21: 94–98.
  1978. On the universal character of phonetic symbolism with special reference to vowels. *Studia Linguistica* 32: 80–90.
Fonagy, I. 1983. *La vive voix. Essais de psycho-phonétique*. Paris: Payot.
Fox, M. W. 1970. A comparative study of the development of facial expressions in canids: wolf, coyote and foxes. *Behaviour* 36: 49–73.
Goldstein, U. 1980. An articulatory model for the vocal tracts of growing children. PhD dissertation, MIT.
Guthrie, R. D. 1970. Evolution of human threat display organs. *Evolutionary Biology* 4: 257–302.
Hermann, E. 1942. *Probleme der Frage*. Nachrichten von der Academie der Wissenschaften in Göttingen. Philologische-Historische Klasse, nr. 3/4.
Van Hooff, J. A. R. A. M. 1962. Facial expressions in higher primates. *Symposium of the Zoological Society of London* 8: 97–125.
  1967. The facial displays of the Catarrhine monkeys and apes. In D. Morris (ed.) *Primate Ethology*. Chicago: Aldine, 7–68.
  1972. A comparative approach to the phylogeny of laughter and smiling. In R. Hinde (ed.) *Non-Verbal Communication*. Cambridge: University Press, 209–238.
Izard, C. E. 1971. *The Face of Emotion*. New York: Appleton Century Crofts.
Jakobson, R. and L. R. Waugh. 1979. *The Sound Shape of Language*. Bloomington: Indiana University Press.
Jespersen, O. 1933. Symbolic value of the vowel *i*. In *Linguistica. Selected Papers in English, French and German*. Copenhagen: Levin & Munksgaard, 283–303.
Kahane, J. C. 1978. A morphological study of the human prepubertal and pubertal larynx. *American Journal of Anatomy* 151: 11–20.

Kahn, M. 1975. Arabic emphatics: the evidence for cultural determinants of phonetic sex-typing. *Phonetica* 31: 38–50.
Liberman, M. 1978. *The Intonational System of English*. Bloomington: Indiana University Linguistic Club.
Lieberman, P. 1967. *Intonation, Perception and Language*. Cambridge, MA: MIT Press.
   1972. On the evolution of human language. In A. Rigault and R. Charbonneau (eds.) *Proceedings of the Seventh International Congress of Phonetic Science, 1971*. The Hague: Mouton, 258–272.
MacKay, D. M. 1969. *Information, Mechanism and Meaning*. Cambridge, MA: MIT Press.
Morton, E. W. 1977. On the occurrence and significance of motivation-structural rules in some bird and mammal sounds. *American Naturalist* 111: 855–869.
Negus, V. E. 1949. *The Comparative Anatomy and Physiology of the Larynx*. New York: Hafner.
Newman, S. S. 1933. Further experiments in phonetic symbolism. *American Journal of Psychiatry* 45: 53–75.
Ohala, J. J. 1970. *Aspects of the Control and Production of Speech*. UCLA Working Papers in Phonetics 15.
   1977. The physiology of stress. In L. M. Hyman (ed.) *Studies in Stress and Accent. University of Southern California Occasional Papers in Linguistics* 4: 145–168.
   1978. The production of tone. In V. A. Fromkin (ed.) *Tone: A Linguistic Survey*. New York: Academic Press, 5–39.
   1980. The acoustic origin of the smile. *Journal of the Acoustical Society of America* 68: S33.
   1982a. Physiological mechanisms underlying tone and intonation. In H. Fujisaki and E. Garding (eds.) *Preprints, Working Group on Intonation, Thirteenth International Congress of Linguists, Tokyo, 29 Aug.–4 Sept. 1982*, 1–12.
   1982b. The voice of dominance. *Journal of the Acoustical Society of America* 72: S66.
   1983. Cross-language use of pitch: an ethological view. *Phonetica* 40: 1–18.
   1984. An ethological perspective on common cross-language utilization of F_o in voice. *Phonetica* 41: 1–16.
   1990. Respiratory activity in speech. In W. J. Hardcastle and A. Marchal (eds.) *Speech Production and Speech Modelling*. Dordrecht: Kluwer, 23–53.
Paget, R. 1930. *Human Speech*. London: Routledge & Kegan Paul.
Roberts, T. S. 1880. The convolution of the trachea in the sandhill and whooping cranes. *American Naturalist* 14: 108ff.
Roederer, J. G. 1982. The search for a biological survival value of music. *Journal of the Acoustical Society of America* 72: S92.
Ryan, M. J. 1980. Female mate choice in a neotropical frog. *Science* 209: 523–525.
Sachs, J. 1975. Cues to the identification of sex in children's speech. In B. Thorne and N. Henley (eds.) *Language and Sex: Difference and Dominance*. Rowley, MA: Newbury House, 152–171.
Sapir, E. 1929. A study in phonetic symbolism. *Journal of Experimental Psychology* 12: 225–239.
Schenkl, R. 1947. Ausdrucksstudien an Wölfen. *Behaviour* 1: 81–129.
Scherer, K. R., H. London, and J. J. Wolf. 1973. The voice of confidence: paralinguistic cues and audience evaluation. *Journal of Research in Personality* 7: 31–44.
Schön, M. A. 1971. The anatomy of the resonating mechanism in Howling Monkeys. *Folia Primatologica* 15: 117–132.

Shipley, C. O. 1981. *Development of vocalization on Northern elephant seal bulls*. PhD dissertation, University of California, Los Angeles.

Shipley, C., M. Hines, and J. S. Buchwald. 1981. Individual differences in threat calls of Northern Elephant Seal bulls. *Animal Behavior* 29: 12–19.

Subtelny, J. D. 1957. A cephalometric study of the growth of the soft palate. *Plastic Reconstructive Surgery* 19: 49–62.

Tembrock, C. 1968. Land mammals. In T. A. Sebeok (ed.) *Animal Communication*. Bloomington: Indiana University Press, 338–404.

Thorndike, E. L. 1945. On Orr's hypothesis concerning the front and back vowels. *British Journal of Psychiatry* 36: 10–14.

Uldall, E. 1960. Attitudinal meanings conveyed by intonation contours. *Language and Speech* 3: 223–234.

Dimensions of meaning in intonation. In D. Abercrombie, D. B. Fry, P. A. D. MacCarthy, N. C. Scott, and J. L. Trim (eds.) *In Honour of Daniel Jones*. London: Longman, 271–279.

Ultan, R. 1969. Some general characteristics of interrogative systems. *Working Papers in Language Universals*, Stanford, 1: 39–63a.

Size–sound symbolism. In J. H. Greenberg, C. A. Ferguson, and E. A. Moravcsik (eds.) *Universals of Human Language*, vol. 2: *Phonology*. Stanford: University Press, 527–568.

Usnadze, D. 1924. Ein experimentelle Beitrag zum Problem der psychologischen Grundlagen der Namengebung. *Psychologische Forschung* 5: 24–43.

Welmers, W. E. 1973. *African Language Structures*. Berkeley: University of California Press.

Westermann, D. 1927. Laut, Ton und Sinn in westafrikanischen Sudan-Sprachen. *Festschrift Meinhof*. Hamburg: Kommissionsverlag von L. Friedrichsen, 315–328.

Whitaker, K. P. K. 1955–1956. A study on the modified tones in spoken Cantonese. *Asia Major* 5: 9–36; 184–207.

Williams, C. E. and K. N. Stevens. 1972. Emotions and speech: some acoustic correlates. *Journal of the Acoustical Society of America* 52: 1238–1250.

Winn, H. E. and J. Schneider. 1977. Communication in Sirniens, sea otters, and Pinnipeds. In T. A. Sebeok (ed.) *How Animals Communicate*. Bloomington: Indiana University Press, 809–840.

Woodworth, N. L. 1991. Sound symbolism in proximal and distal forms. *Linguistics* 29: 273–297.

Zajonc, R. B. 1985. Emotional and facial efference: a theory reclaimed. *Science* 228: 15–21.

23
*Sound symbolism and its role in non-human vertebrate communication**

EUGENE S. MORTON

23.1. Introduction

It is ironic that sound symbolism – the non-arbitrary connnection between the sound shape of a vocalization and its function – has been a neglected topic in both linguistics *and* biological studies of communication. Expressive sound symbolism (henceforth ESS) is a fundamental trait of animal signals but, until recently, ethologists ignored the phenomenon. The irony lies in the reason for the neglect: ethologists adopted concepts underpinning their studies *from* mainstream linguistics (e.g. Marler 1961, Smith 1977). In biology as in linguistics, the physical structure of signals has not been an important consideration, except as a vehicle (with an arbitrary physical form) for "information" transfer.

There is nothing basically illogical about asking what "information" is being "transmitted," but basic biological methodology requires the logic to be empirically based, objective, and to follow rules of the logic of natural selection. A causal account of communication would be cumbersome, involving neurophysiological description and statistical relationships found in communication systems (Markl 1985). "Information" should be used metaphorically as a descriptive term, a shorthand, rather than a causal agent. Information should not be used for something that is "conveyed" or "shared," i.e. causing something.

Since linguistic logic is anthropocentric, the application of information as a causal agent to non-human communication is likely to violate the logic of natural selection, especially by confining us to the here-and-now timescale. An individual can only be said to be favored by natural selection through an assessment of its contribution to future populations relative to other conspecifics. This logic compels us to ask why an individual's genetic material has been, on average, favored by natural selection when it uses signal X in situation Y. The perceivers of these signals provide a major source of natural selection on communicants. They define the "situation," but are often described as mere respondents when information is used causally. In this paper, by attempting to reintegrate sound symbolism into biolinguistic theory, I hope to further the prior efforts of linguists who have sought to unite linguistic and biological priciples (e.g. Chomsky 1977; Lenneberg 1967; Lieberman 1984; Lightfoot 1984; Ohala 1984) and the efforts of biologists who have stressed the inadequacies of classic ethological approaches (e.g. Dawkins and Krebs 1978; Morton 1982; Snowdon 1982).

From an evolutionary perspective – which asks "why," not "how," an animal communicates as it does – communication has two levels. Level one is concerned with the proximate physiological bases that induce an individual to produce a signal (i.e. a living animal in the present time); level two is concerned with the multi-generational timescale or the history of the individual's genetic material that favored or selected for those proximate physiological mechanisms. This is called the ultimate timescale in biology. The proximate or immediate physiological and anatomical causes of a signal, of course, contain the answer to the "how?" question. To answer the "why?" question, i.e. to take the evolutionary perspective, one must take into account both the proximate and the ultimate causes. Most animal signals are genetically determined, permitting ethologists to account for vocal signals in terms of genetic fitness in a manner similar to studying the heritability of morphological features. This, and the large number of non-human species, affords us the opportunity to compare species, an option not available for linguists. Nottebohm (1975: 61, 62) stresses the potential importance of comparative studies when he states:

Phenomena of vocal communication in animals are not likely to answer questions about language phenomena in man. But comparisons between the two can prompt us to look at familiar facts in new ways, ask new questions, and gather new kinds of information. Cross-taxonomic comparisons render suspect some of the circular and fruitless "theories" woven around the uniqueness of man and his speech behavior.

Comparisons between human language and animal communication must take into account vocal characteristics such as intonation, pitch, and amplitude, usually included under "paralanguage", as well as vocalizations such as laughter and crying. Paralanguage may be easy to homologize with animal communication; it conveys information about sex, age, and individual identity. . . . Intonation and amplitude may convey information about the emotional state of the signaller, and this kind of information may be compared with animal sounds associated with play, escape, aggression, and so on.

Nottebohm (1975: 68) also provides us with an example of the evolutionist's proximate/ultimate approach:

It is argued that the first months of an infant's life are a period of adjustment of his immature nervous and digestive systems to life in the outside world. According to this interpretation, the stresses of adjustment lead to crying (Spock, 1968, p. 183). This argument may correctly represent the immediate causes of crying; it does not address itself to the adaptive significance (ultimate causation) of the behavior itself.

Parents habituate little to the crying of their offspring and, as a result, spend many a miserable day and night during the infant's first months. We may wonder whether crying is not a device evolved by infants partly at least to discourage reproduction, and thus delay the arrival of the next sibling.

Nottebohm's suggestion is not *ad hoc*, for it is based on the logic of natural selection: the infant would only share, on average, 50% of its genes with the next sibling. So, sibling competition is delayed in those infants genetically prone to frequent and compelling crying. Since it is known that infant mortality rises upon weaning, any behavior that prolongs access to mother's milk will be favored by natural selection. These hypotheses are testable. Nottebohm asks: "Might deaf mothers stop nursing prematurely and have an earlier recurrence of postpartum ovulation?"

23.2. Occurrence of ESS

Animal signals can be categorized by their use in either short or long-distance communication. Those that function over long distances are relatively more stereotyped in structure, since sound propagation over large distance is affected by habitat acoustics (Morton 1975). ESS is a dominant feature when communicating animals are close enough to permit the variations in signal structure to be perceived. First, I briefly describe the empirical evidence to support the idea that non-human terrestrial vertebrates use similar sounds in similar ways and then describe my model (Morton 1977, 1982) of motivation-structural rules (M-S rules) in the next section.

In tables 23.1 and 23.2, sounds given by aggressive and appeasing birds and mammals are listed. The list is not meant to be exhaustive, simply a sample chosen to show that the occurrence of ESS is not restricted to a subset of animals. These motivational contexts are at opposite ends of a continuum. Aggressive animals utter low-pitched often harsh sounds, whose most general function is to increase the distance between sender and receiver. Appeasing animals use high-pitched, often tonal sounds, whose most general function is to decrease the distance or maintain close contact by reducing the fear or aggression in the receiver. Why these signal structures accomplish their function is discussed below. The continuum of sound structures between these two "endpoints," with structures approaching one or the other, provides the most frequent raw material for signals. Most species do not have a complete set of possible sound structures, but that is to be expected if signal repertoires are under the control of natural selection. Greater signal complexity is not automatically favored by selection. It is this continuum of *possible* sound structures that I depicted in a model of the relation between signal structure and sound functions (M-S rules). As mentioned in the introduction, the notion of a direct correspondence between a signal's physical structure and its function was a new emphasis. I suggest that the signal's structure *predicts* its function for the

Table 23.1 *Avian sounds used in hostile or "friendly," appeasing contexts*

Species (family)	Hostile	Friendly or appeasing	Source**
White Pelican, *Pelicanus erythrorhynchus* (Pelicanidae)	Harsh nasal growls*	Not given	Schaller 1964
Mallard, *Anas platyrhynchos* (Anatidae)	Loud harsh *gaeck* (♀)	Soft whimpers: *kn* and *quais* (♀)	Abraham 1974
Sparrow Hawk, *Falco sparverius* (Falconidae)	Harsh *chitter*	Whine	Mueller 1971
Bobwhite, *Colinus virginianus* (Phasianidae)	Loud, rasping "caterwauling"	*Tseep*; *squee*	Stokes 1967
Ring-necked Pheasant, *Phasianus colchicus* (Phasianidae)	Hoarse *krrrrah*	Squeak (♀)	Heinz and Gysel 1970
Solitary Sandpiper, *Tringa solitaria* (Scolopacidae)	Harsh, metallic sound	Rising shrill whistle	Oring 1968
Stilt Sandpiper, *Micropalama himantopus* (Scolopacidae)	*Trrrr*	*Toi, weet*	Jehl 1973
Cassin Auklet, *Ptychoramphus aleutica* (Alcidae)	Growled *krrr krrr*	Kreek	Thoresen 1964
Orange-chinned Parakeet, *Brotogeris jugularis* (Psittacidae)	*rrrrr*	Low intensity "chirp"	Bower 1966
Burrowing Owl, *Speotyto cunicularia* (Strigidae)	*rasp*	*eep*	Martin 1973
Red-headed Woodpecker, *Melanerpes erythrocephalus* (Picidae)	Chatter, rasp	Not given	Bock et al. 1971
Harlequin Antbird, *Rhegmatorhina berlepschi* (Formicariidae)	Growling *chauhh*	*chee*	Willis 1969
Chestnut-backed Antbird, *Myrmeciza exsul* (Formicariidae)	Snarling nasal *chiungh*	Musical chirps: *cheup*	Willis and Oniki 1972
Eastern Kingbird, *Tyrannus tyrannus* (Tyrannidae)	Harsh *zeer*	High-pitched *tee*	Smith, W. J. 1966
Barn Swallow, *Hirundo rustica* (Hirundinidae)	Deep harsh stutter	Whine call	Samuel 1971
Purple Martin, *Progne subis* (Hirundinidae)	*zwrack*	*sweet*	Johnston and Hardy 1962
Mexican Jay, *Aphelocoma ultramarina* (Corvidae)	Not given	Variable *weet*	Brown 1963
Scrub Jay, *A. coerulescens* (Corvidae)	Harsh rattle	*whew, scree*	Brown 1963
Dwarf Jay, *A. nana* (Corvidae)	Harsh rasp	*shreeup*	Hardy 1971
Common Crow, *Corvus brachyrhynchos* (Corvidae)	Growl	Soft and plaintive	Chamberlain and Cornwell 1971
Carolina Chickadee, *Parus carolinensis* (Paridae)	Click-rasp	Lisping *tee*, soft *dee*, high *see*	S. T. Smith 1972
Blue-gray Gnatcatcher, *Polioptila caerulea* (Sylviidae)	*peew*	*spee*	Root 1969
American Redstart, *Setophaga ruticilla* (Parulidae)	Snarl	*zeeep*, high-pitched *titi*	Ficken 1962
Yellow-headed Blackbird, *Xanthocephalus xanthocephalus* (Icteridae)	Harsh, nasal *rahh-rahh*	*pree pree pree*	Nero 1963
Crimson-backed Tanager, *Rhamphocelus dimidiatus* (Thraupidae)	Rasping harsh hoarse notes	*Sseeeeeeet*	Moynihan 1962
Brown Towhee, *Pipilo fuscus* (Fringillidae)	Snarling throaty notes	*Seeep*, squeal duet	Marshall 1964
Common Redpoll, *Acanthis flammea* (Fringillidae)	Harsh *cheh cheh cheh*	*sweeeee*	Dilger 1960
African Village Weaverbird, *Ploceus cucullatus* (Ploceidae)	Harsh growl	look!see!; high squeal	Collias 1963

* Verbal or onomatopoeic (italics) renditions of sounds quoted from source author's descriptions.
** See Morton 1977 for references listed in Table 23.1 and Table 23.2.

Table 23.2 *Mammalian sounds used in hostile or "friendly," appeasing contexts*

Species (family)	Hostile	Friendly or appeasing	Source
Virginia Opossum, *Didelphis marsupialis* (Didelphidae)	Growl	Screech	Eisenberg et al. 1975
Tasmanian Devil, *Sarcophilus harrisii* (Dasyuridae)	Growl	Whine	"
Wombat, *Vombatus lasiorhinus* (Phascolomidae)	Deep growl		"
Guinea Pig, *Cavia porcellus* (Caviidae)	Grunt, snort	Squeak, *wheet*	Eisenberg 1974
Mara, *Dolichotis patagonum* (Caviidae)	Low grunts	Inflected *wheet*	"
Curu curo, *Spalacopus cyanus* (Octodontidae)	Growl	Short squeaks	"
Degu, *Octodon degus* (Octodontidae)	Growl	Inflected squeak	"
Spiny Rat, *Proechimys semispinosus* (Echimyidae)	Growl	Twitter, whimper	"
Agouti, *Dasyprocta punctata* (Dasyproctidae)	Growl, grunt	Squeak, *creak-squeak*	Smythe 1970
Pocket Mouse, *Heteromys* (2 sp.) (Heteromyidae)	Low scratchy growl	Whining squeal	Eisenberg 1963
Pocket Mouse, *Liomys pictus* (Heteromyidae)	Low scratchy growl	Whining squeal	"
Desert Pocket Mouse, *Perognathus* (4 sp.) (Heteromyidae)	Low scratchy growl	Whining squeal	"
Kangaroo Rat, *Microdipodops pallidus* (Heteromyidae)	Low scratchy growl	Whining squeal	"
Kangaroo Rat, *Dipodomys* (6 sp.) (Heteromyidae)	Low scratchy growl	Whining squeal	"
Lemming, *Dicrostonyx groenlandicus* (Cricetidae)	Snarl, grind	Whine, peeps, squeals	Brooks and Banks 1973
Uinta Ground Squirrel, *Citellus armatus* (Sciuridae)	Growl	Squeal	Balph and Balph 1966
Maned Wolf, *Chrysocyon brachyurus* (Canidae)	Growl	Whine	Kleiman 1972
Bush Dog, *Speothos venaticus* (Canidae)	Buzzing growl	Squeal	Kleiman 1972
Coati, *Nasua narica* (Procyonidae)	Growl	Squeal	Kaufmann 1962
Large Spotted Genet, *Genetta tigrina* (Viverridae)	Growl-hiss	Whine or groan	Wemmer 1976
African Elephant, *Loxodonta africana* (Elephantidae)	Roaring, rumbling sounds	High-frequency sounds	Tembrock 1968
Indian Rhinoceros, *Rhinoceros unicornis* (Rhinocerotidae)	Roaring, rumbling	Whistling	"
Pig, *Sus scrofa* (Suidae)	Growl	Squeal	"
Llama, *Lama guanacoe* (Camelidae)	Growl	Bleat (long distance only?)	"
Muntjac, *Muntiacus muntjac* (Cervidae)	Not given	Squeak	Barrette 1975
Squirrel Monkey, *Saimiri sciureus* (Cebidae)	Shriek calls, err	Peep calls, trills	Schott 1975
Spider Monkey, *Ateles geoffroyi* (Cebidae)	Growl, roar, cough	Tee tee, chirps, twitter, squeak	Eisenberg and Kuehn 1966
Rhesus Monkey, *Macaca mulatta* (Cercopithecidae)	Roar, growl	Screech, clear calls, squeak, nasal grunting whine, long growl	Rowell and Hinde 1962

sender. This is important because a prediction can be tested as we observe animals communicating and perform experiments (see References (2) for studies testing the M-S rule model predictions).

23.3. The origin of size symbolism in animals

I hypothesize that the fundamental unifying principle of the vocalizations in tables 23.1 and 23.2 is how they function to convey an impression of the size of the vocalizer. In evolutionarily older animals (amphibians and reptiles), which continue to grow after sexual maturity, the fundamental frequency of calls may directly reflect body size (based on the laws of physics relating fundamental frequency and mass of the vibrating tissue). Biological competition in these continuously growing animals differs from that in birds and mammals: individuals differing in size compete for mates. Since a larger animal generally wins in an aggressive contest over resources, selection should favor the production of vocalizations that reflect size. This is valuable to both larger and smaller animals, if the smaller are more likely to suffer injury from fighting. The size attained before an animal begins to vocalize could be predicted from game theory to be that size at which roughly half the animals are larger and half smaller than the individual. Animals smaller than the median size should not call. They may still attempt to mate, but take up tactics that do not provoke aggressive confrontations. This is known in several frog species wherein silent "satellite" males wait near calling males to grab females attracted to a larger male's call (e.g. Fellers 1979).

The prediction that continuously growing vertebrates use sounds reflective of their size has been shown in several amphibians (Arak 1983; Davies and Halliday 1978; Ryan 1980; Sullivan 1982). This relationship now seems well established. However, before we call this ESS, one must question whether the sound can function apart from the body size we are suggesting is being "symbolized." Davies and Halliday (1978) did this by showing that an artificial playback of a larger toad's call does repel a smaller toad. Thus, we can say that the sound alone is sufficient to produce the effect "desired" by the caller.

Vocal communication was probably well established, and had taken on more complicated social functions in animals, as long ago as the Cretaceous, 60–130 million years ago. We can know little for certain. However, Hopson (1975) hypothesized that crests found in lambeosaurine dinosaurs functioned as acoustic resonators. (Lambeosaurine dinosaurs compose a subfamily of the hadrosaurs, the most abundant and diverse group of large terrestrial vertebrates of the Northern Hemisphere in the Late Cretaceous.) Fossil evidence suggests rather intricate social behavior, including close parent–offspring ties (Hopson 1977, Horner and Makela 1979, Currie and Sarjeant 1979). Weishampel (1981) used resonance analysis and auditory anatomy to analyze these fossil crests for their potential as acoustic resonators. He suggested that lambeosaurines vocalized over a wide, but predominantly low range of frequencies in adults. He suggested that sexual dimorphism in vocalizations was present in some species. Juveniles vocalized at higher frequencies than adults, and potential auditory sensitivity at high frequencies in adults suggested a high degree of parent–offspring vocal communication, similar to that still found in crocodilians. Since the size–sound frequency relationship in lambeosaur vocalizations is likely, ESS was probably well established in these evolutionary precursors of today's birds and mammals. Vocal communication was more widespread in dinosaurs than it is now in reptiles.

Bird and mammal vocalizations illustrate ESS unambiguously because adult body size is relatively fixed at sexual maturity, and there is little age-related increase in body size after the adult stage is reached. The use of low or high-frequency sounds does not directly reflect differences in actual size between communicating individuals. Instead, the vocalizations are generally thought to reflect differences in motivation. This is why I term the code suggesting the relationship between sound frequency and motivation "M-S rules."

There is every reason to suspect that the motivational control of signal structure in birds and mammals is based on ESS, even though there is no *a priori* reason why it should be. If motivational control were not based on the code I have proposed, one should find many examples not fitting the predictions. This, and the law of physics that predicts winners in aggressive competition (the larger) and the pitch of larger resonators or sound producers (the lower), combine to form an empirically sound and heuristic framework. If, as I suggest the evolutionary origins of ESS in animals is ancient, we may surmise that its genetic basis is homologous throughout the animal kingdom. However, we will probably not be able to prove this until the genetic material underlying it is identified, since there are no fossils. However, signals found in birds and mammals should be derived from pre-existing attributes of their ancestors. This is no more difficult to imagine than the proven derivation of ear ossicles from primitive jaw bones and gill arches. But it is prudent to ask if ESS in vocal signals might occur through convergent evolution, originating *de novo* thousands of times when different species undergo similar selection pressures. This is not likely. Consider, for example, the occurrence of vocal learning in birds. Vocal learning is known from three of the orders of birds: songbirds (Passeriformes), parrots (Psittaciformes), and some hummingbirds (Apodiformes). Nottebohm (1975) suggests that, since the three groups with vocal learning are unrelated, vocal learning must have developed independently in each. He further suggested that the alternative hypothesis, "that vocal learning was discarded by the remaining 24 orders of birds, is highly improbable." This argument in reverse applies to the origin of ESS in extant species of animals: it is highly unlikely that any widely held biological trait developed *de novo* in each species. Of course a trait can be selected against and disappear from certain species (e.g. vultures are mute); the trait must have some universal benefit to be maintained by positive selection. The lack of

The biological bases of sound symbolism

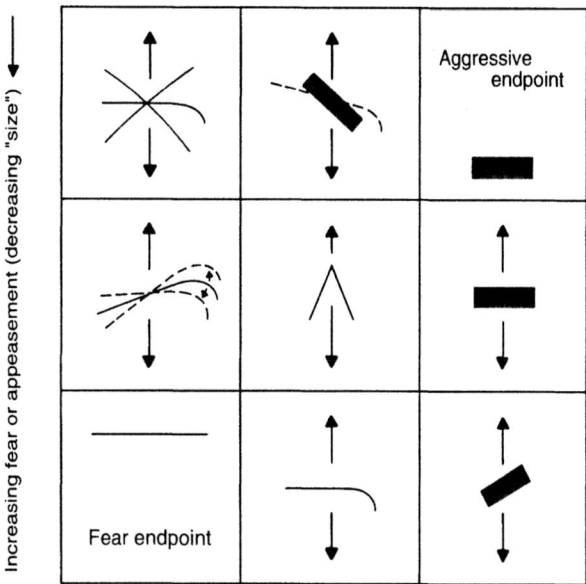

Figure 23.1. A diagrammatic representation of sound structures to illustrate the motivation–structural (M-S) code. Each block shows a hypothetical sound spectrogram (vertical scale, frequency; horizontal scale, time), with thin lines depicting a tonal sound, and thick lines harsh or broadband sounds. The arrows mean that the frequency of the depicted sound may vary up or down, approaching either the low or high-frequency endpoints.

In the upper left block, motivation is weakly tending toward fear if the thin line slopes upward (its frequency rises) or weakly toward aggression if the slope is downward. In the middle left block, closer to the fear endpoint, sounds rise variously upward, between the dashed lines, and are tonal. The three blocks on the aggressive (right) side of the diagram are all broadband, but the frequency is rising in the "distress" call, where fear and aggression are interacting. The center block depicts a chevron, since the motivation point along the continuum and its sound structures are not nearer one endpoint than the other. This structure forms the ubiquitous "bark," which has diverse functions.

functional eyes in a wide taxonomic range of animals living in lightless caves is an example of the loss of a trait through selection pressure acting against genes for eye development. Because the relatives of these cave animals have functional eyes, we say that they are lost in the cave species, not that they arose independently in all the non-cave-inhabiting species.

The universal significance of higher-pitched and tonal calls in appeasement or "friendly" contexts (distance-decreasing) or in fear is less obvious than that of low, harsh calls. I originally suggested an association with "infantile" behavior, implying a release of parental care responses in otherwise dangerous rivals that might reduce their aggression toward the caller (see also Ohala 1983). All young are smaller than adults and produce higher-pitched calls. But young animals are not safe from the aggression of adults simply because they are infants (there is no "taboo" against the killing of infant animals by conspecific adults). Infanticide has been documented in a wide variety of animals (see Hausfater and Hardy 1984). Therefore, I would like to emphasize the ESS basis of the tonal "endpoint" of the M-S code. Through the use of high tonal signals an animal may remain where it is, approach another, mate, warn kin, elicit protection; through the symbolic representation of small size through high pitch, it is perceived as non-threatening and/or fearful.

23.4. The M-S rules model

The M-S rules model is depicted in figure 23.1. The "endpoints," already discussed, are indicated. What should be emphasized in the model is its predictions that sound structures vary toward the endpoints in two dimensions. (A third and fourth dimension, not depicted, are the rate of delivery and amplitude of a signal, which may indicate the intensity or likelihood of behavior associated with the signal. Since only signal structure is related to ESS [see below] I will not discuss these further.) One dimension pertains to sound quality and ranges from broad band (harsh) to narrow band (tonal). The second dimension pertains to the fundamental frequency or spectral distribution of the sound energy. Figure 23.1 illustrates the relationship between sound structures and motivation showing the "endpoint" (lowest harsh and highest tonal) sounds with the intermediate sounds depicting a variety of intermediate vocal expressions. An aggressive motivation is expressed through a low, usually harsh, vocalization, and a fearful or appeasing motivation with a high, tonal sound. The model depicts static "spectrograms" out of graphic necessity; I emphasize that these representative sound structures may be graded or be combined as "composite" signals. The theoretical combination of sound qualities and frequencies is enormous, and the model should not imply that all species use all of the signal structures. The significance of the large potential number of signals is that there is ample room for signal structures to be species-distinctive.

The M-S rule model supplies two entities important to a comparative study of animal communication. First, the model is the first general theory of signal structure and communication. It provides a basis upon which the signals of a diverse array of species can be compared. Second, it provides testable hypotheses concerning the function of the signals in the natural communication of individual animals or species. The information in a spectrogram of a close-contact signal may be used to produce testable hypotheses about a signal's function in communication based on the predictions of the model. A high-pitched tonal signal (relative to other signals in the animal's repertoire), for example, predicts that the animal is fearful or appeasing. When data on the natural use of this signal are obtained, one is able to determine if fear is in fact being communicated. One can then ask why selection would favor the communication of fear in the situations in which the animal gives the call.

In the Carolina wren (*Thryothorus ludovicianus*), for example, all of its eleven types of close-range signals are predicted by M-S rules (Morton 1982). Additionally, seven of these signal classes grade extensively or can be combined with signals from a second class to form composite signals. One, the *chirt*, is used for predator surveillance and also for intraspecific interactions (Morton and Shalter 1977). In the presence of a hawk, the caller presents *chirts* in bouts of two to five at the rate of around seven per second. The second *chirt* is higher in pitch than the first or later *chirts*. However, if the hawk moves even slightly, the *chirts* remain at the higher pitch; if the caller then moves to escape, the *chirts* rise in pitch even more. In intraspecific contexts, *chirts* are lower in pitch and noisy when the caller has chased a conspecific from its territory, or higher and more tonal when it is contacting and attracting its mate. When the mate approaches, the *chirt* forms a composite signal with *pi-zeet*, a signal used in close mate contact and appeasement. Both frequency and sound quality vary in these signals with their contexts as predicted by M-S rules. We do not, of course, know what emotions the bird is feeling, but the contexts and the bird's behavior are consistent with the allocation of specific motivations. The bird escapes from a hawk and appeases its mate, using relatively high-pitched and tonal signals; it chases an intruder and *rasps*, *growls*, and grades *chirts* into low, harsh forms.

The M-S rule model has been used by a number of biologists: in all cases, the predictions of the model have been correct. Researchers may have discovered a new form of symbolism in certain mammals. Mammals are unique, of course, in having the female provide nutrition to infants through suckling. Some mammals, especially carnivores, produce a rather low pitched and noisy pulsed sound as adults that is used in "friendly" interactions (Peters 1984). Sieber (1984) suggests for raccoons (*Procyon lotor*) that these calls (the chitter, churr, and purr), used in body contact and accompanying long-lasting interactions (copulating, social grooming, nursing), are linked with vibrations of the whole body in the rhythm of the pulses of the call. He suggests that the tactile stimulation is more important than the acoustic event in stimulating the partner. Sounds used together with the close body contact during suckling in mammals are more related to tactile stimulation than vocal communication. His data for signals not associated with body contact or near contact follow M-S rules:

> The structural similarity of the calls applied in similar motivations is striking. All distress calls are relatively high in frequency and either tonal or have tonal components. Hostile calls are noisy and only grunting may have a tonal element . . . Between the different distress and

hostile calls, structure and motivation interplay largely as predicted by Morton. The increasing frequency from growl to bark to snort parallels a change from aggression to a conflict between aggression and fear as indicated by the facial expression. The basic frequency of cries and screeches, calls given under high distress, are higher than those of whistles, a call uttered while mildly distressed. Intra-call variation shows similar trends in some calls: e.g., grunts, given by a female facing an intruder are noisy, while those uttered before the intruder is spotted (and by a female more likely to be fearful) contain tonal elements.

In summary, the M-S rule model predicts a universal relationship among the signal structures used by birds and mammals in close proximity. The empirical data show that signal classes (called "displays" by ethologists) fall into appropriate places on the two dimensional model (figure 23.1) and variations in signal structure within classes, like the wrens' *chirt* call, likewise follow the specified code. The signals of "lower" terrestrial vertebrates suggest that the origin of M-S rules is in these more primitive animals.

23.5. The use of voiced and unvoiced sounds

Voiced or vocal sounds are produced by a structure that evolved specifically for the production of signals. The syrinx or larynx has virtually no other function, and the signals they produce are under the control of the central nervous system. If we accept that the M-S code is part of this system, the evolution of unvoiced signals requires separate explanation. I suggest that unvoiced close-range signals evolved *specifically to avoid* the neural control underlying the M-S rules.

There are numerous contexts in which a signal may be favored by selection because it does *not* indicate the motivation of its producer. For example, when a fox encounters a goose incubating eggs the goose is "between a rock and a hard place." Under most close fox encounters, the goose would escape and "bark" while doing so. But she has invested much energy and her genetic future in the eggs. How does she communicate her tendency to both flee and defend to obtain the best result, given that the fox has its own, quite separate, genetic future? She assumes a posture used to threaten another goose: neck extended with the beak ready to bite, with wings raised slightly to show their potential to beat with bone-breaking force. She would perform these same behaviors toward a rival goose but would add a vocal threat, a low-pitched, drawn-out sound. But to the fox she adds an unvoiced sound component not used intraspecifically: she hisses. I suspect that a vocal signal in this context, if produced, could not have been the one most effective to accompany her posturing. She could not produce a low-pitched sound, since she would "rather" escape, though this might help to ward off the fox. She might produce a high-pitched signal, for she could be frightened, but she would not benefit by symbolizing small size. The hiss, I suggest, functions to threaten the fox specifically because it does not encode motivation. The hiss is used in similar situations by many species in a multitude of taxa: as a signal that, on average, benefits by masking motivation that, if voiced, would not be adaptive.

There are, of course, many other types of unvoiced signals in addition to the hiss. A major difference between human and non-human auditory communication is the separation of voiced and unvoiced signals in animals and the combining of them in human speech. Animals might be said to use motivation, indicated through vocal signals, quite differently from all non-vocal signals. A signal expressing motivation is an "honest" one, produced whenever it manages the behavior of perceivers or produces an assessment by perceivers that is beneficial to the sender.

Non-vocal signal use seems to be adapted for a wide variety of situations and not tied to specific motivational states, or to motivation at all. Primitive mammals such as tenrecs (insectivores restricted to Madagascar) produce stridulation sounds through specialized quills (Eisenberg and Gould 1970). Stridulation is necessary for young to locate their mother. It occurs over a wide range of motivational states. Marler (1972) describes the wide range of uses the black and white colobus monkey (*Colobus guereza*) has for unvoiced "tongue clicks." These are produced as the mouth is thrown open and the tongue is "clicked down the roof of the mouth to the floor." Tongue clicks may occur singly or in pairs or triplets. They are used by an animal approaching another in an early stage of aggressive interaction, often associated with glaring and lunging. They may be given before or after an animal moves, especially when making a long leap. A "softer version" is given when "one animal approaches another in a friendly way." And "after two animals have been fighting they may approach each other, both tongue clicking, to interact peacefully." Marler concludes that tongue clicking is "associated with a general state of arousal which .. need not have aggressive connotations and may actually introduce peaceful activities."

ESS following the M-S code suggests that non-human animals separate vocal and non-vocal signals, both in perception and production, to a much greater extent than is the case in human speech. Voiced and unvoiced elements are central to the discrimination of phonemes, indeed of speech itself (i.e. voice-onset timing). If I am correct that animals decouple voiced and unvoiced signals to accomplish quite different ends in communication (hiding or indicating motivation), the combining of these signals in human speech is quite special. Human speech, confluent with its abstraction of sounds and meaning, must have had to overcome a considerable phyletic inertia to combine unvoiced with what, in other animals, are motivationally based vocalizations.

Human speech is not unique in its emphasis on categorial perception of graded signals (Marler 1975) but is different in its joining of vocal and non-vocal elements. Signal grading is not a "problem" for animals, since M-S rules predict a universal "understanding" of gradations of signals. It follows that monkeys discriminate between voiced and voiceless consonants (Waters and Wilson 1976) from their wider separation of voiced and unvoiced sounds than is the case in speech.

If the coupling of voiced and unvoiced sounds is important to the evolution of human speech, specific neural processing of the two sound types may be crucial. The ESS in animal voiced signals must be combined with unvoiced signals, that I suggest are used to mask motivation, in some special way. There is evidence that different classes of phonemes are neurally processed in different ways. Those with more unvoiced elements in their definition seem to be processed more in the left hemisphere. According to Petersen's review (1982: 178)

> Stop consonants yield the largest REAs (right ear advantages) (Shankweiler and Studdert-Kennedy 1967, Studdert-Kennedy and Shankweiler 1970); fricatives (Darwin 1971) and semivowels and liquids (Haggard 1971) elicit somewhat smaller REAs; and vowels (except under special conditions, Darwin 1971, Studdert-Kennedy 1972) generally produce no ear advantage (Shankweiler and Studdert-Kennedy 1967; Studdert-Kennedy and Shankweiler 1970). Paralinguistic features like pitch and intensity, which are introduced simultaneously with phonetic information that is processed predominantly by the left hemisphere, yield strong LEAs, suggesting a preeminent role for the right hemisphere in their analysis (Darwin 1969, Haggard and Parkinson 1971, Carmon and Nachson 1973, Nachson 1973, Blumstein and Cooper 1974).

In summary, the use of voiced signal in animals is associated with ESS while the unvoiced signals are not. The significance of this for human speech, which combines these two types of sounds, is suggested to entail a decoupling of ESS from phoneme production as part of the abstraction phenomenon in words. I suggest that this is either necessary for the evolution of grammar, or was caused by the evolution of grammar.

23.6. Speculation on selection in favor of the decoupling of the M-S code from unvoiced sound in human speech

This section will focus upon a "level 2" view of the evolution of speech; it is quite beyond my purview to discuss mechanisms of speech. I would only like to comment briefly upon the significance of post-pubertal loss of speech-acquisition ability (Lenneberg 1967). Of interest is the lack of ability of post-pubertal humans to learn a new language without a notable "foreign accent." One suggested hypothesis, using the logic of natural selection, is that this lack of ability was favored by natural selection specifically to enable more successful dispersal. The prediction is that dispersers are more likely to reproduce after dispersal if their speech is phonetically different from that in their "new" group. Two potential advantages might accrue: the dispersing person would not be expected to know the details of cultural rules of conduct, and the person would be identified as genetically new to the group.

This idea takes on added meaning when we realize that in mammals, and especially in primates, inbreeding is avoided through the dispersal of males from their natal group to some new one. The proximate causes of dispersal is aggression toward them from dominant males, and their chances of reproducing are enhanced by moving. But apart from avoidance of inbreeding depression in reproduction, any genetic lineage relatively more successful at dispersing has a greater chance of surviving over time and contributing to the gene pool of its species.

Intelligence, tool use, long childhood dependency and other aspects associated with speech were present in hominids for at least a million years before speech is thought to have developed. Selection for dispersal ability, even if dispersal was not a common event (but given sufficient time), might underlie the evolution of universal grammar. Hominid groups were developing a wide variety of "grammar-like" organizations in protospeech; those dispersers with the most general form of such organization would most likely succeed in acquiring the specific protospeech of the new group. The spread and eventual universality of grammar requires both a high heritability and successful dispersal of individuals carrying the genetic material for it. In this sense, then, the genetic attributes of successful dispersing would more or less automatically select for some sort of universal grammar. It is unlikely to have arisen anew many times independently. Those with provincial types that were too specific for outsiders to acquire would be selected against, since dispersers from such groups would be less likely to disperse successfully (i.e. reproduce). In any event, it might have been advantageous to be marked as carrying new genetic material by speaking with a "foreign dialect," and our poor ability to learn new language post-puberty now may reflect the dispersal-ability origin of universal grammar.

NOTE

* The Smithsonian Institution Scholarly Studies program, Fluid Research Fund, Research Opportunities Fund, and Friends of the National Zoo helped support this report. I am grateful to Leanne Hinton, John Ohala, and Johanna Nichols for the invitation to participate in the Sound Symbolism Conference and for their many courtesies.

REFERENCES

(1) *General references*

Arak, A. 1983. Sexual selection by male–male competition in natterjack toad choruses. *Nature* 306: 261–262.

Blumstein, S. and W. Cooper. 1974. Hemispheric processing of intonation contours. *Cortex* 10: 146–158.

Carmon, A. and I. Nachson. 1973. Ear asymmetry in perception of emotional nonverbal stimuli. *Acta Psychologica* 37: 351–357.

Chomsky, N. 1977. *Essays on Form and Interpretation.* New York: North-Holland.

Currie, P. J. and W. A. S. Sarjeant. 1979. Lower Cretaceous dinosaur footprint from the Peace River Canyon, British Columbia, Canada. *Palaeogeography, Palaeoclimatology, Palaeoecology* 28: 103–115.

Davies, N. B. and T. R. Halliday. 1978. Deep croaks and fighting assessment in toads, *Bufo bufo. Nature* 274: 683–685.

Darwin, C. 1969. Auditory perception and cerebral dominance. PhD dissertation, University of Cambridge.

　1971. Early differences in recall of fricatives and vowels. *Quarterly Journal of Experimental Psychology* 23: 46–62.

Dawkins, R. and Krebs, J. R. 1978. Animal signals: information or manipulation? In J. R. Krebs and N. B. Davies (eds.) *Behavioural Ecology: An Evolutionary Approach.* Oxford: Blackwell, 282–309.

Eisenberg, J. F. and E. Gould. 1970. The Tenrecs: a study in mammalian behavior and evolution. *Smithsonian Contributions to Zoology* 27: 1–137.

Fellers, G. M. 1979. Aggression, territoriality, and mating behavior in North American treefrogs. *Animal Behavour* 27: 107–119.

Haggard, M. 1971. Encoding and the REA for speech signals. *Quarterly Journal of Experimental Psychology* 23: 34–45.

Haggard, M. and A. Parkinson. 1971. Stimulus and task factors as determinants of ear advantages. *Quarterly Journal of Experimental Psychology* 23: 168–177.

Hausfater, G. and Hardy, S. B. 1984. *Infanticide: Comparative and Evolutionary Perspectives.* Hawthorne: Aldine.

Hopson, J. A. 1975. The evolution of cranial display structures in hadrosaurian dinosaurs. *Paleobiology* 1: 21–43.

　1977. Relative brain size and behavior in archosaurian reptiles. *Annual Review of Ecological Systems* 8: 429–448.

Horner, J. R. and R. Makela. 1979. Nest of juveniles provides evidence of family structure among dinosaurs. *Nature* 282: 296–298.

Lenneberg, E. 1967. *Biological Foundations of Language.* New York: Wiley.

Lieberman, P. 1984. *The Biology and Evolution of Language.* Cambridge, MA: Harvard University Press.

Lightfoot, D. 1984. *The Language Lottery: Toward a Biology of Grammars.* Cambridge, MA: MIT Press.

Markl, H. 1985. Manipulation, modulation, information, cognition: some of the riddles of communication. In B. Holldobler and M. Lindauer (eds.) *Experimental Behavioral Ecology and Sociobiology.* New York: Sinauer, 116–194.

Marler, P. 1961. The logical analysis of animal communication. *Journal of Theoretical Biology* 1: 295–317.

Marler, P. 1972. Vocalizations of East African monkeys II: black and white colobus. *Behaviour* 42: 175–197.

Marler, P. 1975. On the origin of speech from animal sounds. In J. F. Kavanagh and J. E. Cutting (eds.) *The Role of Speech in Language.* Cambridge: MIT Press, 11–37.

Morton, E. S. 1975. Ecological sources of selection on avian sounds. *American Naturalist* 109: 17–34.
  1977. On the occurrence and significance of motivation-structural rules in some bird and mammal sounds. *American Naturalist* 111: 855–869.
  1982. Grading, discreteness, redundancy, and M-S rules. In D. K. Kroodsma and T. H. Miller (eds.) *Acoustic Communication in Birds.* New York: Academic Press, 183–212.
Morton, E. S. and M. D. Shalter. 1977. Vocal responses to predators in pairbonded Carolina wrens. *Condor* 79: 222–227.
Nachson, I. 1973. Effects of cerebral dominance and attention on dichotic listening. *Journal of Life Sciences* 3: 107–114.
Nottebohm, F. 1975. A zoologist's view of some language phenomena with particular emphasis on vocal learning. In E. H. Lenneberg and E. Lenneberg (eds.) *Foundations of Language Development*, vol. 1. New York: Academic Press, 61–103.
Ohala, J. J. 1983. Cross-language use of pitch: an ethological view. *Phonetica* 40: 1–18.
  1984. An ethological perspective on common cross-language utilization of F_0 of voice. *Phonetica* 41: 1–16.
Peters, G. 1984. On the structure of friendly close range vocalizations in terrestrial carnivores (Mammalia, Carnivora, Fissipedia). *Zeitschrift für Saugetierkunde* 49: 157–182.
Petersen, M. 1982. The perception of species-specific vocalizations by primates: a conceptual framework. In C. T. Snowdon, C. H. Brown, and M. R. Petersen (eds.) *Primate Communication.* Cambridge: University Press, 171–211.
Ryan, M. J. 1980. Female mate choice in a neotropical frog. *Science* 209: 523–525.
Shankweiler, D. and M. Studdert-Kennedy. 1967. Identification of consonants and vowels presented to left and right ears. *Quarterly Journal of Experimental Psychology* 19: 59–63.
Sieber, O. J. 1984. Vocal communication in raccoons (*Procyon lotor*). *Behaviour* 90: 80–113.
Smith, W. J. 1977. *The Behavior of Communicating, An Ethological Approach.* Cambridge, MA: Harvard University Press.
Snowdon, C. T. 1982. Linguistic and psycholinguistic approaches to primate communication. In C. T. Snowdon, C. H. Brown, and M. R. Petersen (eds.) *Primate Communication.* Cambridge: University Press, 212–238.
Spock, B. 1968. Baby and child care. New York: Hawthorn.
Studdert-Kennedy, M. 1972. A right-ear advantage in choice reaction time to monaurally presented vowels: a pilot study. *Haskins Laboratories Status Report on Speech Research* 31/32: 75–82.
Studdert-Kennedy, M. and D. Shankweiler. 1970. Hemispheric specialization for speech perception. *Journal of the Acoustical Society of America* 48: 579–594.
Sullivan, B. K. 1982. Significance of size, temperature, and call attributes to sexual selection in *Bufo woodhousei australis. Journal of Herpetology* 16: 103–106.
Weishampel, D. B. 1981. Acoustic analyses of potential vocalizations in lambeosaurine dinosaurs (Reptilia: Ornithischia). *Paleobiology* 7: 252–261.

(2) *Literature testing or describing M-S rules*

August, P. V. and J. G. T. Anderson. Submitted. Mammal sounds and the motivation-structural rules: a test of the hypothesis.

Barclay, R. M. R., M. Brock Fenton, and D. W. Thomas. 1979. Social behavior of the little brown bat, *Myotis lucifugus*. *Behavior, Ecology, and Sociobiology* 6: 137–146.

Brady, C. A. 1981. The vocal repertoire of the bush dog (*Speothos venaticus*), crab-eating fox (*Cerdocyon thous*), and maned wolf (*Chrysocyon brachyurus*). *Animal Behavior* 29: 649–669.

Brand, L. R. 1976. The vocal repertoire of chipmunks (Genus *Eutamias*) in California. *Animal Behavior* 24: 319–335.

Conner, R. N. 1985. Vocalizations of common ravens in Virginia. *Condor* 87: 379–388.

Harris, M. A., J. O. Murie, and J. A. Duncan. 1983. Responses of Columbian ground squirrels to playback of recorded calls. *Zeitschrift für Tierpsychologie* 63: 318–330.

Harrington, F. H. and L. D. Mech. 1978. Wolf vocalizations. In R. L. Hall and H. S. Sharp (eds.) *Wolf and Man: Evolution in Parallel*. New York: Academic Press.

Harrington, F. H. In press. Aggressive howling in wolves. *Animal Behavior*.

Hauser, M. 1993. The evolution of the nonhuman primate vocalizations: effects of phylogeny, body weight, and social context. *American Naturalist* 142(3): 528–542.

Hill, B. and M. R. Lein. 1985. The non-song vocal repertoire of the white-crowned sparrow. *Condor* 87: 327–335.

Jurgens, U. 1979. Vocalizations as an emotional indicator: a neuroethological study in the squirrel monkey. *Behaviour* 69: 88–117.

Kleiman, D. K. 1983. Ethology and reproduction of captive giant pandas (*Ailuropoda melanoleuca*). *Zeitschrift für Tierpsychologie* 62: 1–46.

Ledger, D. W., D. H. Owings, and D. L. Gelfand. 1980. Single-note vocalizations of California ground squirrels: graded signals and situation-specificity of predator and socially evoked calls. *Zeitschrift für Tierpsychologie* 52: 227–246.

Maier, V. 1982. Acoustic communication in the guinea fowl (*Mimida meleagris*): structure and use of vocalizations, and the principles of message coding. *Zeitschrift für Tierpsychologie* 59: 29–83.

Miller, E. H. 1985. Communication in breeding shorebirds. In J. Burger and B. L. Olla (eds.) *Breeding Behavior and Populations*. New York: Plenum, 169–241.

Nelson, D. A. 1984. Communication of intentions in agonistic contexts by the pigeon guillemot, *Cepphus columbia*. *Animal Behavior* 32: 145–189.

1985. The syntactic and semantic organization of pigeon guillemot (*Cepphus columbia*) vocal behavior. *Zeitschrift für Tierpsychologie* 67: 97–130.

Nugent, D. P. and D. A. Boag. Communication among territorial female spruce grouse. *Canadian Journal of Zoology* 60: 2624–2632.

Payne, R. B. 1979. Song structure and sequence of song types in a population of village indigobirds. *Animal Behaviour* 27: 997–1013.

Peters, G. 1984. On the structure of friendly close range vocalizations in terrestrial carnivores (Mammalia, Carnivora, Fissipedia). *Zeitschrift für Saugetierkunde* 49: 157–182.

Pflumm, W., H. Comtess, and K. Wilhelm. 1984. Sugar concentration and the structure of the sunbird's song. *Behavioral Ecology and Sociobiology* 15: 257–261.

Robinson, J. G. 1982. Vocal systems regulating within-group spacing. In C. T. Snowdon, C. H. Brown, and M. R. Petersen (eds.) *Primate Communication*. Cambridge: University Press, 94–116.

Scherer, K. R. 1985. Vocal affect signalling. A comparative approach. In J. S. Rosenblat, C. Beer, M-C Busnel, and P. J. B. Slater (eds.) *Advances in the study of behavior.* New York: Academic Press, 189–244.

Shy, E. 1983. The relation of geographical variation in song to habitat characteristics and body size in North American tanagers (Thraupinae: *Piranga*). *Behavioral Ecology and Sociobiology* 12: 71–76.

Sieber, O. J. 1984. Vocal communication in raccoons (*Procyon lotor*). *Behaviour* 90: 80–113.

Viljoen, S. 1983. Communicatory behaviour of southern African tree squirrels, *Paraxerus palliatus ornatus, P. p. tongensis, P. p. cepapi* and *Funisciurus congicus. Mammalia* 47: 441–461.

Index

ablaut, 7
  consonantal, 16–21, 45–50
  vocalic, 17, 24–36, 67, 122–4, 163, 249–260
  tonal, 132–133
acoustic frequency, 78–81, 91, 333–336; *see also* Frequency Code
acoustic parameters, of sound symbolism, 4
adverbials, 120, 125, 126, 169, 181, 302
adverbs, 108, 121, 152–154
aesthetics, 180, 237–247
affective speech, in tone languages, 116–119
affixes, 169–170, 250, 258–259, 290
affricates, 69, 209, 211–213, 223–235, 255, 283
African languages, 178–200, 237
age, and size of vocal tract, 338–342
aggression, 329–332, 342–343, 350–352, 356, 361
Akan, 185
allofamy, 128 n.14
allolanguage, 222–223, 228–231; *see also* expressive language
amplitude, acoustic, 281–285, 317–320, 343
amplitude, of imitated sounds, 281–286
animal vocalization, 10–11, 329–331, 339–342, 348–361; *see also* bird calls
animal sounds, representation of, 85 n.1, 189–190, 279
animal names, 77–92, 124, 190, 257 *see also* bird names
animal speech, in narrative, 18–19, 25, 31
animals, calls to, 228
animals, non-vocal signals of, 332–335, 359
animate imitatives, 293–305
anthropology, and sound symbolism, 12
antonyms, 76, 133–137
Apalái, 86–88
aphonia, 313
apophony, 179
Arabic, 209, 211–212
Aragonese, 216 n.19

arbitrariness, 1–2, 4, 7–8, 11, 180, 263–264, 325–326
  in Chinese philosophy, 130
  evolutionary value of, 11
  and ideophones, 161, 180, 189
  motivation and, 40–41
  see also iconicity
areal aspects of sound symbolism, 102–103, 164–167, 249, 259–260
aspect, and ideophones, 163
assonance, 276, 277, 280, 282, 286–290
Attic, 254
attitudinals, 118–120, 125, 229
augmentative-diminutive sound symbolism, 15–16, 21 n.1, 42–53, 57, 299; *see also* diminutive sound symbolism
aural images schemata, 277–292; *see also* imitatives; onomatopoeia
Australian languages, 161–176, 179

baby talk, 19, 26, 28, 33, 34, 44, 128 n. 17, 229
Bahnar, 109–114
Bakhtin, M. M., 52–53, 59 n.11
Bambara, 180
Bantu, 182, 183, 185, 187, 195
beards, 330, 339, 342
Benue-Congo languages, 187
Benveniste, E., 54
Bhacu, 190
Biakpan, 195
Bini, 192–193
biolinguistic theory, 349
biology, and sound symbolism, 11, 309–322, 325–344, 348–361
bird calls, 11, 339–342, 354, 357
bird names, 16, 77–92, 257, 279
bisyllables, *see* disyllables
blends, 6, 235 n.15, 276–290 *passim*
Bloomfield, M., 5, 6

Index

Bloomfield, L., 214–215
Boas, F., 55–57
Bolinger, D., 5, 82, 92, 140, 182, 287, 326, 327
borrowing, *see* loanwords
boundary marking, 7
Bow Wow theory, 40
bright/dark symbolism, 8, 15, 21 n.1, 42–53, 57, 299
Broca's area, 311
Brown Corpus, 264–274
Bulu, 182, 183, 184, 188, 190, 195–196
Burmese, 122, 125, 127 n.11, 128 n.19

calling-out forms, *see* vocatives
Cantonese, 132–133, 137–141, 142 n.8
cartoons, 2, 280–281, 288, 293, 301–302
Castilian, 217 n.22
Caucasian languages, Northeast, 234 n.7
Chaga, 187, 190
Chao, Y. R., 116–117
Chechen, 234 n.7
Cheremis, 259
chiaroscuro coefficients, 241, 243
Chicomuceltec, 65
Chinese, 115, 125, 130–144, 155
Chinook, 40–59
Chipewyan, 34–35
ChiTumbuka, 181, 185, 187
Chukchee, 35
classifiers, of shape and path, 276, 289
clicking, 359
clicks, 196, 289
clipping, of vocative forms, 24–25, 33; *see also* shortening
cognates, sound-symbolic, 164, 165
consonant alternations, *see* ablaut
consonant clusters, 44–5, 124, 163, 276–277, 283; *see also* phonotactics; syllable structure
consonant symbolism
  of affricates, 69, 209, 211–213, 223–235, 255, 283
  of back consonants, 17, 48
  of clusters, 276, 277, 282–283
  of continuants, 9
  of coronals, 48, 154–155, 223–226
  of ejectives, 69, 192
  of finals, 276–288 *passim*; *see also* rime
  of fricatives, 9–10, 96–97, 163, 190–191, 297–300
  of geminates, 250, 252
  of glides, 96–97, 121, 299–300
  of glottal stops, 124, 167
  of initials, 96–97, 276–288 *passim*; *see also* assonance
  of labials, 163, 190–191, 197, 280
  of laterals, 16
  of liquids, 98–99, 287
  of nasals, 10, 46–47, 81, 138, 166, 284–285, 303–305
  of obstruents, 299–300
  of palatals, 4, 148–149, 154–155
  of resonants, 12, 96–99, 294, 299–300
  of sibilants, 96, 123, 209–213
  of stops, 9, 96–97, 192, 280, 297–298
  of trills, 163, 197
  see also feature symbolism
conventionalization, of sound-symbolic speech, 3, 4, 5–7, 281–290 *passim*
coronal consonants, 48, 154–155, 223–226
corporeal sound symbolism, 2–3, 8, 11
Cree, Plains, 36
creoles, 179, 198
Cretan, 225
cries, abnormal, 312
Crioulo, 198
crying, 349–350
Cypriot, 226, 227

Dalabon, 165
Danish, 191
darkness, *see* bright/dark symbolism
Darwin, C., 332
deformity, representations of, 225–227
deixis, 263
descriptives, *see* expressives
Dhuwal, 164–167 *passim*
diachrony, and sound-symbolic forms, 32–3, 63–75, 170, 197–198, 249–260, 299–300; *see also* etymology; sound change
dialects, *see* variation
dictionaries, 119, 293
Diegueño, 36
Difficulty Hypothesis, 138
diminutive sound symbolism, 4, 8, 10, 263–264
  consonants in, 16
  in English, 234 n.6, 284, 292 n.12
  in Greek, 224
  in Lahu, 121–124
  in Nez Perce, 16–20
  and tone, 132, 137–139, 329
  see also augmentative–diminutive sound symbolism; hypocoristics
Ding Dong theory, 40
dinosaurs, vocalizations of, 353–354
Diola, 193
diphthongs, 121–124, 250–251, 296–297
diseases, diagnosis of by sound, 309–322
distance symbolism, 263
disyllables, 99–100, 119, 150–154, 156 n.3, 162, 291 n.4
Djaru, 165, 167
Doke, C. M., 180

Index

doubling, *see* lengthening
doublets, 232–233
downstep, 184
dysprosody, 311

echoic words, 81, 293
echolalia, 312
echo-vowels, 126, 128 n.15
echo-words, 178–179
ejectives, 69, 192
elaborate expressions, in Tibeto-Burman, 120
emotion, 118, 239–247, 309, 312, 315–320
emphatics, 117, 172, 179; *see also* imitatives
English, 189, 208, 234 n.6, 263–274, 276–292, 293–306
ethnozoological nomenclature, *see* animal names
ethology, 325–344, 348–350
etymology, of sound-symbolic forms, 32–33, 207–218, 222, 226–227, 252–254, 299–300; *see also* diachrony; sound change
evolution, and sound symbolism, 11, 354
Ewe, 191, 193
Ewondo, 195
exclamations, 293–305
experiments, *see* psycholinguistic experiments
expressive language, 180, 185–186, 193–195, 214 n.2, 222–322, 228–233
expressive sound symbolism, non-human, 348–361
expressives, 7, 108–114, 178; *see also* imitatives

facial expressions, 326, 332–335
familiarity, 132, 137, 139; *see also* hypocoristics
Fang, 195
feature shuffling, 115–116
feature symbolism
 of glottalization, 68–69
 of gravity, 133, 137–141, 239–247
 of height, 4, 17, 224, 254
 of length, 8, 44, 126
 of nasalization, 96–97, 124–125
 of pharyngealization, 234 n.7
 of rounding, 251–252, 254, 259
 of voicing, 46–47, 98, 163, 292 n.12, 359–364
 see also consonant symbolism; vowel symbolism
Finnish, 249–260
fish names, 77–92, 257
Francis, W. N., 264
Frankish, 214 n.5
French, 207–208, 209, 210, 254
Frequency Code, 10, 83, 91–92, 140–1, 191–193, 317, 330–344
 reversals of, 107–114, 192–193
 see also size symbolism
fricatives, 9–10, 96–97, 163, 190–191, 297–300

functional load, 42–44, 121–122
fundamental frequency, 183, 278, 283–284, 325–332, 315–320, 353
 symbolism of, 116–117, 140, 317, 320, 350–352, 255–256

Gã, 191
Galician-Portuguese, 211
Gbaya, 179, 180, 182, 190–193 *passim*
gemination, 43–44, 124, 250, 252; *see also* lengthening
German, 208, 252
Germanic languages, 254–255, 289
Germanic classifiers, 289
gesture, 181, 196, 331, 343 n.2
Gilyak, 35, 249, 2562–60
giongo, 148
giseigo, 119–120, 148
gitaigo, 119–120, 126, 148
glides, 96–97, 299–300
glottal stops, 116, 124, 167
glottalization, 46–7, 68, 122, 167
graphic ideophones, *see* cartoons
grave/non-grave symbolism, *see* feature symbolism
Grebo, 188
Greek, 36, 210, 212, 222–235
Guaraní, 7, 94–103
Gupapuyngu, 164, 165

habitat acoustics, 350
Hainan Chinese, 133
Hausa, 180, 182–187 *passim*
Hebrew, 189
Hindi, 326
Hispano-Romance, 211–212
hissing, 358
Hmong-Mien, 115
homonyms, 207–213
Huambisa, 76–92
Huastec, 63–74
hypocoristics, 17, 132, 214 n.3, 224; *see also* diminutive sound symbolism

Ibibio, 187, 190, 196
iconicity, 108, 112–113, 180, 192–194, 287–288, 291 n.1
ideophones, 108, 180–181, 228, 302
 unusual grammatical aspects of, 167–168, 178, 181–196
 in African languages, 178–200
 derivation of, 197–198
 dialectal variation and, 195–198
 grammar of, 167–168, 188–194, 194–196, 197
 kinship of verbs and, 186
 in lexicon, 179–180

368

Index

as parts of speech, 168–172, 178, 179–180, 180–181, 187
as punctuation, 170–172
reconstruction of, 195
resistance of, to phonological processes, 184
synonyms for, 108, 178–179
taxonomy of, 196–197
in Yir-Yoront, 161–176
see also imitatives; interjections; onomatopoeia
Igbo, 179, 188, 192, 194, 196
Ijo, 182
images, 277–292
imitatives, 3–4, 9–10, 15–16, 212, 293–305; *see also* expressives; ideophones; onomatopoeia
imperatives, 124, 172
impressifs, 108, 179; *see also* imitatives
inanimate imitatives, 293–305
indexicality, 42, 50–52
Indosphere, 127 n.2
informal speech, 141
Ingush, 234 n.7
intensification, 125, 132–133, 139, 299
interjections, 117, 161, 171, 228, 293, 302; *see also* ideophones
intonation, 6, 141, 325–344
and ideophones, 168, 170–172
in tone languages, 116–117
Italian, 210

Jakobson, R., 214 n.2
Jamaican English, 179
Japanese, 15, 108, 119, 123, 125, 127 n.10, 148–160, 189, 258
Jespersen, O., 81, 130–131
Jingpho, 127 n.12
Jivaroan languages, 76–92

Kanuri, 183–184, 187
Kham, 127 n.1
Khoisan languages, 197
Kikuyu, 184
Kisi, 179, 182–291 *passim*, 196
KiVunjo Chaga, 187, 190
Korean, 108, 110, 119, 237
Krio, 179
Kučera, H., 264
Kuniyanti, 163
Kuuk-Thaayorre, 164
Kwakiutl, 32
Kyoquot, 32

labials, 163, 190–191, 197, 280
Lahu, 115–129, 179
Lakoff, G., 227, 234 n.4
Langala, 179

language acquisition, 154, 255, 259, 315, 360–361
language, evolution of, 40, 325, 360–361
language-specific sound symbolism, 8, 74
Lanham, L. W., 195
Lappish, 35
larynx, 337–339
laterals, 16
Latin, 209–218 *passim*, 289
lemma, 264
lengthening, vowel
diminutive, 43–44
expressive, 4, 117, 126, 132, 183–186, 193–194, 256–257
vocative, 34–36
lenition, 164
Liberian English, 179, 198
Linnaeus, 91–92
lip pursing, 255, 259, 299, 332–334; *see also* rounding
liquids, 98–99, 287
lisping, 19
literature, 11–12, 199
loanwords
in Australian languages, 165
in English, 301
in Greek, 231
in Japanese, 149, 152–155
in Kikuyu, 184
in Lahu, 125
in Romance languages, 211–212
local sound symbolism, 8, 74
Lolo-Burmese, 115–116, 127 n.5
Lulubo, 182

Makah, 24–28
Malay, 179
Mandarin Chinese, 117, 130–144, 254–255
Mangarayi, 167
Mari, 259
markedness, 7, 9, 33, 258–260, 283
Marpurg, F., 315–317
Mayan languages, 63–74, 86–88, 179
McCawley, J., 149
medicine, and sound symbolism, 11, 309–322
Meillet, A., 208
metacommunicative symbolism, 7–8
metalinguistic symbolism, 6–8, 265–274
metaphorical extension, 102
metaphorical sets, 45–46
Miao-Yao, 115
Middle English, 179, 300
mimesis, *see* imitative sound symbolism; onomatopoeia
Miwok, 34
Mohawk, 35

Mongolic languages, 259
Mon-Khmer languages, 109, 127 n.11
monosyllables, 149, 276, 288, 289, 294
morphology, 50–52, 290, 100–102, 288–290
    unusual, 50–52, 66–67, 109, 178, 185–186
morphosymbolism, 7, 207
Morton, E. S., 140, 329–330, 333
motivation-structural (MS) rules, 354–361
movement symbolism, 3–4, 16, 66, 276
Mphande, L., 181–182
music, and sound symbolism, 4, 212, 315–317

Náhuatl, 35
Nama, 197
narrative discourse, 52–55, 57, 118–119, 171–172, 257
nasalization, 121, 124–125, 138
nasals, 10, 46–47, 81, 138, 166, 284–285, 303–305
natural selection, 330, 338, 348–350, 360–361
Nembe, 179, 191, 194
Newman, S., 131
Nez Perce, 15–20
Ngambai/Ngambay-Moundou, 188
Nguni, 182, 195
Nitinat, 28–29
noise words, in Guaraní, 94–103
noises, 189–90, 293–306, 309–310
non-arbitrariness, 7–8; see also arbitrariness; iconicity
Nootka, 23–36
Nottebohm, F., 349
nouns, and back vowels, 264–274
Nupe, 179, 191

o-face, 332–334
obstruents, 12, 294, 299–300
Ohala, J., 10, 81–83, 91, 107, 140, 191, 317
Ojibwa, 279
Old English, 300
Old French, 207–208, 209–210, 214
Old Provençal, 210
Old Spanish, 209, 211, 212, 213
Olgol, 164
onomatopes, 119–120, 230; see also imitatives, onomatopoeia
onomatopoeia, 3–4, 8, 189–191, 279–281
    in Greek, 228
    in Guaraní, 100–102
    in Lahu, 119–120
    in Huambisa animal names, 81–55
    in Huastec roots, 66–74
    in particles, 55–57
    see also ideophones; imitative sound symbolism
Otontepec, 64–65

pain words, 224–227
palatalization, 122–124, 148–160, 185, 255
palatals, 4, 148–149, 154–155
Pama-Nyungan languages, 165–167
paralinguistic phenomena, 196
particles, 55–56, 118, 303
parts of speech, 6 7, 9, 10
    and expressives, 108
    ideophones as, 180–181, 187
    syntactic categories and, 101–102, 263–274
    weak differentiation of, 33
path, 276, 292
pauses, 185
Peircean images, 290 n.1
pejorative forms, 51–52
perception, 277
pharyngealization, 234 n.7
phonation type, 115, 144 n.25, 184, 329–330
phonemes, sound-symbolic
    acoustic properties of, 76–81, 83–85, 335–336
    distribution of, 70–74, 162–163, 223, 230, 263–274, 296–297
    and functional load, 42–44, 121–122
    hemispheric processing of, 360
    historical newness of, 70, 249, 255, 260
    in metalinguistic symbolism, 6–7
    rare or unusual, 9, 46, 121–122
    and resistance to sound change, 70–71, 165, 172, 197–198, 208–218, 331
phonesthemes, 5, 6, 182, 287
    as index of productivity, 252–254, 255
    and lexical analysis, 56–57
    recombinatory, 194
    and suffixes, 258–259
    see also aural images
phonetic intensives, see phonesthemes
phonetics, of ideophones, 197
phonological symbolism, in Yir-Yoront, 163–164
phonology
    resistance to, 184, 198
    unusual, 46, 109–110, 178, 181–185, 198, 223, 249
phonosymbolism, 207–208; see also sound symbolism
phonotactics, 95–98, 117–121, 149–154, 162–164, 223–226, 252–257
    English, 288, 295–297, 300–301, 305
    see also consonant clusters; rime-assonance analysis; syllable structure
Pidgin Sango, 179
pidgins, 179, 198
pitch, see fundamental frequency; intonation
plurality, 286
poetics, 12, 41, 237–247
point of view, narrative, 52–54
politeness, 118, 140, 327–329

370

Index

polysemy, 235 n.13
polysyllables, 291 n.4, 294
Pomo, 9
Pooh Pooh theory, 40
Portuguese, 209–218 *passim*
Potosino, 64–65
pragmatics, 10–11, 53–58, 180, 194–196
prefixes, 34, 169–170, 250, 290
productivity, 123–124, 252–254, 289–290
prosody, 170–171, 183, 326, 311
Proto-Lolo-Burmese, 122–123
Proto-Sino-Tibetan, 122–123
Proto-Tibeto-Burman, 122–123, 125
Provençal, 210
psychiatry, 309
psycholinguistic experiments, 76–77, 131, 198, 237, 309, 327–328, 335–336
Pyrenean, 216 n.19

questions, 118, 326, 331

rapid speech, 313
reduplication
  in African languages, 185–186, 193, 197–198
  in Bahnar, 109
  in Chinese, 132–133, 139
  in English, 284
  in Gilyak, 256–259
  in Greek, 224–255, 228–230, 235 n.12
  in Guaraní, 99
  in Japanese, 148–149, 152–155, 156 n.3
  in Lahu, 119–120
  in Middle English, 179
  in Nez Perce, 16–17
  in Yir-Yoront, 175 n.2
reduplicative symbolism, 4, 16, 99, 109, 185, 193, 343
register, sociolinguistic, 231–233
relatedness networks, 227
resonance analysis, 333, 337, 353–354
resonants, 12, 96–99, 294, 299–300
rhinoglottophilia, 117, 125
Ribagorzan, 216 n.19
Rice, C., 181–182
rime, 66–7, 276, 280, 284–289
rime-assonance analysis, 286–290
Ritharrngu, 164
Romance languages, 209–218 *passim*
rounding, affective, 254–255
Rumanian, 35
Russian, 179, 237–247, 252

sad/bad symbolism, 239–247
Sahaptin, 19–20
Samarin, W. J., 179, 278
Sanskrit, 35

Sapir, E., 21 n.1, 76, 83, 92, 131, 192, 336
Saussure, F. de, 40–42, 130, 325
"scanning" speech, 311
screams, 311; *see also* crying
semantic extension of imitatives, 302–304
semantic fields, 9–10, 10–11, 226–227
semantics, 7, 10–11
  of ideophones, 167–168, 188–194
  unusual, 188–194
  of vision, 276
semiosis, 42, 49
semiotics, 231–233
semi-wild vocabulary, 281–284, 290, 294
sexual dimorphism, vocalic, 91, 140, 326, 336–343
Shangaan-Tsonga, 184, 185
shape, 276
ShiNzwani, 187, 190
Shona, 180, 184, 186
shortening, 34–36
shoulder, amplitude, 281
sibilants, 96, 123, 209–213
sign language, 170
signal structure, 350–353, 356
simplex words, English, 277
Sinosphere, 115–116
Sino-Tibetan languages, 115–129
size symbolism, 4, 107, 140–141, 263
  anomalies in, 109–113, 237–239
  biological basis of, 329–331, 353–356
  and bird names, 83–92
  and diminutives, 124, 132, 223–224
  in expressives, 107–114
  and feature [grave], 138
  see also Frequency Code
slow speech, 312–313
smiling, 140, 332–335
soft/warm symbolism, 137, 141, 237
sonorants, 12, 96–97, 98–99, 287, 294, 299–300
Sotho, Southern, 187
sound change, 20, 155, 198, 230–231
  resistance to, 70–71, 165, 172, 197–198, 208–218, 331
  see also diachrony; etymology
sound propagation, and distance, 350
sound-symbolic forms, unusual properties of, 8–10
  in morphology, 50–52, 66–67, 109, 178, 185–186, 288–290
  in phonology, 46, 178, 181–185, 198, 223, 249
  in pragmatics, 194–196
  in semantics, 188–194
  in sound change, 70–71, 165, 172, 197–198, 208–218, 331
  in syllable structure, 95, 162–164
  in syntax, 100–102, 178, 187–188

371

Index

sound symbolism, 1–11, 40–42, 107–108, 325–326
  conventional, 8
  iconic theories of, 40, 108
  methodology for describing, 45
  and perception, 277
  recognition of, 44–45
  studies of, 76, 131, 263–264
  types of, 1–6, 278–281
  universals of, *see* universals
  see also sound-symbolic forms
Southern Min Chinese, 133
Spanish, 207–213 *passim*, 326
statements, 326–327
stops, 9, 96–97, 192, 280, 297–298
stuttering, 312
style, 231–233
submissiveness, 329–331, 332, 350–352, 356
submorphemes, 287
suffixes, 250, 258–259, 260
suprasegmentals, 2, 9; *see also* amplitude; fundamental frequency; intonation; lengthening
Swahili, 179–180, 188, 190
syllable structure, sound-symbolic
  in aural images, 276–292
  in ideophones, 163–164, 166, 179, 182–183, 239–247
  in imitatives, 99–100, 295–297, 300–301
  and onomatopoeia, 115–129
  unusual, 95, 162–164, 182–183
symptomatic sounds, 2, 309–322
synchrony, 222
synesthetic sound symbolism, 4–5, 66, 189, 237–239, 276–277, 287–288
  in animal names, 77–92
  in ideophones, 191–193
syntax, 100–102, 165–167, 178, 180–181, 187–188, 264–274, 301–302

Tai, 115
takwidi, 179; *see also* imitatives
tame vocabulary, 3, 279–292, 294
tanakali za sauti, 179; *see also* imitatives
Taos, 36
taxis, 288–289
Taylor, K. I., 76
Taylor, M. M., 76
Temne, 183, 187, 191
Tera, 180, 183, 187
terms of endearment, 17, 234 n.5; *see also* hypocoristics
Thai, 118, 125, 133, 141
Tibeto-Burman languages, 115–129
Tolman, A. H., 92
tonal polarity, 184–185, 329–331

tone, 115–129, 142 n.8, 181
  and ideophones, 183–184
  intonation and, 116–119
  morphology of, 132–133
tone symbolism
  and diminutives, 121–122
  metalinguistic, 132–133
  and size, 10, 138, 190, 192–193, 329–331
tonogenesis, 115–116, 122
Toura, 184, 193
trills, 163, 197
Trubetzkoy, N., 7
Turkic languages, 259
Tuscan, 209, 210
Twi, 191, 192
Tzeltal, 86–88

Ukrainian, 244
Ultan, R., 4, 263
umlaut, 128
universals, 8–10, 17, 33–36, 197, 263–264
  animal names as indicators of, 91–92
  and conventional sound symbolism, 237–239
  incorrect claims for, 325–343
  vs. onomatopoeia, 81–85
  and pitch, 140

Vai, 183, 193–194
variation, dialectal, 19–20, 64–66, 68–70, 195, 198
Venda, 196
verbs, and front vowels, 264–274
vielezi miigo, 179; *see also* imitatives
Vietnamese, 115
vision, semantics of, 276
vocal anatomy, sexual dimorphism in, 140, 326, 336–343
vocatives, 2–3, 8, 23–37
voiceless sounds, evolution of, 359–364
voicing, 46–47, 163, 292 n.12
vowel alternations, *see* ablaut
vowel change, 17, 48, 122–124, 249–260; *see also* ablaut
vowel harmony, 17, 95, 183
vowel length, 8, 24–36, 44, 126, 183; *see also* lengthening
vowel quality, 83–92, 110–112, 265–274
vowel symbolism
  of back vowels, 96–97, 123–124, 190, 259, 263–724
  of diphthongs, 121–124, 250–251, 296–297, 303
  of front vowels, 81, 96–97, 122–123, 190, 263–274
  of high front vowels, 10, 78–81, 98, 124, 263, 284

Index

of high vowels, 4, 17, 78–92, 111, 193, 224, 256–259
of long vowels, 8, 44, 126
of low vowels, 17, 78–92, 96–97, 224, 256–259
of nasal vowels, 96–97, 124–125
of raising, 254
of rounding, 251–252, 254, 259
see also feature symbolism; tone symbolism
Voznesenskij, A., 241

Wahlgren, E. G., 208
warmth, *see* soft/warm symbolism
Wasco-Wishram, 40–59
Wayampí, 86–88
Wernicke's area, 311
Wescott, R., 222–223
West African languages, 191, 237
wheezing, 310
whispering, 8
Whitney, W. D., 40

Whorf, B. L., 277
Wik-Mungkan, 164
wild vocabulary, 3, 9, 279–292, 294, 301–302
Wiyot, 16
Wolof, 188
women's speech, 117, 141, 344 n.4
word categories, *see* parts of speech
Wororo, 36

Xhosa, 195, 197

Yag Dii, 179, 187–188, 190, 191, 192
Yana, 7
Yir-Yoront, 161–176
Yoruba, 179, 180–183, 191, 193, 194, 331
Yurok, 36

Zande, 180–181
Zoque, 279
Zulu, 179, 183, 186, 192

Printed in the United States
53515LVS00003B/175-192